A PROPER SENSE OF HONOR

A PROPER

SENSE OF

HONOR

Service and Sacrifice in

George Washington's Army

Caroline Cox

THE UNIVERSITY OF NORTH CAROLINA PRESS | CHAPEL HILL AND LONDON

© 2004 The University of North Carolina Press
All rights reserved
Manufactured in the United States of America

Designed by April Leidig-Higgins
Set in Carter & Cone Galliard by Copperline Book Serices, Inc.

The paper in this book meets the guidelines for permanence
and durability of the Committee on Production Guidelines for
Book Longevity of the Council on Library Resources.

Library of Congress Cataloging-in-Publication Data
Cox, Caroline, 1954–
A proper sense of honor: service and sacrifice in
George Washington's army / Caroline Cox.
p. cm.   Includes bibliographical references and index.
ISBN 0-8078-2884-X (cloth: alk. paper)
1. United States. Continental Army — History.   2. United States.
Continental Army — Military life.   3. Soldiers — United States —
Social conditions — 18th century.   4. United States. Continental
Army — Officers — Social conditions.   5. Honor — United
States — History — 18th century.   6. United States — History —
Revolution, 1775–1783 — Social aspects.   I. Title.
E259.C695 2004   973.3'4 — dc22
2004003689

08 07 06 05 04   5 4 3 2 1

CONTENTS

Preface ix

Acknowledgments xxi

CHAPTER ONE
Take the Length of Every Soldier: Servants, Sons,
and Gentlemen of the Continental Army 1

CHAPTER TWO
A Proper Sense of Honor:
Educating Officers and Soldiers 37

CHAPTER THREE
Necessary and Excusable Measures:
The Policy and Practice of Punishment 73

CHAPTER FOUR
Oh the Groans of the Sick:
Health, Status, and Military Medicine 119

CHAPTER FIVE
The Last Duty to the Dead:
Death and Burial in the Continental Army 163

CHAPTER SIX
Onspeakable Sufrings Such As No Man Can Tell:
Status and the Treatment of Prisoners of War 199

Conclusion 237

Notes 253   Bibliography 291   Index 327

ILLUSTRATIONS

Lieutenant Elisha Bostwick's journal 5

Two 1778 illustrations of American uniforms by Friedrich von Germann 57

Drawing of a wooden horse 87

Warrant signed by George Washington to carry out a capital sentence 111

Late eighteenth-century medicine chest 130

James Tilton's design for a hospital 161

Burial site memorials in Langhorne, Pennsylvania 191

Frontispiece to *The British Prison-Ship* 201

PREFACE

> In the morning sow thy seed, and in the evening withhold not
> thine hand: for thou knowest not whether shall prosper, either
> this or that, or whether they both shall be alike good.
>
> ECCLESIASTES 11:6

IN JUNE 1775, JOSEPH WARREN, a doctor and patriot leader, was killed at the Battle of Bunker Hill near Boston. The British, victors of the battle, buried Warren along with thirty other American dead in unmarked graves where they had fallen defending the redoubt. When the British left the area in March 1776, Warren's friends and family and the members of the Masonic Lodge of which he was Grand Master decided to reinter his body with pomp and circumstance. However, they had to find it first. After a few days' search, they identified his remains by two artificial teeth. His body was then buried with "great respect, honor, and solemnity." One observer noted that the ceremony was attended by "a very Large Concourse of people" and involved full military honors. There was "a Considerable Number of armed men with 3 Drums & fifes marched Before then a great Number of free masons walk[ing] before the Corps which was followed by the Relations & Surgeons & then the Clergamen & other officers boath Civil & millitery." Then, after prayers and an oration, "a great Number of guns" were fired.[1]

In July 1998, twenty-six years after he was killed in Vietnam, Air Force lieutenant Michael Blassie's remains were interred at the Jefferson Barracks National Cemetery in St. Louis, Missouri. He had been buried with military honors fourteen years earlier in the Tomb of the Unknowns at Arlington National Cemetery in Virginia. The remains—four ribs, a pelvic bone, and the upper part of an arm—had not been enough to identify him in 1984, but they sufficed for modern DNA testing. To his family's relief, he was moved nearer home. Attending his reinterment were William S. Cohen, U.S. secretary of defense; Missouri congressman Richard Gephardt, the House minority leader; and hundreds of others. A twenty-one-gun salute and a fly-by of four F-15 Eagle fighter planes, with one peeling off in the "missing man" salute, completed the full military honors of the ceremony.[2]

THESE INCIDENTS, though separated by more than 200 years, reveal ways in which bodies and the public rituals associated with them can contain many meanings and values for a society. In these examples, the private grief of the families and the actual burials were only a small part of larger socially and politically significant events. Warren's interment helped focus public attention on the heroic sacrifice made by one of the town's leading citizens at a moment when the American patriot community was trying to rally material and human resources to continue the military struggle against Britain. Blassie's ceremony can be fully understood only in the context of the social divisions of the Vietnam War, the ongoing political debate over the place of that war in American history, and the continuing struggles over American foreign policy. Both examples show that funerals can be and are invested with political and social meaning.

Funerals are not the only arena where the physical treatment of the body becomes the locus of social values and meanings. As one historian has observed, "Parading is politics," and any occasion that puts treatment of a human body at the center of a public occasion will be rich with meaning. Any high school teacher knows that reprimanding a student in front of classmates has an impact on the whole class. Students watching understand that the punishment has meaning for them, even though they are not being punished. They are made aware of the teacher's values and standards for conduct and the penalties for not complying. This is as true today as it was in the days when classroom infractions resulted in corporal punishments such as paddling or whipping. With or without violence, when the treatment of a body is at the center of a public occasion, it will have a range of meanings for everyone present.[3]

However, the body does not need to be at the center of a public event for its treatment to have meaning. Sometimes, treatment is equally revealing when the body is the center of public policy debates but removed from the eye of the crowd. For example, the subject of overcrowded prisons puts the treatment of prisoners' bodies at the center of debates over status, freedom, race, and justice. Medical care in a hospital setting — away from a crowd but in public nonetheless — also places physical treatment at the center of policy debates. Issues such as the level of care given to the indigent or illegal immigrants and the kinds of intervention done to maintain life are all to be understood only in the context of larger concerns over status, immigration, taxation, and ethics. Examining the public or private physical treatment of bodies, then, is a way of exploring the values of a society.[4]

The connection between physical treatment and social values is not a new discovery in modern academia; astute social observers in the past also recognized it. In the eighteenth century, English writer George Osborne observed that "as in the natural body . . . so in the body politic." He was commenting on a public punishment, fully conscious of the potential of such events to encourage people to respect public or religious authority. However, he also recognized that these public events could provide occasions for challenges to that same authority. The crowd might be sympathetic to the accused or use these public occasions to express other kinds of discontent. Consequently, all groups attending had the potential to influence the occasion. Osborne, like other writers of the era, used the body as a metaphor for political society but also saw it as a symbol with meanings that went beyond the immediate occasion.[5]

The treatment of people's bodies, then, tells us something about the status of the individuals involved, the power arrangements that surround them, their value to public policy, and whether the individual or others contested that value. For historians, this analytical approach has an additional advantage: it enables us to depart from the written historical record and learn something of the values of the people who could not write. We can also learn about the values that those who could write rarely articulated and about the gap between any written expectations and daily realities.

For such an approach, there are few richer settings to examine than the military in time of war. Historian W. Frank Craven once observed that "every aspect" of a society is "pertinent to military history." The converse is also true: that every aspect of military society is pertinent to social history and so understanding the tensions and values within the military community will help us understand the larger society. However, it is important to keep in mind that each serves a different purpose. The larger civil society exists to maintain order, stability, and security. The military society exists to kill and destroy property when necessary, and everything about its organization and its values must serve that end. This, of necessity, creates a certain insularity, and military culture is often identifiably separate from that of the rest of society. However, both are so closely connected that each must be kept in view to completely understand either one.[6]

The military community is a complex and sometimes contradictory world. It is a legally isolated community within the larger society, yet it is not a socially isolated one. It is a community in which relations among the different ranks are codified, that is, written into military law, within a larger society that has some degree of fluidity. Yet, despite these formal relations, all who belong are united in a sense of mission and shared experience in ways that are rarely felt by the larger society. The military community has its own separate traditions and values, but its ceremonies are largely public. And while there is often consensus as to its purpose, there is often little agreement as to how that purpose is to be achieved. Historically, the main source of an army's strength lay in the physical bodies of its soldiers. Even in our own age in which modern technology has increased the killing potential of an individual soldier, the physical bodies of soldiers are still a main source of an army's power. Using that power effectively requires tight control and discipline, treatment of the sick and wounded, and, in the event of death, burial that, if possible, reflects the importance of the sacrifice. If the treatment of the physical body is indeed the place in which complex social values are ascribed and contested, an army in general and particularly an army in wartime should provide a fertile field of study.

There is another advantage in studying the military community in time of war. While physical treatment in public settings can help us understand the unspoken tensions within a society, it is helpful to have a written record from government bodies or key figures in the community about what they understood the values and meaning of an event to be. By comparing their expectations with the events themselves, we can more fully understand the tensions and contradictions in the society. Scholars have access to those thoughts when they study the military community. Many societies that create armies have self-consciously struggled with the legal status to accord their warriors and have left us records of those debates.

The nature of the debate is also a product of its social and political context. In 1775, William Tudor was the judge advocate general of the newly established Continental army, which was the regular American army that would fight the British in the Revolution. Tudor wrote to Congress about the dilemma that the legislature faced coming up with appropriate punishments and procedures for the officers and ordinary soldiers of the new army, noting that "[w]hen a man assumes a Soldier, he lays aside the Citizen, & must be content to submit to a temporary relinquishment of some of his civil Rights." Exactly what "some" should be was the essence of the problem with which Tudor and Congress wrestled, given that the men were to be recruited to fight for liberty.[7]

It was a problem with which the new nation would continue to wrestle. In 1949, shortly after World War II, the House Armed Services Committee held hearings on a bill to consolidate the military laws of the various branches of the armed services into a single Uniform Code of Military Justice. Secretary of Defense James Forrestal, testifying to the committee, wanted to be sure that whatever level of punishment the committee arrived at would provide "for maximum military performance and maximum justice." General Franklin Riter, testifying for the American Legion, a veterans organization, wanted to be sure the committee considered the special problems of an army in which soldiers served for short terms. Since such soldiers moved between being citizens and soldiers, the loss of civil freedoms should not be too great. There always had to be an appropriate "public relationship" so the men could return to civilian life "as friends and not as enemies" of the state. The status of free men and women in service to their country had new weight in the light of postwar ideological struggles with Communism that gave added importance and political meaning to the rights of freedom.[8]

These examples emphasize the way societies — in particular, Americans — self-consciously struggled to define the legal status of their servicemen and -women and how the political circumstances of the periods shaped the discussion. With these kinds of debates available to us, then, the military setting is a rich one for studying physical treatment. We can see the policy debates and legislation that ascribed status and look at them alongside the ways these values were physically enacted and, if they were contested, the ways they were resisted.

The soldiers and officers of the Continental army in the American Revolutionary War are good subjects for such an analytical approach because both they and the larger society have been the subject of controversy and historical debate. There is broad agreement that the Revolutionary Era was one of many rapid social transformations within a century of change and that the army and its participants were an important center of that change. However, it has been difficult to understand these transformations precisely. There are many reasons for this, not the least of which is that the participants themselves were often confused by the changing world around them. The problem is compounded for historians because the written records available are patchy. Fairly complete government records exist; however, the Revolutionary Era was generally a less bureaucratic age than our current one, and record-keeping was inconsistent in many aspects of public and private life. Other written sources are mostly from elite families or from a particular region, such as New England, where there were more towns, churches, or enterprising individuals running schools that offered basic education to men and women below the highest social levels. Not surprisingly, people from the lower levels of society produced the fewest written records. This is due not only to illiteracy but also to a lack of materials or opportunity for writing. For the most part, then, the contemporary written records leave frustrating gaps.[9]

Some of these gaps can be filled by soldiers' pension applications. Congress first awarded the Revolutionary War veterans pensions in 1818, initially based on need and then simply awarded for service. Since the earliest applications were made more than thirty-five years after service, these recollections are naturally colored by the passage of time. Additionally, illiterate or marginally literate men dictated their applications to others. However, for the period when pensions were need-based, the applications provide some statements about service from poorer men who are otherwise not well represented in other kinds of historical records, such as letters and diaries.[10]

Any understanding of the soldiers and officers has been further clouded by events after the war. In the postwar victory celebrations, few people acknowledged the role the soldiers had played or saw them as heroic. Instead, Fourth of July orators celebrating the nation's independence credited the success to a general uprising of outraged citizens and presented the struggle as a people's war, regardless of who had actually done the fighting or how the new nation had treated its warriors when the victory was less certain. Celebratory rhetoric only increased as the United States grew in confidence and power. When the new nation found itself divided over a variety of issues in the succeeding decades, memories and celebrations of the Revolution provided an important source of shared experience and community. Only with the passage of time were the soldiers themselves acknowledged as heroes. As the Revolutionary generation aged and died, Independence Day speeches and veterans' obituaries revered the former soldiers as "heroes of the Revolution" who "in the dark days of 1776 [had] buckled on the sword of liberty."[11]

The physical treatment of servicemen's bodies in the areas of punishment, sickness, and death provides a way to pierce through the problems of the written record and postwar layers of meaning. Such an approach allows us to see the men who served and the values imposed on them and claimed by them during their service. During that period of service, they responded to a new set of circumstances, new experiences, and the exigencies — that is, the pressing necessities — of war. We can see that, for the most part, those who stayed in the service, or who repeatedly enlisted, accepted the hardships of military life and the fact that those hardships were not evenly distributed but were borne most heavily by those at the bottom of the ladder. Army life subjected them to a world of restrictions, punishments, medical care, and burial practices that would be considered degrading to free citizens and were harsher than those legally used for servants and slaves, the lowest members of colonial American society. However, servicemen did, wherever possible, struggle to add dignity to their experiences and assert control over their own bodies. They also offered appropriate respect to their comrades. Thus, physical treatment in daily military life provides a rich view of value imposed, resisted, or accepted.

Although soldiers in the Continental army accepted a level of treatment below that of the lowest members of society, they occasionally resisted or protested other kinds of physical treatment that they believed was disrespectful. To us today, some of the distinctions they made may seem trivial, yet they were deeply felt by the men concerned. It is important to distinguish these complaints concerning physical treatment from those concerning legal or contractual rights, such as pay or terms of service. These contractual complaints were what General George Washington, the commander in chief of the army, was complaining of when he noted that the men were "apt to reason upon their rights." The focus of this project is not those contractual rights but rather the subtler and less obvious rights connected to respect and daily dignity.[12]

Understanding this distinction matters. Colonial America was a world in which daily acts of social interaction — how one treated other people and how one was treated by others — were of profound importance. Everything about the way an individual conducted himself or herself in speech, manners, and dress designated social status. While colonial American society may have been more fluid than British or European societies, that did not mean that these badges of status mattered less. In fact, there was a great deal of social anxiety about status, and those who were attempting to move up in the world were self-conscious about having exactly the correct manner and style. Even at the lowest levels of society, the presence of slaves and other kinds of unfree labor, such as servants and transported convicts, made people sensitive to even small distinctions in treatment.

In the Continental army, the most important distinction of status, indeed the foundation of its organization, was between those who were officers and those who were not. Officers were, by legal definition, gentlemen. In the larger society, those who claimed the status of gentry saw themselves as distinct, superior, and able to lead others. Officers shared those assumptions. In the army, it was not just a convenient and familiar social arrangement; it was the cornerstone of military discipline and backed up in military law. Officers, whose function was to lead, held their posts by a commission from Congress or a state legislature. All officers, of course, were not equal. Distinctions among the different levels within the officer corps were important to all concerned, socially as well as military. Ideally, the distinctions were clearly defined and observed. When they were not—for example, when there was confusion over such issues as seniority among the different branches of the armed forces or dates of commissions—the matter was sharply contested. Despite tensions surrounding seniority, promotion, or personality, all officers learned to share certain manners, expectations of treatment, and a code of conduct. All ordinary soldiers and noncommissioned officers—that is, corporals and sergeants who held minor leadership positions without formal commissions—were, by definition, not gentlemen. They were, therefore, subject to a completely different, and lower, set of standards for behavior and treatment.

The army, then, was a conservative organization with strict hierarchy. Every level of military rank had honors, duties, and responsibilities. Military law clearly spelled out the deference, the actions or signs of respect, that was due superiors. Despite this essential conservatism, however, the army could also be a vehicle for dramatic social change. It accelerated upward social mobility by providing a vehicle for talented, literate, and ambitious men to advance, and in this way, it undermined the hierarchy it was creating and attempting to reinforce.

In the first two chapters of this book, I shall examine the attitudes and expectations that the colonists brought to military life following their experiences with militia service and serving alongside and observing the British army. I shall look at how these experiences influenced the way the colonists conceived of and recruited for the Continental army. From those experiences, they created not only a service with a strict hierarchy but also a hierarchy of different kinds of military service. Militia service was where men served as soldiers for very short terms, usually thirty or ninety days, with the least loss of liberty to the exigencies of military life. Even though Continental army soldiers often looked down on the militia as poorly trained and thus militarily inferior, the militia enjoyed a higher social and legal status than the Continentals, which was reflected in their physical treatment. Regular army officers also looked down on militia officers because they lacked professional status. Militia officers were not considered equal to their Continental equivalents, even though they shared many rights and privileges. Militia officers were acknowledged as gentlemen, but because they were gentlemen who did not belong to the Continental officer corps, they were offi cers of a lesser sort. Continental army officers showed them small slights to assert the difference. In the regular army then, the officers were more elite and the soldiery, to use the eighteenth-century word, were more subordinate than in the militia.

The creation of an officer class with distinct rights and privileges and a subordinate body of soldiers was the foundation on which the Continental army was built. Subsequent chapters of this work turn to the issues of punishment practices, medical care, and burial to see how these distinctions were played out. In the final chapter, I shall explore how all these distinctions were both exacerbated and occasionally blurred when men found themselves prisoners of war. These chapters show that in each of these areas, the gap in kinds of treatment between officers and soldiers were profound and visible. Soldiers and officers were always aware that the struggle for liberty never involved equality. While soldiers did seek, and indeed demanded, certain standards of treatment, their demands were modest.

The level of treatment that soldiers accepted indicates that they came mostly from society's lowest ranks. Those men who accepted standards of treatment on a par with and sometimes below the most degraded members of society were presumably those who did not see such conditions as a shameful decline. However, simply to cast all soldiers as the lowest of the low would be misguided. Certainly, if men felt degraded both by the standards of treatment and by the indignity of serving with men who accepted those standards, they could desert or simply fail to reenlist when their terms were up. This did not mean that men above the lowest levels in society were missing from the ranks of ordinary soldiers. Some men would have stayed in the service motivated by the cause itself. Some would have been motivated by a sense of adventure or by friends serving. Perhaps others perceived service as a means of moving up in society, of becoming a noncommissioned officer (NCO) or even a commissioned officer when the rare opportunity presented itself. All would have been encouraged by the bounty (a cash payment for enlisting), pay, and, as the war progressed, the promise of land. As a British officer of the time wisely observed, "[N]othing reconciles being shot at to one, so much as being paid for it." Whatever their backgrounds or motivation, they had to be prepared to serve with men from the lowest levels of society and to be perceived as such themselves by the larger world.[13]

Men of low status were indeed recruited, but they possessed a broad range of experience and attitudes. This is evident in the ways they tried to shape the physical treatment to which they were subjected. As noted above, the minimum standards on which men insisted were low, but asserting even that low level involved tenacity, resourcefulness, and desperate effort, which speak to the fact that such standards mattered deeply. In all the aspects of treatment on which I shall focus, but especially in the area of medical care, men exploited all available resources and drew on networks of family and friends in and outside of the army for support and assistance, even when a long way from home. They assessed their comrades and found them worthy of respect when the world gave them little.

By examining physical treatment, we find some middle ground in the historical debates that surround the study of the Revolution and the Continental army. Quantitative studies of the social status of servicemen have reached contradictory conclusions. Some historians, studying the available tax rolls, recruitment lists, and other community and military records, have found evidence that the status of recruits declined rapidly from as early as 1776. They concluded that for such poor men, money must have been the prime motivation for service. After all, at the time, a man had to own property to have the right to vote, and so men without property would have had few immediate rewards from the political struggle in which they were engaged. Perhaps, in this circumstance, as one scholar has argued, poor soldiers developed the beginnings of class-consciousness, seeing themselves as exploited workers. There is, however, no consensus that the soldiers were poor men. One detailed study for the town of Peterborough, New Hampshire, showed that throughout the war, Peterborough's enlistees "represented a cross section of the town's society" and concluded that the men were motivated by the political cause. Others have argued that even if soldiers were society's poorest men, they might not have had purely mercenary motives. Since they were prepared to risk their lives, and indeed stayed despite harsh conditions and infrequent pay, they might have had ideological motivations too.[14]

This study draws a less polarized and more nuanced picture. The Continental army was, like all European armies of the time, an organization that reinforced order and rank. Yet it came into existence just at the time when existing social arrangements and patterns of deference were increasingly challenged by the "Tumults & Commotions" of war and when political rhetoric embraced the equal rights of men. Men of all ranks probably navigated their way through unfamiliar terrain without any clear sense of direction. Physical treatment was the most visible distinction among the officers themselves and between officers and men, so it became an area where the values of the army were both instilled and challenged. It was the arena in which the tensions between a deferential society and egalitarian political rhetoric were most visibly played out. As with other kinds of evidence, there is no clear picture that emerges. Some men made a rigid claim to distinctions of treatment and the social value those distinctions represented. Others tried to undermine them. Others still moved inconsistently between the two positions, unsure how to fit the world they knew into their military circumstances. The one certainty is that the struggle between democracy and deference was an ongoing one, not only within the society and the army but also within each individual.[15]

This book focuses on the experiences of officers and soldiers of the Continental army rather than of the militia. However, occasionally, the experiences of the militia are crucial to our understanding and are included where necessary. Historian Holly Mayer used the phrase "Continental Community" to embrace people such as wagoners and camp followers, mostly the wives and other female relatives of soldiers who lived, worked with, and were dependent on the army. The phrase serves us well, too, but for different purposes. The differences in treatment between militia and Continental service were distinct—especially in terms of punishment—and yet the men of each were frequently in close contact, and in sickness and at death, the men and their friends faced some of the same problems. The ways in which these differences were resolved are important and make it worth our while to keep both in view, as did the participants themselves.[16]

In 1778, John Laurens, a lieutenant colonel in the Continental army from a wealthy South Carolina family, wrote to his father, Henry Laurens, the president of the Continental Congress, suggesting that slaves might be recruited in their home state to serve in the Continental army in exchange for freedom. Henry Laurens questioned his son's right "to remove a Man from one state of slavery to another." He felt that army service for a slave would indeed be "a state of servitude which will be esteemed by him infinitely worse than Slavery," as he would be enslaved but with a high risk of dying. Although Continental service was not slavery, exactly what it was to be was always contested. William Tudor and the Continental Congress defined the legal status of soldiers, and by their enlistment, soldiers agreed to that condition. Once they were in the army, soldiers then had to clarify their relationship to each other, their officers, and the state. In the daily marks of dignity they demanded for themselves and gave to their comrades, we see them wrestling with the contradictions of their situation as temporarily unfree men fighting in the name of liberty.[17]

ACKNOWLEDGMENTS

THE WRITER OF ANY BOOK incurs many debts. The people to whom I owe thanks for kindness and support would themselves form a small army. First and foremost among them is Robert Middlekauff. He directed this project when it was a dissertation and has since offered his unfailing enthusiasm, criticism, and friendship. It is an association that is a privilege to enjoy. He is an outstanding scholar and teacher, and he has continually given me a model to which I might aspire.

I have also benefited from the wisdom and encouragement of other scholars and colleagues at different times. Some of them have died too young and are sorely missed. The late James Kettner, whose teaching and scholarship inspired me as an undergraduate, gave me much-needed direction and guidance when this project was a dissertation. The late Jack Pressman and the late Jenny Franchot helped push the project forward and offered their enthusiastic support. I would like to thank Harold Selesky, Don Higginbotham, Fred Anderson, and John Shy for their thoughtful criticisms and comments. Jacqueline Carr, Diane Hill, and Michelle Krowl all know that the many hours spent chatting about this book over cups of tea were a key part of the intellectual process. Kevin Grant, Patricia Lin, Edith Sparks, and Alexa Weinstein asked me the right questions at the right times, even though they may not have realized it.

I have been the beneficiary over the years of much-appreciated financial assistance. As a graduate student at the University of California at Berkeley, I received support from the Preston Hotchkis Chair, Phi Beta Kappa, and the Andrew W. Mellon Foundation Fellowship in the Humanities. More recently, I have been the recipient of generous funding from the David Library of the American Revolution. I especially want to thank David Fowler, the former director of the David Library, for providing such a wonderful opportunity for study and for many

hours of fruitful discussion. The University of the Pacific in Stockton, California, also provided generous funding through a faculty research grant.

Unlike many scholars, academia is my second career. Sometimes, others help
you imagine the way your life might be. Cathy Hardy was the first to encourage
me on a new journey. Laurie Buntain, Paul W. Jones, and Philip C. Stapleton
helped to make my dream a reality. And none of this could have happened at all
without the active assistance and cheerleading of Holly Levison. She not only
encouraged me but also made my switch to an academic life possible. I have been
the happy beneficiary of her friendship and her editing pen for many years. She
and Sharlene Messer have been meticulous readers of this manuscript, and the
book is better for their valuable criticism. I owe them both a considerable debt.
Lastly, many thanks to my husband Victor Ninov, for being there.

A PROPER SENSE OF HONOR

CHAPTER ONE

Take the Length of Every Soldier

Servants, Sons, and Gentlemen of the Continental Army

Praise ye the Lord for the avenging of Israel,
when the people willingly offered themselves.

JUDGES 5:2

IN 1775, SHORTLY AFTER the first shots were fired in the American Revolution at Lexington and Concord, colonial governments and the Continental Congress went about the business of creating an army. At those first April alarms, the Massachusetts militia, which included men from all levels of society, vigorously defended their communities and acquitted themselves well. At the Battle of Bunker Hill in June of the same year, troops from a number of colonies acted with honor on the field of battle. Although defeated, they made the British pay dearly for the victory.

As the siege of Boston began in the spring of 1775, colonial Americans from a variety of social and economic backgrounds participated in the struggle as ordinary soldiers became caught up in the *rage militaire*, the great military enthusiasm, of the time. This broad participation marked a sharp divergence from usual practice. In colonial provincial armies raised to fight alongside the British in imperial wars, and indeed in the armies of Britain and Europe of the time, the men who usually became soldiers were those without property. This war seemed to be different, with men of all stations in life shouldering their weapons in the defense of liberty.[1]

One young prosperous Pennsylvanian officer, Major Ennion Williams, however, was a patriot who expected this war to be fought by the men who had always fought wars: the poor. His diary in 1775 noted the subtle way in which he thought the new political circumstances would change recruitment. Williams was traveling through New York on his way to join his regiment when he saw a recruiting sergeant and six men "beating up for soldiers about the streets as the regulars used to do." He found the sight and its British associations "ridiculous and . . . disagreeable" among American freemen. Given the noble cause of liberty, he was sure "the poor would cheerfully offer to join" without the recruiting sergeant's efforts.[2]

Williams's comment conveys some of the contradictions patriots wrestled with throughout the Revolution. Experience had taught them that poor men would enlist as soldiers, but now, men such as Williams thought, they would go with a different state of mind. No longer enticed into the service of a distant monarch by a recruiting sergeant's bounty and liquor, they would fight voluntarily in the public interest. The colonial world, however, was one in which poor men had little political stake. Recruiters told potential soldiers they were the "future grandeur of the western world." Some officers and citizens saw them as "worthy" and "gallant." Others saw them as "damn'd riff raff," dissipated, and dangerous. With these confusions, it is hardly surprising that we have a difficult time understanding who the soldiers were and what they were about.[3]

Let us then try to sort through some of the confusion about who the soldiers were. Samuel Bixby, a private from Massachusetts and one of the soldiers besieging Boston, had heard that captains had been asked to "take the length of Every Soldier"—that is, get their histories. He noted in his diary that soldiers were to give "the town in which they Belong and where they was born & where they are Servants or Sons & how old and when inlisted." Unfortunately, no such detailed, complete census remains of the men who served except for very few places and times. So, in order to "take the length of Every Soldier" now, we need to review not only the available information on the social and economic status of the soldiers and officers but also some of the attitudes and assumptions that the colonists brought to the army. We can see many contradictions running through plans for recruitment and also one overriding assumption the colonists made as they set to work organizing their army: that all men in society and therefore the army were divided into two groups, those who were gentlemen, or who claimed to be, and those who were not.[4]

THE UNTHINKING DECISION to divide the army into officers who were gentlemen and soldiers who were not reflected a central division in colonial and

British society. It also matched the organizing principles of the British and European armies with which the colonists were familiar. It was understood that armies had to be hierarchical in order to be disciplined and successful. However, in the decades after the Revolutionary War, this hierarchical reality disappeared somewhat from the imagination of the American public. Nineteenth- and early twentieth-century writers celebrated the accomplishments of the Revolution and remembered it as a people's war. Historians of the era, Fourth of July orators, and politicians created a national mythology in which military arrangements reflected the Revolutionary rhetoric of political rights, liberty, and independence. Celebratory egalitarian stories of Massachusetts soldiers electing their officers and, in one instance, of an officer shaving one of his soldiers helped to create this image of a democratic army.[5]

There is an element of truth to this conception. Some of the Massachusetts soldiers did elect their officers, following in their militia tradition. However, historical studies of the militia before the Revolution suggest that in practice, this made little difference to military hierarchy. Elected militia officers of Massachusetts were usually of the same social status as appointed officers in other colonies. So, even if men elected their officers, social deference was the order of the day. Similarly, the shaving incident did indeed occur in 1776, but as the war progressed, such leveling incidents became rare, and few officers acted in an egalitarian way toward their men. Indeed, they vigorously demanded the marks of respect and distinction that military law required.[6]

There is also a grain of truth in the perception that citizens of all kinds were represented in the army, that it was a people's army. In the rush to participate in the great drama that was unfolding, men of varied social ranks shared military service. Young men of middling rank, farmers and craftsmen, enlisted when that first military enthusiasm gripped the country. However, after the military setbacks of 1776, the social status of recruits declined rapidly. High mortality rates, military discipline, and the rigors of camp life discouraged men from reenlisting and others from joining. Increasingly, bounty money—a cash payment for enlisting—was used to induce young men of low social and economic status and those with few other options into the ranks of the army.[7]

Very quickly, the army took on the social structure that some Revolutionaries, such as Major Ennion Williams, expected. In South Carolina, Captain Barnard Elliott went out recruiting in 1775, deliberately targeting propertyless men whom he and the communities to which he traveled saw as "very proper for the service." Captain Alexander Graydon of the Pennsylvania line shared that opinion when he was out recruiting early in 1776. He found that citizens in one community had in mind as potential soldiers not only the poor but also community troublemakers. His recruiting party met a gentleman who encouraged them to enlist a local "worthless dog" who would "do to stop a bullet as well as a better man." He told Graydon the neighborhood would be much indebted to him for taking the fellow away. So, even while the patriots were living in the midst of a new kind of war and a new kind of political struggle, some thought it would be the same people doing the fighting who had always done it, that is, poor men.[8]

Just how many poor men made up the Continental ranks and how many were men of property or the sons of such men remain a subject of controversy among historians. Buying property and paying property taxes are two activities that leave a paper trail for historians to follow. However, prior to their service, soldiers either did these things inconsistently in the communities in which they enlisted or not at all. Historians, therefore, have to draw on other kinds of records to find information about the soldiers who served. Ideally, these would be firsthand accounts from soldiers themselves in the form of letters or diaries. However, there were many practical problems that prevented soldiers from writing, such as opportunity; access to paper, pen, and ink; and, most importantly, limited literacy. Many soldiers, particularly those from the southern states where there was no public education and few other educational opportunities in churches or urban centers, were barely literate, if at all. So there is a scarcity of records from soldiers about their service. Additionally, even those who did write were usually recording present events and excitements and not reciting their economic histories. Muster rolls and other military reports add to our knowledge about the war but only occasionally provide useful details about a soldier's life.[9]

Memoirs are another source of information about soldiers' lives; however, these were usually written decades after the war and are obviously colored by the passage of many years, as are another rich resource, soldiers' pension applications. Congress first awarded the Revolutionary War veterans pensions in 1818, initially based on need and then simply awarded for service. Since the veterans or their widows frequently had no formal discharge papers in their possession or other written records of service, soldiers had to validate their claims by giving details such as whom they had served under and where they had been. They also had to produce testimony from neighbors who remembered their service. Some veterans have left us wonderful, detailed narratives of a memorable event or encounter with a famous figure, but most have simply given bare-bones information. Very few give us any clue to their lives before enlistment. The vast majority are richest in the genealogical information they provide, as the application files became repositories for testimony by widows, children, and other related par-

Sometimes military diarists found themselves short of paper. Lieutenant Elisha Bostwick, a Connecticut Continental, wrote his journal on his commission from Congress.
Courtesy Revolutionary War Pension Files, RG 15, National Archives.

ties who wanted to stake a claim to veterans' benefits or land bounties decades
after the war. All these historical sources can be augmented by what we know
of contemporary attitudes, the actions of recruitment officers, draft legislation,
and other recollections.[10]

The low expectations of recruiting officers such as Captains Elliott and Graydon reflected contemporary attitudes about soldiers. These came from knowledge of European armies, observing the British army, and colonial experiences
of raising their own provincial troops during earlier imperial wars. Provincial
forces differed from the militia. The militia served locally, only within a colony's
boundaries. Provincials were troops raised within a colony but for distant service beyond its borders. These forces sometimes operated alone but more commonly served alongside the regular soldiers of the British army.

Consequently, the British troops were the regular soldiers with whom the
colonists were most familiar, either through personal contact or by reputation,
and they were held in low esteem. Even British noncommissioned officers, who
rose from the ranks of private soldiers, got little respect. A Virginia officer in

1775 was surprised that a British sergeant taken prisoner "seems a very intelligent person for his station," his "station" being perceived as lowly. This officer presumably had even lower expectations for the intelligence of the mass of British soldiers, understood to be drawn from, and living at, the lowest levels of British society. Certainly British recruitment practices and those of its European counterparts meant that colonial perceptions were not too far off the mark. In the seventeenth century, Gregory King, an English scholar, made a study of family income. He listed all the categories of occupation in the country and ranked them by status and earnings. By social "degree," soldiers came almost at the bottom, below day laborers, seamen, and paupers, ranking only above vagrants. Ranked by income, only paupers and vagrants made less.[11]

Soldiers made little upward progress in the following century. Imperial wars with high mortality rates from both battle and disease, compounded by manpower losses from desertion, meant that the British were continually engaged in recruitment. In that effort, recruiters cast their nets wide and deep. Colonists at the time and many people since believed British soldiers to have been mostly vagrants or criminals. Some probably were, but more often, soldiers came from the working poor. The enlistment bounty and regular pay was an attractive inducement to young men trapped in the uncertainty of seasonal or casual labor. Recruiting parties certainly recognized their opportunities in poor communities. When British general James Wolfe had been a lieutenant colonel, he was optimistic when his recruiting party went into one neighborhood where the people were so poor, he thought they might "turn soldiers through sheer necessity." British army recruiters also searched for troops in Scotland, Ireland, and colonial America. Although resentment by the poor at being targeted occasionally resulted in violence, the British were mostly able to meet the country's manpower needs through these recruiting parties and did not have to turn to a draft. The Prussian army experienced similar pressing needs for men. It too turned to men of the lowest social ranks, as a variety of exemptions enabled a man with any skills or connections to avoid service. The Prussians also turned to foreign mercenaries who eventually made up more than 40 percent of the troops.[12]

Apart from their knowledge of the kinds of men who served as soldiers elsewhere, the colonists had plenty of local experience to shape their ideas of who should be soldiers. Organizing colonial militias and providing provincial troops to the empire, particularly for the Seven Years' War (1756–63), had given them ample opportunity to develop their own traditions of military service that reflected community sentiments.

The legislation that governed militia and provincial troops and their recruiting strategies reveals some of these attitudes. The colonists had inherited from seventeenth-century English Whigs a distrust of standing armies, that is, those that exist at all times, not just when there is war with an external enemy. This suspicion of a standing army was based on the assumption that, without a foreign enemy, such an army might be used by a government against its own citizens. As Whig writer John Trenchard argued in 1698, such a fear made sense in the face of "not only our own Experience" but also that of other societies. Trenchard was thinking of the not-too-distant past when considering "our own Experience." During the brief reign of the Catholic king James II from 1685 until he was deposed in late 1688, the king had used the army to try to consolidate his power. Two rebellions early in his reign gave him the perfect excuse to add to the army's strength. He announced to Parliament that he had doubled the size of the army, demanded appropriate funds to pay it, and, most worryingly, had staffed the army with Catholic officers, who, by law, should have been excluded from serving. During the rest of his reign, the army not only was a symbol of the king's power but also seemed on occasion to stand as an actual threat to liberty. That was certainly how it appeared to a number of leading citizens when, for example, in 1686, the king kept 13,000 troops near London.[13]

Though the king was deposed and went into exile two years later, the events of his brief reign consolidated sentiment against standing armies. Englishmen of all political stripes in England and its colonies celebrated the virtues of the militia, citizens called to service for short terms to attend to immediate threats to their communities. In turn, they denigrated the role of soldiers who served longer terms, if not life terms, in the service of the monarch. While soldiers might accomplish glorious things overseas for the state, at home they were a threat to the citizens. Consequently, Englishmen in England and America thought that if a standing army was necessary, it should be stationed somewhere else, preferably a long way from them.[14]

Colonial assemblies, like the British Parliament, sharply differentiated between militia and other kinds of military service. Most colonial militias required the service of able-bodied white men, usually between the ages of sixteen and sixty. Militia muster days, when the militia assembled to practice drills and maneuvers, often became festive occasions for men and their families, who otherwise rarely had an opportunity to see each other. Most colonial legislation defined the militia's duties as local, assisting counties in need for brief emergencies, and not as a force that left the colony. In fact, during the seventeenth century, frontier conflict against native peoples was the primary military reason for the militia to be called out. When military need changed and the British requested that colonists fight imperial wars against European powers in North America, troops were required for longer, more distant service under harsher conditions. Since soldiers had to leave the colony in which they were raised, colonial governments enacted special legislation to recruit and govern those provincial troops. In recruiting for distant service, they often drew on those who were the least essential to the economic life of their communities — the young, the propertyless, and the rootless.[15]

In contrast, over the course of the eighteenth century, militia service increasingly came to be seen as a badge of full economic and social community involvement and began to exclude a variety of individuals. In Georgia, during the Revolution, the legislature enumerated "lunaticks, Idiots and madmen" as among those unfit for militia service. Before the war, however, most colonies also left out an increasing number of able-bodied men such as friendly local Indians, free African Americans, servants, and vagrants. It was exactly these men who were perhaps more willing to go for more prolonged and distant military service in exchange for a bounty and regular pay when the colonies raised provincial troops.[16]

Historians have done a variety of studies of the men who served in the provincial forces in the Seven Years' War. The source material, as one might imagine, is incomplete, but overall they see colonial legislatures reaching down into the "mudsill" of society for their soldiers. Connecticut started using bounties to attract soldiers for imperial service as early as 1709. Since the practice had worked well, it offered money consistently afterward. Bounties increased significantly during the Seven Years' War, with special bonuses for veterans to rejoin. However, once enlisted, the rate of pay was low. Colonists in Connecticut recognized that offering financial incentives was effective but also realized that they were appealing to mercenary elements. One man was concerned that Connecticut was recruiting soldiers who served themselves rather than "their country." They also recognized that the money was most appealing to those who, financially, "are not the most prudent men." In other words, the ranks filled with those of "weak or corrupt character."[17]

In Connecticut, the ranks were open to all men, including free blacks and Indians. These men, who were among the society's poorest, were always among the volunteers and indeed were encouraged to enlist. However, when Connecticut was finally forced to go to a draft, unable any longer to rely on volunteers, it specifically excluded such men, almost certainly as an act of racial prejudice. However, as in all drafts of the era, a draftee could hire a substitute to serve, and prosperous draftees did hire African Americans and Indians as substitutes.[18]

Connecticut was not alone in offering bounties, moving to a draft, or reaching down into the lowest levels of society to fill troop quotas. Many colonies did all or a combination of these things. In 1754, North Carolina targeted "idle dissolute Persons wandering abroad" and explicitly saw provincial military service as the "useful" task of otherwise "disorderly" young men. Virginia too used a draft early in the conflict but, in response to resistance from those targeted, opted to use enlistment bounties in conjunction with drafts to secure recruits. The Virginia legislature, like its southern neighbor, specifically provided for the impressment of "idle, vagrant or dissolute persons."[19]

Still, the colonial Virginia government preferred volunteers. As Governor Robert Dinwiddie observed, "300 Men rais'd voluntarily will do more Service than 800 Men of the Militia forc'd on Service." As in Connecticut, the men who served in provincial troops outside of Virginia's borders were mostly those who had been outside of the militia system. The young Virginia lieutenant colonel George Washington had at least informally "taken the length" of the soldiers under his command in the provincial service and found that they were "loose, Idle Persons that are quite destitute of House, and Home, and I may truely say many of them of Cloaths." Despite the enlistment bounties, and the draft that targeted the idle, Virginia had trouble recruiting enough men. Poor pay and stories circulating from deserters and veterans of harsh discipline and miserable conditions kept many men out of the service. As a result, the colony had to cast its net wider into neighboring colonies. By 1756–57, fully 50 percent of the men serving were born elsewhere. Almost one-third of the troops were over thirty years old, aged by the standards of eighteenth-century armies. Also, service records indicate that men of mixed African and Indian ancestry and a few mulattoes enlisted. Given that Virginia was a society in which slaves made up approximately 40 percent of the population and that associated racial attitudes denigrating nonwhites were deeply entrenched, few white men with alternatives would have chosen to serve alongside them.[20]

In contrast to the Virginia experience, a study of Massachusetts soldiers in the Seven Years' War indicates that enlisted men reflected the makeup of the larger society and that the ranks were not more heavily weighted with transients or other marginal men. This study, however, was done for the first years of the war, and it is possible that the status of enlisted men declined as the war progressed. Certainly by 1759, Massachusetts had passed legislation that not only drafted "strolers" but also specifically targeted those who "may strole from town to town," deliberately attempting to avoid drafts in Massachusetts and other colonies. However, even contemporaries saw the colonial troops from different perspectives. British general James Abercromby saw the Massachusetts provincials, both officers and men, as made up of the "Lowest Dregs of the People." The governor of Massachusetts, on the other hand, wrote that the "soldiers in the ranks are freeholders, who pay taxes; that these are the sons of some of our representatives, the sons of some of our militia colonels, and . . . sons of some of our principal merchants." Of course, both men had reason to be partial in their assessment.[21]

In all their recruiting efforts, the colonies were competing with the British regulars who were also looking to fill their own ranks that had been depleted by disease, battle, and desertion. All over the colonies, unhappy indentured servants, poorly treated apprentices, and criminals found the British recruiters' offer tempting. In Philadelphia, a man calling himself John Smith who was in court facing a heavy fine he was unable to pay accepted a remission on the condition "that he enlist himself a soldier" in the British army.[22]

Whatever the actual status of colonial men serving as provincials in the Seven Years' War, taxpayer or vagrant, son of an artisan or convicted criminal, colonists already had no high opinion of it. Social rank was fluid in North America, but it was still a critical distinction, and the divisions of social status were respected. When colonial assemblies passed legislation to draft criminals and vagrants and opened the ranks to nonwhites, it was a sign that white property-owning (that is, voting) colonists held the status of soldiers in no high estimation. British colonel Henry Bouquet found this out when he led regular and Virginian provincial troops to Charleston, South Carolina, where his redcoats were treated no better than slaves. This attitude might have been due to hostility to British policies, the army's disruptive presence, or the perceived low social status of the soldiers themselves. Whatever the reason, local civilians made "no great difference between a soldier and a Negro." As the Massachusetts study suggests, there may have been times and places in the Seven Years' War when artisans and farmers joined laborers and transients as privates in the provincial service, but overall, colonials knew that young men living in poverty with little prospect of improving their situation were promising recruits for their own regiments, as they were for the regulars, and they pursued them accordingly. Such men increasingly made up the soldiery of the Continental army during the Revolution.[23]

In 1775, during the first months of the Revolution, recruiting parties went out "beating up" for recruits and had little difficulty finding them, due to the enthusiasm for the military struggle. Such parties were usually led by newly commissioned junior officers who set off with a sergeant and perhaps a few soldiers or drummers to raise men for their companies, the smallest administrative unit in a regiment. The recruiting party went to a tavern or town square and sounded a drum roll to attract the attention of a crowd and, they hoped, potential recruits.

Prospective candidates were plied with ale and regaled with tales of glory and adventure. When the first Virginia riflemen were recruited, two newly commissioned captains, Hugh Stephenson and Daniel Morgan, engaged in a friendly competition to see who could raise his company faster. Both companies were raised in less than a week, and the winner was never determined. One of their recruits, Henry Bedinger, later a commissioned officer himself, remembered that the standard of recruits was high and "none were received but young men of Character, and of sufficient property to Clothe themselves completely, find their own arms, and accoutrements."[24]

Propertied or not, those who most readily responded to the recruiters' offer were the young and the restless. In 1776, Thomas Painter, a sixteen-year-old orphan, had lived in his uncle's household for five years and was learning a shoemaker's trade from him. Despairing of the hard future he would have in that trade, Painter "thought it best to try my fortune by a Roving life, and having (as, is common in young Boys) an inclination for a Soldier's life, I Enlisted." Sixteen-year-old Joseph Plumb Martin was also restless living with his grandparents and working on their farm. He was tempted to become a soldier, but a year's enlistment seemed too long; he hesitated to commit to something he had not tried before. "I wished only to take a priming before I took upon me a whole coat of paint for a soldier." As soon as six-month enlistments were available, he signed up.[25]

Any hesitations Martin had were teased away by his friends. Like many young men, he enlisted with others from his community. As Martin told it, when he went to enlist, he found a number of acquaintances there. "The old bantering began—come, if you will enlist I will, says one; you have long been talking about it says another—come now is the time." Many others also enlisted with friends or siblings. Virginian Henry Bedinger enlisted with his brother George. Jonathan Burrows of Lebanon, Maine, enlisted in 1777 with two other men from his town, and brothers Israel and Ichabod Ide set off to enlist with their friend Jacob Abbey from Westminster, Massachusetts. When seventeen-year-old Austin Wells of Connecticut enlisted in 1776, he joined up with seven other young men he knew, and they all served together during their one-year enlistment.[26]

Sometimes very young boys were taken into the army with their fathers and served as drummer boys or ran errands for officers. Young Israel Trask joined that way. At age ten, he enlisted and served as a cook and messenger in the regiment in which his father was an officer. He served for about eighteen months before setting off, at the ripe old age of twelve, to go to sea. When, as an old man, Trask applied for a pension, he recalled himself volunteering for service, and indeed he may well have joined his father enthusiastically. Because of his age, though, it would have been his father who signed his enlistment papers. The young Alexander Milliner Maroney, however, appears to have been sent away. Maroney's exact age is unclear, but his stepfather apparently enlisted him as a drummer in a New York regiment when he was around eight or ten years old. The boy's mother opted to travel with the army as a washerwoman to be near her son. So, army life may sometimes have been an option in dealing with misery at home.[27]

Boredom, friendship, the recruiter's bounty offer, a desire for "a Roving life," a longing to be free from family supervision, and indeed the political cause itself attracted young men into the Continental army all through the war. But, as time passed, it became steadily harder for recruiters to find them. Even in the summer of 1776, when Henry Bedinger, now a young lieutenant, was out "to recruit and refill the old Company" in Virginia, it took five weeks rather than the one week Shepherd and Morgan had each taken the previous year. A correspondent to the *Connecticut Courant*, writing to encourage enlistment in the summer of 1777, chided his readers for their lack of public zeal. He criticized people who encouraged the recruiting of "the children and servants of their neighbors" but forbade their own "to engage." He also mocked those recruiting officers who wasted their time trying to recruit at "assemblies and balls." Even though this correspondent wanted all free men to respond to their country's need, he knew that assemblies and balls were where people of consequence met, not where plentiful recruits were to be found.[28]

Colonial experience had already shown who would do the fighting if it went on for any length of time and took place away from home communities: the men of low social status. Colonists were also fearful of standing armies close to home, so they were slow to allow longer-term enlistments to build an experienced army. But events quickly showed that seasoned soldiers performed better than seasonal ones, and when, in the fall of 1776, Congress decided to recruit for either a three-year term or the duration of the war, the states turned to the men they had turned to in earlier colonial emergencies.[29]

Recent studies of several communities, although indicating some regional variations, reflect similar patterns of a steady decline in status of recruits. A study of Concord, Massachusetts, showed enlistees as young men of property in the first year of the war, but by 1777, the men who signed on for three years were mostly the poor of the town. By 1780, they were the transient poor. A study of New Jersey troops from late 1776 to 1780 showed that most were in the eighteen- to twenty-two-year-old age group, and 46 percent owned no taxable property at all, more than twice the proportion in the general population. About 20 percent were from out of state or were foreign-born with no apparent connection to New Jersey society. Somewhere between 20 and 40 percent were serving as substitutes for others. A study of a sample of Virginia soldiers showed that the recruits were predominantly in the fourteen- to nineteen-year-old age category for each of the war years. Over 80 percent were Virginia-born, and half still lived in the county of their birth. They were mostly sons of poor farmers or farm laborers who went as substitutes for a father or older brother.[30]

Hiring a substitute was a way for men of even moderate means to buy themselves out of a state military draft. There was no stigma attached either to hiring one or serving as one, and the payment to a substitute was privately negotiated between the two parties. However, not all substitutes were paid. As the Virginia study above indicates, substitution was also a mechanism by which a family could shift the burden of military service within itself without any money changing hands. Also, a few men who were drafted sent their slaves to serve as a substitute. Benjamin Coe of Newark, New Jersey, did just that, sending his slave, Cudjo, to serve in his place.[31]

We cannot assume that all those serving as substitutes were slaves, sons serving for older family members, or men drawn from desperate poverty. For some men, substitution presented a good opportunity. Joseph Plumb Martin, mentioned above, who initially signed on for a six-month term, went as a substitute in 1777. He was not hired to replace a particular man but to replace someone who was to be drafted from a "class." The procedure in Connecticut and a few other places was that men from a certain county—usually those eligible for militia service—were grouped into classes or "squads," as Martin called them. Each squad had to produce someone from the group to serve as a Continental soldier, or, if none wanted to go, they could hire a substitute and share the burden of the cost. Martin, still only sixteen years old but already a veteran, had been flirting with the idea of serving again. His townsmen heard of his interest and began to lobby him. Writing his memoirs years later, Martin could not remember what he had been paid but thought it had perhaps been "enough to keep the blood circulating during the short space of time which I tarried at home after I had enlisted." Martin's service as a substitute was hardly lucrative, and in his account of it, the fee represented only an additional inducement to do something he was already inclined to do.[32]

Another man who took what seemed and indeed proved to be a good opportunity was Absalom Hughes, who served as a substitute for Barnabas Hailey from Virginia. In 1776 at age sixteen, Hailey enlisted for three years. He had already served out eleven months of his enlistment when his family hired Hughes as a substitute for him. The boy was very reluctant to go home, but "owing to the great distress [his service] gave his mother," his father and grandfather had already contracted to give the substitute a hundred acres of land in Charlotte County, Virginia, and so Hailey had no option but to return home. The generous substitution payment of good farmland in the community in which they all lived speaks to the fact that Hughes was negotiating from a position of strength, not weakness. Fortunately for Hughes, his bargaining paid off. He survived the Battle of Brandywine and the remainder of the term of enlistment and lived to enjoy his land.[33]

Evidence suggests that men, such as Martin and Hughes, substituting for or serving with men they knew from their home communities was less common as the war progressed. A Maryland regiment studied for the year 1782 showed that 40 percent of enlistees were foreign-born, many either indentured servants or transported convicts, with the majority coming from either England or Ireland. Since many convicts had been sent from Britain to the Chesapeake Bay region over the years, their presence among the Maryland troops was not surprising. The records of the first South Carolina regiment indicated the presence of a significant number of Irish-born troops at Fort Moultrie, outside Charleston. On March 16, 1778, Colonel Charles Pinckney ordered that "tomorrow being St. Patrick's day such non-Commissioned officers & Soldiers as are Natives to the Kingdom of Ireland are to be Excused Duty." While the statistics are not available, Pinckney would not have given a unilateral holiday if he were to lose the bulk of his troops by doing so. However, the numbers involved must have been significant enough for the Irish to be an easily identifiable group.[34]

One place of note was Peterborough, New Hampshire, a frontier town settled mainly by Scots Irish immigrants and with a strong tradition of military service. In that community, all levels of society participated in the Continental army throughout the war. While Peterborough, on the surface, appeared to be drawing on nonresidents for service, a detailed community study showed that such men did in fact have ties of friendship or family to the town. It also showed the town's leading citizens to be engaged in the army actively throughout the war. As the war dragged on and moved farther south, however, men with family commitments appear to have decided to stay home. Peterborough's enlistees did get younger, and while a few of these young men were propertyless, many were the sons of property owners. The Peterborough experience is important to examine in order to prevent any generalizations about social status from becoming too sweeping. Certainly this detailed community analysis reveals that men who were occasionally identified in the tax rolls of other communities as nonresidents or transients might in fact be connected to the communities for which they were serving.[35]

Elsewhere in the new United States, the steady pattern of draft or recruiting legislation indicates that states were having great difficulty finding men to serve. As time passed, they offered steadily greater inducements and targeted men of low social status. In its reorganization of the army in late 1776, Congress authorized cash bounties and postwar land grants as incentives. By the following year, manpower shortages were so severe that some states introduced a draft in order to meet their troop quotas set by Congress. Some states were already offering additional incentives to snag recruits. In Maryland, legislation in the fall of 1777 offered recruits an additional state bounty of forty dollars and further tempted them by granting "a pair of shoes and stockings . . . , over and above the continental allowance." In 1779, the state increased its incentives to new recruits and now offered a shirt, hat, and pair of overalls in addition to the shoes and stockings. North Carolina, by 1780, had added the bounty of a "prime slave" to a land and cash bounty. These bounties were probably tempting. The Maryland regiment studied for the year 1782 shows that for native-born recruits for whom information was available, the enlistment bounty equaled almost one-quarter of the total assessable property of the recruit or his family, indicating that the bounty alone might have been a meaningful inducement.[36]

Extra inducements were not by themselves evidence of the declining status of soldiers. Many men of moderate wealth might have been tempted by property and cash bounties. However, such men who were thinking of serving would find themselves in low company indeed, as the new draft laws clearly showed. As early as 1777, Maryland recruited "such disaffected persons that were arrested, or hereafter shall be arrested," offering pardons in exchange for three-year enlistments. In 1778, the House of Delegates passed a law stating that "every idle person, who is able bodied, and has no fixed habitation nor family, nor any visible means of getting a livelihood, ought to go as a soldier." The only discretion left to such a man was whether "he will be enlisted for nine months, or three years, or during the war," and if he chose the shortest term, he was denied a bounty. In South Carolina, in 1779, "a law was passed to take up vagrants and idle disorderly persons who had no visible method of maintaining themselves." In order to determine if an individual qualified, there was "a trial to be held before one justice and six freeholders." Although the act did promote a "spirit of industry in some idle persons" and restrained others from "disorderly practices," contemporaries were aware that such a system was open to abuse. David Ramsay, a South

Carolina physician, thought that, in a few cases, the system was "perverted, by the private resentments of partial judges, to the distress of some individuals who did not answer the character described in the act."[37]

Army service was denigrated to the point where a three-year term was the punishment for failure to comply with militia or draft laws, particularly in the southern states. In North Carolina in 1778, failure to turn out for the militia as required resulted in a term in the Continental army for the duration of the war. Also in North Carolina, even the legislation to draft men for a nine-month term of service for the Continentals provided a penalty of service for the duration if one failed to turn up as required. North and South Carolina and Maryland punished those harboring deserters from the Continentals with service in the army. In South Carolina, those guilty had to serve out the deserters' time or pay a fine if they were above service age, and the crime was forgiven only if one was the father or son of the deserter. In Maryland, three years' service was the punishment, and even being the father of a deserter or above recruitment age was not an excuse. In such a case, the offender had to provide a substitute. Clearly, service was not a badge of honor if it was the mark of a lack of public spirit at best and treachery at worst.[38]

Initially, a few patriot leaders hoped to see men above the lowest levels of society in the ranks fighting for the cause. General Lachlan McIntosh in December 1776 ordered his recruiters to avoid men who were "notorious Rogues." A year earlier, General Charles Lee felt that some poor men were not suitable. He had a low opinion of some of the "Common Soldiers" and was especially worried about the Pennsylvania riflemen, whom he described as "damn'd riff-raff—dirty, mutinous, and disaffected." William Tudor, the judge advocate general of the new army, shared his low opinion of riflemen. "Many of them are Irish & foreigners & are thus wid[e]ly suspected of being transported convicts."[39]

Among the poor men serving were free African Americans who were often trapped by racial prejudice in society's worst paying jobs. Probably as many as 5,000 black men served the patriot cause over the course of the war. Many military leaders feared that the sight of black soldiers would prevent whites from enlisting, and, accordingly, even though some were already in arms in October 1775, Congress did "not incline to inlist" them again. However, white men were failing to enlist for a variety of reasons, and it was in response to this failure that states turned to blacks to meet their troop quotas. By the end of 1775, the shortage of manpower in the Continentals was already acute, and free blacks, already present in the service, were then invited to reenlist.[40]

By the end of 1776, in New England at least, the tide of sentiment turned in favor of using black troops, slave and free. When in 1777 the Continental Congress fixed troop quotas for each state, northern states began to turn a blind eye to race in an effort to get men in the service. Connecticut and Rhode Island passed bills offering freedom to slaves in exchange for service, and by early 1778, the Rhode Island legislature voted to organize two separate battalions of African American troops. Elsewhere, African Americans, either already free or serving as substitutes in exchange for freedom, served in integrated regiments throughout the war. The only complete survey of Continental army personnel, by General Alexander Scammell in 1778, shows that at that time almost 10 percent of Continentals fit for duty were African American, and they appeared in regiments from Massachusetts to North Carolina. Even Maryland, with enslaved blacks making up about 40 percent of the population, accepted enslaved men serving with the consent of their masters by 1780 and, by 1781, extended the draft to include free African Americans.[41]

Racial attitudes that held blacks in low esteem complicated the attitudes of citizens toward soldiers and complicate our own assessment of soldiers' sense of themselves. A Continental army council of war, consisting of the army's highest ranking officers, rejected the use of black troops, apparently fearing that the presence of such men would inhibit white recruitment. Any truth to this belief comes from the observations of officers. Captain Graydon from Pennsylvania, surveying the qualities of the troops he was encountering on a journey through New York in 1776, was struck by the sight of a number of black soldiers in the regiment headed by John Glover of Massachusetts. This, he observed, "to persons unaccustomed to such associations, had a disagreeable, degrading effect," even though he thought Glover's troops were well disciplined and far superior to the otherwise "miserably constituted bands from New England." It would seem to have been Graydon who was unaccustomed.[42]

Despite the anxieties of Graydon and high-ranking officers, there is no evidence from soldiers' diaries and letters to believe that men who served alongside African Americans in the same companies or regiments considered their presence racially offensive. Most found it a point unworthy of comment. In fact, in many integrated regiments, there were few occasions when "negro" or "mulatto" was noted in muster rolls, even by the adjutant, a junior officer who did the administrative paperwork of a military unit. Historians have determined which soldiers were African American by identifying distinctive names or by connecting names with later records such as tax, census, or pension applications in which a veteran's race was identified.[43]

This omission complicates our own understanding of how race influenced the way men understood their own status. We cannot tell if the lack of comments was due to low literacy rates or if race was simply not a distinction that mattered to them. However, given the prevailing racial and social attitudes of the time, it was more likely that the free white men who served were of such low status that they did not see themselves as socially superior to free blacks. In fact, if white soldiers were being drawn from the ranks of local troublemakers, British deserters, vagrants, or convicted criminals, the larger white society probably made little or no distinction either.

There is little evidence, then, of racial anxiety from white soldiers who served alongside blacks. However, there is evidence that all soldiers were anxious that their status not be confused with slavery. In October 1775, when senior officers and Congress were considering how long a period of time soldiers should engage for, General Nathanael Greene felt strongly that the period should be "fixed and certain." He argued that without a defined period, men would see their service as "a boundless gulph, where the fruitful Imagination creates ten thousand nameless horrors." With a set term, men felt their "confinement" in the army was one with safe limits and was clearly removed from the condition of the slave.[44]

While soldiers throughout the Continental army left little indication of how they felt about race, there is other evidence from the lower south (South Carolina and Georgia) that soldiers were concerned about racial status. There, community and racial politics meant that soldiers were going to be poor and white. In both places, there were large slave populations; in fact in South Carolina, there was a slave majority. In such a setting, fear of slave revolts meant that arming even free blacks was not considered. While recruiters elsewhere could draw on men from a variety of social levels during the initial war enthusiasm, that was not the case in South Carolina, the colony with the greatest social stratification. As Josiah Quincy of Massachusetts noticed when he traveled to coastal South Carolina in 1773, the population was divided into "opulent and lordly planters, poor and spiritless peasants and vile slaves." With rich planters vigorously pursuing commissions in the officer corps and few white men of moderate wealth, the poor were left to fill the ranks.[45]

The racial and social politics of the region presented two other dilemmas. One was that soldiers were reluctant to perform labor they perceived as "servile." The other was that soldiers chafed under the rules governing camp life, which were similar to those of the slave quarters. General Charles Lee, dispatched in 1776 to help defend Charleston as it faced British attack, tackled the problem head-on. He arrived to find the community in desperate straits and in great need of his military experience and organizational skill. He also found soldiers reluctant to do the necessary labor constructing defenses on the grounds that such work was beneath them. In his orders, he told both the militia and the South Carolina troops that they had to labor. "Courage alone will not suffice in war," he told them, and "true soldiers and magnanimous citizens must brandish the pick-axe and spade, as well as the sword, in defence of their country." Lee hoped his patriotic words would get the soldiers to overcome their resistance to doing work they perceived as beneath them.[46]

The regulation of camp life presented similar problems. From the beginning, the men were subject to treatment that, while it served military purposes, must have been particularly galling for white men in South Carolina and reinforced the low regard in which they were held. From the first days of the conflict, soldiers were required to enlist for long terms, three years or the duration, unlike the much shorter contracts available elsewhere. They had to carry passes when they left camp, just as slaves did to leave the plantation. Also, an act passed in April 1776 empowered any "free white person" to stop any soldier without a pass. Free whites were offered a cash reward for turning such men in as deserters, just as they were rewarded for seizing runaway slaves.[47]

Passes were required not only to prevent desertion but also to control behavior. When Colonel Pinckney in Charleston heard of "some very Hedious & Disorderly behaviour Committed by the Soldiers up the path," he required that in the future, the men were "absolutely forbid to go up the path with out Leave in Writing from an officer of this Regt." He also insisted that officers meeting any soldier in town "Inquire for his pass & if he have none Immediately to Confine him."[48]

Until this time, only black slaves had had their freedom of movement circumscribed and were compelled to carry passes. After the Stono slave rebellion of 1739, the South Carolina legislature had passed a law requiring slave owners to furnish slaves leaving the plantation or town of residence with a "letter superscribed and directed, or a ticket." The legal penalty for a slave being found without a pass was a whipping not exceeding twenty lashes (although of course slaves could be punished outside of the courts and could never rely on the protection of due process). The penalty for soldiers absent without leave, prescribed in the 1776 articles of war, the body of law that governed the army, was up to 100 lashes. If any soldier was in doubt about his subordinate status, the pass system and its penalties must have clarified it. These rules put their status, in terms of movement, on a par with the most degraded members of the community.[49]

All over the new United States, soldiers were held in low regard. The recollections in pension applications testify to the depth of these attitudes. When Susan

Bateman, the former widow of William Asberry, applied for a pension, she needed testimony from neighbors and relatives to verify that she had indeed been William's wife, as she had no papers to prove it. One relative particularly remembered the wedding in Fauquier County, Virginia, in 1782 because the bride's family had objected to William "because he was a soldier and was thought a disipated man." The family thought that his "habits as contracted in the army were such as to unfit him for marriage." The marriage went ahead and lasted twenty years before Asberry's death. Whether Susan's family's concerns were justified remains unknown.[50]

The presence of soldiers occasionally seemed to create both anxiety and disgust among civilians. One farmer drafted a letter to George Washington to complain about the "rude manners of common Soldiery." One family in Madison County, Virginia, had heard a great deal "about the bad conduct of soldiers in many instances," so much so that they even feared what might happen when their soldier son, Private Samuel Carpenter, returned home. He was traveling with several other soldiers, all of whom stayed the night before moving on. Samuel had been away a long time, and his family had been anxious about him; indeed, they had even heard reports that he had died. However, his return did not prompt them to celebrate. In light of all the stories they had heard, having strange soldiers in the house "caused the family much uneasiness." Consequently, Samuel's father stayed up all night to make sure nothing untoward happened.[51]

Revolutionaries seemed to have no difficulty holding their soldiers in low regard and yet having great expectations of them. In March 1776, the Reverend William Linn, in a rousing address to a gathering of Continentals and some residents of Carlisle, Pennsylvania, managed both to exhort the troops to glorious action and to denigrate them, apparently without skipping a beat. He urged the troops to imitate the actions and courage of the "bold Montgomery and intrepid Warren," two heroic figures who had already been killed in action, Richard Montgomery at Quebec and Joseph Warren at Bunker Hill. Linn told the troops that they must "assert the glorious cause" in which these men fell. Despite this glory they were being called on to exhibit, Linn suspected that the soldiers might not equal Warren and Montgomery in moral character. He warned them against "drunkenness, lying, stealing, profanity, and debauchery of every kind," and then commended them for exchanging "the field of labor for the field of battle."[52]

Linn had a very different view of the officers commanding the troops. He praised their "laudable enthusiasm for liberty." He was sure they had given up their professions or "the delightful scenes of rural life" in order to follow "the rugged paths of war," and he only cautioned them to add religion as an officer's

"finishing accomplishment." Otherwise, he was reluctant to "so much as insinuate a suspicion" as to any failings in their courage, character, or honor.[53]

In these comments, Linn's audience would have heard nothing unusual or
noteworthy. Colonial Americans came to their Revolution knowing from experience what an army looked like and what kind of young men became soldiers.
From the earliest days of the war, but especially as they faced declining recruitment, state legislatures went after exactly those men. There indeed may have
been men above the lowest levels of society, as the Peterborough study suggests,
who continued to serve for political, economic, or personal reasons, but when
they did, they had to be willing to serve among the poor and degraded and be
prepared to be viewed by civilians as dissipated and dangerous at worst and as
suspect at best.

Colonists came to the war assuming that poor men would be soldiers, but
they also assumed that the officers leading them would all be gentlemen. From
colonial knowledge and experience and observations of the British army, officers
were gentlemen. Indeed, officers were gentlemen by definition; it was written
into the British articles of war. The articles of 1765, the ones in place at the time
of the Revolution, required that officers who behaved "in a scandalous infamous Manner, such as is unbecoming the Character of an Officer and a Gentleman, shall be discharged from Our Service." The British knew what they expected their officers to be, and Americans did not think twice about copying
them. Patriots changed the phrase "Our Service" to "the Service" but otherwise
took the passage verbatim. It was used in the Massachusetts articles of war, enacted in April 1775, the first Continental articles of June 1775, and the revised
Continental articles of September 1776, in place for the duration of the war. Indeed, U.S. military law in force today still punishes officers for "conduct unbecoming an officer and a gentleman."[54]

Much more than courtesy rested on the fact that officers were gentlemen. It
was essential to military discipline. Senior Continental officers and political leaders shared the attitude of European military officers that a gentleman made a good
officer and that social hierarchy would cement the military one. It was commonly held that discipline was "the life of an army" and that it could not be accomplished "without due subordination" of the soldiers. Washington believed
that soldiers would respect only gentlemen. Anyone less, he wrote in 1776, they
would regard as "no more than a broomstick." Gentlemen officers were, therefore, "essentially necessary to due subordination."[55]

Many Europeans and colonial Americans believed that a man's qualities as a
gentleman gave him an inherent ability to lead. A correspondent to the *Pennsyl-*

vania Packet in 1778 thought that to be a good officer of any rank required only "[c]ommon sense and the deportment of a gentleman" and not "supernatural talents." Patriot leader John Adams, in considering the qualities Congress should look for in its generals, did think a candidate should be an educated man but also thought that he should be "a Man of Address and Knowledge of the World." Washington thought that the starting point for an effective officer corps was recruiting "Men of Character."[56]

Having an officer corps of superior social status to the soldiers was not the only means by which an army could create a disciplined fighting force. The British army, in which a number of the Continental army's senior officers had served during the Seven Years' War, was again the model to which Americans turned for guidance; it was the one with which they were most familiar and the one they most admired. In it, social hierarchy indeed supported military hierarchy, but the military hierarchy was additionally supported by harsh military law. British and European soldiers surrendered many civil liberties when they entered the service for life terms and were routinely subject to harsh and bloody punishments. But how were discipline and subordination to be instilled in the Continental army when soldiers served for short terms, were sometimes citizens and sometimes soldiers, and the rhetoric used to recruit and inspire them centered on liberty?

The answer was that respect for rank was to be the cornerstone of military discipline and "due subordination" of the soldiery. Washington believed that having gentlemanly officers whom the soldiers naturally respected as their superiors would instill this. As in the British army, public punishment—either capital, corporal, or shaming in some way—would support this. However, punishment was never as harsh as Washington and others believed necessary to be truly effective. As a result, respect for military rank became critical to instilling obedience. A strong military hierarchy, supported as far as possible by social hierarchy, would, as Washington noted, be "essentially necessary."

This organizational framework was successful only when those who served could clearly see distinctions of social status among themselves and among those above and below them. It did not take long for some astute observers to identify the problem the Americans faced. In December 1775, James Sullivan, a prominent lawyer, wrote to his brother General John Sullivan concerning the Massachusetts troops. He argued that the narrow social gap between officers and men undermined discipline. When junior officers commanded men who were lately their neighbors and social equals, and "as the soldiery in this country are by no means dependent on the army for a living," the result was a "prevailing uneasiness" that undermined discipline and effectiveness.[57]

So the declining social status of the soldiers facilitated discipline and subordination as did the development of a self-confident, assured officer corps. These developments were certainly not the only reason for improved discipline and efficiency as the war progressed. The increased length of enlistments, developing professionalism, and the arrival of the Prussian drill master Baron Friedrich von Steuben were also key. However, having soldiers who saw themselves as inferior to officers who conducted themselves in the manner of gentlemen was an important factor contributing to improved discipline.[58]

Attracting gentlemen, "Men of Character," to serve as officers became problematic, not because there were not enough men who wanted to be officers—indeed, of these, the country had a surplus—but because there were not enough who could immediately be recognized as gentlemen. The discipline and subordination of soldiers was to rest on social hierarchy in a country where that hierarchy was weaker and more fluid than that of Britain or any of the European powers to which Americans might look for a model on military affairs. Wealthy American men who accepted commissions as senior officers knew their social rank as gentlemen matched their military one. However, there were many more positions than there were true gentlemen, so the ranks of junior officers filled with ambitious young men whose social standing prior to service was less secure. Anxious to advance and to secure the recognition of their rank as officers and gentlemen, those who were accepted into the officer corps fiercely defended their rights and privileges both to differentiate themselves from soldiers and to define their status among each other. For young men of moderate means and less certain social status, the claiming of gentlemanly status was central to their experience in the officer corps.

This stands in striking contrast to the attitudes and opportunities of junior officers serving with provincial troops in the Seven Years' War. If they had pretensions to claiming the status of gentlemen, there were two groups that worked against them. The first was British officers, who treated them with poorly disguised contempt. The British had decided that among provincial and British officers of equal rank, the man who had held his commission the longest had seniority. This automatically made almost all provincials inferior to their equivalents in the regulars. This treatment conformed to the low opinion already held by the British of colonial officers. An aide to British general Edward Braddock, Robert Orme, observed that the British could have little expectations of the Virginia soldiers "given the lowness and ignorance of most of their officers." With this frame of mind, British officers dealt out daily slights that provincial officers deeply resented. As a result, most provincial officers served only one year.[59]

In New England, provincial soldiers also kept the ambitions of junior officers in check. While officers might be sensitive to the nuances of rank among each other, the New England provincial soldiers prevented too much distance from being established from themselves. While some soldiers came from the lowest levels of society, noncommissioned officers (NCOs) and some privates would have come from an officer's own community. Some of these men were not too removed from junior officers in social status, which made it hard for officers to separate themselves. New England studies indicate that many junior officers were craftsmen or farmers who, while landowners, were hard-working men, often cash poor, and, like their soldiers, drawn by the pay. Such men found it hard to lead their troops by asserting respect for rank the way the British did and led instead by example. Also, the punitive actions of the British toward both provincial officers and men drew both groups together. Many junior officers, like their men, had had enough after one year of service, forcing some colonies, such as Connecticut, to offer bounties to veteran officers to serve again.[60]

For most, years of service as junior officers did not translate into postwar political or social success. The colonies, as imperial possessions, were places in which advancement and patronage came largely through British connections, not colonial ones, and these veterans still did not have those connections. As ever, the information is incomplete, but even at the local level, they seemed to make little headway. Only 6 percent of Connecticut provincial officers went on to become militia officers before the Revolution. Only seven men, just over 1 percent, went on to serve in the legislature. We shall never know how many might have desired elective office, but certainly few achieved it. Only the most heroic or senior of provincial officers had their reputations made by their service.[61]

The Revolutionary War was to be different. Years of political activism through protest and committee work had brought men of lower social status into contact with those who held political power. Indeed, some of these had been junior officers in the Seven Years' War and had been radicalized by British slights to their rank. Now their sons and other young men again considered the rewards and opportunities military service might offer. This time, they were anxious for there to be no slights from the British. In all their dealings with European powers in the war, patriot leaders and the officer corps itself wanted to meet their enemies and friends as equals.[62]

George Washington was the both the epitome of a gentleman and the greatest proponent of a gentlemanly corps. He insisted that officers be gentlemen with pay, conditions, and treatment that confirmed that status. In 1776, he wrote to John Hancock that he hoped that the service would take on as officers only "Gentlemen of Character & liberal Sentiments." However, he also knew he could draw less financially secure gentlemen by practical means. Good pay and the distinctions of rank "gives a Man consequence & renders him fit for Command."[63]

Distinctions of rank were the foundation on which the discipline of the army rested, as it was in every European-style army of the time. The officers and the institution of the army enforced military hierarchy through every aspect of military life. Standards of dress, manners, and style of living; making deference to rank a legal requirement; and of course physical treatment were all ways in which social distinction was reinforced. In all of these areas, daily practice closely followed lines of military rank.

The army thus codified the social distance between officers and men in military law. Consequently, the army became a vehicle for reinforcing lines of social hierarchy for a generation of young men. At the same time, it accelerated mobility. It emphasized to ambitious men of even moderate means the advantages of separating themselves clearly and emphatically from the lowest levels of society and gave them a vehicle for making the transition.

As they created their new army, the Revolutionary leadership consciously articulated some of the dilemmas they faced. As they struggled to recruit, create new legal codes, supply the army, create a hospital system, and fight a war, army and political leaders juggled the competing tensions they faced. Torn between civilian standards and military exigencies, political and religious beliefs, and the tenuous nature of an army organized in rebellion, they tried to find workable solutions. The unthinking decision was to create an army divided along the line of gentlemanly status. They did so because it was how they understood armies to be organized from the British and European example and because that social division was fundamental in their own lives.

The distinction of gentry status had been a key social division in American life for many years, but it was increasingly important as the eighteenth century progressed. Gentility was a social division that existed between the wealthiest families and everyone else. While there was a correlation with wealth, education and manners could sometimes help an individual or family of lower economic status claim to be gentry. Members of the gentry spent enormous amounts of time — if not their entire lives — refining their manners, appearance, and homes, continually affirming the social distance between themselves and those beneath them. They constantly policed themselves and others for the bearing, speech, dress, and manners that separated them from everything they considered coarse or awkward.[64]

The word "gentility" had a kaleidoscope of meanings in the eighteenth century. A person might describe an object such as a dress, table, or vase as genteel if it enhanced the perceived gentility of the user. While its meanings extended to consumer items, its most important meanings related to character and behavior. It meant having refined manners, but it also meant being sensitive to beauty and elegance. It involved personal restraint, managing one's emotions to avoid any unpleasantness. Personal diaries and journals attest to the fact that unexpressed emotions often led to those emotions being felt more intensely, but genteel society preferred domestic tranquillity to emotional disruptions.[65]

One person who offered a definition of genteel good manners was Lord Chesterfield. His letters of social advice to his son were collected and published in both Britain and North America as a courtesy book, an eighteenth-century version of a self-help, "how-to" manual for good manners. Genteel manners, he wrote, were *"the result of much good-sense, some good-nature, and a little self-denial for the sake of others, and with a view to obtain the same indulgence from them."* They were indeed that, and so much more. To be a gentleman required possession of a long list of desirable traits, from bearing, dress, and table manners, to remembering to avoid bragging or embarrassing others, to "Think before you Speak" and to "spit not in the Fire." Lord Chesterfield advised his son that personal "address, manners and air" were of "great consequence to every man." "An awkward address," he wrote, "ungraceful attitudes and actions, and a certain left-handiness (if I may use that word) loudly proclaim low education and low company."[66]

Courtesy books such as Lord Chesterfield's were a critical means by which socially ambitious people could learn correct behavior. Such books went back to the courts of early modern Europe, but by the seventeenth century, the courtly ideals had been refined and reached far beyond the world of ambitious aristocrats. Books, such as Francis Hawkins's *Youth's Behavior, or Decency in Conversation among Men*, went through many editions, and their advice was read and absorbed by several generations.[67]

Hawkins's book was part of a rising tide of courtesy books. The first to be published in the colonies in the late seventeenth century was Richard Lyngard's *Letter of Advice*, published in New York in 1696. Lyngard wrote that his manual was essential for those who were not fortunate enough to possess the *"Native Discretion"* that might "prevent them from *gross absurdities* in conversation." Eleazar Moody, a Boston schoolmaster, published his courtesy book, *The School of Good Manners*, in 1715, and it went through numerous printings all over the colonies in the succeeding decades. The popular *Tatler* and *Spectator* magazines also carried advice on genteel conduct, and Lord Chesterfield's *Letters* to his son, which appeared in print in 1774, was an immediate best-seller on both sides of the Atlantic.[68]

It is hard for us now to grasp completely all the meanings of gentility, but people in the eighteenth century could recognize it at a glance. The journal of Major Ennion Williams showed how easily someone alert could read the signs. While Williams was traveling through Connecticut, he lodged at a tavern and there struck up a friendly conversation with a man whom he discovered was a Connecticut assemblyman. Williams recognized him immediately as a gentleman. He did not do so because the man held public office. Being an assemblyman did not automatically qualify him for gentry status. After all, a gentleman could be an assemblyman, but not all assemblymen were gentlemen. Rather, Williams drew on subtle clues. He detected that the other guest was "a man of property, of good education, of good sense and sociable disposition, and behaved politely. His person is lusty and well proportioned. His features pleasing and his complexion ruddy." Williams never did learn the other guest's name, but the guest also did "not ask us any such impertinent questions as is usual here." Following the unknown gentleman's lead, Williams "therefore avoided it too." Despite this mutual ignorance of identity, they each recognized the other as a worthy companion and "spent the evening happily."[69]

George Washington was as conscious of the rules governing correct behavior as any man of his generation. At fifteen, he wrote down his own guiding principle for conduct, which came largely from Hawkins, and tried to follow the rules he had set down all his life. Most of them related to respect for rank and regard for feelings. He noted that in speaking to those of higher rank, it was important to keep a certain distance from them and not lean too close to them. Deference to rank also meant walking a respectful distance behind one's superiors, "pulling off your Hat to Persons of Distinction," and making "a Reverence [bow]." It also regulated seating arrangements, who could speak first, and the order of movement from room to room.[70]

Regard for feelings allowed for sensitivity toward those who would feel offended if treated wrongly. As Washington's first rule noted, "Every Action done in Company, ought to be with Some Sign of Respect, to those that are present." Its location at the beginning of his list was indicative of its importance. A gentleman was required not only to be respectful to social superiors but also to show condescension—humility—to inferiors. To be both respectful and to receive respect from others was essential to all social interactions.[71]

This sensitivity was the basis of the refined sense of personal honor that gentlemen were assumed to possess. A gentleman's sensibilities moved along a spectrum from honor to shame, with accomplishments requiring public acknowledgment and criticism public vindication. In this cultural context, as one historian has observed, "everything mattered all the time." The young Aaron Burr, while at college around 1770, gave some thought to the behavior of a gentleman. His guiding principle was to act in such a way as to conceal "natural defects" and to avoid being "exposed to the scorn and ridicule of the less honorable part of mankind."[72]

Fear of scorn and ridicule governed the behavior of men who were or who aspired to be gentlemen, and such men who joined the Continental army as officers carried these sentiments with them. British humorist Francis Grose mocked exactly these feelings in his satire of British military life, *Advice to the Officers of the Army*. The book's epigraph could have been applied equally well to the Continentals: "Safe from the Bar, the Pulpit, and the Throne, / Yet touch'd and move'd by ridicule alone." The actions of Continental army officers indicate that they were as moved as any gentleman by fear of ridicule.[73]

In this context, the matters of who became an officer and who did not, who was promoted and who was not, what exactly the trappings of rank were to be, and relative seniority among the different branches of the service became matters of immense importance to the individuals involved. When Congress and Washington were trying to decide who might qualify for the officer corps, they again looked to European models and their British experience for guidance. The French and Prussian armies, which preferred their officer corps to be of noble birth, were not models available to American imitation. In the British army, the officer corps was largely made up of gentlemen, with only those possessing high birth, wealth, and influence advancing into the highest ranks.

The background of British officers fell into several main categories. The first was the younger sons of the nobility and landed gentry who usually possessed all three elements of success and therefore had the best promotion prospects and held the majority of colonelcies and generalships. Most regimental officers came from the second group, the lesser gentry, families involved in professions or trade or who were yeomen farmers. Although many of this group were like one officer who described himself as "a private Gentleman without the advantage of Birth and friends," they often had patrons to facilitate their advancement. A third group consisted of foreigners who lacked money and interest but were born to gentry families and were educated. Members of the fourth group were not gentry; they came from the ranks of long-serving, experienced noncommissioned officers who usually gained their commissions in wartime, filling vacancies created by death or when a new corps was raised. A fifth group cut across all of these categories: the sons of officers. No matter how their fathers had acquired commissions, sons had access to commissions through networks of friendship and regimental fraternity.[74]

In the British army, all commissions from a colonelcy upward were by appointment, usually determined by seniority. Commissions to lower ranks were purchased. These might be bought from colonels in newly raised regiments who had new commissions for junior officers or from officers who were leaving the service. An officer was not bound to serve for any specific period and therefore could resign and sell his commission at any time. Although the crown frowned on the practice, commissions were frequently bought and sold through a commission broker operating out of a coffeehouse or through newspaper advertisements. Commissions not purchased were usually held by the fourth group mentioned above, former long-serving NCOs. Since these men had been appointed as officers and had not purchased their commissions, they had nothing to sell in order to advance and were stuck at that rank unless another emergency led to their promotion.[75]

For the American Continental army, the right to appoint officers was divided between Congress and the state assemblies. Since all commissions were by appointment, they could not be bought or sold, but officers, like their British counterparts, were not bound to serve for any specific period and might resign their commissions at any time. Commissions could be obtained only through influence, contacts, and recommendations. Appointment of field grade officers (colonels, lieutenant colonels, majors, and lower ranks) was a privilege retained by the assemblies in the state in which a regiment was raised; the assemblies often confirmed the recommendations of influential men. Congress retained the right to appoint men to the rank of general but had difficulty agreeing on even those appointments. It had to consider the competing claims of merit, seniority of serving officers, and recognition of states where the most troops had been raised. The difficulty Congress faced with these relatively few high-level appointments probably induced it to defer to the assemblies for the others.[76]

Political connections were central to getting senior commissions. For example, as Maryland raised regular troops early in 1776, its leading officers came directly from positions of political leadership. Colonel William Smallwood and five other officers had served in the Maryland Convention, the new colonial government. The Continental Congress also turned to men of influence when it wanted to recruit in specific communities. For example, when the British secured Hessian troops to fight with them in North America, Congress wanted to counter that by enlisting German colonists in a separate German battalion of the Continental army. It recruited heavily among the German communities of Pennsylvania and Maryland and appointed leaders of the German community— George Stricker, Nicholas Hausegger, and Ludowick Weltner—to be the battalion's highest ranking officers.[77]

For the New Jersey regiments, political connections combined with military experience secured high rank. While Congress had the right to appoint field grade officers, it simply approved the New Jersey assembly's recommendations of Lord Stirling and William Maxwell. The two were both important political figures in the colony and had had experience in the Seven Years' War. Other high-ranking officers were similarly well connected. A study of a sample of New Jersey officer corps shows that 84 percent of them came from the wealthiest third of society and 32 percent from the richest tenth. Since men had to apply to the legislature for commissions, it is not surprising that they went to those men who could offer letters of recommendation from prominent people. Only those who moved in the right circles would have access to such letters. None of the poorer men in this sample advanced beyond the rank of captain.[78]

Sometimes the benefits of political connections were not enough to smooth the path of an officer's life. John Trumbull, a deputy adjutant general, was the son of Connecticut governor Jonathan Trumbull and brother of the deputy paymaster general, Jonathan Trumbull Jr. John had been appointed to his post in September of 1776, but when his commission was formally conferred by Congress, it was dated February 1777. This interfered with any future calculations of military seniority, and John Trumbull immediately objected and wrote to Congress asking for a new commission. Despite having a supporting letter from his commander, General Horatio Gates, Congress refused. Fed up after receiving too many complaining letters from army officers, Congress was "highly piqued at the style and manner of your demand," a friend told Trumbull. Trumbull in turn was piqued, resigned the commission, and left the army.[79]

There were some regimental appointments that could be made without such intense political wrangling. The infantry, artillery, and light horse regiments that were raised directly under Continental authority rather than through the states were completely under Washington's control. He thus had more say in who became officers. Even so, the criteria for appointments were never straightforward, as illustrated in the following 1777 letter from Washington to the twenty-five-year-old Colonel George Baylor, a fellow Virginian. In it, Washington advised Baylor, who had just been given the command of a new regiment of dragoons, on choosing officers. Since Baylor would bear the burden of their honor or disgrace, Washington wrote that

> I shall vest you with the power of Nominating the Officers of your own Regiment — except the Field Officers, and those of the Troop commanded by Geo:Lewis . . . and except a Lieutenancy in some Troop for little Stark [a fellow Virginian]; . . . I would have it understood, that, I reserve to myself a negative upon a part or the whole, if I have reason to suspect an improper choice.
>
> I earnestly recommend to you, to be circumspect in your choice of Officers — take none but Gentlemen — let no local attachments Influence you — do not suffer your good nature (when an application is made) to say Yes, when you ought to say No. . . . Do not take old Men, nor yet fill your Corps with Boys — especially for Captains — Colo. Landon Carter sometime ago recommended a Grandson of his to me — if he still inclines to serve, & a Lieutenancy would satisfy him, make him the offer of it.

The competing claims of honor, interest, and local attachments must have caused even Baylor, who was from the highest ranks of Virginia society, to hesitate.[80]

It was not only Washington and his senior officers who wanted to be sure that the officers were "none but Gentlemen." Officers themselves wanted those around them to confirm their status. Lieutenant Isaac Bangs, a young Massachusetts officer, expressed concern about the social status of the officers of Captain Jacob Allen's company, which he was to join in 1776, since he "was entirely unaquainted with any Person." To avoid any discomfort, he "had previously enquired of my Friends as to their Characters before I engaged to serve, & found that the Capt & his other Officers had the Charracter of civil & agreeable Gentlemen." To Bangs's delight, he "found their Good Characters to surpass my expectations." In Pennsylvania, Alexander Graydon had not applied for a commission in the first months of the war as the officers in the first regiment organized "were not of my set of acquaintance." However, when a subsequent regiment was organized, he indicated to his uncle who sat on the committee that recommended men for commissions that he was finally ready to serve and received his commission in January 1776.[81]

Similarly, groups of officers had opinions on whom they might welcome into their circle. In 1780, General Francis Marion, in an exchange of letters with Major Isaac Harleston concerning the appointment of officers, had difficulty placing a Lieutenant Langford, as, when he had previously applied to the Second South Carolina Regiment, "the Gentlmn Disapprov'd of him & is not agreable now to

them." Captain John Lacey of Pennsylvania, on the other hand, could easily recommend a young man of his acquaintance for an ensign's commission in a Pennsylvania battalion in 1777, as he was "a young Gentleman well known to us, and
of good character and family." All these men had a clear idea of who was appropriate and what was expected of them.[82]

Those appointed senior officers usually had no difficulty in meeting the require-
ments of gentlemanly status. Men of considerable social prominence held the
highest ranks. However, junior officers from all the states brought a variety of
backgrounds to their new profession. Captain Lacey wrote that the army's officers were mostly "the sons of Farmers or Mechanicks." He himself fell into this
category. He was able to trace his lineage back several generations, and his connections to a number of families, "all reputable," had a long history of public service. He worked, however, in his father's gristmill, cooperage, and sawmill from
the age of thirteen or fourteen. His family's prosperity and political connections
helped him overcome the deficiencies of education when it came to military service. It is clear from his memoirs and correspondence that he possessed refined
manners and a keen sense of honor. Another young officer, Thomas Posey, who
rose to the rank of major by the end of the war, was without education or financial resources and had been only a saddlemaker. However, he was not without
connections. His father was a Virginia landowner who had fallen deeply in debt,
and George Washington was both Posey's father's nearest neighbor and principal
creditor. Although the young Posey had settled on the frontier, he maintained
the "civility, decorum and social graces" of his former social circle. He was also
politically active, sitting on his local committee of correspondence. Although
the family had fallen on hard times, Posey's manners and interest, combined
with ambition and talent, ensured his success.[83]

Some men of modest social status seized the opportunities to claim gentry status by becoming officers and insisting on the social distinctions that came with
it. Junior officers such as Lacey and Posey, artisans and farmers, were as likely as
their more socially secure counterparts to insist on the prerogatives of rank. Like
officers of all ranks, they were careful to separate themselves from soldiers. This
separation did not take place only in their living arrangements and social activities; it was also reflected in their private writings. Their diaries and journals indicate no interest in the activities of their men and rarely mention them. Rather,
their writings are filled with information on dinner engagements, clothing, comforts, and pleasant flirtations.[84]

Soldiers, while they noted something of their officers' activities in diaries, also
clearly saw their military superiors as being in a different world. Zebulon Vaughan,

a Massachusetts private, referred in 1779 to his regiment being mustered by Colonel Sprout of Middleborough. Since that was Vaughan's hometown, Sprout was known to him, and he noted parenthetically to himself in his diary, "Ebenezer Sprout formerly." Even in the pages of his diary, Vaughan gave Sprout the respect of his rank. While there would have been a social gap between them in the civilian world, Vaughan's comment acknowledged both the community connection and the social distance at the same time.[85]

Some individuals did leap across this social gap and go from being private soldiers to officers, usually holding an intermediate rank as a noncommissioned officer, but they were few. In the New Jersey sample, less than 2 percent of officers rose from the ranks of the common soldiers. The later years of the war provided greater opportunities to reward an NCO's good service or recruiting efforts with a commission. These openings occurred as experienced officers resigned their commissions exhausted, fed up, or desirous of pursuing the more lucrative opportunities that the war presented at home.[86]

The men who succeeded in moving up through the ranks and finally joining the officer corps had diverse backgrounds but shared one important skill: they were all literate. Some were barely so at the beginning of the war but exploited the opportunities the army presented to become more competent. One such man was Jeremiah Greenman, who began his army career as an unskilled seventeen-year-old. In his first period of war service, he was a private with a Rhode Island regiment on the Quebec expedition and spent time as a prisoner of war. Home again, but still without a trade or other skills to offer except his military experience, he signed on for a second time as a sergeant for the duration of the war. Over the next two years, he worked briefly as a recruiting sergeant and showed his loyalty during the first of the Rhode Island regiment mutinies of 1779. His diary showed no sympathy with the mutineers: "part of ye Regt this Evening peraded under arms under pertence [pretense] of giting thair rights"; they were, he noted, "soon dispearst by ye Genl on perad." He became an ensign, the lowest rank in the officer corps, in May 1779 and ended the war as a lieutenant.[87]

Another who made the transition was Benjamin Gilbert, rising from a fifer in 1775 to a lieutenant by war's end. Born in Brookfield, Massachusetts, Gilbert came from a farming family of moderate wealth and had probably attended the local school for several years where he acquired a high degree of literacy. Although more prosperous than Greenman, he was no more skilled or settled, and at nineteen, when the war began, he was quick to join up. Again like Greenman, when he signed up for a three-year term at the end of 1776, his year of experience as a soldier earned him a sergeant's rank. Gilbert brought two other important ingredients to his military experience that helped his upward mobility. One was that he served for much of the war with men from his community. The other was that he was a Freemason, and attendance at lodge meetings, where he knew and mixed with men mostly above or equal to him in social rank, was a regular part of his life. He was a social young man who loved drinking, music, and dancing. His diary, begun in 1778 when he was a sergeant, showed him mixing easily with his fellow NCOs and junior officers. This by itself was extraordinary, for NCOs and officers would rarely have socialized together. He received an ensign's commission in February 1780 and was immediately aware of the change in his social as well as military rank. His regimental commander, Colonel Rufus Putnam, was a neighbor in Brookfield. Gilbert's diary recorded only one social invitation to Putnam's home: that was in February 1780, just after Gilbert received his ensign's commission and joined the officer corps.[88]

Young officers who did not come from gentry backgrounds were anxious to learn appropriate behavior and sometimes matters of more substance. John Lacey, also from a humble background, worried in case "the defects of the want of a liberal Education become conspicuous." Gilbert and Greenman, who had to travel a greater social distance than Lacey, took considerable pains to learn what it took to be an officer and a gentlemen. Greenman, from the time of his first commission, read widely. In addition to newspapers and "the Spectator," he read "Tom Jones," "Cato's letters," and the "2nd. Vollum of Guil Blas." Unlike Greenman, Gilbert was more focused on improving his manners rather than his mind. His diary in 1783 recorded a day spent reading Lord Chesterfield's *Letters*. He also began a letterbook in late 1780, just after he became an ensign. A letterbook was a record of all of a person's correspondence. Gentlemen and merchants of the time commonly kept one so they could keep track of their social and business affairs. So, for Gilbert, starting a letterbook was a sign of status-consciousness by itself, as his diary indicates that he was a frequent letter-writer to a large circle of friends long before then. He also changed his style of writing and began to use pompous language in his letters. This was clearly intended to impress the recipient. In one letter to a cousin, he apologized for his brevity by noting that "[t]he frigorific season and multiplicity of business, prevents me from expiating on the above or any other subject." Gilbert clearly saw his transition to the officer corps as one that required a significantly different kind of behavior and language.[89]

Despite this self-education by young officers, their ideas were often unformed and awkward. Washington had hoped that the qualities of a gentleman would be the starting point. From there, he would work to shape an effective officer. He quickly realized he might have to teach more than military matters. In his earlier military service during the Seven Years' War, Washington had shown his skill and willingness to teach both. Determined to make his Virginia provincial officers into gentlemen, he reminded them that a young officer had to know that there was "more expected from him than the *Title*." An officer's good conduct required learning, and Washington thought that "there ought to be time appropriated to attain this knowledge." He encouraged his officers to more appropriate behavior with "this friendly admonition."[90]

Twenty years later, as commander in chief of the Continental army, Washington's admonitions would not be so friendly. Some guidance for junior officers would be informal. Senior American officers, true gentlemen, would model appropriate conduct, as would British officers and those from other European armies in the military conflict. However, the institution of the Continental army also played an important role in educating its officers. Through levels of pay, clothing, accommodation, and physical treatment, the army would enforce the distinctions of rank in every detail of daily life. It would teach gentlemanly style by example if it could and through the courts if necessary.

CHAPTER TWO

A Proper Sense of Honor
Educating Officers and Soldiers

A good name is rather to be chosen than great riches,
and loving favour rather than silver and gold.
PROVERBS 22:1

JUST AS IN OTHER ARMIES over the centuries, much of Continental military life was spent waiting for something to happen. Soldiers and officers, in their separate social worlds, made their own entertainment in order to pass the long hours. Officers, such as Lieutenant Samuel Armstrong of Massachusetts, sometimes met friends and "made a frolick, each fetching his bottle of wine." While wine and women were often part of a "frolick" for all servicemen, so too was song. Perhaps with the accompaniment of a fife, a small flute, or just other voices, songs were a way of either celebrating or commiserating about the great and small events of life. Men took songs from the British military tradition, changing the words where appropriate or adding military refrains to old folk tunes. The songs told tales of distant homes, lost or present loves, great heroes, and, frequently, the harsh realities of military life.[1]

In these songs, honor was the perennial military and social virtue. One popular song indicated that military honor was the barometer for a man's actions in other aspects of his life:

> A Soldier is a Gentleman
> His Honour is his Life
> and he that Wont Stand by his Post
> Will not Stand by his Wife.

Another told the story of a soldier separating from his new love. The hero goes to the aid of his "Country Bleeding" but has to leave behind his "Weeping maid." He tells his love: "I go where glory calls me & danger points the Way / Tho coward Love upbraids me, yet honour bids Obey." In songs, honor was something that all men possessed, and the need to hold onto one's honor through military service always triumphed over the immediate needs of heart and home.[2]

A man's sense of honor was something that patriot and military leaders exploited to enjoin all men to serve the cause of the American Revolution. They were exhorted to serve with honor that they might receive the thanks and recognition of posterity. Before the Battle of Long Island, George Washington told the troops that it was on them that "the Honor and Success of this army, and the safety of our bleeding Country depend." He reminded them "that you are Freemen, fighting for the blessings of Liberty—that slavery will be your portion, and that of your posterity, if you do not acquit yourselves like men." Yet, calls to honor were used with the recognition that the word had different meanings for men of different social status. All men had honor, even poor men, but a gentleman's honor was of a more refined and delicate nature.[3]

The word "honor" had a wide range of social meanings. Even in the present day, the *Oxford English Dictionary* takes two pages to define it. In the eighteenth century, its meanings were equally complex. It was something that could be possessed, given, or received. It included glory and fame, compassion, and integrity but also extended to having a reputation for being responsible with money or respectful to parents. An essential component of honor was to have the rank you claimed respected by those around you and for you to offer appropriate respect to everyone else above and below you on the social scale. This was a complicated business and occasionally required a careful social dance. For example, one of Washington's maxims covered the etiquette for having a houseguest: "To one that is your equal, or not much inferior you are to give the cheif Place in your Lodging and he to who 'tis offered ought at the first refuse it but at the Second to accept though not without acknowledging his own unworthiness." Clearly, pulling off this complex set of maneuverings successfully required an adept reading of all the nuances of social behavior. Failure to do so carried the risk of offending someone's sense of honor.[4]

Respect for rank, one's own and that of others, was a key ingredient in honor. Even the poor potentially could claim an honorable reputation in the community provided that, in addition to their personal qualities, they showed appropriate respect to those above them in status. Those higher up the social scale completed their claims to gentry status not only by showing respect to social superiors but also by showing condescension, which in the eighteenth century meant humility and cordiality, to social inferiors. In addition, wherever they were on the social scale themselves, they always had to be careful to make the appropriate distinctions of rank among others. Gentlemen and gentlewomen found that their reputations for honor were fragile and had to be protected attentively. This was necessary because having a good and honorable reputation was absolutely essential to acceptance in polite society. Consequently, they would always strive for the highest standards of personal conduct to secure their reputations.

For men serving in the army, a similar complex range of qualities was required in order to have an honorable reputation. Of course, bravery in action was the most obvious way to be recognized as honorable. Men of all ranks gloried in their military accomplishments. Private Zebulon Vaughan of Massachusetts was thrilled to have a chance to enjoy "the glory of a fiet [fight]" and to show the enemy at Saratoga in 1777 that American "[b]oys can fight." After the victory at Cowpens in 1781, General Daniel Morgan wrote with the news of the victory to General Nathanael Greene and of the bravery of his men. Morgan wanted "to mention the Name of every private Centinel in the Corps" so the world would know of their actions. Instead, as a way of honoring the soldiers' "Bravery & good Conduct," he followed the convention of the time and sent only a "List of their officers from a Conviction that you will be pleased to introduce such Characters to the World." Even after defeats, such as that at Quebec early in the war, newspapers extolled the virtues of "truly brave" and "excellent" officers and duly named them to give them appropriate public recognition and honor.[5]

But in eighteenth-century wars, battle was a relatively rare occurrence. Daily conduct therefore was an equally important barometer of a man's military honor. Poorer men, serving as private soldiers, needed to behave in a "soldier-like" manner: smart, dutiful, and respectful of superiors. Officers had to be equally dutiful. General William Smallwood valued Enoch Anderson, a subaltern (junior officer) under his command, because Anderson was "punctual and faithful" to his duty. Consequently, Smallwood was able to overlook the fact that the young man was "a little wild" and too fond of dancing. (Not surprisingly, Anderson thought the general "a man of excellent understanding.") In addition, officers had to pay meticulous attention to the distinctions of rank to secure their reputations as men of honor. With all these attributes, gentlemen serving as officers in the army would be worthy of the respect of their fellow officers and soldiers, and their gentlemanly honor would make them strive continuously to act in ways that improved their reputations.[6]

Recruiting such natural leaders was essential in an army that had limited means of compelling obedience from its soldiers. Without brutal punishments, the respect that soldiers would show officers was essential for discipline. As noted earlier, soldiers and officers being socially "too nearly on a level" had to be "cautiously guarded against" as it undermined military hierarchy. As Washington observed, "the Person commanded yields but a reluctant obedience to those he conceives are undeservedly made his Superiors." Ideally, officers should be true gentlemen so that social rank could easily be "transferred from civil Life into the Departments of the Army," or, if not true gentlemen, they should at least possess important gentlemanly qualities.[7]

Washington was sure that the only quality that mattered was honor. Outside of the army, there was no consensus as to which gentlemanly quality was the most vital. Indeed, there was some regional variation in the way people assessed a gentleman's qualities, with a greater premium placed on sociability in the South and piety in the North. One New England courtesy book from 1776 counseled that Christian faith was central to the character of a "True Gentleman." In addition to being "GOD's Servant," he also had to be "the World's Master, and his own Man," not dependent on the favors of others. But that was not all of a true gentleman's attributes. Additionally, "Virtue is his Business, Study his Recreation, Contentedness his Rest, and Happiness his Reward." Washington wasn't sure he needed officers to be such paragons of Christian virtue. In an exchange of letters advising Patrick Henry, the governor of Virginia, on the recruitment of officers, Washington wrote that "the true Criterion to judge by . . . is to consider whether the Candidate for Office has a just pretention to the Character of a Gentleman, a proper Sense of Honor, and some Reputation to loo[s]e." Honor mattered, then, because officers would be compelled to good conduct by the threat of having any pretensions or weaknesses exposed.[8]

A proper sense of honor was to be the cornerstone for creating a self-confident officer corps and a subordinate soldiery, but several problems remained. How were honorable gentlemen to be encouraged to join and stay in the army, and how were less qualified men who aspired to be officers and gentlemen to be transformed into gentlemen worthy of respect? And how were soldiers, recruited to fight in the name of honor and liberty, to be reminded of their subordinate status, and would they resist when they were? On the soldiers' side, recruitment from the lowest levels of society facilitated their subordination. For ambitious young men who looked to the officer corps, the widespread transmission of gentry values through popular courtesy books facilitated their social and military ambitions. Yet neither of these could be relied on to accomplish the mission at hand: disciplining a new army in time of war.

The institution of the army and its principal officers would be the agents by which the appropriate values of honor and status would be taught. Certainly some young officers read military texts to educate themselves in appropriate behavior. More commonly, they were guided by the model of American officers who were true gentlemen and of British officers observed as enemies and prisoners. Even more important was the role of the institution of the army itself. By providing different standards of living for officers, noncommissioned officers, and enlisted men and by providing a pay scale to support these differences, the army emphasized the distinctions of rank in every aspect of daily life. Clothing, food, and housing all reflected military status. These different standards were not only required but also enforced through military law. It was an offence for soldiers to act in capacities above their prescribed status and for officers to do tasks that were beneath them. In short, anything that was prejudicial to "good order and military discipline" could result in a court-martial.[9]

Soldiers also played their part in reinforcing the social division. They shared the expectation that officers should be men they could look up to, and they complained about, or were disrespectful to, those who failed to meet that standard. For soldiers, the army was a teacher to any who failed to show the courtesies due to rank. In patterns of daily interactions and the rigors of camp life, the army taught any who were in doubt about their social status. In civilian life, harmony reigned when people knew their place in the hierarchy, accepted it, and acted accordingly. In the military world, a clearly understood and accepted hierarchy was essential not only to harmony but also to efficiency and, consequently, to military success.

THE NEW UNITED STATES was not the only nation that had to train its officers and soldiers in matters of order, discipline, and military life. In European societies, where social divisions between the men who made up the soldiery and those who were officers were more sharply drawn, this task was certainly easier. However, that did not mean that men generally, and the officer class in particular, came to their service with relevant military knowledge. Men of high social rank may have come to the army with the "Character of a Gentleman," but they were usually clueless about what being an officer actually meant and what tasks were involved. Historians have made much of American inexperience in this regard, and certainly senior Continental officers continuously lamented the lack of knowledge and what we might now call management skills among the officer corps. However, many European armies faced similar problems. Armies in which promotion rested on who you knew and not what you knew gave officers no incentive to educate themselves in military matters. All Western armies struggled with the problem of how to create a competent officer corps.

By the time of the American Revolution, many European powers had founded academies to address this issue. The French introduced training for officer cadets in 1682. By the middle of the eighteenth century, there was a military academy in Turin, Italy, and one for the Austro-Hungarian army at Weiner Neustadt. Karl Eugen of Württemberg established the Karlsschule for his officers in 1771. These institutions taught such things as rules for discipline and good order, tactics and strategy, and mathematics in order to construct fortifications and calculate artillery trajectories.[10]

All this left the British far behind. They had founded a military academy at Woolwich in 1720 to train artillery officers, but only a small number of cadets passed through it, and their training rested heavily on acquiring gunnery skills, knowledge of surveying, and the manners of gentlemen. However, some senior officers, such as General James Wolfe and Lord Cornwallis, recognized the need for broader training. They read widely themselves and encouraged others to do so. Since French and German officer training was far superior, it is not surprising that many military books, such as Sébastien Le Prestre de Vauban's classic *Treatise on the Attack and Defense of Fortresses* and King Frederick of Prussia's *Instructions* to his generals, written in French and German respectively, were not available in translation. So fluency in a foreign language was a prerequisite to get beyond a rudimentary military education. Only instruction in the basics of drill was available in English. The British army produced a text, *The Manual Exercise*, and General Wolfe authored his own handbook, *Instructions to Young Officers*, which included such necessary information as "the orders and signals used in embarking and debarking an Army by flat-bottom'd boats." But essentially, the British relied heavily on "on-the-job" training. New officers were introduced to daily military order and the rituals of long regimental tradition. Some of this was done through the social rituals of the regimental officers' mess where officers of all ranks often dined, smoked, and conversed together. Additionally, senior officers, ideally those with talent and experience, modeled desired conduct and instilled appropriate values. And seasoned noncommissioned officers monitored and directed the daily running of the camp, showing young officers, often many years their junior, the ropes. In such ways, young officers slowly gained confidence and skill.[11]

The institutional ingredients that the Americans lacked, then, are clear. Without military academies, well-established regiments and their social and dining rituals, or experienced noncommissioned officers (at least until after the first year of the war), Americans had to rest heavily on the daily routine of army life, military law, the model of senior officers, and the few available books to train officers. Judging by the books that were circulating in the country, either imported before the armed conflict began or rushed to print after, officers and armchair generals were eager to learn about the art of war. From 1773 onward, there were a flurry of colonial editions of the British army's *Manual Exercise*, which often included Wolfe's *Instructions* as an appendix. Roger Stevenson's *Military Instructions for Officers Detached in the Field*, printed in London in 1772, was quickly picked up by an American printer once the fighting began. Colonel Lewis Nicola, a French-born Continental officer, translated two military treatises into English, published in 1776 and 1777 respectively, and also wrote his own *Treatise of Military Exercise, calculated for the use of the Americans*. Finally, in 1779, Baron Friedrich von Steuben, the Prussian officer who volunteered his services to the Continental army, gave the officer corps an official manual. Washington intended that Steuben should train the army in "a Uniform System of useful Manoeuvres and regularity of discipline," and his *Regulations for the Order and Discipline of the Troops of the United States* gave officers all the basic information they needed.[12]

These instruction manuals were basic indeed. They did not go into explanations on how to construct fortifications or calculate artillery trajectories. Rather, they told young officers what words to say when giving commands to arrange camp life and how to care for equipment. They included instructions for organizing and participating in military funerals, dealing with insubordination from soldiers, organizing a camp, and inspecting the men. In these manuals, a young, inexperienced officer could find the commands to have soldiers practice loading and unloading their weapons or to drill, the latter being essential for the close-order tactics of eighteenth-century warfare. Steuben showed officers how to organize men for guard duty and gave an example of a worksheet that might be used that would record who was on duty when.[13]

Senior officers encouraged the reading of these military texts, and certainly some books seem to have reached their intended audience. General Lachlan McIntosh, in 1776, distributed some military books he had received to his officers, and the following year, Washington instructed his commanders to encourage their officers to read military texts, as there was "a great deal of useful knowledge and Instruction to be drawn" from them. And indeed the books were circulating. In 1775, John Adams, at the time a Massachusetts representative to the Continental Congress, was eager to know "what Books upon Martial science were to be found in the Army." He asked his friend William Tudor, the army's judge advocate general, to tell him if the great military books of the age were available to officers who wanted to become "Masters of the Profession." Adams asked Tudor about a long list of books that included Marshal de Saxes's *Rêveries*, Guillaume Le Blond's *Treatise of Artillery*, and William Young's *Manoeuvres or Practical Observations on the Art of War*. In reply, Tudor told him that most of them were at headquarters but "not more than two of them are in any officers hands." But in hands they were. Jeremiah Greenman, having crossed the great divide from soldier to officer, recorded in his diary that he was reading Stevenson's *Military Instructions*. A Hessian officer, Johann Ewald, part of the German forces fighting as British allies, was impressed by the reading American officers were doing; the Hessians were regularly finding military books in captured American baggage. He claimed that the Hessians had found Frederick of Prussia's *Instructions* "more than a hundred times."[14]

Still, Captain Ewald's observations and the translating labors of Colonel Nicola notwithstanding, it is unlikely that military texts were reaching more than a small minority of officers. If any text gained wide currency, it was Steuben's, which covered the basics of camp life, drill, and military organization rather than tactics and strategy, which was information the Continental army probably needed more. Reading about army life was not going to train the army. Rather, living the army life would have to do it. By insisting on sharply different standards for pay, clothing, and style of living, the distinctions of rank and due respect for those distinctions were instilled in American officers and men.

Of course, distinctions in standards of living among social ranks were the norm in civilian life, and colonial Americans carefully considered the needs of the different social levels as they created their army. Letters concerning army pay make some of these perceptions explicit. Pay levels, of course, were a key difference among ranks. Officers' pay had to be substantially more than that of soldiers to support a higher standard of living. However, the pay scale also reflected the perceived differences in the social needs of the two groups.

The men who would serve as soldiers, already clearly identified in the colonial mind, could be encouraged, Washington thought, to enlist for mercenary motives. General Charles Lee at the outset of the war maintained that soldiers' pay was a "fortune to the low wretches who live like the Common Soldiers," and General Nathanael Greene concurred. He thought the pay so high that it amounted to bribery. Colonial newspapers agreed the pay was good. The *Connecticut Courant* did not think the pay "equal to intentions of bribery," but it did think that the money offered was "equal to all the purposes of comfortable and manly subsistence" and encouraged enlistment.[15]

Despite Lee's and Greene's claims and the public rhetoric, soldiers' pay was never as much as could be made by free men who had steady employment as laborers. Even the additional value of an army food ration, largely consisting of flour and beef of poor quality, probably did not tempt more than a few. The prospect of an army uniform did not add value to the recruiter's offer, either. Apart from the clothing offered by some states as part of the bounty, uniforms, when available at all, were charged to the soldiers. Still, for those who faced the uncertainties of seasonal labor, a soldier's pay was probably tempting. Even so, state legislatures had to resort to a variety of bounty inducements to entice those in need of ready cash. It was still not enough to tempt older family men. Certainly, concern over providing for a growing family kept Boston shoemaker George R. T. Hewes out of the army. A patriot by sentiment but already in his thirties with four children at home at the beginning of the war and six by the end, the promise of land did not meet his immediate need to provide for his growing family. But patriot leaders hoped that for younger men, especially those without family responsibilities, bounties in some form would draw them into service. Washington understood that "such People as compose the bulk of an Army" were never recruited "by any other principles than those of Interest," that is, material gain. His advice to John Hancock, the president of Congress, was that any expectation that such people would fight for principle was "to look for what never did, & I fear never will happen."[16]

If material gain was going to spur those who normally became soldiers to join and stay in the army, it might also inspire "Men of Character" to apply to be officers, and indeed it did. However, Washington thought it did so for different reasons. Officers needed money so they could live like gentlemen, entertain and dress in a manner appropriate to their rank, and yet be financially independent of the mercenary world around them. "There is nothing that gives a Man consequence, & renders him fit for Command," Washington wrote, like financial independence. Also, an officer, in contrast to the common soldier, had to be rewarded for taking on the risks of service. For a soldier, this was seen as just another job for pay. An officer, on the other hand, if indeed he was a gentleman, might never have worked for pay before. He would have supported himself from income from his investments or from property farmed or labored on by others. An officer therefore was seen to be risking himself in ways he had not previously done. By becoming an officer, Washington observed, a gentleman put "his life in his hand — hazards his health — & forsakes the Sweets of domestic enjoyments" by serving his country.[17]

Of course, not all men who claimed gentry status or who aspired to it had such complete financial independence. Many took an active role in farming or commercial affairs, or were prosperous craftsmen, or the sons of such men who had worked for pay. So, good pay was seen as essential to augment other income and was by itself perceived as a way society valued the service and sacrifice of "domestic enjoyments." In a letter to John Hancock in 1776, Washington had another, less noble reason for wanting generous pay. Since he suspected that all his officers were not paragons of virtue, he hoped that with pay to support a gentleman's lifestyle, they would not stoop "to the low, & dirty arts which many of them practice to filch the Public." The "dirty arts" he was referring to were crimes such as embezzling funds that were intended to support and pay soldiers. For example, a year earlier in 1775, Captain Oliver Parker of Massachusetts was cashiered — dishonorably discharged from the army — for "defrauding his men of their advance pay" and "drawing more Rations than he had men in his company" and selling the excess. We do not know what drove Parker to his crime. Later, Washington clearly suspected that when officers defrauded the public, they were driven to do so by financial necessity; however, since such crimes were not unknown among British and other European officers, pay alone was probably not going to solve this problem.[18]

Congress, when organizing the army, created a pay scale that reflected social distinctions and the different responsibilities of officers and men. During the war, however, this scale changed to bolster the needs of officers and to tempt them to stay in the service. It was also part of the continuing process of subordinating soldiers. The change in pay indeed worked to the detriment of the private soldier. In 1775, Congress set the pay for all ranks. The pay for privates, ordinary soldiers, was set at six and two-thirds dollars per month. The pay of an ensign, the lowest rank of commissioned officer, at ten dollars per month, was one and a half times higher. The pay of a colonel, at fifty dollars per month, was seven and a half times that of a private soldier and five times that of the most junior officer.[19]

In 1778, Congress finally addressed the concerns of officers and patriot and military leaders about pay. This followed the disastrous winter at Valley Forge, which had led to widespread officer resignations. Congressional resolutions substantially widened the gap between the pay of officers and men but narrowed the relative pay among officers themselves. A private soldier continued to be paid at six and two-thirds dollars per month, but now an ensign received twenty dollars, about three times that of the private, and a colonel received seventy-five dollars, more than eleven times that of the private but less than four times that of the ensign. This legislation also continued this pay differential into the postwar years. It provided at war's end, following service for the duration of the war, a "gratuity" payment of eighty dollars to privates and NCOs. That was a year's pay for a soldier and eight months' pay for a sergeant. Officers, in contrast, were to receive half-pay for seven years.[20]

Grievances over pay were legion among both officers and men, but the relative differences of the pay scale were not in question. Rather, complaints centered on concerns they all shared. Officers, representing their own interests and those of their men, lobbied state and national legislatures over the form of pay (whether specie — hard coin — or paper of questionable worth), its late delivery, and its depreciating value. The last issue was resolved in 1780, when Congress required states to pay their own Continental soldiers. Most arranged conversions for depreciating currency, although the formulas they came up with for this left most men of all ranks unhappy. Unrest over pay issues culminated in the mutinies of January 1781 and concerned the grievances noted above, not the pay differentials between soldiers and officers.[21]

Officers had to have pay to support the life of a gentleman because it was generally understood that they should not have to share the great physical hardships soldiers endured. Soldiers' lives were often grim because of two particular problems they faced. The first was disease. Poor sanitation and hygiene practices resulted in the proliferation of camp diseases with high mortality rates such as dysentery and typhus. This was a problem that would not be completely resolved until the twentieth century. The second cause of hardship was the inability of even the most powerful nations to harness effective systems of organization and supply in the changeable circumstances of war. Even when nations, such as Britain, were occasionally able to accomplish it, frequent breakdowns occurred that could and did lead to catastrophe. When the system worked well, it was usually the result of a harmonious convergence of factors. First, there needed to be an effective and respected leader who had the support of a dynamic quartermaster-general, the highest ranking officer in charge of supply. Next, the quartermaster-general had to be capable of coordinating and administering his organization, and he in turn needed to have under him a bureaucracy of effective agents. To facilitate their work, they also needed strict discipline among troops and an energetic officer corps. But even if all of this was in place, the entire army and its campaigns could be supplied only if there was a good measure of political will to finance the enterprise. Without all of these elements, which even the British with their considerable experience could muster only periodically, soldiers were doomed to suffer periods of short rations, clothing unsuited to different seasons, and poor equipment of every kind.[22]

In the face of intermittent and inadequate supply, soldiers frequently lived in horrific conditions. From their experiences in imperial wars, colonial Americans already knew about them either firsthand or secondhand. In the Seven Years' War, provincial soldiers had experienced great hardship, and some had been shocked at the precariousness of camp life. Joseph Nichols of Massachusetts noted that "[o]ur provincial forces die more or less, almost every day; but people who are used to camps tell me that they never knew a more healthy time in an army." Sickness in the army was compounded by malnourishment as food supplies were irregular. Sometimes soldiers found themselves in situations where there was simply no food available to them anywhere. At other times, they could use their own money to make up for the army's deficiencies. In 1758, another Massachusetts soldier, William Sweat, wrote in his diary that "our alowence is very short, for wee have not more than half alowance, & wee were forced to Buy the Rest."[23]

As this observation shows, the low pay of soldiers compounded their problems. When supply was deficient, they relied on their own meager financial resources to augment their diet. When this ran out, they were forced to sell whatever they had. On an expedition to Fort Edward in 1760, hungry soldiers waited for supplies, but as one Massachusetts provincial soldier noted in his diary, "[N]o wagen came and we had no alounc." The next day, another soldier "[s]ould his Shirt for half a Doler and Bought Sum Backen [bacon] Bones for us to eat." The ragged Virginian provincials at Fort Necessity in the Ohio country also went hungry as the colonial governor Robert Dinwiddie lamented that the colony's finances prevented him from providing more food. He suggested that the troops use "Ind[ia]n Meal, w[hi]ch is a hearty Food and comes much cheaper than Flour." It was indeed cheaper, which, as the governor and the luckless troops knew, was why it was usually given to slaves. In these circumstances, it is not surprising that soldiers bought food when they could and stole when they had to, preying on any farms or communities that might alleviate their distress.[24]

This led to a vicious cycle. Soldiers were perceived as dangerous and thieving and their camps the locus of disease and despair. Civilians in the Seven Years' War and during the Revolution were happy to have soldiers somewhere else, out of sight—and sometimes also out of mind. This was compounded by the general suspicion of standing armies and the fact that those serving were poor men without a direct political voice. Consequently, it required energetic souls indeed to see the problem in its totality and muster the political will required to bring about an efficient system of supply. Without the political will to alleviate soldiers' suffering, there was no hope of resolving the administrative and financial problems of coordinating supply, and so soldiers suffered accordingly. Colonial Americans came to their Revolution knowing these problems but without a solution in mind.

The experience of the Revolutionary War did not provide the answer, and, for the army, the war years were marked by unpredictable supplies, intermittent suffering, and occasional catastrophe. The colonists faced the fundamental problem of having poor infrastructure. They simply lacked adequate roads, wagons, and teamsters to wage a prolonged war over great distances. Even when there was a political will to ameliorate supply problems, there was rarely a way it could effectively be brought to bear. Congress initially tried to have the states supply the army. It did this partly from inexperience, not realizing the coordination and administration required to supply goods on this scale, and partly from an expectation that the war would be short. But, it also looked to the states because it feared centralized power and because most members of Congress had a local worldview. By 1778, when the suffering of the army was apparent, there was the political will to transform the system of supply and concentrate power at the national level. However, this failed to solve anything, because the structural problems were not well understood and because national power was weak and newly appointed department heads had to work with local communities and not override them. Also, local authorities preferred to listen to the needs, rights, and interests of their constituents rather than those of the army. Soldiers serving in the Continental lines of their home states were not a constituent interest that needed representing.[25]

Some believed that state legislatures were serving not only the interests of their constituents but also their own interests. For example, Nathanael Greene thought that in the Rhode Island legislature, "[i]gnorance, confidence and obstinacy" were the hallmarks of the government. Like cynics of every age, he observed the old proverb that "when the political Pot boils the scum rises." Greene was not accusing the legislature of corruption but rather concluded that some members had their own prosperity in mind more than the good of the nation or the condition of the army.[26]

For all these reasons, the army remained poorly supplied. All during the war, food was unreliably provided; warm clothing was scarce; and tents, blankets, and clean straw were hard to come by; and the soldiers duly suffered. Officers occasionally suffered, too, and complained vigorously when they did, but for the most part soldiers and officers lived in very different circumstances. Americans inside and outside of the army were quite clear on the distinction between the standard of living for soldiers and officers. When John Williams wrote to his uncle Elisha Porter, a Massachusetts officer at Crown Point in New York, he was concerned about his uncle's health and asked him, "[W]hat is your Situation? do you live as officers, or under the Hardships and Fatigues of soldiers?" Similarly, Samuel Adams, a prosperous Massachusetts doctor serving with the Continentals (not the patriot politician of the same name), complained to his wife that on one occasion he lived "[s]oldier like indeed." He could be sure she would know what he meant and sympathize with him accordingly.[27]

Officers lived the lives of gentlemen. Occasionally, this meant living in specially built huts in camp, particularly when the army was in winter quarters. More commonly, it meant that they billeted in nearby homes with local families, coming into camp to supervise their men. Lieutenant John Bell Tilden and his fellow officers, near Parker's Ferry in 1782, found some pleasing accommodation at a Mr. Orwell's where "we are used politely by him and his lady." Captain Persifor Frazer of the Pennsylvania line also found some creature comforts while on Long Island in the summer of 1776. He lodged with some other officers "at a private House near the Camp, a very genteel commodious, pleasant place as ever I saw, and the people extremely agreeable." Physicians in the Continental army enjoyed a status equivalent to officers, and so Doctor Samuel Adams also enjoyed staying in genteel homes and found the comforts both material and social. So nice were his accommodations at Mount Independence in the fall of 1776 that he promised his wife that, should she visit, he and the officers would be able to offer her tea "in a genteel manner." Two years later, while at "Artillery Park," a camp in Fredericksburg, Pennsylvania, he enjoyed not only the "friendship of the officers in general" but also the "acquaintance in some of the best families in the vicinity."[28]

Some officers also had servants, sometimes called waiters or valets. These were usually soldiers assigned the task, but they could be servants or slaves brought from home, or even a young son brought by an officer both to serve him and to give the child the adventure of being away from home. Ten-year-old Israel Trask served with his officer father and did a variety of chores for him and the other officers. He was a messenger, he looked after the baggage, and when the officers were on duty, he was to "take the edibles prepared at the mess to the officers on duty, which in some instance [were] miles distant." In the case of Joseph Rundel, who enlisted in 1778 at age sixteen in the Connecticut line, duty as a servant was given in a protective way to keep him out of harm's way. When General Israel Putnam inspected the troops shortly after Rundel enlisted, he caught sight of the young man and told Rundel he "looked too young . . . to go to the line and said he would take me as his waiter."[29]

Servants smoothed the path of military life. Lieutenant Tilden and his fellow officers near Parker's Ferry had servants attending them. The officers were staying at the Orwells' house while waiting for "our valets" to bring down the tents in which the officers were to camp for a short time. It was a leisurely time. Tilden spent one day relaxing and "reading Spanish novels" while waiting for all this to happen. Lieutenant Isaac Bangs in New England also had a servant to make his life easier. He noted that he and his fellows were inconvenienced for a time when their "waiter," the soldier Simeon Chubbuck, was "very ill of the camp disorder [dysentery]." Without him, they were "in great confusion."[30]

Officers, even while they cared for and were active on behalf of their men, accepted the differences in accommodations. Even Jeremiah Greenman, who, recently promoted to the officer corps, might have been expected to sympathize with the suffering of his men, was quick to exercise the privileges of rank. Settling in for the hard winter at Morristown in December 1779, he made them move so he could have the more comfortable accommodation they had snagged. Captain Moses Greenleaf, with the retreating army after the British took Ticonderoga in the summer of 1777, was pleased that he "[l]odg'd well Last Night, blessed be God for it," but noted that "our men have no Blankets nothing but the Heavens to Cover them." Colonel John Brooks of Massachusetts was deeply moved as he observed the distressing condition of his soldiers on the march to Valley Forge. He felt helpless and wrote to a friend that seeing them "bare footed, bare-legged, bare-breeched, &c, in snow, in rain, in marches, in camp, and on duty, without being able to supply their wants is really distressing." Brooks was a compassionate man who felt their pain, but as an officer he did not share it.[31]

Soldiers lived in a very different world. Occasionally they were in log barracks in winter quarters, but much more commonly they found themselves under canvas in tents or, when on the move, under the night sky. Joanna Eliot wrote to her soldier husband simply asking if he had any "comfort of Life or no." Usually the answer was no. For many men, that sometimes meant "hardships sufficient to kill half a dozen horses," especially in winter when the ground was cold and wet and blankets and warm clothing scarce. Sergeant Moses Moody described a miserable night in January 1777 that he and his men spent near Kingsbridge, camped in the woods without tents or other shelter. That night, there was "[a] Snow

Storm So bad that we were Forced to Stand up from twelve o'Clock till morning over the fier [fire] we Could not lay down because it was so weet." Even when
kind local residents offered accommodation, soldiers, embarrassed by their
ragged and filthy state, sometimes refused. For food, flour and beef, often salted
or dried, made up the core of the soldiers' diet, augmented by potatoes, rice,
peas, and whatever else could be had, all washed down with rum or ale. Occasionally the meat had seen better days and was referred to by the soldiers as "car-
rion beef," that is, rotting meat, which they considered better than none. Bread
too could be unpalatable. The son of one Virginia Continental, Thomas Bailey,
remembered his father telling about the time the soldiers had received "sour
bread" and that they had made a complaint to George Washington. Washington had tried it and said that "it was true that it was bad but it could yet be eat."
The soldiers had duly made do. There were periods when there was sufficient
food and blankets and dry hay for bedding, but deliveries of these treasures were
unpredictable.[32]

Soldiers who did not desert in the face of these hardships grumbled, but they
accepted, mostly without comment, the differences in circumstances between
officers and men. Young Continental Joseph Plumb Martin remembered that,
as his unit sought shelter from a thunderstorm for the night, "We were ordered
into some barns nearby, the officers as usual ordering themselves into the houses."
For Martin, who did not hesitate to vent his many grievances in his war memoir, that was as close as he got to a complaint on the subject. He understood that
that was just the way things were.[33]

Despite putting up with great hardship, there were certain kinds of treatment
that soldiers did protest vehemently in their diaries and letters, if not vocally at
the time. These occasions involved treatment from officers that they perceived as
additionally or unnecessarily disrespectful while they were suffering from "marching and countermarching, starving and freezing." Lemuel Roberts of the Massachusetts line accepted many hardships but hated it when officers were indifferent
to soldiers' suffering. In 1776, as the army moved through New York, he found
officers cruel when they were "unconscious of our fatigue," resting in comfort
while soldiers slept "on the hard ground, with nothing but the canopy of heaven
for their covering, and that too in the month of December." Roberts especially
resented the disregard General Alexander McDougall had for the comfort of the
troops. Unlike most soldiers, Roberts had a chance for revenge when, one cold
January night, he was assigned sentry duty outside the general's door. "I kept such
a stamping on the loose boards of the stoop, as to prevent his sleeping, and at

length he sent the colonel out to still me; this gentleman, judging rightly of the existing facts, came out with a case bottle of whiskey, which he left with me for the service of the sentries on the stand, with a request that they be as still as possible, and his politeness very much favored the churlish general's repose."[34]

Most soldiers had to seethe more discreetly. Sometimes the available records just hint at deep-seated resentment. One soldier wrote home to his family to advise that they should "do all that Lies in your power to keep your Sons from going into the Service for numbers of reasons I could give but time will not allow at present." Zebulon Vaughan, barely literate, confided more explicitly to his diary that "we ar yoused wors than Beests or hogs att home." The previous year he had lamented that he was billeted in "the Stabel whare the hors feeds this is the way Soldiers ar yused for thare good Conduck." It was enough, he wrote, "to mak Solders Cuse [curse] the day thay Listed." It was hardly surprising that, around the same time, Vaughan noted that there were "dsarteres plentey."[35]

What little we know of Vaughan marks him as the kind of poor man who was filling the ranks of the army. His literacy, marginal as it was, did not help him make his way in the world. He was about thirty-three when he signed up for a three-year term in 1777, and he had already served two short terms, one in Massachusetts and another in New York, putting him among the army's older soldiers. Despite the fact that he had married in 1765, his pattern of service implies no close ties to home, and the New York service indicates mobility. His lengthy diary makes no reference to his home life, nor does it indicate any awareness of the political cause. He did not desert when some in his regiment did and in fact guarded some who were captured. He put up with great hardship and noted at the end of 1779 that he was "tired of this war and want a Discharg." His discharge came in May 1780, exactly three years after his enlistment, and Vaughan had served out his time doggedly. Vaughan noted on a number of days through 1778 and 1779 "dutey very hard and provishon very short," and there were occasions when a day or more passed with no food. However, it was only the indignity of being billeted in the stables with the animals that prompted him to complain that "[s]olders Never was yused woss [worse] than thay been thes days" and to "[r]epent" of his enlistment.[36]

Soldiers' diaries often noted appreciatively small improvements in their daily conditions that help us see what they understood to be the norm. One Continental teamster had clear expectations of a soldier's lot. He recorded his delight in his diary on the few occasions he got a bed to sleep in, and in May 1778, he celebrated a day when he had also got plenty to eat. "I live well for a Continentel," he noted with satisfaction. And a sergeant with the artillery serving as an as-sistant adjutant realized that while he had that duty, he had been a "feather bed soldier."[37]

The state militia also knew that living conditions had to be taken as they came, even for temporary soldiers such as themselves. One Pennsylvania militiaman told of the night that his whole company, all thirty-three of them, slept in a two-room house with the householder, his wife, and their four small children. The men found the house "not very clean and sweet"; however, since they were very tired, they were not fussy and slept wrapped in their blankets on a floor "which did not appear to be clean'd since the house was built." They knew the alterna-tive was the wet ground outside, and so our diarist looked on the bright side and noted that the dirt made the lodging "soft," which was not "a bad circum-stance in soldiering."[38]

Officers occasionally shared the conditions of their men when the circum-stances of a campaign required it. Most had difficulty adjusting. In May 1776, one Pennsylvanian lieutenant, James McMichael, was surprised on the first night after his company mustered to find that he was "denied a bed." He was so un-used to this that he spent a sleepless night. There would be more than a few nights when he was unable to get a bed, but that only made him determined to get "agreeable quarters" whenever he could. Officers grumbled when they along with their men were issued meager rations, as when the Massachusetts troops arrived exhausted and hungry at Valley Forge. Lieutenant Samuel Armstrong observed that the soldiers put up with this "bad Usage" well, partly, he thought, because they had the pleasure of knowing that "the Officers Endured the Same and in-deed there was more mutiny among the Officers than among their men." When Lieutenant Ebenezer Huntington found himself in the summer of 1780 living like a soldier, he was outraged. He wrote to his family that he was "in Rags, have lain in the Rain on the Ground for 40 hours past" with hardly any food. He was disheartened and bitter and felt abandoned by his civilian countrymen. He wished he "could say I was not born in America, I once gloried in it but am now ashamd of it."[39]

Though sometimes an officer had to live like a soldier, it was unusual for him to dress like one, and Huntington's comment about being clothed in rags was almost certainly hyperbole. He was probably just not as appropriately dressed as he would have liked to be, as he was from a prosperous Connecticut family. Dress was the most immediately visible mark of distinction that officers had, and as such, a great deal of attention was devoted to it. Genteel men dressed elegantly in and out of the army. Luxurious fabrics, such as satin, silk, or velvet, and decorative touches of lace were badges of wealth, fashion, and gentility for men and women alike. Indeed, it was socially acceptable for men to be as fussy about their clothing as women were without compromising their masculinity.[40]

This attitude meshed nicely with the military uses of dress. In the European tradition, uniforms served a greater purpose than merely warming body and soul and distinguishing friend from foe. Since much of an army's duty was public display that reinforced the power of the monarch, such as marching in parades at ceremonial occasions, uniforms became smart and fashionable and sometimes almost theatrical in the amount of decoration and adornment they had. Even battle itself, usually an event that everyone could anticipate and prepare for in advance in the eighteenth-century world, was a dress-up occasion that required fastidious attention to appearance. Uniforms in bright colors with insignia and accessories not only helped to differentiate among regiments and sides in the smoky confusion of battle but also impressed the enemy with the military prowess, poise, and power of the state represented.[41]

Colonial Americans brought these attitudes about dress to their own army. While the problem of supply and funding interfered with an appropriate "soldier like" appearance for privates, and while officers themselves sometimes lacked supplies and the cash to dress with requisite flair, the goal remained a stylish uniform that both served a functional purpose on the battlefield and reinforced the distinctions of rank. The British relied on a range of decorations and adornments, such as differing colors of facings, linings, waistcoats (vests), hat lace, cockades (a ribbon or feather in a hat), epaulets (shoulder straps often made of strips of cloth, sometimes fringed), gorgets (badges hung about the neck), and so on, for distinctions among officers and regiments. Washington followed the British pattern and used different colors of linings and facings to distinguish different regiments from different states. However, while he simplified some of this ornamentation for the Continental army, he went further than the British in coming up with distinctions among officers. After a brief period when the different state troops followed their own paths, Washington settled on different colors of sashes for generals, different colors of cockades for each rank of officer, and epaulets for NCOs. After the French joined the war as American allies, Washington made some changes, principally for high-ranking officers. In the summer of 1780, general officers added stars on the epaulets of their uniforms, just as the French did. With this adjustment, the additional establishment of a broad range of epaulets for various ranks, and other minor alterations, he made the final uniform changes of the war, "both for the sake of appearance and for the regularity of service that the different military ranks should be distinguished from each other."[42]

We know from Washington's specific instructions in his general orders and from a variety of government documents what the uniforms of officers and men of the various state lines were supposed to look like. But, the convictions of some modern reenactors and Hollywood directors notwithstanding, we have very little certainty about what they actually did wear. Sometimes, the perfect, prescribed uniform was worn. One of the few that has survived the centuries belonged to Lieutenant Colonel Tench Tilghman, a senior staff officer. Tilghman had been a wealthy Philadelphia merchant before the war and, after joining the army, was on Washington's personal staff. His surviving uniform conforms almost exactly to the army's specifications.[43]

However, despite this example, we know from written memoirs, eyewitness observations of both enemies and allies, newspapers, and a few extant drawings that the complete uniforms were almost never worn. Even the highest-ranking officers probably did not regularly wear the uniforms they wore when they were immortalized in the oil paintings left to us by portrait artists of the day. One clue to their attire is a set of drawings that survive, probably made by a Hessian officer taken prisoner after the British defeat at Saratoga in 1777. His images show an American officer and soldier in a mixture of military and civilian clothes, with only the jackets being in military style. Even when they had the outfit, officers sometimes lacked the sophistication to wear it appropriately. Perhaps the best indication that Continental officers frequently fell short of military perfection in their dress is the number of occasions commanders in their daily orders congratulated officers on appearing "clean & genteel on the parade." One can imagine that off the parade ground, with or without the correct uniform details, they often failed to achieve this standard.[44]

While they might not have been fussy about cleanliness, American officers were, like their European counterparts, fussy about the distinctions of rank between themselves and soldiers and among each other. While there may have been variety in clothing depending on their finances and available materials, the distinctions of rank were always preserved. One young officer in 1776 had to suffer a court-martial for wearing the wrong color cockade on duty. Lieutenant Benjamin Holcomb, who should have worn the green cockade of junior officers, was charged with going on guard duty wearing a yellow cockade, thus "assuming the rank of a Captain." Fortunately for Holcomb, the court accepted that he acted "thro' misinformation and want of experience" and released him.[45]

The dress of soldiers, by prescription, was strikingly different from that of officers, but it is even more problematic for historians to reconstruct. Clothing was frequently in short supply, leaving the men in rags, so there is a considerable

An American Soldier.
1778
Kail.   F.v. Germann

An American Officier
1778
Kail.   F.v. Germann

Two 1778 watercolor illustrations of American uniforms by a Hessian
officer, Friedrich von Germann. Courtesy Print Collection, Miriam and
Ira D. Wallach Division of Art, Prints and Photographs, The New
York Public Library, Astor, Lenox and Tilden Foundations.

difference between Washington's guidelines for specific uniform colors, with different color facings and linings to distinguish the different states, and the daily reality. In the earliest days of the war, it was not surprising that the troops stood in "great want of cloathing." It takes a while to harness resources on a large scale. However, the problems continued. For Joseph Plumb Martin, in 1776, the discomfort and distress of "hard duty and nakedness" even outweighed lack of food. The fact that the army, when not in winter quarters, was almost constantly on the move was hard on shoes and stockings, and sleeping in the open was hard on clothing. However, the levels of supply varied enormously at different times, with soldiers of individual states experiencing either feast or famine. The soldiers' problems occasionally went unrelieved when other states refused to share any surpluses that they occasionally had. A few years later, in 1780, Martin, now well clad, was able to make fun of troops he saw on the road who were dressed so raggedly that they looked like a "caravan of wild beasts." In 1777, it was Massachusetts soldiers who went "without Stockings, Breeches or Shoes," and, General John Glover observed, they too were being "[p]ick'd upon" by the troops of other states.[46]

Despite this intermittent hardship, there were periods when the army was supplied. Once Washington determined uniform specifications, Congress and the states bought thousands of them, both from within the new United States and from France. Some of these were pilfered along the way to their destination, but there were times when soldiers did have uniforms. However, when the troops had them, they sometimes did not hang on to them. Soldiers took an entrepreneurial approach to army property, occasionally selling what they had to civilians (who also found clothing in short supply) for food or liquor, cutting up older uniforms to make patches for other items, or trading any recent clothing issue for whatever they might need.[47]

Consequently, even when clothing was issued, it was sometimes held under lock and key for special occasions. This was partly done to preserve clothing, but it was also done so high-ranking officers could be sure that soldiers had an appropriate appearance when they paraded in public. Public display of troops in full dress was a way of reinforcing confidence in the state and its power. When some of Colonel Francis Marion's South Carolinians were to go into Charleston, he gave the junior officers two days' notice to have the men "get their Cloathes clean" so they would look presentable. When his men were to be part of a funeral parade, he ordered that they were "to be as Clean as possible" and were to "receive their Coats out of the store." However, the officer commanding these soldiers had "to take an Account of the men who receive their Coats to see they are return'd before they are discharged." Marion knew that a "soldier like" appearance not only helped build confidence in the institution of the army but also helped soldiers feel confident and have pride in themselves. However, if the latter was indeed a motive, having to give the coats back may have undermined the strategy.[48]

So the question remains: What were soldiers wearing when they were not in uniform, which was most of the time? Letters, diaries, and newspaper advertisements for deserters offer some sources of information. These all describe a hodgepodge of military and civilian clothing and confirm that, throughout the war, soldiers were more concerned with acquiring clothes than caring what color or style they were. They were happy to wear any item, even British uniforms taken from seized enemy stores, with appropriate changes to avoid confusion. However, the principal item of clothing that soldiers wore was the hunting shirt. This practical garment, popular with backwoodsmen, was striking to soldiers who had first seen it worn by Virginia riflemen. In the beginning, some saw it as a "rustic uniform" and made fun of it, but it became the default service uniform for the Continental army. Worn over leggings, the loose-fitting, thigh-length shirt could be made of deerskin, linen, duck, or wool and easily dyed to any color. Washington thought it was a practical alternative when uniforms were not available. "No Dress can be had cheaper, nor more convenient, as the Wearer may be cool in warm weather, and warm in cool weather by putting on under-Cloaths which will not change the outward dress, Winter or Summer." Even this versatile garment was sometimes in short supply. However, by allowing and encouraging its use, Washington achieved some uniformity of appearance, which he felt necessary to order and discipline; soldiers avoided rags; and more costly uniforms were protected from the wear and tear of daily use and consequently lasted longer. The only function of uniforms not met by this garment was the ability to impress the enemy with troops in full military regalia, but Washington felt even that might not be a problem. As the hunting shirt was associated with riflemen, he thought the enemy might be intimidated by the possibility that each of his soldiers was "a complete marksman."[49]

Even while junior officers may have sometimes failed to be as clean and smart as their commanding officers hoped, and soldiers were frequently much more patched together than Washington would have liked, the two groups would never have been confused. Officers, even on their worst day, would have cut a very different appearance from the men under their command, and officers were quick to insist on the distinctions among each other. The officers of the Delaware line, in a petition to the state assembly concerning the supply of their uniforms, pointedly complained of a serious error in the uniform order: the assembly had forgotten to order officers' hats. The officers had to remind the assembly "how necessary a part of an officer's dress a hat is." Without a hat with the right cockade, officers would have difficulty securing the appropriate respect from those around them.[50]

Occasionally, the exigencies of war or intermittent supplies meant that the gap in the standards of living for officers and men narrowed. However, these circumstances did not mean that distinctions disappeared or that officers and men interacted with each other any differently. The army was quite clear that there was to be no fraternizing between soldiers and officers under any circumstances since, as Colonel Lewis Nicola observed, discipline and subordination were "the life of an army." Senior officers set a good example, and orders of the day reminded junior officers of their rank. These reminders in orders were presumably issued because a transgression had been observed. General John Sullivan in 1777 warned his officers against any undue "familiarity" that would lessen their authority. To that end, no officer was to "[e]at or drink with his Men, or play at any games with them." Officers who disobeyed "will not be Counte-

nanced, but removed from the Regiment as unworthy to hold a Commission."
When daily orders failed, military law gave the final lesson: courts-martial were
used to reinforce any lines of distinction that blurred.[51]

A few officers faced courts-martial for conduct unbecoming an officer and a
gentleman for their fraternization. In 1777, a court-martial found one Lieutenant
Cummins of the First Virginia Regiment guilty of "[m]essing with common
soldiers" and sentenced him to be reprimanded by the commanding officer at
the head of his regiment. The court acquitted Cummins of other charges that
throw light onto his state of mind. At the same time as he committed this crime,
he was accused of speaking disrespectfully of his commanding officer, for which
the court found no evidence, and "carrying" away a soldier of his regiment. When
the court heard that the soldier he had carried away was in a "bad state of health"
and "the peculiar circumstances of the matter," they forgave him this transgression. While the details of this incident are lost to us, it seems that Cummins's
compassion caused him momentarily to forget his station. Sometimes, it was
entertainment rather than compassion that caused officers to transgress. In April
1779, Lieutenant Michael Daugherty was court-martialed, found guilty, and
cashiered for two crimes: sending a captain a challenge to fight a duel, which was
illegal under the articles of war, and "playing ball with sergeants." The record
does not show which offense the court considered the more serious.[52]

Fraternizing was not the only act prohibited by military law; courts-martial
were also used or threatened to prevent officers from forgetting their status and
taking on tasks beneath them. As late as 1780, Washington was dismayed that
there were still instances, though he conceded "they are not numerous," where
officers performed duties "derogatory to their rank." He asked all his senior
officers to join with him in preventing this from happening. In 1776, a Lieutenant Whitney was sentenced to a public reprimand by General James Brickett
at the head of his brigade for "infamous conduct in degrading himself by voluntarily doing the duty of an Orderly sergant in violation of his rank as an officer."
In South Carolina, at Fort Moultrie, the daily orders of Colonel Charles Pinckney reprimanded Major Barnard Elliott for ordering a private "to take power
[on]ly due to an Officer." The commander assured the regiment that "if an Officer suffers his Preroga[tive] to be trampled upon which he ought to [not su]p-
port," he would consider him unfit to hold a commission. He also warned that
if "a Private shall dare to obey any[?], but such as have a right to command
[hi]m, he shall suffer for his obedience." Soldiers had to share responsibility with
officers for enforcing the distinctions of rank.[53]

Through dress, accommodation, clothing, and pay, the army taught and insisted on the appropriate and honorable style of living for officers and men. This was an important part of the subordination of the soldiers and the creation of a self-confident officer corps. Part of this self-confidence was a keen sense of what it meant to be a gentleman and have a "proper sense of Honor," and that, ironically, created great tension and anxiety. Officers claimed honor while they labored on a very public stage. On or off duty, they inhabited a cultural world where every action was the subject of scrutiny. Additionally, for most officers, the community of the army was larger than any in which they had previously lived. There were now many more people watching every move, ready to criticize.[54]

One important group of observers was the officers of the British and Hessian armies. These men, despite the fact that they could sometimes be arrogant and supercilious toward Americans, remained models of appropriate conduct to admire and copy, and they were the men that the Continentals desperately wanted to impress. The British had set a standard for the behavior of military gentlemen in North America for years, especially in the Seven Years' War and later during the army's sometimes unwelcome presence in American cities. During that time, and during the Revolution itself, Americans believed themselves qualified to judge gentlemanly behavior. Accordingly, they judged some officers favorably and others not. So deeply ingrained in American sensibilities was the appropriate conduct for British officers that South Carolina historian David Ramsay, writing after the war, was able to note the decline in quality of the British officer corps during the war. The "old officers of the British regiments in America were for the most part gentlemen," he observed, but the corps began to fill up with a "new set greatly inferior in fortune, education and good breeding."[55]

Individual British officers who joined the American cause sometimes transmitted standards of conduct for military gentlemen directly to the Continental army. One who did this was General Richard Montgomery, who was killed early in the war at the siege of Quebec. He was an Anglo-Irishman who had been a captain in the British army and a friend of the British general Guy Carleton. Montgomery was a recent immigrant who had resigned his commission in the British army only in 1773. His rank and experience made him a valuable addition to the Continental army, and he was second in command to General Philip Schuyler on the Quebec expedition. His military experience was not the only asset that he brought to the army; he was also an important model of a military gentleman, admired for his "fine military presence . . . , winning manners," and bravery.[56]

Direct British influence was felt not only at the highest levels. John Holland, an adjutant with the Delaware Continentals, had a profound influence on the junior officers in his regiment. He had been a captain in the British army and had resigned his commission over a matter of honor and immigrated to the colonies before the war. The young Enoch Anderson, a nineteen-year-old second lieutenant in the Delaware regiment, relied heavily on Holland's advice, as did other young officers, and often "consulted my friend Holland" on a variety of matters.[57]

When British, European, and American officers encountered each other on occasions such as surrenders or parleys under flags of truce, they tried to impress each other with their gentlemanly qualities. Each party wanted to assure the other of his ability to act as a gentleman. American general Philip Schuyler pleased a number of witnesses with his graciousness toward British general John Burgoyne when Burgoyne surrendered his troops after the Battle of Saratoga. Burgoyne had reason to be embarrassed at Schuyler's kindness, as he had ordered a number of the Schuyler family homes burnt, which one observer thought was done "without any necessity." Burgoyne was moved. "Is it to *me*, who have done you so much injury, that you show so much kindness!" "That is the fate of war," Schuyler replied, "let us say no more about it." Schuyler's behavior conformed to the standard advice of the courtesy books. "Shew not yourself glad at the Misfortune of another though he were your enemy." The rules said that it was all right to be inwardly pleased at the misery of a "Suffering Offender," but one should "always shew pity."[58]

Showing an enemy kindness in defeat and having that magnanimity recognized was something that all officers prized. During the Seven Years' War, when the French baron Jean-Armand Dieskau was mortally wounded and taken prisoner at Lake George in 1755, Sir William Johnson, who headed the New England provincial forces, treated him with "utmost Humanity & generous Delicacy." Dieskau, even near death, impressed all observers with his reciprocal kindness, "decent Composure," and his bearing as "the philosopher, the Soldier and the Gentleman." Peter Wraxall, Johnson's secretary, was moved by the gracious conduct of both men and related it to Henry Fox, then the British secretary at war.[59]

Similar cases of model behavior during the Revolution also circulated widely. The gracious behavior by American commanders toward the Hessian colonel Carl von Donop, who was mortally wounded in the attack on Fort Mercer in October 1777, and Donop's reciprocation touched many Americans. People were moved by the respect and courtesy of his supposed last words. On his deathbed in American custody three days after the battle, he was reported to have said to a brother officer: "I fall a victim to my own ambition & to the avarice of my prince; but full of thankfulness for the good treatment I have received from my generous enemy." Whatever the truthfulness of this story, Americans were willing to believe it. A number of American military diaries and letters of the period noted Donop's ceremonial burial by his captors. Jeremiah Greenman, one of the privates who moved up to the officer corps, was still a sergeant when he wrote Donop's last words out in his diary. He was clearly touched by the graciousness of the language and sentiment.[60]

Sometimes British and American officers tried to impress each other with the relative delicacy of their sense of honor. The following exchange between American Robert Howe, a colonel at the time, and British naval captain Henry Bellew shows how such exchanges could sometimes border on the ridiculous. Bellew was about to attack Norfolk, Virginia, in December 1775. He told Howe he had no option but to do so as "the honour of my commission" would not allow him to tolerate armed rebellion. Howe responded cordially. "I am too much of an officer to ask you to do anything incompatible with the honour of your commission," he told Bellew; therefore it was all right for Bellew to attack. But Howe also added that he was bound by what he believed to be his own duty. Therefore, he would "be unworthy of the respect of a man of your character" if he did not resist Bellew's attack.[61]

It was not surprising that American officers asserted their status given the precariousness of their military situation and the uncertainties of their rank. American officers envied the security of British and European officers' positions. It was not the legitimacy of the Continental commissions themselves that were in doubt. Surprisingly, those had gained immediate recognition and respect in colonial society, a testament to the widespread public support for the cause and the political process by which commissions were assigned. Still, officers found themselves uncertain of the paths for advancement. The Continental army was a national force operating along state lines, which complicated matters of seniority and preferment. When vacancies occurred in one state at a particular rank, men might be promoted quickly, while officers in another state's regiments could serve for much longer periods without the opportunity for promotion. Whether militia service prior to Continental service added to seniority, how seniority was calculated when officers left the service and then returned, and what the comparative status was of officers from different branches of the service (infantry, light horse, and artillery) were all issues that compounded the already daunting divisions along state and national lines. Sometimes merit rather than seniority led to promotion, but even that might be seen by the jealous as favoritism. An officer might be promoted after demonstrating bravery in the field; however, that proved to be a source of tension too as some officers thought that that was a matter of luck, as had they been there, they too would have acted bravely.[62]

Thomas Burke, a Congressional representative from North Carolina, saw the need for clear guidelines, especially if the national government was to decide on promotions. If officers saw their honor resting "at the precarious pleasure" of Congress, he argued, they would have to direct their energy toward courting that body, since "[o]fficers hold their honor the most dear of anything." Unfortunately, Congress came up with a vague resolution that said it would take seniority, merit, and troop quotas into account. The matter would always be a source of conflict.[63]

In this environment, anxiety over rank and other kinds of public recognition were severe. When some of General Anthony Wayne's senior officers felt slighted when they were not accorded the recognition they thought they deserved in his reports after the Battle of Stony Point in 1779, they wrote to him to express their sentiments. Colonel Return J. Meigs wrote that "[o]ur feelings in these matters are exquisite." Lieutenant Colonel Isaac Sherman took the part of all the officers who were injured — injured in reputation, that was. He told Wayne that "my blood boils at the thought" of their "trampled" feelings. Sherman explained his reasons for taking up their cause. "I thought we were viewed of no consequence in the scale of Beings. The thought awoke all my sensations — it would have animated a dead man."[64]

In the face of this sensitivity, senior officers found themselves having to be resolute in defending their decisions. Wayne, in this case, decided the best defense was a good offense, and he accused the officers who wrote to him of challenging his honor. He reminded one that he too "was tanacious of my *honor* — which is now slighted." To another, he wrote that "for altho' I don't wish to Incur an[y] Gentlemans displeasure, I put up with no mans Insults." In 1782, when Lieutenant Colonel Henry Lee accused General Nathanael Greene of slighting him, Greene took a gentler approach. "Whatever may be the source of your wounds, I wish it were in my power to heal them," he wrote, but "I am far from agreeing with you." Lee was a good friend of Greene's, and their dispute was painful to both of them. When, later the same year, a challenge came to Greene from a group of lesser men, officers of the Pennsylvania line, he responded more aggressively. The officers were objecting to a reorganization of the line that left them feeling "injured subjects" with their "rights infring'd on." Greene's response was swift and unequivocal. "You are under military not civil government," he wrote. "Your grievan[c]es are imaginary."[65]

Sensitivity concerning rank and honor occasionally provoked officers into disputes with each other over perceived slights that resulted in charges that could be settled only by courts of inquiry and courts-martial. Junior officers were not the only ones involved in this behavior. One court of inquiry had to sit to take facts on an incident involving a brigade major and a major, with the former having been arrested by the latter who thought he had been insulted. In another instance, a captain requested a court of inquiry because "the Officers of his Corps have from some misunderstanding refused to do duty with him." He wanted the court to determine whether he had "committed any Action which makes him worthy of the Neglect." He asked the court to acquit him of any misconduct, which it duly did.[66]

Commanding officers used their authority to confirm courts-martial decisions to try to stamp out these petty squabbles. They tried to teach that, although the troubles were rooted in matters of honor, the nature of the disputes were themselves dishonorable. They reprimanded officers for inappropriate actions, even when the court acquitted them. In South Carolina in 1777, a dispute between two lieutenants over perceived insults resulted in the accused being acquitted, as his words were "in no wise Criminal but rather indelicate." In confirming the acquittal, General William Moultrie took the opportunity to note that even indelicacy was wrong "in a profession So pure as that of a Soldier" as it was "inconsistent with that nicety of honour which gives dignity to the Caracter." The following year, Washington confirmed the sentence of an ensign discharged from the service for "challenging" a captain. Having done that, he restored the ensign to his rank and reprimanded both men for conduct "that does neither of them much Honor."[67]

Senior officers used the verdicts of courts-martial both to reprimand and educate young officers on appropriate standards of gentlemanly conduct. General McDougall, while pardoning an officer sentenced to be cashiered in 1779, rebuked him for exhibiting "a temper more like a petty fogging Attorney than the nice & delicate principles of honour which should always govern every Officer concerned with the Continental Army." Washington severely reprimanded an ensign in his general orders in 1780 for calling his colonel "a damn'd liar and Rascal." Although the charge was "not fully supported," the court found that Ensign Russel had used "highly indecent and illiberal" language. Washington confirmed the sentence and said that Russel's behavior was "diametrically contrary to the rules of good breeding" and "entirely disrespectful considering the relative situation between him and Colonel Sherburne." On the counts of manners and deference to rank, this young officer had offended.[68]

Educating officers in appropriate conduct was also done in more benign ways, such as the quiet example of superiors. Washington and other senior officers led the way in demonstrating gracious conduct. Captain Persifor Frazer was impressed by the manners of General Nathanael Greene, who he thought was an "accomplished, fine gentleman." Greene and others, as true gentlemen, also had to show appropriate condescension, and junior officers were grateful recipients of such treatment. Young Lieutenant John Bell Tilden of the Pennsylvania line was very sensitive to the small courtesies of life. He joined the officer corps in 1779 as an ensign after graduating from Princeton when he was eighteen and became a lieutenant a year later. He recorded in his diary when Colonel John Lamb gave him "a cordial shake by the hand." At this time, shaking hands had not yet replaced the bow as a greeting. A handshake was a mark of intimacy and affability, and Tilden recognized it as a compliment. He was also impressed when Washington behaved with similar cordiality. The commander in chief had joined the troops at Williamsburg. After reconnoitering the lines, he invited the officers of the Pennsylvania line to his quarters where "he received them very politely and shook each officer by the hand."[69]

General Sullivan offered direct encouragement to his officers when he wanted them to learn "the salute with the sword." Lieutenant Erkuries Beatty and other officers of the Pennsylvania line were eager to get it right and, in response to the general's orders, duly turned out one Sunday morning to learn and practice. Sullivan himself came out to inspect the results, led by "curiosity," Beatty suspected. The officers wanted a reward for their efforts and, after they were dismissed, approached the general and asked him to give them a keg of rum. Sullivan must have been impressed or, as Beatty thought, "in one of his generous thouts which he is but seldom possess'd of," for he not only granted the request but made it six kegs instead of one.[70]

Knowing the rules of appropriate behavior gave officers confidence to navigate the various complex paths for promotion and made it easier for them to advance in the military hierarchy. This was one of the central contradictions of genteel society and, in turn, the army that absorbed its values. The rules of honor and deference instilled a respect for rank, and that respect was a critical tool for social harmony. Society functioned most harmoniously when everyone knew his or her place and acted accordingly. Yet knowledge of the rules gave people the ability to move up socially. So the acquisition of the skills essential for social and military stability and harmony was in itself socially disruptive and a tool for the private end of self-advancement.[71]

A number of gentlemen of the army were quick to criticize perceived overtly ambitious behavior in others. John Lacey, certainly ambitious himself but feeling slighted after his honor was dented in a dispute with General Wayne, saw some of his colleagues as his enemies. He had thought that men were "simple as myself." He never dreamt of the designs of "Men of Craft and cuning swindlers and deceptive knaves, of Mean Sycofants, Toad-eaters, & spittle lickers to great Men, Flatterers & Buffoons." Lewis Beebe, a Continental doctor on the Quebec expedition, also had no kind words for those he saw as only interested in "promotion & honour." He described the senior officers with his party as "a Sett of Haughty, ambitious aspiring miscreants."[72]

Ambitious miscreants or not, all officers had to be shown respect, especially from soldiers. The army taught and insisted on appropriate "reverence," that is, bowing, saluting, or other marks of deference from soldiers. In South Carolina, the appropriate marks of deference were published in 1777 in the front of orderly books that the officers were to use. An order book or orderly book was one in which a commander or adjutant recorded all the daily orders down through the chain of command. This book instructed a soldier not to bow or "touch his cap" while under arms but at all other times to "touch his cap to all officers, without bowing or taking it off." It laid out in great detail the "[h]onours to be paid to different Officers" by the guards. A major general could expect "rest arms, beat 3 ruffles" on a drum but no salute unless he was a commander in chief. A brigadier, on the other hand, only received one ruffle and rested arms. When Baron von Steuben's *Regulations* was published in 1779, giving standardized instructions to the Continental army, he included a section with similar information. Under local and then standardized rules, all sentries had to "present their arms to general officers, and to the field officers of their own regiments; to all other commissioned officers they stand with shouldered arms."[73]

Soldiers were expected to show deference to rank on guard duty and in formal situations on parade. They were also expected to show it at every encounter with an officer, although the order books indicate that they were sometimes lax in doing so. Colonel Pinckney, at Fort Moultrie outside Charleston, South Carolina, was forced to respond when it was drawn to his attention "that Several of ye Men when they are in Town do not pay the Officers of the other Regts the Compliments which is Due to them. Every non Commissioned officer and Private is Therefore hereby Ordered to touch his Cap & give the wall to every Continental officer whome he Shall meet." This order complied with standard advice from the courtesy books of the time, which spelled out the details. When three people walked together, the middle place should go to the highest ranking person. If two walked together, "the wall is usually the most worthy." When two people passed each other, it was important for the lesser to step aside and give way to the superior so that he might easily pass. [74]

Despite these constant reminders of their subordination, soldiers were en-

couraged to think of themselves as honorable men. They were exhorted to obedience and service as a matter of personal honor and the honor of the cause in
a wide range of matters other than combat. Washington made honor the basis
for preventing marauding. After the victory at Trenton, he noted that his troops'
"humanity and tenderness to women and children will distinguish brave Americans, contending for liberty, from infamous mercenary ravagers, whether British or Hessians." On another occasion, soldiers who behaved badly were reminded
that they would be exposed "to the Censure of the Country." New Hampshire
soldiers were encouraged to be as attentive to their appearance as British soldiers were. After all, they, as Americans, had the honor to fight for "Life Liberty
Property and our Country" and were therefore "Superior to Mercenary troops
that are fighting for two or three pence pr. Day only." Brigade orders recorded
by the adjutant of a Virginia regiment attacked the honor of any soldier thinking of deserting. How "can any man be so deserted of Honour as to dessert [*sic*]
a cause he has pledged his reputation to be faithfull in by taking a reward for his
service & swearing a most solemn oath to defend[?]"[75]

In a few instances, soldiers' diaries reflected their possession of a dignified, even
gentlemanly, sense of honor. When they recorded efforts to assert their honor, it
was usually in opposition to behavior they saw as inappropriate from an officer,
noting that their own standards were higher. Private Elisha Stevens was disgusted
by a new captain assigned to his company. Captain Mills, he wrote, "seamed to
be Voyd of all Grace and he cared [carried] on to a very High Rate Singing all
manner of Pordy [bawdy] Songs." A month later, Mills spent a "Knight Drinking and Corousing Desturbing all," and Stevens and his fellows could stand it
no longer. "We thought it was time to Enter Complaint a Gainst Him for we
Had sufered it long a Nuf."[76]

Young soldiers with a gentlemanly sense of honor could find military life
hard. One incident involved seventeen-year-old John Adlum of Pennsylvania, a
young militiaman who stoutly asserted his personal honor against daunting odds.
His story reflected the difficulties that men like him faced and showed why they
might be reluctant to join the Continentals. Adlum was considered dutiful and
strong-willed enough for his brigadier general to ask Adlum's help in catching
some officers who were leaving the camp at night against orders. The brigadier
made Adlum acting sergeant of the guard for the occasion. The officers leaving
camp told Adlum at the guard post that they were going out for "a frolick" and
that they expected him to let them back in before reveille. Adlum warned them
that he would do no such thing, but they laughed at him, then got angry with
him, and continued on their way out. Adlum recognized that they "intended to

intimidate" him, ignored their taunts, and duly did his duty on their return by asking them to surrender their swords and telling them they would be confined. Most of the officers went along quietly with Adlum, but one was furious and objected, at which point Adlum had the guard take the officer's sword forcibly and confine him to the guardhouse. At this, the officer concerned was "enraged nearly to madness." Fortunately, the brigadier arrived and reprimanded the officers. The blustering officer asked for his sword back, but Adlum refused. The young soldier insisted that the officer remain under arrest as he "had not acted like a gentleman, that he had threatened the General, Adjutant Howe and my-self and had called me by improper names." Since the insults had been delivered in the presence of the guard, Adlum required an apology in their presence. The brigadier backed him up and had the officer give the appropriate apology. Ad-lum credited his standing firm on this matter to the "tutorage" of his sergeant named Murray, a Scotsman of "both education and talents," who had offered him "a great deal of good advice." Murray had instructed him "never to insult any person nor to suffer myself to be insulted with impunity."[77]

Adlum had learned his lesson well. In this instance, his determination was aided by the support of his commander and the outrageousness and public na-ture of the offending officer's discourtesy. Adlum and Elisha Stevens were both literate, so they and men like them were already, socially, a step above many of their comrades in arms. We cannot say if this heightened their awareness of gen-tlemanly sensibilities or just their ability to record them. Adlum was a particu-larly unusual young man whose intelligence and attention to duty had gained him the recognition of other senior officers. After a period as a militiaman and then a prisoner of war, he wanted to serve again but only as an officer. He held out for a lieutenant's commission, which he never received, and so spent the re-mainder of the war in his hometown. His memoir of service was written many years later, after he had some fame and prosperity. It is possible his later success and social status colored his recollections and helped him see his role in that past night's events in a more heroic light. However, his defense of his reputation and his desire to serve only with a commission speak to his refined sense of honor and set him apart from the men who served as Continental soldiers.

Despite the efforts to enforce military hierarchy, there were factors that blurred distinctions between officers and men of the Continental army. One of these was the connections of extended family and community and the practical neces-sity of sending news and letters, which men of all ranks did for each other. The ties of a common folk culture, music, and song also bound the army. Another factor that worked against sharp distinctions of rank was officers' compassion and admiration for soldiers' patience and endurance. John Laurens, Washington's aide-de-camp, who very much wanted his own command, wrote to his father in 1778 that if he got one, he "would cherish those dear, ragged Continentals, whose patience will be the admiration of future ages, and glory in bleeding with them." Similarly, Lieutenant Ebenezer Huntington was heartbroken at the treatment his soldiers received from the country. Huntington was moved "by the too just & Repeated Complaints of those who seldom Murmur." In these hard circumstances, men of all ranks felt the neglect of the larger society that seemed oblivious to their suffering.[78]

Both Huntington and Laurens showed tender concern for the soldiers under their command and, to a degree, identified with them. Hardship (albeit unequally endured), loneliness, sickness, and the death of friends from disease or wounds were all part of a shared experience that wore away at the lines of social separation. However, the kind feelings of officers toward their men should not be confused with any leveling sentiment. Men such as Laurens and Huntington were as conscious of rank as any officers, but they were active on behalf of their men's suffering and their own. In a letter, Huntington begged his relatives to use their influence to improve the terrible conditions officers and soldiers labored under and not let others profit "by the distress of their brave Countrymen, in the field." Unusually, he presented their suffering collectively. "Dont drive us to Despair—we are now on the Brink—Depend upon it we cannot put up with such treatment any Longer."[79]

Occasionally soldiers and officers came together as they tried to alleviate their mutual suffering. Although stealing food from local civilians was strictly forbidden, enterprising soldiers sometimes did what they had to do to keep body and soul together with the tacit approval of their officers, who also benefited from their actions. Sergeant John Smith, serving with a Rhode Island regiment, enjoyed the goose brought in by "the Rest of my Brother Soldiers who . . . Resolv'd to Live By their industry." So delighted was he by the feast that when out on patrol later with some soldiers, they "took up a Sheep & two Large fat turkeys not Being able to Give the Countersign & Brought [them] to our Castel where they was tryd By fire & Executed By the whole Division." The officers were not to be left out of this feasting. The next day, the lieutenant and ensign came by and "brought the two turkey Prisoners out of their Confinement and set them Before the whole Assembly to be Examined further & Behold they were speechless then we consumed them." The mutual delight in this charade that transformed the turkeys from contraband to prisoners of war made difficult circumstances more bearable for all involved.[80]

However, some of these factors also worked to divide the army. Community connections would have lessened once towns started meeting their drafts with men who were not long-term residents. The ties of music and song would have slackened once too many of the recruits were foreign-born. The hardship was never equally experienced, no matter how disgusted Huntington was with his situation. Soldiers grumbled when they were treated with what they believed was unnecessary cruelty but otherwise accepted the fact that they lived in different worlds from the officers who commanded them. Even the adventure with the contraband fowl would have ended with officers eating separately from their men.

Many officers would have shared General Israel Putnam's feeling that since they were all in the service of "our bleeding & distressed Country" and were "to mingle their Blood with each other in Defence of her Common Liberty against one Common Enemy," all should live in harmony together. Harmony, though, meant that everyone knew his place. Being prepared to bleed with his soldiers on the battlefield, as Laurens was, did not mean being willing to sleep in the same hut, eat together, or play together. Nor did it mean being held to the same standards of conduct or being treated the same way when they failed to meet those standards.[81]

Guided by the civilian standards of gentlemanly honor and taught by the army to maintain the distinctions of rank under all circumstances, the men of the Continental army respected military hierarchy and accepted the different standards of living dictated by that arrangement. Resistance by soldiers and officers came only against acts they saw as adding insult to injury, acts that seemed to be disrespectful to their rank, however low it was, and their personal honor. Harmony reigned when everyone knew their rank and acted accordingly. If any person was in doubt, the institution of the army guided them by example or by military law. Harmony existed in their social relations, even in a playful situation such as the petty theft described above. The soldiers were able to do something the officers might have thought of but were prohibited by their rank from doing. The officers' participation gave the soldiers a measure of protection in their theft in that they would not be betrayed and punished. However, had the owner of the turkeys complained or caught the offenders in the act, the army would have instructed not only against the theft but also in the social separation of rank. The army set strict rules against stealing from civilians and would have punished the offenders. In doing so, it would give its most graphic lesson in the respective status of soldiers and officers.

CHAPTER THREE

Necessary and Excusable Measures

The Policy and Practice of Punishment

He who loves his son will whip him often, in order
that he may rejoice at the way he turns out.
ECCLESIASTICUS 30:1

THE MOST ENTERTAINING war memoirs from the Revolutionary era offer tales of adventures and hair-raising escapades that often have nothing to do with pivotal battles or great leaders. John Blatchford wrote one of the best. He was about fifteen years old when he enlisted as a cabin boy on a Continental navy ship, the *Hancock*. The next month, a British naval vessel captured the *Hancock*. Its crew was taken to Halifax, Nova Scotia, in British Canada and imprisoned; shortly after this, the British transported Blatchford and some of his fellows to Sumatra, a British-controlled island in the Indian Ocean, where they were forced to do soldiers' duty. Suffering horribly from the heat and hard labor, they decided to try to escape but were caught and court-martialed, and three of them, Blatchford included, were sentenced to death. On the day of their execution, they were marched to the parade ground and made to stand beside three coffins as the firing squad formed in front of them. Blatchford and another prisoner as young as himself were reprieved at the last minute. The third prisoner was executed in their presence. Blatchford later wrote, "I cannot describe my feelings upon this occasion, nor can it be felt by anyone but those who have experienced some remarkable deliverance from the grim hand of death."[1]

Blatchford's narrative is one of the few accounts we have that expresses the thoughts of a condemned man at the moment of his reprieve. Years later, he could tell his story proudly as his court-martial and close encounter with execution were the result of honorable service and resistance to British injustice. Few others could do the same. Most men who experienced such a narrow escape at the gallows or in front of a firing squad, or who had endured any other kind of public punishment, kept quiet about the experience and the shameful events that led to it.

Not surprisingly, in letters home and in later pension applications, soldiers, if they had ever been punished for military crimes, chose to remain silent on the subject. These were hardly things you told your family at home or your grandchildren on your knee. If a soldier committed a crime, there was a range of punishments he might receive. An offender might be fined, docked pay, reduced to the ranks (if he was a noncommissioned officer), or publicly humiliated in some way. But the cornerstones of military punishment in the eighteenth century were either corporal or capital sentences. A corporal punishment is one inflicted on the body, and the sentence was usually that the offender be lashed. A capital sentence saw the offender executed either by hanging or by firing squad. For officers, there was no corporal punishment. Instead, a private or public reprimand from a superior officer was the norm with dismissal from the service being the harshest punishment. In corporal or capital punishment or with sentences that involved public humiliation, other soldiers inflicted the punishment, which was, by order of the court, carried out in front of assembled soldiers. We have few records about what soldiers thought or felt about observing such punishment or inflicting it.

Despite the limited information, a careful reader finds the story of military discipline and punishment in many records from the period. Soldiers' and officers' diaries, orderly books, or later recollections are filled with minutiae about camp life. Amidst the details of the weather, food, friendship, and hardship are references to the relentless sittings of courts-martial and subsequent public punishments. While men almost never offered any emotional response to what they were observing, the constant repetition in diaries indicate that like food, weather, and living conditions, punishment was something that made its presence felt in the experience of officers and men.

Had he known, General George Washington would have been gratified. He wanted the potential for punishment to be a part of the soldiers' daily experience. Punishment in a military setting served many purposes, not the least of which was to create an obedient, effective fighting force in the field. However, it was also an essential ingredient in creating daily discipline and order; it added to the distinctions of rank; and it furthered the subordination of soldiers. Punishment was not a tool that could be used to excess as it was in the British or Prussian armies in which men serving for long terms could be treated brutally. The Continentals were an army of mostly volunteers, serving for short terms, who, if they did not desert, always had the option of reenlisting. Washington and other military and patriot leaders needed to find a level of punishment that could establish discipline and subordination yet avoid provoking mass desertions or rebellion against officers.

On the surface, a clear policy was quickly reached with little discussion. Congress, when it created the Continental army in June 1775, followed in the British and colonial military tradition and created a military body that was legally separate and subordinate to all other social institutions. Congress provided a framework for military justice in the articles of war, the legislation that laid out military regulations. In them, traditional crimes, such as desertion, mutiny, theft, and offenses that weakened the lines of military hierarchy, were spelled out and assigned appropriate punishments.

This early legislative clarity belied the complicated task ahead. Even with some legislative changes, increased formality in procedures, and experience, officers still found they had to be creative. In practice, officers in the field frequently had to use their initiative, especially when they were operating at a distance from general officers or the commander in chief. Colonel Lewis Nicola explained his discipline strategy in a letter to Washington. At the time, Nicola was an older man and commanded a regiment of invalids in Philadelphia, which he had put to work training recruits. He had years of military experience and was a man of the world. "My only guide," Nicola wrote, "is the resolves of Congress, and, occasionally, particular directions from the Board of War, where these fail I am governed by such principles of discipline as I have imbibed from long practice." In addition, Nicola drew on the example of the British army, whose "customs and manners" were useful as an example for him to follow.[2]

Most officers sitting on court-martial panels, and legislators in Congress and state assemblies drafting military regulations, drew on a similar broad range of influences when writing legislation, enumerating crimes, and establishing sentences. In addition to the British military tradition, the militia and provincial army codes, the practical experiences of the Seven Years' War, and, certainly, the contemporary practice in civilian life all played a role in shaping policy and practice. Regional variations in punishment practice existed; however, throughout the colonies, punishment was influenced by the demographic makeup of the population, theological doctrine that followed biblical guidelines for punishment, contemporary philosophical attitudes toward crime and punishment, and the social status of the accused. Colonial Americans brought all of these ideas and attitudes to their army.

It is necessary to take a comprehensive view of civilian and military justice in studying the Revolution, even though punishment served different purposes in military and civilian settings. In civilian life, it reinforced social order and the power of public authority. In military life, it was also a statement of authority and a tool for reinforcing hierarchy. However, rather than simply reinforcing order, military punishment was a tool for instilling subservience, blind obedience, and unqualified respect for rank. So, the different purposes behind punishment, the different social makeup of the populations regulated, and the greater variety of options open to civilian authorities make a direct comparison difficult. Doing so, though, enables us to look comparatively at physical treatment, particularly to understand the connection between the application of punishment and social status, to see regional differences, and to understand the relationship of officers and men to each other and to the larger society.

Policies for punishment involved the active participation of many layers of the military and political community. Punishment was prescribed under military law written by civilian authorities, handed down at courts-martial by junior and senior officers, ratified by generals, and carried out by soldiers on each other. As its punishment policies evolved, it was clear that the Continental army was a new kind of military institution. In its legal structure and its practices, the army was a bridge between the British military legal tradition, colonial militia and provincial ones, and accepted civilian practices. As the army's creators were marking out new legal territory, the men who considered enlistment had to decide if they could live with these arrangements.

WHEN COLONISTS CREATED their army, they brought to the task three fundamental assumptions. The first was that loss of liberty went along with military service; the second was that punishments should be more severe than those meted out in civilian life; and the third was that those punishments should be unequally applied, that is, that they should fall only on soldiers and not on officers. In these assumptions, patriot leaders followed the English legal tradition and the organizing principle of British and colonial militia and provincial armies.

Loss of liberty, this legal subordination of the military, came from the traditional fear of a standing army that was deeply rooted in British and colonial culture. The reasoning behind this fear was that a standing army posed a threat to a legally constituted government, since it might serve the interests of a king or prince rather than the elected body. It might even come to serve its own interest and promote its own authority. One way this threat could be lessened was to restrict the officer corps to men of property and standing who would be more likely to have a stake in the existing political structure. Another was to require those serving in a standing army to surrender many civil rights upon entering the service. In the British army, this principally meant that officers and soldiers lost the right to a jury trial. They were subjected to courts-martial in which the presiding panel was both judge and jury, and not necessarily peers of the accused. Also, those accused were brought more speedily to trial than in civilian life. For capital crimes, a two-thirds majority could give the death sentence rather than the unanimous decision required in civil law. And, for soldiers, the corporal punishments to which they were subjected were much more brutal than anything likely to be handed down by a civilian court. This last fact had not always been the case; in earlier times, when soldiers commonly had some property, they were fined as punishment. But, as one Englishman noted, "Soldiers of the present times having nothing but their bodies can only be punished corporally." So, heavy use of corporal punishment was an indication of the poverty of recruits. The brutality relative to civilian practice was a reflection of the extent of their subordination to the larger society.[3]

This assumption that loss of liberty went along with military service did not apply only to a standing army; militia service required some loss of liberty in Britain and its colonies. As the New York militia law of 1746 explained, this was essential to create the "due & Proper regulation" required for "Security & Defence." However, since militia service was conceived of as local in nature and with the purpose of responding to an immediate threat to life and property, a short-term loss of liberty was considered no great threat or inconvenience. Militia punishments were generally less severe than those in civilian life, and infractions against military regulations were usually punished only by a fine. The main loss of liberty came through the compulsion to serve and the requirement of a court-martial rather than a jury trial.[4]

The much greater legal subordination of the standing army and its harsh punishments were matters that troubled some Englishmen, and they had spoken out about the dangers of organizing an army this way. They believed that such treatment only added to the potential for the army to be a threat to liberty. John Trenchard, the Whig writer and pamphleteer, objected because it made soldiers men whose interests were separate from those of the rest of society. Liberty was only secure when "the Interest of the Governors and Governed [are] the same."

As long as soldiers or any group were, in the words of the jurist Sir William Black-stone, "reduced to a state of servitude in the midst of a nation of freemen," they were a danger to liberty because they lived "in a state of perpetual envy and ha-tred towards the rest of the community."[5]

While these comments came from thoughtful men writing decades apart, they were not part of a widespread challenge to this legal arrangement. The British did wrestle with the political and philosophical issue of having a stand-ing army, but the debate largely centered on the army's cost and the perceived danger of its allegiance to a monarch rather than to Parliament instead of the legal condition of its officers and men. The British got around the dilemma of any danger the army might pose to society by keeping most regiments stationed in overseas imperial possessions, a long way from home. If officers got fed up with their status and their overseas posting, they were free to sell their commis-sions, leave the service, and return to civilian life to enjoy their full civil rights. Soldiers, on the other hand, served with subordinate status for life terms. One Englishman wrote sardonically that a gentleman, on becoming an officer, tem-porarily bartered away his civil rights "for a laced coat and a feather." Soldiers bartered them away for a lot less and a lot longer.[6]

Colonial Americans were aware of this legal structure and its risks as they cre-ated their army. Of course, they already had a degraded group, black slaves, in their midst whose presence made some white Americans nervous, particularly those in the South, for exactly the same reasons that Blackstone suggested. How-ever, only a few patriot leaders made any reference to slavery as they considered the legal structure of the army. They saw their dilemma as twofold. On the one hand, they had to subordinate the status of free men while they were in an army fighting for liberty because subordination and discipline were essential to the creation of an effective fighting force. For that purpose, a soldier was so subor-dinate that his body was, literally, at the disposal of his commanding officers. On the other hand, they could not subordinate soldiers so much that they stopped fighting or that when the fighting was over, they returned to civilian life so em-bittered by their treatment that they became enemies of the state.

That soldiers might not lose liberty through service to their country never se-riously entered the thinking of political and military leaders. William Tudor, the first judge advocate general of the Continental army, simply stated as fact that "[w]hen a man assumes a Soldier, he lays aside the Citizen, & must be content to submit to a temporary relinquishment of some of his civil Rights." Exactly how much "some" should be was the focus of debate. These political and mili-tary leaders recognized the contradictions of subordinating an army whose purpose was to secure liberty; yet they also saw the potential threat to liberty that came from a body in which troops stood in obedience to their officers and not the civil authority that had organized it. They were quite clear that the rules governing this new entity had to be more stringent than those that governed the militia, and as a result, punishment practices became the focus of their debate. They considered the punishments that could be inflicted and on whom, and what crimes should be capital. The other conventional losses of liberty—loss of a jury trial and so on—were never reconsidered in the halls of government.[7]

In Pennsylvania, a few radical souls were thinking in very different ways about military service, and although their experiment was short-lived, they deserve consideration. Because of its history of Quaker political control and that group's commitment to pacifism, Pennsylvania was the only colony to come to the war without an entrenched militia tradition. The colony had faced pressing needs for defense in the past, such as against pirates in 1747 and again on the frontier in 1755. However, these crises had been resolved by the creation of temporary, voluntary militia associations, and those who participated had been closely tied to existing political factions and struggles within the colony. In 1775, following the bloodshed at Lexington and Concord and without an institutionalized militia heritage to limit them, some men from Philadelphia from all social ranks met. They formed themselves into military bodies for the purposes of defense, and they conceived of their military association in innovative ways.[8]

The Associators, as they became known, wrote their "Articles of Association" collectively, so their governing rules were not imposed by a social and political elite; rather, they were produced for self-government. In other colonies, electing their own officers was the limit of self-determination for members of the militia, but that was the starting point for the Associators. They conceded that "just regularity, due subordination, and exact obedience to command" were essential components in a military enterprise, so they were willing to relinquish some rights "for the defence of American Liberty." They even conceded the necessity for courts-martial. The articles provided for panels to be made up of six officers and six privates with an additional officer as president who also had a vote.[9]

The Associators were clearly trying to think about ways in which the full civil liberties of citizens might be translated into the military setting without compromising the rights or needs of either. The desire of the Associators to have a court-martial panel that was as close as possible to a panel of peers is evident. Some of the debate surrounding this and later militia legislation indicates that even this balanced court-martial panel was a reluctant compromise. Some radical Associators wanted privates to sit in judgment over privates and officers over officers; that is, they wanted to hold on to the right to be tried by peers. Possible punishments that could be imposed by a court-martial were dismissal, fining, or degrading, literally demotion to a lower grade. There was no provision for corporal punishment as was common in civilian life and which appeared occasionally in the militia laws of other colonies.[10]

These articles of association had a brief life. Officers, usually men of higher social status, lobbied for greater disciplinary measures, and by later in the year, the assembly had taken control of matters. It wrote legislation to raise and regulate militia, which took on more conventional forms. But the radical impulse was not smothered so quickly. Not every militiaman embraced the new regulations wholeheartedly, and some still worried about their relationship to military authority and wondered whether they were truly bound to comply with all orders, especially those they found demeaning. However, elsewhere in the colonies, there is little indication that men considered the possibility that this might be another arena where the world might be made over again.[11]

As colonial political and military leaders examined their options in the spring and summer of 1775, they operated within the British and colonial military tradition that expected liberty to be lost through service. If they felt any caution, it focused on resisting the brutal levels of corporal punishment used by the British. If the radical ideas of the Associators crossed anyone's mind as Congress drew up legislation to create the Continental army, no record of it remains. They wrestled consciously with the needs of shaping an army organized in rebellion against what was then the most powerful nation on earth. That project alone seemed radical enough. While for soldiers, there is some indication that the harsh realities of military service, including its discipline, kept some out of the service after the initial war enthusiasm, there is no indication that they conceived of the army being organized otherwise. Officers and soldiers committed themselves by their enlistment to this subordinate legal state, and many, such as Private Joseph Plumb Martin, simply looked forward after their service to "becoming citizens" again.[12]

In colonial America, there were a number of circumstances in which people lived with a temporary loss of liberty. Indentured servants and apprentices lived under special legal conditions for their terms of service and had laws that regulated their treatment. Convict laborers, though working involuntarily, also lived under special legal codes that gave them few liberties. In the case of slaves, of course, their loss of liberty was permanent and without any legal protection whatsoever. The kind of unfree labor colonists were most familiar with varied from region to region. Most transported convicts labored in the Chesapeake region. Immigrants who were indentured servants lived in all colonies in the seventeenth century, but by the middle of the eighteenth century, most made Pennsylvania their destination as it was seen as offering better opportunities. Pennsylvanians were particularly familiar with a kind of indentured servitude known as redemption, and the people who came as redemptioners were mostly German immigrants. These people had the same kind of contracts as indentured servants; the only difference was that they signed their contracts when they arrived in the colonies. In their case, shipmasters sold them off to recover the cost of the passage if no family members or friends could pay cash to redeem them. Apprenticeship, which generally consisted of a seven-year indenture whereby one acquired a skill, existed everywhere in the colonies; however, it was most common in small towns and the few colonial cities, which meant that the middle and New England colonies were more familiar with it. And slavery, although more central to the southern economy, was legal and practiced all over British North America. So, some kind of labor with limited freedom was familiar to all colonists.

The legal status of soldiers was a hybrid of these. At first glance, soldiers, with their short terms of service, appear to have had more in common with indentured servants and apprentices. They all bound their labor for a specific period of time to a master who stood in loco parentis with obligations to feed, clothe, and discipline. However, servants and apprentices retained their civil liberties while indentured and had recourse to the law if they were not provided for appropriately or if punishment was excessive by local standards. Convicts had no protection but did retain the knowledge that their term was finite. A slave's status was lifelong and hereditary with no civil rights at all. Soldiers retained their right to due process, if little else. Like slaves, however, soldiers were subject to punishment that was beyond accepted levels in the larger society. While the law subjected slaves in Virginia, for example, to mutilation and dismemberment for certain crimes, the limits to the number of lashes that were enumerated by the slave codes stayed well within the levels used on free men and servants. Soldiers, although never subjected to dismemberment, were subject to lash punishments well outside civilian norms.[13]

Civilian practice, along with military practice in the British army, colonial militia, and provincial troops, guided local assemblies and the Continental Congress as they considered the range of possible military punishments. Potential Revolutionary soldiers also knew these practices as they considered whether to enlist or not. Civilian practice varied considerably from colony to colony and changed over time everywhere, but there were some fundamental attitudes and practices shared by all. Nowhere had the idea of punishment or reform through incarceration appeared; that was to be a nineteenth-century phenomenon. Fining was a common punishment for less serious infractions for those who had the money to pay. Otherwise, whipping, public humiliation — such as putting criminals in stocks on public display, branding, and cropping (chopping off the tops of the ears) — and hanging were all part of the punishment repertoire inflicted on white criminals. All took place in public.[14]

In the British legal world, punishments differed according to the social status of the accused. Despite a much-vaunted claim that there was equality before the law, only the most heinous of crimes, such as treason or murder, would ever cause gentlemen to be sentenced to death. When a gentleman committed a lesser crime, he was often dealt with in an extralegal manner. This might be done in a variety of ways: through a private reprimand by a respected social equal; by the threat or reality of making the crime public, bringing shame and tarnishing his highly valued sense of honor; or by the requirement that the offender leave the area. If a gentleman was brought to trial, he was much more likely to be acquitted than a person of lower rank and, if convicted, was usually punished by a fine or monetary restitution. Although there are one or two cases of English gentlemen being executed for murder, celebrated as examples of the fairness of British justice, the cases are famous because they stand alone.[15]

In Britain and North America, courts used the death penalty for a broad range of offenses, from murder to repeated petty theft. The day of execution was an important public occasion complete with pomp and circumstance in order to awe the onlookers with the power of authority and to act as a deterrent. In the American colonies, particularly New England, an important part of the public ritual was the execution sermon. One minister, Noah Hobart, warned the crowd that "excessive wickedness was the way to an untimely death." He chose as his text Deuteronomy 19:20: "And those which remain shall hear, and fear, and shall henceforth commit no more any such evil among you." These execution sermons were often published so that the clergyman's warnings reached a wider audience than the watching crowd. Through these, colonists would have been familiar with the ritual and meaning of executions, whether they had witnessed one or not.[16]

Those who lived in larger towns would have had an opportunity to attend one. In colonial cities, small as they were, few years passed without the gallows being set up. Some of the crowd would, as Hobart wanted, have heard and feared, but the event could also have a festive feel. It brought people together, vendors sold food, and there was sometimes street entertainment. Still, it was an event in which the centerpiece was not only death but terror. The condemned did not always go gently into that good night. Even the most cavalier prisoners could choke or wet themselves as death approached. In this setting, the minister's words brought familiar rituals and meaning to a tense public occasion.[17]

A great number of the condemned, perhaps as many as 50 percent, were reprieved, usually at the last minute. With many capital sentences handed down, authorities did not want to appear brutal by carrying them all out. The crowd had to share the court's view that the punishment was just, and any sympathy from the crowd had the potential to weaken respect for law and authority. Imagine the throng at the hanging of one Thomas Goss. He had murdered his wife, but as he went to his death, observers described him as "a poor deluded wretch." It is possible that those watching were tempted to pity him.[18]

The condemned was more likely to be reprieved if some citizens could plead his or her worth or if there were extenuating circumstances. The provincial council in Pennsylvania found nothing to recommend the reprieve of Edward Hunt, who was convicted of counterfeiting. In fact, they could see "no Service at all that a Reprieve to so miserable a life could be to him." But friends of Catherine Reynolds, condemned for the murder of her "Infant Bastard," was seen as "a fit object of Mercy."[19]

When not resorting to capital sentences, colonial courts used fines, various forms of public humiliation, and the corporal punishments described above, reserved of course for those who were not part of the gentry. These corporal punishments were used in varying degrees even within a given colony. Most colonies adhered to biblical injunctions that limited lash punishments. Deuteronomy 25:3 laid out the limit for whipping: "Forty stripes he may give him, and not exceed." Paul noted in 2 Corinthians 11:24 that "[o]f the Jews five times received I forty stripes save one." It was understood that the Jews gave thirty-nine lashes in order to stay comfortably within divine law. Most colonies followed that example and only occasionally exceeded it, as in Pennsylvania, for example, where fifty lashes were sometimes given for third offenses.[20]

When colonies consistently departed from this thirty-nine-lash limit, two factors converged: weak or inefficient judicial institutions and the presence of slaves. Only New York and the Carolinas shared both these attributes. In these colonies, lash punishments for whites regularly rose above 39 lashes, ranging as high as 150 in New York and to several hundred during the vigilante Regulator movements in the Carolina backcountry. In both places, the most brutal punishments were directed toward the black slave population. A master's punitive power over his slave was limited only by his own property and labor interest in the slave. However, when a slave committed crimes against other whites in the community, courts got involved in punishment practices. While court-ordered punish-ments for black slaves for property crimes were often comparable to those for whites of low status, crimes against social order, such as conspiracy to rebel, brought brutal sentences. In New York, some of the slaves convicted of conspir-acy in 1712 and 1741 were burned alive, one was ordered to hang in chains until dead from starvation and thirst, and another was to be "broken on a wheel." This last punishment was a military one in which the prisoner was tied spread-eagled on a wagon wheel, usually for a day or two, to suffer discomfort, thirst, hunger, and the indignity of fouling his clothes with his own excrement. How-ever, in sentencing this particular slave for conspiracy, the court ordered him to stay on the wheel "until death." In South Carolina, the heads of slave offenders were occasionally severed and publicly displayed.[21]

In response to weak judicial institutions, the mostly white Carolina back-country was, from approximately 1768 to 1771, torn by violent vigilante move-ments formed to bring law and order to the region. In its desire to restrain out-laws and the "lower people," the vigilante Regulator movement used excessive violence. In fact, participants drew heavily on British army punishments, and many saw themselves as engaged in a war. The violence of the movement matched the cruelty of the "desperate villains" it sought to subdue. The *South Carolina Gazette* reported that, in one instance, the Regulators gave two criminals 500 lashes each, a punishment in keeping with British military practice.[22]

In coastal South Carolina, the need to contain a slave majority and to disci-pline poor whites set up contradictions that were hard to resolve. Since whip-ping was generally used against slaves, its use for whites added to the shame of punishment. It had to be administered with restraint, however, so that the vic-tim was shamed only in the eyes of whites. A similar problem existed in the Chesa-peake region, but there great planter families dominated the court system to a degree unmatched by other colonial elites. Standing in authority over a close-knit, white social world, the courts were usually able to use the lash sparingly. High conviction rates, low recidivism, few requests for jury trials, and the fre-quent use of good behavior recognizances — that is, a commitment to the court to behave well and usually reappear before it — all speak to the court's authority and effectiveness.[23]

Throughout the colonies, corporal punishment not only reinforced the au-thority of the state but also aided in defining social status. Members of the gen-try, as noted above, were usually treated differently from those beneath them. The poorest laborers and servants, without access to money to pay fines, could be punished only with either longer terms of servitude or corporal punishment.

Slaves, at the bottom of the social ladder, experienced only corporal punishment; the greatest restraint against excessive punishment was their inherent value as property, protection they lost when their actions were perceived as a threat to the security of white society. Long before colonial Americans came to their Revolution, punishment practices helped define the contours of social and race relations.

Reformers of the period were beginning to think about other ways of punishing criminals, but none were concerned with egalitarianism. Their concerns lay in other directions. Some, in keeping with a new respect for the human body associated with eighteenth-century philosophers of the Enlightenment, were revolted by the brutality. Others focused on the lack of flexibility in sentencing. They felt that high rates of capital sentences and pardons undermined the effectiveness of punishment. During the second half of the eighteenth century, civilian reformers such as William Eden, William Blackstone, Cesare Beccaria, Benjamin Rush, and Thomas Jefferson wrote extensively on the subject in Britain and North America. They wanted courts to consider a broad scale of punishments below a capital sentence that gave them room to maneuver. Not all reformers shied away from corporal punishment, but some expressed concern that public punishment numbed everyone to violence.[24]

These ideas circulated widely in the Revolutionary era. It would be the end of the century before these reformers' thoughts coalesced to direct public policy away from public punishment that humiliated to prisons that reformed. What is striking for our purposes is that while these intellectuals, lawyers, and doctors were turning their energies to reforming civilian punishments during the second half of the eighteenth century, they paid little attention to military practices. From the Seven Years' War onward, assemblies had many occasions to debate the kinds of punishments to be given to men serving in either militia, provincial, or Continental forces. They continually differentiated among the different branches, steadily eliminating any corporal punishment for militiamen while laying a heavier hand on those serving for longer terms or at a greater distance. Even when they were actively considering, as the new nation formed in 1776, whether bloody, cruel, or unusual punishments should be prohibited in civilian life, they were able to require exactly those punishments in Continental regulations. Whenever they were in doubt, legislators looked to British army practice, not reformers, to guide them.

One reason reformers ignored military practice was the historic subordination of a standing army, but there were others. One was that contemporary battlefield strategy relied heavily on immediate, blind obedience to facilitate actions fought in tight formation. Additionally, the perception that soldiers were poor, young, disorderly, inclined to criminality, and disrespectful toward their officers all reaffirmed the belief that they had to be ruled with a firm hand. For the British army, judging by their court-martial sentences, there is little evidence that British officers embraced any new philosophical respect for the body. Certainly there were attempts to increase flexibility in sentencing. As in civilian life, the army rested heavily on capital sentences and also found it had to issue too many pardons to avoid unrest or low morale. However, the British army showed no inclination to shy away from brutal punishments with the lash. "Lash averages" (an efficient phrase that historians use to mean the average number of lashes assigned in court-martial punishments) showed no evidence of declining through the end of the American Revolution.[25]

Following on the legal tradition throughout the British and colonial world, officers as gentlemen were subject to a different assortment of punishments. In contrast to the severe corporal punishment inflicted on soldiers, officers could receive legally only punishments that ranged along a scale from a private reprimand from a superior officer, to a public reprimand in front of the soldiers, to a discharge from the service. It is noteworthy that for officers, a severe punishment was to be thrown out of the army, but for soldiers, it was to have the period of service extended. While the British articles of war, colonial provincial articles, and the Continental articles of war all allowed capital punishment for both officers and soldiers for a few enumerated crimes, in practice only soldiers ever received such sentences. This stark separation in treatment reflected and reinforced the gap in social status between each group. While equality before the law existed in theory rather than practice in civilian life, there was not even a pretense of it in the military one. There, inequality was codified.[26]

In the British army, like other admired armies of the age, "the trinity of justice, terror and mercy" maintained discipline for soldiers. The court-martial process provided for justice, punishments provided the terror, and pardons, usually at the last moment, offered the possibility of mercy. So that punishment was as effective as possible, it had to be inflicted in front of the largest number of soldiers that could be easily assembled to watch. All punishments were harsh. The death penalty could be used for a number of crimes, but there were also a range of brutal corporal punishments. One was riding the wooden horse, in which soldiers had to sit on a wooden frame for a prescribed number of minutes with their ankles tied to prevent movement. Other punishments were the lash, branding, running the gauntlet, and piquet, also called picket.[27]

These last two were among the most brutal of the British military practices.

Drawing of a wooden horse from Francis Grose, *Military Antiquities
Respecting a History of the English Army*, 1788. Courtesy Bancroft
Library, University of California at Berkeley.

Since both were later adopted by the Continentals, albeit on a smaller scale, they
are worth a detailed examination. Running the gauntlet required a soldier to pass
between two rows of his fellows, sometimes as many as 100 on each side, each
of whom had to beat the man with sticks or a strip of hide as he passed through.
We have a detailed description of how the British applied this punishment from
Levi Hanford, an eighteen-year-old American prisoner of war during the Revolution. He and other prisoners were required to watch the punishment of a
British guard whose crime had been fraternizing with them. First to enter the
gauntlet were the drummers of the regiment, who marched slowly and beat a
long drum roll (both to add tension and to conceal the screams of the victim).
Then came an officer who walked in front of the prisoner with his sword drawn,
preventing the victim from running through the rows too quickly. Finally, the
prisoner entered, and the lashes rained down on him. An officer patrolled outside the gauntlet to make sure none of the other soldiers spared their comrade.
Enduring this, Hanford wrote, "the prisoner at first walked firmly and erect, but

he soon began to queck and droop, then to writhe and convulse, until at length
his lacerated body was thrown into contortions, and was literally streaming with
blood."[28]

Piquet was more efficient, although no less brutal. It involved tying a prisoner
by one arm to a tree branch or gibbet, with his feet hanging about twelve inches
above the ground for a specified period of time. Driven into the earth beneath
him was a stake with a sharp point. The only way the man could relieve the in-
tolerable pressure on his arm was to stand upon — impale himself on — the sharp-
ened wood beneath him. An English writer, Francis Grose, noted in 1788 that
piquet was no longer used in the British army, "it having lamed and ruptured
many soldiers."[29]

By far the most common tool in British military discipline was the lash, usually with a cat-o'-nine-tails, which was used with "lavish abandon." This consisted of nine lengths of whipcord, each two feet long, attached to a wooden
handle. Since the knots that joined the lengths inflicted the most damage on the
soldier, each length sometimes had additional knots tied in it. Twenty-five lashes
was the absolute minimum given, but the average penalty was much higher. There
was no legal upper limit. During the Seven Years' War, the lash average for the
British army was above 720 stripes, with about 40 percent of sentences dictating
1,000 lashes or more. Inflicting the punishment was the task of a drummer; a regimental surgeon stood by so he could call a halt to the proceedings if it looked as
if the prisoner was too close to death. Sentences as high as 1,000 lashes were often
applied in installments so that the offender would survive the punishment.[30]

The few available records indicate that British drummers hated the task. One
referred to it as his "disgusting duty." By 100 lashes, "blood would pour down
his [the prisoner's] back in streams," and the drummer would be spattered with
blood. After the punishment was over, he would run to wash "to rid my clothes
and person of my comrade's blood." Another young British drummer refused to
take his turn at the whip in Boston in January 1775. He flung the whip to the
ground, saying that while he wanted to do his duty, "he never entered the service to be a whipper or hangman." The young man was immediately arrested,
but a court-martial acquitted him of misconduct.[31]

While civilian reformers ignored the military world, within the British army a
few officers were thoughtful about the problems of military justice. In the years
before the Revolution, several books appeared that began to look for alternatives to these brutal punishments. In 1769, Stephen Payne Adye, a first lieutenant with the Royal Artillery garrisoned in New York, wrote a book on the subject. He believed that officers often hid "the lesser crimes Soldiers may be guilty

of" because they hated to see harsh punishments imposed. Like the reformers who wrote on civilian practices, Adye was looking for a greater range of punishments so that courts-martial had more options, and a surviving subscription list for his book showed that other officers shared his interest. Thomas Simes and Roger Stevenson, who both wrote instruction manuals for young officers published in Britain and America, also questioned the effectiveness of harsh punishments. They called them a "very erroneous principal" and claimed that brutality only "excites resentment, revenge, and despair" in those commanded. But mostly British soldiers were out of sight and out of mind and attracted little interest from reformers.[32]

While some colonists were familiar with the British army from earlier imperial wars, it was the Seven Years' War that provided their first prolonged encounter with British military punishment practice. Provincial forces serving alongside the British, and citizens in the towns where the army was posted during the war and after, got a close look. Some were horrified. A Massachusetts merchant, John Andrews, was pleased to hear that a deserter was not to suffer the death penalty but was appalled to discover that the substitute was 1,000 lashes. He was "shock'd to think that mankind can so far divest themselves of humanity as to be instrumental in inflicting such an horrid punishment on their fellow mortals." The hapless soldier was to receive 250 lashes a week until the sentence was completed.[33]

Some citizens objected publicly. Andrew Croswell published a book in 1768 in which he objected to the army's brutality on theological grounds. Drawing on Acts 26:10, Croswell quoted Paul: "[A]nd when they were put to death, I gave my voice against them." The phrase "I gave my voice against them" became Croswell's impassioned refrain. A second edition was published with an anonymous appendix written by a "like minded" person. This person described severe lash punishments as a "[s]hocking barbarity!" and noted that "if any person has a mind to see a representation of hell, let him attend upon this part of the discipline of the Army."[34]

"Like minded" also noted that harsh punishments were not conducive to good discipline since no one "who is not altogether lost, to tender feelings of humanity, will make any complaint against them, when they consider the cruel punishment they must suffer." Since the soldiers knew that, they misbehaved "with impunity." George Hewes, a Boston shoemaker, was one such citizen who had not lost his "tender feelings." He lodged a complaint with the army when a soldier cheated him, but when he learned that the sentence was 350 lashes, he told the court that, had he known, "he would have said nothing about it."[35]

Not all colonists shared the sympathetic attitudes of Croswell and Hewes. They were cautious of the army's presence in wartime, resented it in peacetime, and were concerned about the potential criminal threat from young soldiers. They demanded prompt actions when soldiers misbehaved. The *Pennsylvania Journal* noted in 1766 that a court-martial had sentenced a soldier to receive 500 lashes for assaulting a civilian. The newspaper found the punishment "convincing proof that the military are determined to give ample satisfaction to the inhabitants for any insult that may be offered them by the soldiers."[36]

Massachusetts provincial soldiers serving with the British had to watch brutal punishments regularly, but that did not necessarily fill them with respect for military authority. One young Massachusetts soldier, David Perry, witnessed three soldiers being whipped, one for 800 lashes and the others for 500. Perry was shocked. After 300 lashes, there was a pause. "[T]he flesh appeared to be entirely whipped from their shoulders, and they hung as mute and motionless as though they had long been deprived of life." However, the surgeon, on examining them, told the soldiers, "[Y]ou can bear it yet," and the punishment continued. Perry thought that it was "the most cruel punishment I ever saw inflicted, . . . by far worse than death," and felt he "could have taken summary vengeance on those who were the authors of it, on the spot, had it been in my power to do it."[37]

After the first couple of years of the Seven Years' War, New England men found themselves not just observing British practices but subject to them. In 1757, the British decided that all provincials serving alongside the British regulars should be under the British articles. However, whenever provincials were apart from the regulars, they could operate under their own rules. Colonists began the war, then, believing they could keep their soldiers under separate regulations. The early legislation written by assemblies tells us a great deal about colonial societies. Assemblies had to adapt the disciplinary practices of civilian life, their own military traditions, and what they knew of the British army to organize a large military operation. The issues they struggled with then reveal the tensions that would arise again in the Revolution.[38]

In keeping with the pattern set in their earlier involvement in imperial wars, colonial governments were unanimous in their belief that troops raised for distant service had to operate under much harsher rules than the militia. There was some variation in militia regulations in different colonies, but generally militiamen were subject to courts-martial and occasionally corporal punishment. Such punishment was very limited, however. Usually, fines were the order of the day, since most participants were free men, property holders or sons thereof, or wage earners, all of whom had access to money. In those colonies where servants and apprentices were required to serve, corporal punishment followed, since they had no access to money to pay a fine. By the Seven Years' War, corporal punishment barely existed at all for the militia. In the few cases it was allowed, it was usually limited to around twenty lashes.[39]

Punishments for militiamen were a more sensitive issue in southern slave societies. There, assemblies had to be sure to maintain distinctions between punishments for slaves and those for the free. In Virginia by midcentury, the lash had ceased to be used as a militia punishment, although tying by neck and heels was allowed. That could be excruciatingly painful, but militia sentences were limited to five minutes. Mostly, fines and brief jail terms had become the rule. In South Carolina, the greatly outnumbered white minority felt compelled to allow slaves to be part of the militia, and the 1747 Militia Act invited masters to select those seen as "most faithful." The colony, of course, had to differentiate its punishment practices between that inflicted on white servants, who were also required to serve, and slaves. Punishments for both were corporal. Depending on the crime, servants received up to forty lashes. For slaves, the number was unlimited but "not extending to loss of life or member" and was left to the discretion of officers. Again, any protection the slave had rested in his value as property to his master, who would not want to incur a financial loss.[40]

Colonial assemblies all recognized that provincials had to be punished more severely than militiamen, but they were also concerned over the loss of liberty that service entailed. There were, however, striking regional differences in the way those concerns played out. When Massachusetts raised its regiments, the legislature was quite clear that it did not want its men to be subjected to brutal treatment. The assembly passed a Mutiny Act (articles of war to govern provincial troops) in 1754, which carefully restricted the punishments available to regimental courts-martial. It enumerated only mutiny, sedition, and desertion as capital crimes, far fewer than what was listed in the British articles, and provided a limit of thirty-nine lashes. For Connecticut troops also, punishments stayed comfortably close to civilian practice. For these provincial soldiers from New England, the shift to coming under the British articles in 1757 was a difficult one.[41]

Virginia provincials experienced no such transition. They were already serving under colonial regulations that looked very similar to the British articles. George Washington, serving as commander of a regiment of Virginia provincial troops, was not disturbed by severe punishments. He admired the British articles of war and recommended that Virginia adopt them. Washington expressed frustration at the lack of disciplinary power available to him. He wrote to Governor Robert Dinwiddie complaining of the troops' disobedience and of the need for "putting us under Military Law." When Virginia passed a Mutiny Act in October 1755, it listed only five capital crimes, adding disobeying an order and striking an officer to the Massachusetts list, and it had no limit on corporal punishment.[42]

This was a striking departure from civilian and militia practice. The sketchy information we have on Virginia's recruits indicate they were of low status. The perception that harsh punishment was necessary to keep them in line reinforces this view. The close connection between punishment and status is further emphasized by the fact that, alongside this legislation for the provincials, the assembly removed the last remnants of corporal punishment from the militia. Washington was delighted when he heard about the new rules to govern the provincials. He told his second in command, Adam Stephen, that "[w]e now have it in our Power to enforce obedience."[43]

Stephen did not shy away from the task. A few months later, when he was with his provincial troops at Fort Cumberland with the remnants of British general Edward Braddock's defeated army, Stephen reported to Washington that he had apprehended two deserters. He told his commander he had "wheal'd them till they pissd themselves and the Spectators Shed tears for them" and concluded his report with the hope that this would "answer the End of punishment," meaning that the horrific sentence should deter others from deserting. Washington himself also used harsh punishments and told Dinwiddie he had "flog'd several [soldiers] severely" and had others "under Sentence of Death."[44]

There is no ready answer as to why Washington, Stephen, and other Virginian provincial officers embraced British military punishments so readily. In the first year of the fighting, Virginian officers had been shocked by British punishments, yet they quickly came to embrace them. Perhaps it was because the catastrophe of Braddock's defeat and other setbacks had shown the need for strict discipline. Perhaps it was because the recruits were of such low social status that they stood outside the close-knit Virginia communities in which social deference was ingrained. Perhaps it was because these Virginia gentlemen, stung by the fact that the British gave them an inferior military rank, were determined to emulate and even outdo their counterparts in the British army in order to prove something to themselves or others. Or perhaps the presence of slaves in their society made them more likely to use excessive force against those they perceived as inferior or disrespectful. Probably, a combination of all of these factors led to the ready acceptance of British practice.[45]

When Washington learned the details of Virginia's Mutiny Act of 1755, he was frustrated that it still did not give him the sweeping punishment powers he wanted. He believed there should be more capital crimes allowed and that the restrictions on locations of courts-martial were "inconvenient and absurd." Although the Virginia troops, by 1757, came under the British articles when they were with the regulars, they needed to be under Virginia law when they operated alone. Consequently, Washington again lobbied Dinwiddie for military laws under which firm discipline could be established. He told Dinwiddie that he thought it "quite obvious, that we can prepare no Law more fit than that provided by Act of Parliament [the British articles], as a military code for the government of our Troops." The obstacles to adopting strict disciplinary measures were, he believed, those who were too "tenacious of Liberty, and prone to Censure; [who] condemn all Proceedings that are not strictly Lawful, never considering what Cases may arise to make it necessary and excusable."[46]

Virginia legislators were not the only ones "tenacious of liberty." In Massachusetts, the preamble to its Mutiny Act exemplified the cautious way in which the assembly placed its citizens in the armed service under martial law. The legislature recognized that military life had different needs. It was prepared to bring those convicted at courts-martial "to a more exemplary and speedy punishment than the usual forms of law will allow." But it also stated that "no man may be forejudged of life and limb, or subjected to any kind of punishment by martial law, or in any other manner than by the judgment of his peers, and according to the known and established laws of the province." New Englanders were more suspicious than Virginians of the British articles. When the British brought provincial soldiers under British military law, the Massachusetts agent in London petitioned unsuccessfully to have the decision reversed.[47]

With the outbreak of hostilities in 1775, Americans were again forced to deal with the tensions of military expediency, theology, and separation from civilian life. The earliest articles of war of the Revolution held firm to the commitment to reserve corporal punishment for soldiers only but were more cautious about what kinds of crime were punishable and the nature of the punishment. On April 5, 1775, two weeks before the first armed confrontation at Concord, the Provincial Congress of Massachusetts approved articles of war to govern any troops it might be necessary to raise. Many of the articles were similar to those of the 1754 act. The thirty-nine-lash limit stood. The capital crimes enumerated, however, were not the standard mutiny, sedition, and desertion. Rather, they related to anyone who might "shamefully abandon any post committed to his charge . . . in time of an engagement." This is indicative perhaps of the event the patriots most feared.[48]

The preamble to these Massachusetts articles provides a clue to prevailing sentiments. It noted that the assembly had "great confidence in the honor and public virtue of the inhabitants . . . [that they] will cheerfully do their duty when known, without any such severe articles and rules (except in capital cases) and cruel punishments as are usually practised in standing armies." The resolution "earnestly recommended" soldiers and officers to obey the rules for "their own honor and the public good." A provincial government, operating extralegally, could ask for little more, but never were articles of war more tentatively offered to those whom they would govern. Rhode Island, Connecticut, and New Hampshire quickly passed similar articles.[49]

When the Continental Congress resolved to raise an army in June 1775, it had the tension between military necessity and political liberty very much in mind. When it selected Washington as commander in chief, it gave him discretion "to order and dispose of the said army." However, they wanted him to make it "his special care, in discharge of the great trust committed to you, that the liberties of America receive no detriment"— that is, no detriment to liberty other than what was understood to be essential to the existence of an army, which were separation and inequality.[50]

Congress passed the first articles of war to govern the Continental army on June 30, 1775. The capital offenses were related to military engagement rather than internal army discipline, and the punishments available to courts-martial were enumerated: "That no persons shall be sentenced by a court-martial to suffer death except in the cases expressly mentioned . . . ; nor shall any punishment be inflicted at the discretion of a court-martial, other than degrading, cashiering, drumming out of the army, whipping not exceeding thirty-nine lashes, fine not exceeding two months pay of the offender, imprisonment not exceeding one month." With their emphasis on public shaming and the thirty-nine-lash limit, these punishments have the hallmark of Massachusetts stamped on them. Indeed, with some additions and exceptions, they are the Massachusetts articles.[51]

These articles had a brief life. An amendment to them in November listed the old trinity of sedition, mutiny, and desertion as capital offenses and added other crimes, such as giving information to the enemy. Additionally, the early New England resistance to the kind of "cruel punishments" that others considered essential to standing armies soon disappeared. In fact, William Tudor, the judge advocate general and himself from Massachusetts, suggested to Congress that New Englanders might not be averse to harsher punishments as they were not "so bigoted to *Mosaic* Institutions [biblical authority] as is imagined." Of course, the New Englanders Tudor was referring to were probably political leaders and senior officers and not the men who might be subject to these punishments.[52]

In the summer of 1776, as the army faced a string of military setbacks, Congress set to work revising the articles, and immediately senior officers began a campaign to get the articles changed. Washington complained to Congress that thirty-nine lashes had become more "a matter of sport than punishment." He directed Tudor to lobby Congress, and Tudor wrote to his friend and mentor John Adams, then a Massachusetts representative in Congress, on the subject. The articles were, Tudor argued, "incompetent to the Purpose." He suggested using the British articles with "very few Alterations, such as making fewer Crimes punishable capitally and limiting the Number of Lashes to 1 or 200. The General joins with me in this opinion." Adams did not take any persuading. He was a great admirer of the British articles as he believed they had taken the empire to "the head of Mankind." He told Tudor, "I am perfectly of your opinion." The result, passed by Congress on September 20, was a document that was very close to the British articles. It had no restrictions on the kinds of punishment that could be used, but it had a lash limit of 100 stripes, unlike the British articles, which had no limit.[53]

Adams, Tudor, and Washington were not the only ones who worked for these changes; a variety of senior officers and representatives corresponded all through the summer of 1776 on the subject. Elbridge Gerry, another Massachusetts representative to the Continental Congress and a signer of the Declaration of Independence that summer, agreed that the British articles were a good foundation. He wrote to General Horatio Gates that "[w]e can readily look over the statutes of Britain . . . and find how far the same are applicable to our own forces." General Charles Lee wrote to Edmund Pendleton, head of the provisional government in Virginia, recommending that tough discipline would serve better to keep "refractory spirits in order than the Continental Ordinances." And Colonel Joseph Reed, a successful Philadelphia lawyer before joining Washington's staff, wrote to John Hancock, the president of Congress, to assure him that "the mildness of the Punishments" was detrimental to the service. He stressed that Continental soldiers included men "who would equal if not exceed the King's Troops in all kinds of disorder & Irregularity," and consequently, the army needed "very material Alterations" in its punishments.[54]

Even though the new articles were approved, it was not done without a fight. Many men, such as Gerry, saw the British articles as a useful framework but one that needed to be carefully adapted to the American context. What those adaptations were to be was not easily agreed upon. John Adams wrote about the congressional debate and noted that "[i]t was a very difficult and unpopular subject." Adams, who took credit for getting the new articles approved, complained that "all the labor of the debate on those articles, paragraph by paragraph, was thrown upon me." It was an uphill battle, "so indigested were the notions of Liberty prevalent among the Majority of the Members," but Adams managed it.[55]

Without any restrictions on the kind of punishment that could be inflicted and with the loss of the thirty-nine-lash limit, the new articles were a critical step in the separation of soldiers from the civilian population. While still far short of British military punishments, and not so far beyond what was acceptable for free men guilty of heinous crimes in some parts of the country, it marked a radical departure from civilian practice in most places.

This revision in the articles occurred at around the same time Congress reorganized the army itself. Since most Continental enlistments were expiring at the end of 1776, Congress and Washington hoped to avoid the manpower crisis that had occurred the previous year. In their reorganization, they wanted to create an effective army for the duration of the war, however long that might be. Central to this plan was the recruitment of soldiers who would serve for longer terms in order to create a seasoned and disciplined army. The result of their labors was a reorganized army and new articles that abrogated soldiers' liberties in order to gain a more effective fighting force. Americans already knew from experience that the kind of men who would serve for longer terms would be drawn from the lower levels of society. The tightening of discipline, escalation of punishment, and casting wider for recruits all occurred about the same time. It is unclear now how the patriots linked these ideas. What is clear is that senior officers saw soldiers as the kind of men who could be controlled only by stern discipline. Soldiers, by their enlistment, had to accept that control, whatever their status.[56]

While Continental troop regulation was being steered toward punishment practices more severe than those in most colonies, a different evolution was taking place in South Carolina. In June 1775, that colony opted to form regular state troops and stay outside the Continental army umbrella, but by July 1776, under pressure from the Continental Congress, all South Carolina regulars were under Continental army control. The period of separate administration highlights the close connection between local civilian context and military practice.[57]

While other colonies wrote articles of war framed in tentative language in the first months of the conflict, South Carolina did not hesitate to bring its new body of troops under severe military discipline. Massachusetts hoped that the men it recruited would have "public virtue" so it could avoid harsh military punishments, but South Carolina had no such thoughts about the men it was recruiting. There, the assembly rapidly adopted "Rules & Regulations" for its new colonial troops "grounded upon the British Mutiny Bill." This action was immediately reflected in court-martial sentences. Colonel William Moultrie, near

Charleston, was trying to instill military discipline in his new, all-white troops, and camp courts-martial regularly handed down sentences of 200 lashes. Though these were often partially remitted, the resulting punishments of 50 to 100 lashes were still above the existing Continental limit. Throughout the winter of 1775 and the following spring, lash counts stayed high. In April 1776, a court-martial handed down sentences of 800, 400, 200, and 100 lashes. John Rutledge, president of the South Carolina legislature, pardoned these men. No sentences as high as 800 lashes appear to have ever been carried out. Whatever the sentence — and lash counts were all high at this time — most offenders received a partial remission. In August, a soldier sentenced to 200 lashes for being absent without leave for four days "rec'd 120 on Account of a bad Leg."[58]

The civilian and militia practices give us clues as to why patriot leaders in South Carolina acted this way. We have already seen that the presence of slaves and weak judicial institutions led to more severe or erratic punishment practices in civilian life in the Carolinas. Also, the recruits in that colony, from the earliest days of the war, were poor whites, a number of whom were foreign-born. The lower status of these Carolinian troops is also reflected in the pay scale assigned to them. The pay scale assigned by the Continental Congress to the Continental army in 1775 was that a colonel was paid seven and a half times what a private soldier was paid and five times the most junior officer. At the same time in South Carolina, the pay scale for a colonel was set as sixteen times that of a private but only about three and a half times that of a junior officer. Henry Laurens made it clear that high pay for officers was offered to attract "proper Men for the Service." He made no comment about what that said about the men who responded to the recruiter's drum at the opposite end of the social scale.[59]

From the beginning, soldiers were subject to treatment that, while it served military purposes, must have been difficult for white men in Carolina to accept and reinforced the low regard in which they were held. A year before the Continental Congress considered longer-term enlistments, soldiers in South Carolina had to enlist for three years or the duration. They had to carry passes when they left camp, just as slaves did to leave the plantation. Also, an act passed in April 1776 empowered any "free white person" to stop any soldier without a pass. Free whites were offered a cash reward for turning in such men as deserters, just as they were rewarded for seizing runaway slaves. Additionally, soldiers were subject to lash punishments that would never be imposed on white men in civilian life and rarely on slaves.

As noted earlier, there were a significant number of foreign-born men among the South Carolina troops, particularly from Ireland. Their presence possibly fa-

cilitated the similarities in the treatment of soldiers and slaves. Newer immigrants tended to be poorer, and they might also have been less immersed in the
subtleties of racial politics and therefore less sensitive to the anxieties that native-
born white men might have felt at this treatment. Comments by observers from
outside the colony indicate that perhaps South Carolinians had anticipated who
their recruits would be and had instituted punishment practices accordingly.
General Charles Lee, admiring the colony's tough punishments, thought that
"severity [was] necessary for an Irish soldiery." General John Armstrong, also in
Charleston in the spring of 1776, said the South Carolina government had
thought that the "perverse soldiery of this meridian" had needed harsh punishments to keep them in line.[60]

John Rutledge's willingness to issue reprieves for harsh punishments, however, indicates that he was perhaps consciously juggling some of the competing
pressures of military needs, political circumstances, and racial politics. William
Tudor, more than a thousand miles away, wrote that a soldier had to submit to
being a "temporary slave" when he served his country. For native-born white
men of little property who had grown up in a society with an overwhelming slave
majority, the prospect of even temporary slavery must have been a difficult one
to contemplate. The punishment level that Rutledge and senior officers settled
on reflected the community's tolerance for violence and the low social standing
of the men who were serving.[61]

At the same time, the New England regiments practiced a military discipline
in the early months of the war that was reflective of their culture. The approaches
to discipline of the two cultures stood in stark contrast. In keeping with the more
tightly knit, stable communities there, shaming punishments in conjunction
with lash sentences well within the legal thirty-nine-lash limit were the order of
the day. At the end of June 1775, a Massachusetts soldier was found guilty of de-
faming Washington. Sentenced to be drummed out of the camp with men assembled to witness the event, the prisoner was tied and put in a cart surrounded
by fifers and drummers. At intervals, the cart stopped for the soldier to publicly
announce his crime. After he had gone through the army, he was allowed to go.
In this early stage of the struggle, the soldier's public humiliation was a warning
to others. When the lash was used, it was used sparingly. A New Hampshire soldier convicted of theft was sentenced to ten lashes "to be put in execution as
soon as the weather Will Permit."[62]

Lash averages remained high in South Carolina until November 1776, when
the new articles of war (drawn up in September 1776) were received. In accordance with General Robert Howe's instructions, the articles were "to be read at

the Head of the Regiment. . . . [N]o one to be Absent that is able to stand."
From that time on, courts handed down lash sentences that conformed to the
new Continental limit. The quick South Carolinian response to the new legal
limits was an indication of both the standardization of the army as the war progressed and the presence of General Howe. From North Carolina, Howe had
been active in bringing that colony's Regulator movement under control. While
lash sentences dropped, the South Carolina courts-martial did not shy away
from brutal punishments, and they were among the few who used piquet.[63]

With the passage of the revised articles of 1776, soldiers from New England,
the mid-Atlantic region, and the Chesapeake found themselves subject to a discipline sharply different from the civilian practices they knew. That discipline
was familiar to the military culture of South Carolina, but its worst excesses were
curbed. Riding the wooden horse, running the gauntlet, and lash sentences at
the new legal limit were now commonplace everywhere.

The September 1776 articles stood with only minor alterations throughout
the war. In 1781, following the mutiny of the Pennsylvania line, Washington appealed to Congress for an increase in the lash limit to 500. His arguments would
have been familiar to civilian reformers. He felt there was a "want of a proper
gradation of punishments." With nothing between 100 lashes and death, too
many capital sentences were being passed. Death sentences were "so frequent as
to render their execution in most cases inexpedient," and pardoning rates were
high. Congress referred the matter to a committee, which recommended that
the articles be changed. It was voted down, though the vote was close, both by
delegate and by state count. The voting hints at a North/South division but of-
fers no clear picture. Congressman John Sullivan, a former Continental army
general, wrote to Washington to notify him of the resolution's defeat. He said
that it "was rejected upon the principles Laid Down in the Levitical Law Strongly
urged by Roger Shearman Esqr &ca." The "Shearman" to whom he was referring was Roger Sherman, a delegate from Connecticut, an experienced legisla-
tor, and a man with a reputation for being honest and "a stern puritan." While
the devout had failed to hold the country to biblical injunctions in 1776, a line
had been drawn in the sand. They were not prepared to stray any farther.[64]

But strayed they had. The separation between military and civilian justice became even more pronounced during the war years. Many of the new states had
passed their own state constitutions, some of which reflected reformers' concerns about civilian punishment practices. The new constitutions of Maryland,
Pennsylvania, North and South Carolina, Vermont, and Virginia all had clauses
that prohibited "cruel and unusual punishments" or required that punishments

be "less sanguinary, and in general more proportionate to the crime." These concerns with civilian punishment during the flurry of state constitution writing
did not open up a debate on military punishment. While Washington's request
for a 500-lash limit was indeed voted down, some of the delegates' votes indicate that they were able to delineate clearly the civilian and military worlds. South
Carolina and Pennsylvania both had new constitutions that restricted cruel or
sanguinary punishments, yet all seven of their delegates voting on the 1781
amendment voted in favor of raising the lash limit to 500.[65]

Lash and other punishments well beyond civilian standards and theological
commands were the cornerstones of discipline for Continental soldiers. In contrast, men in the militia continued to be largely free from even the corporal punishments of civilian life. In the September 1776 articles of war, Congress tried to
bring harsher punishments to bear on the militia on the occasions when it was
"joined, or acting in conjunction with" the Continental army. However, there
was a provision that court-martial panels could be made up only of officers from
the militia corps with which the offender served. In practice, then, this did little to alter militia punishments. Courts-martial were few and sentences other
than a fine were rare. When a lash sentence was given, it appeared to be inflicted
on someone outside the community. For example, one lash punishment handed
down in the Massachusetts militia was given to a man described in the record as
"a transient negro," someone who was almost certainly serving as a substitute.
(Substitution was permitted in the militia also but was most commonly a family affair with sons or siblings serving for fathers or older brothers.) In South
Carolina, a militia orderly book from one summer indicates that, in the face of a
problem with desertion, the courts consistently handed down fifteen-lash sentences for the crime, including one for a man named Truelove Brewster. However, all of these were pardoned. Corporal punishment for the most part remained the province of the regular troops.[66]

The effectiveness of lash and a variety of other public punishments depended
not only on the pain inflicted but also on the shame. However, shame was only
possible if a person had a reputation to lose. All men possessed honor. It was a
gentleman's particularly refined sense of honor that made corporal punishment
too degrading for him. In punishing soldiers, corporal and other kinds of public punishment were used because everyone knew that soldiers had honor and
reputation to lose. Washington and others lobbied for an increase in the thirty-
nine-lash limit because the punishment was not severe enough to bring dishonor in the eyes of the individual or the watching crowd. Washington felt that

some men barely considered it punishment and that "for a bottle of Rum" they
would take it again. Some political leaders in South Carolina thought thirty-
nine lashes would be "a light breakfast" for soldiers. Indeed, even after the increase in the lash limit to 100, some thought that soldiers took even that punishment lightly. One sergeant described his men as "old Country men wich are very
bad[. W]e are [forced?] to flog them night & morning a hunder[d] lashes a
piece," and there is no hint in this comment that it was working as a deterrent.[67]

However, not all officers agreed that men shrugged off the shame of punishment. Some, instead, exploited a soldier's honor and used shaming punishments,
which held the offender up to ridicule by making him do something animal-like
or childish. Officers could be quite inventive. Some soldiers were sentenced to
be led about by a halter, to wear their coats inside out, or, like William Telley, a
Rhode Island soldier, to be "tied to a tree Naked & to stand for ten minits."
John Ricky, convicted of disobedience and being verbally abusive to an officer,
had to make a public apology to the officer involved and "wear a board of eight
inches square one day on his back, with a label on the board saying, 'A disobeyer
of orders.'" Sometimes shaming was used in addition to corporal punishment.
Lieutenant Benjamin Beal noted that three New Jersey soldiers, guilty of verbally abusing their officers, had each received seventy-eight lashes and then were
"drumed through the Camps with a halter on their necks."[68]

When men serving together came from a single community, a deeper sense of
honor could be brought to bear. Letters sent home by others carried the news of
disgrace. The army also placed newspaper advertisements in deserters' home
states both to shame the family and to encourage people to turn them in. The
Pennsylvania Evening Post carried such advertisements; sometimes they went into
great details. One for three local deserters was complete with details of where they
were last seen, what they were wearing, and what they looked like, even down
to the color of their eyes. Similarly, the Boston *Independent Chronicle* ran advertisements for deserters and called on "every Friend to his Country" to try to ap-
prehend them. Both newspapers noted the extra incentive of a reward to get citizens to exert themselves.[69]

If the deserters made their way home, the shame could be even greater. Thomas
James of Scituate, Massachusetts, wrote to his brother Elisha at Ticonderoga
with the news that two of their old friends, David and Varsal Turner, had deserted. The men had been advertised and had turned up at home but "with no
honnor . . . [and] thay Dont look up with A good face." Elisha's wife, Sarah, at
home in Scituate with a new baby, knew of David and Varsal Turner's disgrace.

She was anxious for her husband to be home but she wanted him to return with honor. She asked Elisha to "git desmist as soon as you Can but not run away and be advertisd as david and versil ware."[70]

The shame of corporal punishment was so great that some officers acknowledged that under certain circumstances it did more to hurt discipline than help it. When a court-martial convened for the Eighth Connecticut Regiment to punish two men, one older than the other, for being absent without leave for two days, it was reluctant to punish the younger man. The court was sensitive "to the Wound the Whip inflicts on the character of a young soldier." Instead it forgave him and recommended his commanding officer remind the young man "of the Evil consequences of such Company & Conduct." The older soldier was whipped, but the regimental commander confirmed the other man's pardon, "having the most tender feelings for the correction of a young soldier." In South Carolina, too, youth was worthy of consideration. Young Oliver McHaffey was found guilty of being absent without leave and sentenced to sixty lashes, but the court was sympathetic to his youth and inexperience and recommended "him to Mercy being a young Soldier." The commander agreed and remitted twenty lashes of the punishment.[71]

Some officers resisted flogging for theological reasons or because they saw it as an ineffective tool. Excessive flogging was degrading, according to Deuteronomy 25:3: "[I]f he should exceed [forty stripes], and beat him above these with many stripes, then thy brother should seem vile unto thee." Daniel Morgan, who commanded the Virginia riflemen, brought his personal experience to bear in his decision not to use the lash. As a young man during the Seven Years' War, he had been a wagoner with Braddock's expedition. During that campaign, he had struck a British officer in an argument and had been sentenced to 500 lashes. Years later, after the pain and bitterness were long past, Morgan, a colorful and vigorous character, enjoyed telling the story over dinner. He particularly relished the fact that the drummer had miscounted and only given him 499 lashes. As a commander in the Continental army, he refused to use whipping as a punishment as he believed public flogging degraded and disheartened soldiers.[72]

Most officers who sat on courts-martial, however, consistently included the lash and a range of other corporal punishments in their sentencing for soldiers. Early versions of the articles of war had shied away from the degrading, brutal punishment levels of the British army. In the articles of 1776, the Continental Congress limited the number of lashes that could be given to soldiers and enumerated capital crimes, but it avoided specifically mentioning other kinds of punishment. For a number of crimes, the articles stated that the punishment could be simply "such punishment as shall be inflicted upon him by the sentence of a court-martial."[73]

Some American officers in the field quickly adopted the full array of punishments from the British army's inventive range and added a few of their own. With soldiers serving for short terms, some courts added additional years of service to the punishment of the lash. A New Hampshire soldier was sentenced to receive seventy lashes and was then compelled to join the Continental navy "there to serve during the War." One soldier with General Lachlan McIntosh reported in a letter to a friend that discipline was strict. If "a man Dus any thing Amiss," he wrote, "[i]nto the gard house with him & he Must Either [en]List [Dur]ing the War or Receive thirty Nine on his back."[74]

The traditional British punishments of riding the wooden horse, running the gauntlet, and piquet were all used in the Continental army. The gauntlets were usually smaller and the beatings inflicted with branches or switches from trees. Piquet, which was particularly brutal, was rarely used. When Francis Marion commanded the Second South Carolina Regiment in October 1778, he approved a court-martial sentence that subjected a soldier to ninety-nine lashes and the piquet. For the latter, the prisoner was sentenced to endure it for "7 & 8 minutes 2 different days." Marion was not alone in using it. Among others, courts-martial from the Second New York Artillery Regiment and Colonel Samuel Webb's Connecticut Continentals also sentenced men to be "picketed" for brief periods, in the latter case for playing cards. However, these occasions were few.[75]

The revised 1776 articles represented a more complete subordination of the soldiers both to their officers and to the civilian population. For British soldiers, the possibility of a humanitarian response to harsh punishment was inhibited by physical separation. The Continentals were never as separate from the civilian world, but there were no voices raised complaining of punishment levels. While the army was often physically close to the civilian population, it was always carefully segregated. In fact, the army's proximity to the civilian population sometimes led to more stringent discipline as civilians and military authorities feared the consequences of marauding young men about their property and their daughters.

There is no evidence that Continental punishment practices made citizens reluctant to complain against soldiers. Regimental orderly books indicate that civilians were quick to do so and company commanders quick to respond to even the smallest of complaints. Senior officers railed in their orders against soldiers who were "guilty of the most unherd of bad behavior, such as pulling young Corn," "wantonly destroy[ing] the inhabitants fences," or plundering their fruit. One farmer complained to Nathanael Greene of soldiers "gathering and roasting his corn," which prompted Greene to declare that anyone "Detected with Corn" could expect to find himself in the guardhouse. Of course, complaints did not mean that the guilty party could be identified and tried. There were many more admonishments than there were courts-martial for crimes such as these, but even when the perpetrators were caught, there is little evidence that any complainants found punishment levels troubling. Courts handed down lash punishments at or near the legal limit for stealing geese, cows, and hogs, often with orders to pay restitution to the owner.[76]

However, there is evidence that a few people who were not experiencing the depredations of the soldiers were considering the problems of corporal punishments. One was Judith Stevens. She was from an old Massachusetts family and recognized that in giving her opinions to her brother, a Continental officer, she was "wandering from [her] proper sphere." She wrote to him questioning the appropriateness of harsh punishments for men fighting for liberty. Others were concerned for an entirely different reason. Doctor James Thacher, serving with the army, thought that corporal punishment was an appropriate substitution for the death penalty but that otherwise it suppressed a "spirit of ambition and enterprize in the young soldier." More importantly, he was concerned it might lead to social discomfort. If an individual who had had the disgrace of being lashed was later promoted for "meritorious services" to the officer corps, how could such a person ever be considered a gentleman and become an acceptable "companion for other officers"? Neither of these comments represented widespread criticism. Most people accepted the army's punishments without comment.[77]

While civilians did not seem unsettled by Continental punishments, they still appeared to find British practices beyond the pale. In towns held by the British during the war, citizens expressed reluctance to subject soldiers guilty of property crimes to harsh punishments. Robert Morton, a teenager in a loyalist family in Philadelphia during the British occupation in 1777, wrote with great anger about the "ravages and wanton destruction of the soldiery" on local property. However, when the British arrested the men who had broken into the Morton family home, "breaking and ransacking" the contents, the family tried to intercede on the soldiers' behalf. They had no success, nor did another neighbor who had also sought clemency for a soldier who had robbed her.[78]

For the Continental army, civilians and their property had to be protected for political reasons, which added to the tensions surrounding military justice. For civilians, however tenacious of liberty and devoted to biblical injunctions they might be, the prospect of large numbers of armed young men in their neighborhoods was a cause for concern. Troops were supposed to be "the guardians of the property of the inhabitants," and when they preyed on them instead, punish-ment, Washington thought, should be swift and unequivocal. In a letter to the Marquis de Lafayette, who had problems with soldiers plundering, Washington advised, "[Y]ou can make your trial and punishment as summary as need be; and where the latter can be inflicted legally, it is to be preferred." As Washington had observed in the 1757 letter quoted earlier, sometimes going outside of the law was "necessary and excusable."[79]

The casual references to extralegal punishment were a further indication of the reduction in the status of soldiers. Due process, the adherence to legal pro-cedures, was, and is, central to civil liberty. In the British army, the suspension of due process was a regular occurrence. This either took the form of an announce-ment in the general orders of the day that soldiers guilty of certain offenses, like drunkenness, would be punished without court-martial, or by the immediate infliction of a whipping for minor infractions. Threats of punishment without court-martial, principally for desertion, were in Washington's general orders on several occasions. General Israel Putnam, too, ordered that any man caught steal-ing from local inhabitants would be whipped "without the formality of Tryal by a Court Martial." While there was certainly a good deal of informal punishment, such as slapping or punching, which is discussed below, there is little evidence in orderly books, letters, or diaries that many were subjected to the formality of being tied to the post and whipped by a drummer without a court-martial.[80]

If Washington could have done it, he certainly would have. The reason he could not was the soldiers themselves. By their enlistment, they accepted pun-ishment levels in excess of civilian norms and a system of justice that codified in-equality. But, it was a system and it fit in with their sense of their own status and the familiar conventions of indentured labor, which included the right to due process. The only social group punished without due process was slaves. Whether soldiers ever consciously made the association with slavery, we can never know.

Some people certainly thought that the loss of liberty that soldiers were sub-ject to was akin to slavery. As noted earlier, William Tudor and Henry Laurens, president of the Continental Congress and a wealthy South Carolinian, had quickly made the connection. Tudor called the soldiers' status "temporary slav-ery." Laurens, at the suggestion that a regiment of slaves be formed, could not see why slaves would be inclined to exchange one state of slavery for another. Laurens was more paternalistic than most South Carolinian planters and thus perhaps more aware of the burdens of both slavery and military service. But per-haps he did not intend his comment to be taken literally and was simply discour-aging the idea. Certainly, by its voluntary enlistment and short terms of service,

Continental service was not slavery. But Laurens's and Tudor's words indicate that even conversationally, some saw the loss of liberty that went along with service as extreme.[81]

Soldiers accepted and respected the system of military justice that existed but were unwilling to abrogate any of their few rights under it. Certainly the response of one infantryman to an improper punishment carried a strong sense of injustice. Zebulon Vaughan recorded in his diary on New Year's Day 1779 that some soldiers had fired off their guns to celebrate "the hapey New Year." This outraged their commander, Colonel Rufus Putnam, since ammunition was supposed to be carefully husbanded. Vaughan noted (phonetically) that "the old Cus praded th holl Rigment and picked out them and whipt them without aney plea or given them the Benefut of ae Cort marshil and Reseved [received] ten Stripe one [on] thar Naked Back Cus all Such men and Let the Cus foller them to thar grave and six feet under ground." Soldiers were prepared to put up with a great deal of hardship, but Vaughan's comment indicates that their endurance did not extend to losing the right to due process.[82]

In fact, despite Washington's comment, almost all officers of the army, including Washington most of the time, cared as much about the formalities of the judicial process as Zebulon Vaughan. In Charleston in 1779, William Moultrie, now holding the rank of brigadier general, disallowed a sentence on a legal technicality. A court-martial had decided that a soldier charged with desertion was guilty only of the lesser crime of being absent without leave and sentenced him to 100 lashes. Moultrie ruled that the "Court finds the prisoner Guilty of a Crime with which he is not charged and Sentence him a punishment when that Crime did not come before them." The prisoner was immediately freed without punishment.[83]

While soldiers objected to the absence of due process, there is no record that they objected when they were sentenced or subjected to punishments that were illegal under the articles of war. Since all court-martial punishments had to be approved by the commanding officer, it was his responsibility to disallow such sentences. Washington himself was inconsistent. In the spring of 1778, he chided Colonel Thomas Hartley when a court-martial Hartley presided over handed down 100 lashes for each charge of which the accused was found guilty. Washington warned Hartley not to try to "elude" the restriction of the articles of war and allowed a punishment of only 100 lashes in total. However, Washington's general orders of the same day confirmed a 200-lash sentence to the luckless John Clime of the Tenth Pennsylvania Regiment. He was found guilty of "desertion and attempting to make his Escape to the Enemy" and received 100 lashes for each crime. A few sentences simply ignored the lash limit altogether. In 1777, Captain Robert Kirkwood of the Delaware regiment recorded sentences of 400 and 500 lashes, which appear to have been carried out. On the disastrous Florida expedition in 1778, a deserter was spared execution due to "favorable Circumstances." Instead, he was "only" sentenced to 500 lashes, which was "approved & executed accordingly."[84]

We cannot now determine the circumstances that led some illegal sentences to be confirmed while others were disallowed. The nature of the crime, the character of the prisoners, and the tenor of camp life at any given time probably all influenced the decision. A number of illegal sentences were given out during the army's winter quartering at Valley Forge in 1777–78 and on campaigns, such as the one in Florida, when things were going badly. So, harsh punishments were possibly indicative of the fragile state of the army at those times.

While formal lash punishments above the legal limit were rare, informal violence was a regular occurrence and an accepted part of daily life. Officers, standing in the place of parents or masters, assumed a right to hit soldiers, and nothing in the records left by soldiers indicates that they felt there was anything inappropriate about this. Daniel Morgan, who shied away from degrading, formal, public punishments, was known to let fly with his fists when he lost his temper, and this did not prevent him from being well-liked by his troops. Twenty-three-year-old Captain Joseph Bloomfield, a young lawyer prior to serving in the New Jersey line, saw himself in a paternal relationship with his men; he assumed that meant disciplining them as necessary. He felt that the "Men compose my Family," and he used formal punishment sparingly and pardoned soldiers for "being Very penitent." But, as the head of a family, he occasionally saw the need for informal punishment. One day, his guards frustrated him when they were drunk on duty, and one got involved in a brawl. Bloomfield "could not help bilabouring him with my sword, which I did so effectually that I believe He will ever remember it." Bloomfield did not feel his actions interfered with his desire to "gain the Love & esteem of my officers & Soldiers."[85]

Casual physical punishment was an accepted way of life. Like indentured servants who took masters to court when abusive behavior passed accepted local norms, soldiers too appear to have complained only when this violence was excessive or inappropriate. A court-martial found Lieutenant Isaac Barber of Massachusetts guilty "for beating & kicking Lt. Freemans Servant, Edward Bird [a soldier], & rendering him unfit for Duty." In confirming the sentence of a reprimand, General Alexander McDougall noted that it was painful to him "that any Officer in the American Army, raised for the express purpose of defending the Rights & Liberty of Humanity, should so forget his object As to beat a Soldier put under his Care and protection, without provocation."[86]

Without ever articulating what was acceptable, everyone seemed to recognize what was unacceptable when they saw it. For an officer to hit without provocation or to appear to have lost control was unacceptable. In South Carolina, in an effort to control informal violence, William Moultrie forbade any officers from striking soldiers "save the Major & Adjutant, and that tenderly and in the way of their particular duty." In confirming a court-martial sentence of a Captain Van Anglin for striking a sergeant, General John Sullivan gave this observation on informal punishment for soldiers. "Though the General will never countenance soldiers in disrespectful behaviour to officers, and will entertain a poor opinion of an officer who suffers himself to be insulted without immediately chastising the soldier who may attempt it, yet he can never suffer officers to beat & abuse their soldiers wantonly. Blows should never be given except where they are necessary to the preservation of order & discipline, & then unaccompanied with those marks of cruelty & malevolence which were apparent in the whole of Mr. Van Anglin's conduct." While Sullivan never specified what was acceptable, loss of control was not.[87]

When courts-martial failed to discipline officers appropriately for this infraction, senior officers did it anyway. Punishment for officers often was simply a public reprimand. Indeed, Sullivan's comment above on Captain Van Anglin was Van Anglin's court-martial sentence. When a court of inquiry declined to bring a charge against one Captain Lee for attacking a soldier because it considered that the officer had been provoked, the division commander, General Arthur St. Clair, responded in his general orders that he was "obliged to differ" with the court's finding. Captain Lee's "vexation," St. Clair observed, could not be "a sufficient Excuse for his conduct which was not only rash but highly blame worthy." So, despite the court's favorable finding, Captain Lee found himself publicly reprimanded anyway.[88]

In these instances of informal punishment, officers were acting spontaneously in anger. When drummers had to carry out formal punishment, it was an assigned duty. Few Americans have left us an account of what it felt like to carry out this charge. One Virginia militiaman hated to be part of a gauntlet; he remembered it as a "cruel punishment" and thought he would "like to have died" if he had received it. We know that one teenage Continental drummer, a senior officer's son, tried to use what influence he had to get out of the task of inflicting a lash punishment, but "he was obliged to submit and take his turn of the unpleasant duty." Drummers were usually of the same social rank as the men they were punishing, but there is little other evidence that drummers either resisted or avoided the duty. It is possible that if an offender was someone who had preyed on his fellow soldiers, then neither soldiers nor drummers might have been reluctant to watch or carry out the sentence.[89]

While neither drummers nor soldiers challenged punishments, there is evidence that some tried to manage the event a little. One Delaware soldier, Abram Meers, was brought before a court-martial for assaulting a drummer who Meers thought had done his whipping duty too enthusiastically. Meers believed that the drummer should "not have abus'd the man so." Meers told him that if the drummer ever had to inflict a punishment on him and whipped him that hard, Meers would "me[e]t him in a bye place, [and] he would give him a knock that he would not be aware of." The drummer defended himself, claiming he had just done his duty. Meers warned him that he had to be more moderate and not "whip as if he was in A passion or else he would get the ill will of the whole comp[an]y." So, despite their apparent cooperation in the punishment, soldiers were clearly able to separate cooperation from enthusiasm and accepted the former but not the latter.[90]

Memoirs, letters, and diaries often recorded floggings in a matter-of-fact way with little elaboration, but executions elicited more detail. While executions were a regular feature of urban life, many soldiers coming from farms and scattered communities had probably never seen one until they joined the army. One pension applicant, writing fifty years later, offered almost no details of his wartime service except the names of two men he had seen executed.[91]

Some of the trappings of military executions would have been familiar to those who had seen them in colonial towns or who had read about them. Military executions were also intended to instill awe, and so the sentence was carried out with great ceremony in front of as many troops as could be assembled. The condemned was marched in under guard with a minister in attendance. There was also the possibility of reprieve that, for the condemned and the soldiers, added to the tension of the moment. Sometimes, if a number of men were to be executed at one time, one would be hanged as an example and the rest pardoned, adding to the agony of the condemned men as they waited.

As in civilian life, reprieves were an important part of the justice system. Military authorities also had to juggle the needs to conserve manpower and to instill discipline and the desire not to appear brutal, and so capital punishment was used sparingly in the Continental army. Washington took corporal punishment as far as he could, using it as much and as often as possible, rarely pardoning, but with capital sentences he was more cautious. Probably only between 17 and 30 percent of capital sentences were carried out. Like civilian reformers, Washington was frustrated by the lack of a flexible scale of punishment. Since he and many other officers believed that 100 lashes were not enough to subordinate soldiers appropriately, too many capital sentences were handed down. In the fall of 1778, he felt "obliged to remit" the execution of a soldier, even though he believed the death sentence of the court-martial appropriate to the crime. He did so because he had recently approved seven death sentences in different parts of the army and was concerned "lest the frequency of punishment should take off the good effects intended by it."[92]

The similarity to civilian practice ended there. At military executions, attendance by the watching crowd was not voluntary but compelled by military orders. There were no publications of the condemned man's last thoughts and no air of festivity among the crowd. Religion played little or no role. A minister might be present to counsel the condemned man or hear last prayers, but he rarely made any speeches. Some ministers, like the Reverend William Rogers, who was with General Sullivan in the campaign against the Iroquois, played an active role in lobbying for mercy if the accused seemed appropriately penitent. When Rogers first visited two deserters sentenced to death, he found them "very ignorant of things which appertain to religion." In later visits, he was encouraged by their willingness to listen to him, and Rogers was able to recommend to Sullivan that he pardon the men, which he duly did. However, on the parade ground, before the pardon was read, Rogers was an observer only; he was not there to deliver a sermon. In the military world, execution was a secular event. Soldiers watching were to be awed not by the wrath of God but by the power of military authority.[93]

The diaries that noted executions sometimes went into great detail, especially if the event held some unusual feature. A Massachusetts corporal, Ebenezer Wild, witnessed one such execution on the grand parade ground at Valley Forge. The troops formed in a circle around the prisoner, who was brought under the gallows in a wagon. The prisoner spoke his last words, the rope was attached to the gallows, the noose was put around his neck, and then the wagon moved away. The rope broke, and the condemned man had to go through the process a second time. After death, his body was cut down and dropped into a hole that had already been dug under the gallows.

Wild gave details of another execution later in 1778. In this case, the two condemned men were paraded to the site of the execution, walking under guard, and "The Dead March was played behind them." The charges and sentence were read to the pair in front of the assembled troops. Each had to kneel beside his

By his Excellency George Washington Esquire, General and Commander in Chief of the Forces of the United States of America;

To Colonel Richard Hampton Commanding the 11th Battalion of the State of Pennsylvania

Whereas, at a General Court Martial held in the City of Philadelphia on the 8th day of this Month, whereof Col. Rich.d Hampton of the 11th Pennsylvania Battalion was President. Brent Debbadie a private soldier of Cap.t Lang's Company in the 10th Pennsylvania Battalion was charged with DESERTION; And upon a fair and full Inquiry and Examination of the Premisses, Consideration of the Testimony and Circumstances, and hearing the said Prisoner in his defence, he the said Brent Debbadie for the Crime aforesaid stands sentenced to suffer Death; of which said Sentence I have approved— And whereas the said Sentence remains yet to be executed— These are therefore to command & require you the said Col. Rich.d Hampton to cause the said Sentence to be fully executed by shooting the said Brent Debbadie in pursuance thereof on the 8th day of March between the hours of Ten in the forenoon and Three in the afternoon: For which this shall be your sufficient Warrant.

Given under my hand & Seal at Head quarters in Morris Town this 24th day of February 1777—

G.o Washington

Warrant signed by George Washington to carry out the capital
sentence of a court-martial. The prisoner had been tried and
found guilty of desertion. Courtesy Horatio Gates Papers,
Collection of The New-York Historical Society, #74951.

coffin, which was set beside a freshly dug grave, as those in the firing squad loaded their weapons. Moments before the order to fire was given, the two were reprieved and the soldiers dismissed. Wild seems to have been drawn to record the elements that were the most unsettling: in the first case, the breaking of the rope, and in the second, the sight of the men kneeling beside their coffins. Wild's detailed accounts suggest that he was duly impressed by these demonstrations of military authority.[94]

Others also provided detailed recollections of executions that did not go as planned. Sometimes the effect was more disturbing than awesome. That might have been the case with an execution that took place in the 1778 campaign into Florida under General Howe, which involved South Carolina and Georgia Continentals and their state militias. Desertions plagued the expedition, and Sergeant Tyrrel, a Georgia Continental, was sentenced to death by firing squad for encouraging mutiny. Whereas a hanging needed only a few soldiers to be involved in carrying out the execution, a firing squad required the active involvement of fifteen to twenty men. The usual practice was that two-thirds of the squad fired first, then the remaining third would quickly fire a second volley if the prisoner had not been killed. In Tyrrel's case, even that was not enough. Both "[t]he execution Guard & the Reserve failed in putting him to immediate death: A Single Man therefore marched up & blew his brains out."[95]

If the officer recording this, Major John Grimke from South Carolina, was distressed, it was not reflected in his journal. Indeed, this was one of a flurry of executions he recorded in his campaign diary. The campaign was a disaster, plagued by disease, lack of food, and disagreements among its commanders. Between May 21 and May 24, the expedition either hanged or shot seven men, Tyrrel and six deserters, and these executions were around the time four other deserters had been sentenced to run the gauntlet and a fifth sentenced to the lash and fifteen minutes of piquet. Grimke called these punishments "necessary to put a stop to the encreasing Evil" of desertion, which was "prejudicial to [the] Service." Two weeks later, he was pleased to note that there had not been a desertion since the last of these seven executions.[96]

Not all officers were so detached. An account by an officer detailed to lead a firing squad reveals a very different sensibility. After the Battle of Long Island, a devastating defeat for the Americans, a court-martial sentenced Ebenezer Leffingwell, a sergeant in the Connecticut Continentals, to death for running off during battle, although he denied his guilt. In fact, a number of men present recorded the tension around this trial and court-martial as there was a general sentiment that the sergeant had acted according to orders and was being treated unfairly. Companies drew lots to see who would supply the soldiers for the firing squad. Captain Enoch Anderson reported that "the lot fell" on his Delaware regiment. His major told him, "You must go with some soldiers and do this thing." He therefore "chose out twenty men and went on the hateful business." Anderson described the scene:

> I drew near the fatal spot; — the prisoner was kneeling in front of the parapet, with a cap over his eyes. We came within twenty feet of him, — his every nerve was creeping, and in much agony he groaned. I groaned, my soldiers groaned, — we all groaned. I would rather have been in a battle. After he was worked up to a high degree for an example to the army, perhaps, a minister mounted the parapet and cried "a pardon, a pardon!" The poor condemned thing tried to look upward, but could not, — he was bound in fetters. He cried out, "oh! Lord God, oh! I am not to be shot — oh! oh!"
>
> Such are the feelings of sympathy, that the tears of joy run down my cheeks. I was not above my poor boys [soldiers], each also shed their tears. Gloomy as was the morning, the evening turned out crowned with pleasure.[97]

As with executions in civilian life, the mood of the crowd and its response to the criminal and the perceived justice of the sentence played a role in whether the punishment achieved its end of instilling awe in authority. The rapid pace of executions on the Florida campaign seems to have indeed awed the watching soldiers, if only temporarily. In the case of the prisoner Anderson's squad was to execute, a soldier watching remembered that it was just as well Washington had issued a reprieve. He recalled that had the execution been carried out, the prisoner's blood "would not have been the only blood that would have been spilt." It is unclear whether carrying out the execution would have really started a riot or mutiny, but at the very least it was not going to serve the desired end.[98]

Loss of honor was as central to capital punishments as it was to corporal. Men sentenced to death worried about the shame their fate would bring to their families and themselves. The sergeant who received the last-minute reprieve went to Washington and begged not to be sent home in disgrace but rather to be allowed to serve as a private "to retrieve his character." Another deserter, who faced a death sentence from a civilian court for murder, requested that his real name be kept secret. He told a "gentleman who attended him to his execution" that his life had been "notoriously wicked" and he wanted to spare his friends and family from ever knowing "the shocking end to which he came." His request had "much weight" and was honored. Only his initials were made public. Both these men felt the shame of the charges against them, indicating they held deeply that value of the society. Washington would have been pleased. In their final moments, or what they thought were, the men showed a proper sense of honor.[99]

Unlike civilian authorities who occasionally brutalized the most degraded members of their communities at death — for example, slaves whose severed heads were publicly displayed — the Continental army did not inflict this final insult on its soldiers. Occasionally, dead bodies were displayed. For instance, a deserter from the Maryland Continentals was hanged on a tree "in full view of all who passed by." Greater brutality did not regularly occur, but it did cross the minds of some officers and, indeed, happened on at least one occasion. The Virginian Henry Lee, known as "Light-Horse Harry" Lee, who commanded a legion of cavalry and infantry, suggested to Washington that it would be good for discipline if executed deserters had their heads cut off and publicly displayed. Lee thought this final degradation would be an added deterrent to others. Washington, appalled, responded with gentlemanly restraint. It might, he wrote, give "an appearance of inhumanity." His response came too late to prevent one of Lee's captains, Philip Reed, from beheading a deserter. Lee reported the incident to Washington, noting that it had "had a very immediate effect for the better on both troops and inhabitants." Washington was concerned about the response of soldiers and the public, should the incident become widely known. He instructed that the body be quickly buried "lest it fall into the enemy's hands" and be used as propaganda against the American cause.[100]

Washington clearly understood the uses of public punishment but also its limitations. He also understood the limits of tolerance of his soldiers. They had accepted punishment levels beyond anything that was generally acceptable in civilian life, yet they would not tolerate treatment that placed them on a level with the most brutalized and degraded members of the community.

This drama and violence stood in sharp contrast to the punishments handed out to officers. Even officers found guilty of lengthy catalogues of crime were simply discharged from the service. Captain Patrick Duffy of the Fourth Artillery Regiment was charged with conduct unbecoming the character of an officer and a gentleman. The list of his crimes was shocking: drawing a sword on another captain, attempting to stab him, firing a pistol at him while the other was unarmed, seizing another loaded pistol and aiming it at another officer, being drunk, rioting in the street, abusing a French soldier, and behaving in a seditious manner in trying to take a French guard. A court-martial sentenced him to be discharged from the service. Similarly, Captain Joseph Leaunden was cashiered for drawing "more provisions than he had men in his company to consume," stealing a gun, and "threatening the life" of a sergeant.[101]

Even the possibility of a discharge was too disgraceful for some officers to tolerate. In 1776, when the Continental Congress was pressing South Carolina to let its troops be swept into the Continental army, the legislature resisted. Paramount among the legislature's reasons was that it saw the Continental articles, which at the time had a thirty-nine-lash limit, as "too mild" for South Carolina's soldiers. In addition, the fact that officers could be cashiered gave "great disgust." So, it saw the punishments for soldiers as not harsh enough and for officers as too awful.[102]

A key element in the severity of the punishment for an officer was how many people were to witness or be aware of the gentleman's dishonor. One Lieutenant Dukerson, guilty of conduct unbecoming an officer and a gentleman and sentenced to be discharged, had the additional punishment that the sentence "be publish'd in the publick newspapers on this Continent." The Virginian captain George Lambert also had his crime publicly announced. He had stolen a hat from another captain, an important accoutrement for an officer. For this crime, apart from the publicity, he was cashiered and ordered to pay thirty dollars for the hat. However, such publicity was uncommon. One military instruction manual reminded officers that when they were dealing with junior officers in any context, they had to consider that they had "gentlemen to deal with." This advice applied equally well to courts-martial. For some cases, simply the shadow of a charge and a court-martial over an officer's honor was punishment enough. For example, when a court-martial found one lieutenant guilty of neglect of duty, that result was announced in the daily orders. His sentenced reprimand, however, was to be done "by the Col[onel]: in a private Manner."[103]

Only in the most extreme circumstances was an officer held up to ridicule. This happened in the case of Lieutenant Frederick Enslin, who was found guilty of attempting to commit sodomy and of swearing false returns. The charge of sodomy undoubtedly led to the severity of punishment, particularly when compared to that of Captain Duffy noted above. Enslin was brought to the parade ground, under a strong guard, where there was "a very large concourse of people assembled." His crime was read aloud to those assembled, and he was drummed out of the camp, never to return. His shaming did not end there. "His coat was turned wrong side outwards, and then he was drummed off the parade and through the camps down to the side of the Skool Kill, where a guard took him and carried him over the bridge and dismissed him."[104]

As in civilian life, officers enjoyed preferential treatment in that they did not experience corporal punishment and were acquitted much more frequently. The courts did sometimes listen to extenuating circumstances or explanations and were not resistant to acquittal. The patchy records show great variability, but they confirm that the chances of acquittal were significantly greater for officers than for soldiers. The absolute number of officers prosecuted was not high, but they were usually acquitted more than 30 percent of the time. In one Connecticut regiment, that number rose to 70 percent. NCOs also enjoyed high acquittal rates, usually slightly below that of officers but significantly above those of soldiers. For soldiers, acquittal rates ran between 10 and 25 percent.[105]

NCOs were not subject to the indignity of corporal punishment, either. Their status, however, was fragile. Their punishments ranged from fines, reduction to the rank of private soldier, and, for more serious crimes, reduction to the ranks and a lash sentence or shaming. It was only once they had been reduced to privates that it was considered appropriate for them to receive corporal punishment. They did, on rare occasions, receive capital sentences. As noted above, informal punishment was considered appropriate chastisement from an officer to a soldier. However, officers were not allowed to treat NCOs the same way. Captain Van Anglin's court-martial, described earlier, was for striking a sergeant. General Sullivan chastised the officer for his cruelty, but what made "his behavior still more criminal," he noted, was that it "was a non comd officer whom he made the object of his inhumanity."[106]

NCOs and soldiers who served long terms have left scant records giving their opinions on any subject and little on their responses to punishment. What few records there are indicate that grumbling resignation was the order of the day. Zebulon Vaughan recorded his disgust at an illegal lash punishment but carried on. Another private recorded in his diary that "Lt. Johnson swore he would put me under guard unless I paraded, and I paraded." Sergeant John Smith, who "had Some Dispute with Capt. Peek upon ye Soldiers Account," was spared a formal charge and a court-martial because his lieutenant and ensign sided with him in the dispute. However, the captain ordered Smith and another man "to loge in the Crib with a Centinel at the Door untill the Next Day an honour I Did not merit."[107]

Despite the steadily larger social gap between officers and men as the war progressed, there was no noticeable change in disciplinary practices in the later years of the war. Punishment levels stayed constant from the time of the passage of the revised articles and the reorganization of the army in late 1776. While mid-1777 to mid-1778, especially the time at Valley Forge, stands out as a period of severe discipline, it seems to have been occasioned by the fragile state of the cause. It is also questionable if periods of greater severity of punishments or a greater number of courts-martial bore any connection to increased criminality on the part of soldiers. Studies of eighteenth-century civilian criminal justice suggest that changes in pace of prosecution probably had more to do with a government's ability and willingness to enforce the law than changes in criminality, and the same probably holds true for the military setting.[108]

Like the Associators and the militia, Continental army soldiers did not question the conventions of the time, which included the subordination of men in a military force for the sake of order and discipline. Soldiers of the standing army, even a temporary one, who could not accept their subordination either failed to reenlist or deserted. Those who reenlisted accepted a judicial system that, while harsher than civilian life, largely adhered to a process that ultimately became familiar. The men who stayed must not have found the punishments inappropriately severe, unjustified, or unnecessary.

In doling out punishments, both legally and informally, officers were acting in place of a parent or master in guiding soldiers to the correct behavior. Going into the service, few men articulated as clearly as Captain Bloomfield an awareness of their soldiers as family for whom they had parental responsibilities. They would soon become aware that punishment was not the only kind of physical treatment that was an officer's responsibility. Soldiers' health, their personal cleanliness, and general camp hygiene were also under his jurisdiction. All needed close attention to prevent the terrible camp epidemics that plagued eighteenth-century armies. Sickness was almost inevitable, and the treatment of officers and soldiers as they suffered from a variety of diseases was yet another reflection of their relative status.

CHAPTER FOUR

Oh the Groans of the Sick
Health, Status, and Military Medicine

The Lord created medicines from the earth
And a sensible man will not despise them. . . .
And give the physician his place,
For the Lord created him.
ECCLESIASTICUS 38:4, 12

IN THE SUMMER OF 1776, soldiers from the Second South Carolina Regiment were at Fort Johnson. Their commanding officer, Major Barnard Elliott, suspected some of the men were trying to avoid duty by pretending to be sick. Elliott knew how to deal with the problem. He ordered that any soldier discovered feigning sickness "will be physick'd as they deserve." This was a punishment that would have made anybody think twice. Medical treatment in the eighteenth century from either a physician or a folk healer was almost guaranteed to be unpleasant. Both used treatments they thought would cleanse the body of disease. Physicians routinely bled patients, literally draining some blood from the body into a basin, and both physicians and folk healers used emetics, potions that induced vomiting. It was hardly surprising that Elliott thought treatment would be punishment enough for insubordinate behavior.[1]

Elliott wanted to catch soldiers pretending to be sick, but a much more serious problem for the army was the large number of soldiers who really were sick. Doctor Benjamin Rush of Philadelphia observed that it was "a proposition long since established in Europe, that a greater proportion of men perish with sickness in all armies than fall by the sword." Smallpox, scurvy, dysentery, a variety of disorders called putrid fevers (probably typhus and typhoid), and pulmonary and respiratory diseases were facts of military life. Some had their origins in the unsanitary and crowded conditions of a camp. All found fertile ground in soldiers who were malnourished, poorly clothed, and often forced to sleep on wet ground without blankets or straw.[2]

It would be the end of the nineteenth century before there was a complete understanding of why disease thrived in these conditions. However, in the Revolutionary era, physicians, generals, and soldiers made connections between living conditions and disease based on their own observations and experience. A few senior military surgeons thought broadly about the issue and considered diet, weather, poor sanitation, adequate clothing, and overcrowding as factors critical to good health. Most people, however, made smaller, more local connections. General Charles Lee thought that the sickness in his camp was due to soldiers "being expos'd to the Sun in the day time, lying on the damp ground at night, and [drinking] bad water." General Nathanael Greene thought the soldiers needed to have more vegetables in their diet and to keep themselves cleaner. He wanted more soap so they could wash themselves and their clothes more often. Private Joseph Plumb Martin thought he and his friends all got sick from lying on wet ground after a period of "profuse perspiration." Many people were making the connection between certain discomforts and poor health.[3]

The fact that officers and soldiers lived in very different circumstances — officers in private homes and soldiers crowded in camp — had implications beyond the distinctions and comforts required by rank. If good health required access to a clean, dry, comfortable place to sleep and nourishing food, officers, through their status and by having greater financial resources, could more easily and regularly obtain these things. Soldiers lived with limited resources in conditions that left them more vulnerable to disease.

Unlike punishment practices, which were spelled out in military law, there was nothing codified in the articles of war that prescribed medical care for men of any rank. As it evolved in the early months of the war, first informally and then in institutional arrangements, medical care simply followed existing lines of separation and distinction that flowed from other aspects of military life. Officers when sick were cared for in private homes, while soldiers continued to live either in unsanitary camps or languished in overcrowded and equally unsanitary hospitals. However, without being restricted by specific military codes, soldiers had considerable room to maneuver. Provided they were still well enough to direct their fate, soldiers proved resourceful about treating themselves if they could and receiving and giving help to family members, friends, messmates, and townsmen.

Medical care was one aspect of physical treatment where being a militiaman or a Continental made little difference to a man's experience. Infectious disease did not recognize the legal distinction. However, short-term servicemen did have a few advantages. Militiamen probably came to their periods of service rested and well nourished, both good defenses against the diseases of camp. Also, they served with men who were mostly known to them who could offer aid in time of need, compelled by friendship or by family or community connections. But letters and pension applications indicate that the Continentals seemed to have been ready to offer their friends the same courtesy. Certainly the militia frequently operated closer to home, which was an advantage. But when illness struck and walking was the only way to travel, 50 miles could be as insurmountable an obstacle as 500. While we have no statistics showing the differences in the incidence of sickness between militiamen and Continentals, the pension applications of both indicate that they were all very aware of sickness among and around them, whether or not they themselves were ill.

Men of all ranks valued the advice of physicians, but demand for their services was far greater than the supply, and the needs of officers always took priority over those of soldiers. Although there was little that doctors could do by modern standards, people respected their knowledge of medicines and physiology and sought their assistance whenever possible. At this time, college-educated doctors were a small minority of the number of people practicing medicine in the colonies. One other group of practitioners was surgeons, who, since they had a practical skill that was unpleasant to do and involved getting dirty, were considered inferior. There were also midwives, bonesetters, apothecaries who made potions and medicines, and a whole variety of men and women in every community who were respected for their knowledge of herbs and other ingredients that made effective cures for whatever ailed you.

These competing sources of medical knowledge led to a struggle that had a great impact on the health of soldiers. College-educated gentlemen physicians used the war and the organization of a Continental hospital system to help establish their professional authority. They tried to discredit uneducated practitioners of lower social status, and to do so they did whatever they could to set high standards for admission not only to their professional ranks but also to Continental appointments. They also tried to supervise the skills of surgeons serving with regiments in the field. Since a number of patriot leaders were college-educated physicians, they were able to set the country on this path. Respect for them, their profession, and their knowledge led others to defer to them.[4]

This seemingly laudable goal for high professional standards met with some success for the profession but not necessarily for the patients, since doctors had few advantages over other practitioners in either preserving health or in curing disease. This determination by some physicians to subordinate others led to intrigue and public quarrels. It also caused some leading medical men to ignore the significant body of knowledge that had been accumulated by British and European military surgeons.[5]

In these circumstances, the army suffered greatly but not always passively. Some doctors and surgeons tried to buck inflexible rules and think about care for soldiers in innovative ways. Energetic officers did what they could to get their men to keep the camp clean. They acted almost as parents to their troops, chiding them about personal hygiene and treating their minor injuries. Soldiers too used their initiative and whatever resources they could access to help themselves and their friends.

In treating illness, the American medical military world followed conventions from military tradition that reinforced distinctions of rank. It also followed medical practices from daily civilian life where social status determined the standard of care. But while treatment reinforced the distinctions of rank, illness itself had the potential to wear away at them as all men had to confront pain and suffering. A long way from home, officers and men had to deal with their own sickness and mortality. Throughout the war, thoughtful officers, surgeons, and physicians in the field as well as soldiers themselves played a role in preserving the health of the army, each group working within the confines of the resources accorded by its status.

FOR US IN THE PRESENT DAY, it requires a leap of historical imagination to grasp the devastation wrought on armies by disease. Before the twentieth century, disease took a much heavier toll on armies than any weapon ever did. So terrible were the ravages of disease that Hans Zinsser, a bacteriologist and historian, has argued that epidemic diseases, not humans, have determined the outcome of military conflicts and indeed the course of history. Zinsser believed that too often generals and political leaders, and even soldiers themselves, envisioned war as drilling, shooting, tactics, and strategy. However, these things were "only the terminal operations engaged in by those remnants of the armies which have survived the camp epidemics." While Zinsser had a flair for the dramatic, his words starkly conveyed the history of Western military experience.[6]

From the seventeenth century on, able generals and dynamic military surgeons began to direct their energies toward keeping soldiers healthy. This did not particularly come from humanitarian concerns; rather, individual soldiers had become more valuable. By the seventeenth century, new technology and changing military tactics put a premium on an individual soldier's discipline, training, and battle experience. Leaders such as Oliver Cromwell in England, Gustavus Adolphus of Sweden, and Maurice of Orange used tactics that maximized control of movement and firepower. With experienced soldiers, they were able to engage in complex tactical maneuvers and formations, and because of this the soldiers themselves became more valuable.[7]

However, the new weapons also made battles more destructive, and this together with the new usefulness of experienced soldiers caused some nations to pay new attention to soldiers' welfare. The English articles of war of 1688 reflected this new interest. They provided that "[i]f any Soldier be sick, wounded, or maimed in his Majesties Service, he shall be sent out of the Camp to some fit Place for his Recovery, where he shall be provided for by the Officer appointed to take care of sick and wounded Soldiers." After 1684, the Royal Chelsea Hospital in London and the Royal Kilmainham Hospital near Dublin, Ireland, provided long-term care for some permanently disabled soldiers. In France, more than fifty military hospitals were created in 1708 alone, and more followed in subsequent years. In addition, new attention was paid to camp life, and conditions improved throughout the eighteenth century due to the efforts of energetic military surgeons and the new administrative systems of increasingly centralized states that facilitated the delivery of needed supplies.[8]

However, these improvements proved both limited and short-lived. While the health of soldiers in permanent camps on their home territory did get better, soldiers in the field and on the move still died in appalling numbers. Also, as European armies grew in size during the eighteenth century, the greater density of soldiers in the field increased the risk of disease, and overcrowding in hospitals raised the rate of cross-infection. These changes overwhelmed any improvements in camp organization and the supply of provisions. The revised British articles of war of 1765, in force at the time of the American Revolution, had abandoned the clause that assured the soldier would receive care. All that remained was the guarantee, drawn from the articles of 1688, that in the event of his death, his commanding officer would pass the soldier's effects to his representatives. It was a guarantee that British soldiers needed. American soldiers were to need the same assurance and received it in the 1776 Continental articles of war.[9]

When Congress created the Continental army in June 1775, it did not do anything immediately to attend to its medical needs. In that first flurry of military activity, patriot leaders were thinking of battles, tactics, and strategy—what Zinsser sarcastically called "the minor, although picturesquely appealing part" of war. Despite the fact that there was a substantial literature on military medicine by the time of the American Revolution, and despite the country's experiences in the Seven Years' War, Congress was slow to create a Hospital Department. A month passed before Congress turned to it, and even then, the department created was small in size and scope. The country was to learn of the medical needs of an army the hard way.[10]

When they set up the Hospital Department, Congress and the leading medical men who helped formulate it ignored some of the key discoveries and accumulated wisdom of British and European military medicine. Not that the British and Europeans had ideal military medical arrangements; those tradition-bound armies were all slow to respond to the recommendations of their surgeons general. Still, despite the slow rate of change, these senior medical officers had produced a body of literature that connected camp cleanliness, adequate provisions, warm and comfortable clothing, and the health of the soldiers. Writing with the authority of extensive observations and long experience, their books on the subject were widely read in the medical world.

Several great British military surgeons of the eighteenth century elaborated on this knowledge and spelled out what armies could do to improve soldiers' health. Men such as Sir John Pringle, the British surgeon general during the War of the Austrian Succession in mid-eighteenth century; Sir Richard Brocklesby, his successor; and Donald Monro brought a new holistic approach to military health. They wrote little on surgical technique for treating wounds; instead, they extolled the virtues of good food and dry bedding in maintaining the health of soldiers. Their interest was engaged by the details of clothing, not only its style but also the best kinds of fabric to use. Monro believed that for service in northern climates, "it would be right to allow every Soldier on Service a Flannel Waistcoat, a Pair of Worsted Gloves, and a warm woollen Stock, or a neckcloth, to wear when on duty in cold and wet Weather as soon as the Winter begins to set in." Little was beneath the notice of these thoughtful men in their efforts to improve the health of soldiers.[11]

For these British surgeons general, the role of the judicious officer was critical. Since soldiers could only obey orders, their health depended on attentive and energetic nonmedical leadership. Camp hygiene and soldiers' personal cleanliness became the responsibility of officers of the line, not medical men. Officers had to see that soldiers washed, shaved, and had appropriate clothing for the climate and adequate blankets. Some tried to delegate this task to noncommissioned officers, but officers, if they were competent, did it more effectively.

One other cause of sickness and death in an army on which they wrote extensively was the hospital itself. Pringle, considered the father of modern military medicine, wrote in 1752 in his *Observations on the Diseases of the Army* that "the Reader will little suspect that I should mention those very means which are intended for its [the army's] health and preservation." He recognized that all hospitals were subject to overcrowding, "bad air and other inconveniences," which facilitated the spread of disease. Indeed, he realized the deadliness of all crowded places and identified hospital fever as the same disease as what was then known as jail fever and wrote on the transmission of both. He offered advice on preventing cross-infection in hospitals through ventilation, lessening overcrowding, improving sanitation, and burning soldiers' clothes as they entered the hospital.[12]

As an alternative to crowding soldiers in large general hospitals near headquarters, Pringle recommended using smaller regimental hospitals whenever possible. In these hospitals, attached to the regiment from which a sick soldier came, one would be at less risk of cross-infection and could also avoid the discomfort and distress of a longer journey in the back of a cart to the more centralized general hospital. He would also be closer to his friends, who could visit and offer assistance. So, the smaller regimental hospitals were healthier places, even if a physician could not be there and the attendants who were there had little skill. In other words, the environment had a greater impact on the outcome than the skill level of the attendant.[13]

Despite the fame that came to these doctors from their work and their writings, change did not come easily or quickly in the tradition-bound British army. Doctors fought an uphill battle to bring about even small improvements in organization. Since senior officers and a budget-conscious Parliament did not seem to respond to the "Dictates of Humanity" to provide for soldiers' health, these leading medical men took another tack. Surely, Monro argued, "[i]n a commercial Country like our own, where Numbers of Hands are constantly wanted for the carrying on of our Manufactories," it would be in the country's interest to preserve the lives of soldiers in order to lessen "the Number of Recruits who must be perpetually drawn off for the Service of War." The cost of buying the soldiers appropriate clothing might seem high, but continually recruiting and training fresh troops "will cost the Government a great deal more." Brocklesby, surgeon general at the time of the Seven Years' War, also took a practical line, arguing that there needed to be measures to "prevent the sufferings, distresses, and death of many useful members of the Body Politick."[14]

The work of these surgeons general was well known to American physicians at the outbreak of the Revolutionary War. In 1755, Benjamin Franklin arranged for Pringle's work on jail fever to be published in the newspaper he had founded, the *Pennsylvania Gazette*. After Franklin arrived in England in 1757, he and Pringle became friends, and Franklin was pleased to introduce bright young visitors such as Benjamin Rush to him. Other aspiring colonial medical students and physicians joined Pringle's circle and attended his medical dinner club meetings. Many of them later went on to play important roles in the Hospital Department of the Continental army. The leading figures in colonial and Revolutionary medicine — William Shippen, John Morgan, Benjamin Church, and John Jones, soon to be a professor of surgery at King's College (now Columbia) in New York — all knew Pringle during their time in London. Pringle, in fact, was one of John Morgan's sponsors for his election to the Royal Society in London in 1765.[15]

Despite these close connections to Pringle, when it came to the organization of the Continental Hospital Department, many of these colonial doctors forgot the principles of their mentor's most famous works. The Continental Congress and senior physicians created an organization whose central feature was a number of large general hospitals, with very much subordinated regimental hospitals. The Americans would have to learn on their own the problems of the general hospital. The reasons why they ignored the large body of evidence that advised against such a system are complex. Partly, it was a desire for the greater administrative efficiency offered by a more centralized hospital system. It was also due to a desire to keep less skilled medical practitioners subordinated professionally and under the management and direction of general hospital physicians. But it was also connected to the status of the men whom these hospitals would serve and to the low opinion colonial Americans had of the hospital itself.

Most colonial Americans had never seen a hospital. A few towns had them, but they largely functioned as almshouses, providing shelter for the destitute, aged, crippled, and insane. Most people would have been only dimly aware of their existence. Only the sick without financial resources or without family or friends would ever have found themselves in one. Those with any resources whatsoever and still in control of their senses would pay for a nurse or other person to attend to them in private lodgings. In the countryside, or in one's own community, a relative, neighbor, or local widow would be the most likely person to serve as a nurse. Such a person might be a local midwife who was also knowledgeable about potions and salves. Other than those who were completely destitute, only people who had suffered an accident or a sudden overwhelming illness in a strange city would ever end up in a hospital.[16]

Since they viewed a hospital as a place for the destitute and friendless, colonial Americans saw their homes as the place where illness could be best treated. They believed that friends and family, using common sense, could effectively treat many health problems. American colonists brought a reverence for medical learning with them to North America, but they had little or no access to it. Self-help was a way of life. Most medical care was part of the domestic economy passed on by oral tradition, practiced by women and men specializing particularly in midwifery and bonesetting. For those who were literate, a range of manuals and almanacs offered advice to help people fill the gaps in their medical knowledge. As early as 1677, Thomas Thacher wrote a broadside called *A Brief Rule to the Common People of New England How to order themselves and theirs in the Small-Pocks or Measels*. Among the most popular eighteenth-century medical manuals were John Tennent's *Every Man His Own Doctor*, first published in 1734, and Simon André Tissot's *Advice to the People in General, with Regard to their health*, which was translated from French in 1771. By far the most famous was William Buchan's *Domestic Medicine*. First published in Edinburgh in 1769, Buchan's book had its first American printing in 1771 and eventually went into more than thirty editions.[17]

These books firmly asserted the ability of individuals to treat most common diseases by themselves. Written in the vernacular, avoiding Latin and technical terms, the writers emphasized diet, regular habits, and common sense and tried to demystify medicine. The long title of Buchan's work explained his purpose: *Being an attempt to render the medical art more generally useful, by shewing people what is in their own power*. Tennent and Tissot shared that mission. Tennent recommended ingredients for his remedies that "may be procured with little Trouble and Expence," and Tissot advised against doing anything that might interfere with the healing power of nature.[18]

Self-help medical manuals were written not only by physicians; one of the best-selling volumes of the century in Britain and America was *Primitive Physick* by John Wesley, the founder of the British Methodist Church. Although it had its widest circulation in America after the Revolution, it made its first appearance in the colonies in 1764. It had already gone through many editions in Britain, where it had first been published seventeen years earlier. Basing his work heavily on contemporary self-help medical writings, Wesley emphasized the spiritual importance of maintaining a healthy body and, to that end, emphasized steadiness, prayer, and moderation in diet, dress, and exercise.[19]

Buchan and others encouraged a secular and naturalistic view of sickness that divorced disease from any divine, supernatural, or moral cause. How people reconciled this view with their own faith went largely unrecorded. Even ministers, who frequently found themselves the bearers and sometimes makers of medicines, rarely articulated their thoughts. Simply, they seemed to believe that in a world in which physicians had elevated themselves beyond the reach of most people, or were simply unavailable, individuals had a moral obligation to themselves and to God to attend to their own or a neighbor's health. That was how Henry Muhlenberg felt. He was a minister and leader of the Lutheran Church in America and was resourceful in treating any medical household emergency. When his wife scalded herself badly, he and his family made up potato poultices and tried to make recipes from Tissot's book. Muhlenberg thought that, when confronted with sickness, one had to pray as the outcome lay in "the gracious will of God." However, he also thought that, while prayer was "good and necessary," it was important to use remedies "prescribed by God" and take an active role in effecting a cure. Muhlenberg, like others who were literate, embraced the assistance of the commonsense approach, which made people believe that they could indeed be their own doctor.[20]

This did not mean that, in writing these manuals, doctors were relinquishing their professional authority. On the contrary, these writings were an important component of the rise in their professional ambition. In asserting people's ability to care for themselves, the goal was to extend medical professional authority and diminish people's dependence on untrained practitioners. In writings designed for those who could not get to a physician, doctors provided their knowledge to all those who could read a physician's book. Buchan felt that in sharing and demystifying medical knowledge, he could guard against the "destructive influences of ignorance, superstition and quackery." He and other commonsense medical writers wanted all medical practitioners to have a formal education, which would require the subordination of other healers, particularly midwives and uneducated men. However, in the late eighteenth century, doctors' increased knowledge of anatomy and physiology had yet to bring any improvement in patients' lives or treatment. Although people respected a doctor's knowledge, less formally educated practitioners had equal success treating patients. Still, the spread of a commonsense medical culture was part of a vigorous rise in medical ambition.[21]

Some physicians in colonial America also were sensitive to the value of different skills among those with some formal medical training. This was an issue about which medical practitioners in Britain and Europe were equally sensitive. Before the eighteenth century, physicians had viewed surgeons (only recently separated from barbers) and apothecaries (who used to be joined with grocers) as crafts-men, not educated gentlemen, and therefore subordinate. However, while physi-cians were struggling to understand and develop new theories about how the body worked, surgeons were learning from practical experience. By the end of the seventeenth century, gains in anatomical knowledge combined with more finely engineered instruments enabled surgeons to work more deftly. This led to a dramatic improvement in survival rates from surgery, and slowly the social sta-tus of surgeons improved. They were routinely able to perform operations for bladder stones, cataracts, and strangulated hernias (all without any anesthetic, of course). The development of the screw tourniquet by Jean-Louis Petit in Paris in 1718 and the widespread use of his circular cutting technique described in 1736 made amputations more successful. As the century progressed, many leading physicians came to believe that surgical skills might be a great asset to have. Con-sequently, leading figures wrestled with what the implications of that might be for the old craft distinctions and their corresponding social status.[22]

For medical practitioners in colonial America, which lacked the strong craft guilds of Britain and Europe, the situation was more fluid. The small number of college-educated physicians in North America had, of necessity, long since had to combine the skills of physician, surgeon, and apothecary in one person. Most doctors in colonial towns began their careers apprenticed to an experienced prac-titioner, often starting as his apothecary. If the apprentice had the resources, he followed this up with a college education, usually in London or Edinburgh. Only after John Morgan established the Philadelphia Medical School, which con-ferred its first degrees in 1768, and with the founding of King's College in New York shortly thereafter, were colonists able to get medical degrees in the colonies. Outside of urban areas, however, barber-surgeons, surgeon-apothecaries, or other healers were usually still the only medical practitioners available.[23]

The fact that colonial doctors acted as combined physician, surgeon, and apoth-ecary did not mean that they liked this state of affairs or thought the skills were equally valuable. John Morgan made this clear when he gave a speech in 1765 on the future of American medicine and medical education. In it, he recognized the need for physicians to have surgical skill (in fact, he himself was a skilled sur-geon) and envisioned common course work and later specialization into either a career as a surgeon or physician. However, while Morgan foresaw the critical role that surgery would play in the future of medicine, he did not see it on an

Late eighteenth-century medicine chest belonging to Dr. William Shippen Jr.
Courtesy Mütter Museum, College of Physicians of Philadelphia.

equal footing. "How disagreeable!" it was, he thought, for a physician to perform "some painful and tedious operation." It was far better for the task to be
consigned to a surgeon qualified for "the irksome but needful task!" For Morgan, the work of the physician was more intellectual and should not be colored
by low craft origins. In his Philadelphia medical practice, he did not make and

sell his own medicines as his colleagues did because of its low associations with trade. Morgan thought that a physician was like a general who had to understand all aspects of military duty but should not "act as pioneer and dig a trench." He wanted there to be the "proper subordination," that is, the traditional hierarchy connecting the craftsman to the intellectual.[24]

Others agreed. After Samuel Bard received his medical degree from Edinburgh University, he joined his father, a prominent New York physician, in a ready-made practice. He wrote to his friend Morgan that, unfortunately, "[t]here is I own one dissagreable Circumstance attending it, that of keeping a shop." Bard would have liked to copy Morgan and eschew this retail aspect of the profession but did not "think such an innovation would be as easily submitted to here as in Philadelphia."[25]

Most college-educated physicians shared the view that they were superior to other practitioners and that the unqualified should be driven from the field. Peter Middleton, teaching at King's College, had complete contempt for "the *Self-taught Doctors* of this City" who, he wrote, with their "ficticious cures," possessed a "Spirit of Rapacity" and preyed on the "distempered Imaginations of the sick." He thought that doctors should have knowledge of the classics, anatomy, mathematics, and natural philosophy. In addition, they must possess "the *Character* of a GENTLEMAN," as only such a man "could secure the Esteem of his Patients, do Honour to himself, or Support the Dignity of his *Profession*."[26]

It was with these thoughts in mind that college-educated physicians conceived of the Hospital Department of the Continental army. Doctors saw themselves as the social equals of officers and, in terms of skill, superior to all other medical practitioners. They saw hospitals as the repository for the lowest members of society, expecting it to house only soldiers. They knew that officers would be treated separately and that capable soldiers would be able to take care of their own minor medical problems. It is hardly surprising then that they, with the Continental Congress, created the hospital system the way they did. What is surprising is that they ignored so completely the work of the British military surgeons they admired and created an organization modeled on the way the British army was rather than on the way it should be.

During the Seven Years' War, colonists serving in provincial armies had become familiar with British military medicine, seeing the best and worst of it. Pringle's ideas had prompted reorganization to the degree that regimental hospitals were widely used in peacetime. During war, however, a desire for administrative efficiency led the army to continue to use general hospitals extensively and regimental hospitals only when troops were at a great distance from headquarters. Men such as John Morgan were able to observe the best of this system. He joined the provincials with the express intent of improving his surgical skills and had ample opportunity to do so. Eighteenth-century muskets, although not nearly as destructive as the later rifle technology of the nineteenth century, inflicted many more casualties than the hand-to-hand fighting of earlier centuries. Morgan was able to watch great surgeons at work and got more practice himself in a few months than years of private practice might provide. Morgan, only twenty-one years old, also experienced the medical hierarchy within the army and secured an ensign's commission so he could avoid the indignity of being treated like common surgeons who, in the British army, could be ordered about by officers. So, through their service, young colonial medical men such as Morgan learned both about medicine and medical and military hierarchy.[27]

Soldiers were the ones who experienced the worst of British military medicine. When they contracted dysentery, smallpox, or fevers or when they were recovering from wounds, they were mostly swept into general hospitals. The sick infected those who were there with wounds and often picked up a new disease themselves. Life was precarious in camp and in the hospital. Massachusetts provincials, in a few short months of service, were four times more likely to die from disease than they were in a whole year spent at home. Indeed, they were frequently more at risk than in the worst of New England's epidemics. The statistics from Connecticut provincials show similar mortality rates. The only dramatic exception to this level was when Connecticut troops joined the regulars and some other provincials for a campaign in Havana, Cuba, against the Spanish in 1762. There, yellow fever and malaria added to the toll of dysentery and other camp fevers, leaving many dead. Almost 20 percent of the Connecticut men in Havana died, about three times the rate of the worst epidemic years at home.[28]

Young provincial soldiers were shocked at the steady loss of life in and around the camp. Intermittent food supplies compounded soldiers' problems and left weak soldiers vulnerable to disease. However, not all sick soldiers were taken to a hospital. Some died before they could be moved, and others stayed in camp if the nearest hospital was full. Soldiers recorded the steady toll of sickness around them. In his diary, William Sweat of Massachusetts wrote that "it is now very sickly in the army, & the people Dyes very fast." A few days later, he wrote that men "fall Down Ded as thay are traveling." And a few days after that, "[T]hre more men Dyed in our Rigement." His stark comments reveal his growing alarm.[29]

There were no accurate records kept that might show the relative survival rates for soldiers who were in camp or general or regimental hospitals. Of course, in a regimental hospital, they were at less risk of cross-infection, but the risk still existed. On the Ticonderoga expedition in 1758, Sweat was pleased to find himself near his brother Enoch, serving in another Massachusetts regiment. Sweat was glad to help Enoch when he was "very ill: I went to see him, & carreyd some chees to him." Sometimes, regimental hospitals admitted defeat in the face of infection (and made a mockery of reliable mortality statistics) and simply sent sick men home. Sweat wrote that "30 of our sick men were ordered home by the Doctor, the first carts that came." Their fate is unknown.[30]

Twenty years later, during the Revolutionary War, Continental medical officers were sometimes impressed by what they saw of British military medicine, yet little had changed. When Benjamin Rush was allowed to go to a nearby British hospital to attend to American officers taken prisoner at the Battle of Brandywine in 1777, he admired the "order and contentment" of the hospital and the "supreme regard" he saw British officers give "to the cleanliness and health of their men." Rush wrote this in a letter to John Adams in which he was trying to hold up British efficiency and effectiveness in stark contrast to Continental inefficiency. Yet, despite Rush's admiration on this occasion, disease, compounded by supply problems, continued to take a terrible toll on British soldiers. When the army was cut off from supplies of fresh food from farms in the region — during the siege of Boston, for example — scurvy added to the British soldiers' miseries.[31]

Diseases were compounded by the conditions in the British hospitals themselves. One British private noted that, after the Battle of Bunker Hill, many of the wounded in the hospital contracted "a bloody flux [dysentery], which killed numbers of them." Complaints from soldiers on the conditions in hospital ships led British general William Howe to command field officers to inspect the hospital ships each day. A month later, there were still complaints from "men on Board the Hospital Ships, of the want of Necessaries," and Howe instructed the officers again to see to their complaints. One British officer observed that sometimes the journey of the sick to the hospital could be harrowing, as soldiers were often dumped in any cart that was going in the right direction. Consequently, sick or wounded soldiers were very dependent on the kindness of the wagoner, but "the drivers too frequently treat them ill on the road, nay sometimes abandon them sticking them in sloughs." He thought it was necessary "to send careful people with them to prevent this barbarous inhumanity." So, problems still abounded in British military hospitals.[32]

The Revolutionaries measured themselves against perceived British efficiency. All during the war, and for 200 years thereafter, Americans believed that their own efforts at military medicine paled beside those of the British. This view came from positive comments on British abilities from men such as Rush and from the assumption that since the British had years of experience, they would be more efficient and organized. Accurate numbers for casualties for the British in any of its eighteenth-century wars are difficult to piece together. For the Seven Years' War, overall deaths from disease appear to have been about eight times the number of battle deaths. However, this ratio would not have held everywhere. The war was fought in many parts of the world, and there were especially high casualties when soldiers were exposed to tropical diseases. The catastrophe in Havana alone drove up the total disease fatalities considerably. European powers that fought only in Europe experienced disease-to-battle-death ratios of about three to one. While the British in North America were hampered by supply problems and encountered a virulent form of dysentery, it is possible that their total for this theater of the war was closer to the ratios experienced by armies in Europe.[33]

No reliable data exist for the British in the American Revolution, but the army and navy again ended up fighting in tropical climates as the war expanded internationally after 1779. Engaged in combat in Nicaragua, Honduras, Guyana, and the Caribbean islands and besieged on Gibraltar, British servicemen suffered catastrophically from a variety of tropical diseases. Their overall disease-to-battle-death ratio was about eight to one, similar to their ratio in the Seven Years' War. But again, the ratio was probably considerably better in North America, British supply problems notwithstanding.[34]

Whatever the true total for the British, the Americans perceived their own situation to be much worse. The constant complaints of Continental inefficiency from medical men in the army, occasional public scandals over mismanagement during the war, and finger-pointing afterwards, combined with the experience of sweeping epidemics, left Americans at the time and historians for a long time after feeling that medically, the war had been disastrous. In 1777, Rush noted that high mortality rates, which he laid squarely at the door of mismanagement, were so great it seemed they would "depopulate America [even] if men grew among us as speedily and spontaneously as blades of grass." Another doctor who served through the war, James Thacher, observed in his memoir that fully 70,000 men had died during the war in battle and from disease, making the ratio of deaths from disease about nine times those on the battlefield, and his figure became entrenched in histories of the war.[35]

Recent analysis paints a somewhat less bleak picture. A detailed study of war casualties, which has produced the numbers in current use, calculates total American casualties at approximately 25,000. Of these, battle deaths accounted for around 7,000, making the ratio of death from disease about two and a half times those in battle. These numbers, which include those who died of disease while held as prisoners of war, are admittedly conservative. But even if they were to be revised significantly upward, these statistics show that American military forces were just as healthy as those of European armies fighting in Europe in the period and that the Americans succeeded in avoiding the kinds of medical catastrophes that plagued the British in the Tropics.[36]

No matter how the statistics look in the context of eighteenth-century military experience, the daily reality was shocking. Contemporary observers, who we can now see overestimated the mortality rates they were experiencing, were no doubt responding to how these levels *felt*. There were periods when mortality far outstripped the worst epidemics in civilian experience, and relative to the total colonial population, the high mortality rates would indeed have made it seem, as Rush put it, that the country was being depopulated. When, in 1778, Rush suspected the surgeon general, William Shippen, of deliberately understating fatality rates at hospitals, he was outraged because he believed it was blinding people to the catastrophe. Rush resorted to bitter sarcasm. He wrote to his friend General Nathanael Greene that Rush's own numbers must be wrong; he had calculated them from counting coffins going into the ground and had assumed from "their weight and smell" that they contained dead soldiers. If Shippen's numbers were correct, Rush wrote, then soldiers were apparently being buried alive, and Rush hoped that steps would be taken "to prevent and punish the crime." Rush, like some other surgeons, felt outrage at the deaths around him and helpless in the face of mismanagement.[37]

However, not every campaign saw medical catastrophe. Experiences were variable, and there were healthy periods, but the periods of great mortality were the ones that veterans recalled in their pension applications. James Fergus, who served in the Pennsylvania militia in 1776 and early 1777, remembered when sixteen out of the thirty men with whom he served died of smallpox and "spotted fever." Alexander Logan, a Continental private also from Pennsylvania, remembered that in 1776, out of the sixty men in his company, twenty-five died in less than two months when the army became "sickly." In these circumstances, it was hardly surprising that these events left haunting memories with those who witnessed them.[38]

Though disease and the army's medical needs had been little considered by patriot leaders at the beginning of the military conflict with Britain, it was not long before both made their presence felt. As with other legislation governing the army, the Continental Congress had to revise the structure and scale of the

Hospital Department in 1776. The year before, it had appointed a physician/director and four surgeons and had limited the number of surgeons' mates (assistants) to twenty. It had even hoped that the mates did not need to be employed full time but simply could be hired by the day as needed. The legislation of 1776 increased the size of the department and tried to make it more efficient. Congress had to enlarge and reorganize the department again in 1777, then followed that change with alterations in 1778 and 1780. Some of the problems came from poor lines of authority and infighting; more resulted from the failure of Congress and the medical establishment to learn from European experience.[39]

Of course, a fundamental obstacle connected to the health of the army was that Congress was unable to resolve the problem of supply. Consequently, the army intermittently lacked the warm clothing, blankets, clean straw, and adequate food that Pringle, Monro, and others considered essential for healthy troops. As discussed in chapter 2, Congressional supply problems arose from poor transportation networks, inexperience, an expectation that the war would be short, and a fear of centralized power, and these issues remained unresolved for the duration of the war. This meant that even senior men in the Continental Hospital Department felt buffeted by events beyond their control and helpless in the face of the cumbersome machinery of army purchasing and supply. Even John Cochran, a senior physician who later became director general of the Hospital Department, felt frustrated and helpless. He had General George Washington's ear and knew he could complain to him but felt even that was pointless. Washington would "refer the matter to Congress, they to the Medical Committee, who would probably pow-wow over it for a while, and no more be heard of it. Thus we go before the wind."[40]

In the face of these administrative and political obstacles, it is all the more impressive that the American forces were able to end up with disease-to-battle-death ratios that matched those of experienced European armies fighting in or near their home territory. In doing so, the Americans overcame the fact that their soldiers were generally younger than their British and European counterparts and were mostly from remote farms and villages. Consequently, they were more likely to lack any biological defenses against the diseases that lurked in the crowded conditions of camp life. So the army had to overcome political, administrative, and biological disadvantages. Some possible explanations are speculative and can never be proven. For example, it is possible that while Continental soldiers were ill fed, they may have actually fared better than their European counterparts. American forces, when on the move, may have been able to purchase or kill (or steal) more fresh food. Also, because the campaign season meant that they frequently moved, they were able to leave areas they had contaminated with their waste.[41]

However, there is another explanation to be gleaned from the records, which is that, apart from a few places and times, the army improved in health as it gained in experience. This may have been due partly to the fact that those soldiers serving for longer terms slowly built up resistance to some diseases. Additionally, those same men adjusted to the discipline and practice of camp life that were necessary for good health and helped inculcate some of those habits in men serving for shorter terms. Finally—and some observers thought this the most critical —officers learned what they needed to do to instill and direct healthful measure. British military surgeons believed that energetic leadership by officers was essential for enforcing higher standards of camp hygiene. American military medical men quickly concurred. In 1813, James Tilton, a senior army doctor, observed that a great lesson of the war was that able officers could keep a regiment healthy.[42]

Just as for other skills, officers had to be trained for this too, and there were instruction manuals available. A flurry of them were published after the beginning of the war, both for officers and surgeons. The earliest were directed at surgeons and other medical men in the field. John Jones, professor of surgery at King's College and a man at the "head of the profession," published a text on surgical technique and camp and hospital hygiene in 1776. Also, a famous European work by the Dutch physician Gerhard Van Swieten, *The Diseases Incident to Armies*, quickly appeared in English.[43]

It was 1777 before the first important medical text appeared directed especially at officers; this was an essay by Benjamin Rush called "Directions for Preserving the Health of Soldiers." It first appeared in the *Pennsylvania Packet* newspaper, and Nathanael Greene immediately encouraged him to have it printed as a pamphlet so that it might become a "real utility" for junior officers. Rush took his advice, and when the pamphlet was published the next year, the Board of War ordered 4,000 copies to be distributed to officers. In his "Directions," Rush wrote that healthy soldiers required attention to "I. Dress. II. Diet. III. Cleanliness. And IV. Encampments." Without supplies, which were largely beyond the control of line officers, little could be done about the first and second items, but he insisted that officers pay attention to camp hygiene in order to secure the health of their soldiers.[44]

Another influential work was Baron Friedrich von Steuben's *Regulations for the Order and Discipline of the Troops of the United States*, published in 1779. He knew that discipline was not just about drilling and maneuvers. His book noted the importance of separating latrines from food preparation and both from the tents where men lived. He gave step-by-step instructions on how an officer could supervise his men's cleanliness, even spelling out the orders for seeing that the "straw and bedding [are] well aired," the men's hair combed, and "their hands and faces washed clean."[45]

However, by the time these instruction manuals were available, the army was already gaining in experience. In the early years of the war, camp hygiene depended on commands, indeed harangues, from senior officers directed at junior officers and soldiers. From the army's earliest days, Washington and others issued a stream of orders concerning camp health. Washington directed officers "especially to the digging, and fixing the Necessaries [latrines] in the place appointed for that purpose." Experience yielded the connection between foul smells and infection, so it was important that "all obnoxious, and unwholesome Smells, be prevented from infecting the camp." Animals were also present in camp and, when necessary, were killed and butchered. Consequently, orders also targeted that health hazard and required "Dead Carcasses & their filth" to be buried promptly.[46]

Like Pringle and Brocklesby before them, Washington and others sometimes grounded their orders in Mosaic law. Deuteronomy 23:12–14 instructed: "Thou shalt have a place also without the camp, . . . and it shall be, when thou wilt ease thyself abroad, thou shalt dig therewith, and shalt turn back and cover that which cometh from thee: For the Lord thy God walketh in the midst of thy camp, to deliver thee . . . therefore shall thy camp be holy: that he see no unclean thing in thee, and turn away from thee." They hoped that soldiers might attend to camp hygiene as a matter of faith.[47]

Some senior officers badgered the troops into cleanliness as a matter of honor. General Anthony Wayne reminded his officers in general orders that they had to have "necessaries" dug when the troops were to be anywhere more than one night. Any neglect in this matter caused the camp "to become a public Nuisance. And public Reproach to the Great Discredit of the Army—Which in fact is not less Injured in point of health than Reputation by Such Unclainliness and Offensive Smells." And General Robert Howe told his soldiers that their "slovenly, indecent and dirty state" was not only "inconsistent to their health" but also "disgraceful to the army, censurable at all times, and, when on duty, absolutely unpardonable."[48]

In their repeated orders on this subject, senior officers sounded like nagging parents. Daniel Morgan commanded his officers to appear "clean and genteel" as an example to their men, and Francis Marion told them to "See their men Keep themselves Clean decent with their Hair combd & Dressed in a Soldier like manner." Commands to officers to take responsibility for keeping "troops as neat and clean as possible" went on throughout the war. However, by far the greatest torrent of such orders came in the earlier years, indicating that the lessons were slowly learned.[49]

One central problem was that officers and men were generally quite unfamiliar with the experience of living in close quarters with throngs of other people, and consequently most officers had no more knowledge than their soldiers about how to preserve health in camp. In fact, the size of the gathering of men in an army camp was noteworthy to many in and out of the army. One soldier noted in his journal that when the army made camp, "the Neighbours Came all to see us Bringing their Wifes & Children with them who Never Saw so many Men Before together."[50]

The arrival of a large number of men, often equal to the population of a good-sized colonial town, made the camp a curiosity as well as a medical danger, because the contamination and filth of the camp were hard to contain. Men of all levels of society were used to relieving themselves near where they slept at night. Washington repeatedly had to order that "any soldier caught easing himself" anywhere other than the dug latrines was "instantly to be made prisoner and punished by order of a regimental Court Martial." And citizens complained that the soldiers' "want of cleanliness" not only was "irksome" but also exposed people in the neighborhood with "weak Constitutions" to sickness.[51]

Colonial Americans had varying ideas about what constituted cleanliness. Few people of any rank would have immersed themselves in water more than a few times a year. Still, most would have washed much more often than the "old carter, Brown" who was with George Norton of Massachusetts. In March 1777, Norton made a note in his journal about nine weeks after their period of service began that Brown had "washed his face & handes" for the first time since they had left home. Brown "[d]esired to have it set down in the Journal," and George Norton obliged him. However, Norton also wrote it down because it was funny and unusual, not because it was commonplace. If order books and instruction manuals were the guide, the basic level of cleanliness was that men routinely washed their faces and hands and combed their hair.[52]

Soldiers were overwhelmed not only by the filth of massing humanity but also by the remains of dead and butchered animals. General Wayne had to chide officers to "Cause all Ofal to be buried," and Washington had to order fatigue parties to "cause all dead horses in and about the camp" to be buried, too. Moreover, the need for security, both to keep soldiers in and the enemy out, meant that this environment was much more densely populated than any urban area the men might have lived in. Apart from the few older men who had seen service in the Seven Years' War, none would have seen this scale of effluvium before.[53]

Many men were simply in territory unknown to them. A good number probably shared the sentiments of Lachlan McIntosh, commander of the North Carolina Brigade during the winter at Valley Forge in 1777–78. He noted that "[t]his is the first time I ever attempted housekeeping . . . and a most wretched hand I make of it." Men of his rank went through life dimly aware of the household production, cooking, and cleaning that made their lives comfortable. This was, in general, women's work that most men in the services had to learn to do for themselves.[54]

Unlike the British and other European armies, there were comparatively few women in camp to take care of such chores. Women and children were always part of European armies where soldiers served for long terms. In the Continental army, the early prospect of a short war meant that fewer married women joined their husbands. Even when the war dragged on, repeated short terms of service made a wife's decision to go or not one that could be revisited according to family circumstances. Also, the youthfulness of Continentals relative to their British counterparts meant that fewer of them were married. However, as the war progressed, more women joined their husbands in camp, especially when the army was settled in winter quarters. Sarah Osborn joined her husband, who was with his regiment at West Point, shortly after she married him in 1780. Prior to her marriage, she had been a household servant. Once with the army, she washed and sewed for her husband and other soldiers. At Yorktown in October 1781, Osborn and other women were behind the American tents about a mile from town sewing, washing, and cooking, and she "carried beef, bread, and coffee" to her husband and other soldiers in an entrenchment from which they were attacking the town. While young women like Osborn were no more experienced than their husbands in the problems of densely settled camp life, the fact that they washed clothes regularly and were more accustomed to food preparation probably did result in improved health for the men they tended.[55]

Not all men were as helpless as General McIntosh. Some officers and men were able to bring their experience to bear in dealing with difficult conditions. Charles Willson Peale, who after the war won fame as a portrait painter, was resourceful and energetic as a junior officer in the Pennsylvania militia. Before he turned his interests to art in the 1760s, Peale had trained as a saddle maker. When some of his men were barefoot after their hard march from Trenton, he tried to make "Mockasins" for them. One night, when they halted, the men were exhausted. Peale was, too, but he did not rest immediately as he let his men do. First, he wanted to find food for them. He "purchased some beef, which I got the good woman to Boil against I should call for it in the Morning. [A]nd I got a small kettle full of Potatoes Boil'd where we lodged." Peale had an advantage in supplying his men in this way because he frequently had ready cash, acquired by augmenting his pay by painting miniatures for fellow officers, and he enjoyed a steady stream of commissions.[56]

Soldiers could be equally resourceful. A private in the Rhode Island militia endured a starving time along with his company on the march to Quebec in 1775. By killing one of the dogs traveling with them, and then mixing some of that "with the head of a squirll" and some candle wax all boiled together, they "made a very fine Supe without Salt." Continental soldiers on the Florida expedition in 1778 risked ambush by hostile Indians to sneak out of camp to get hold of honey, which they then mixed with rice. This was not just a sweet treat but an important source of sustenance as the expedition's beef supply was exhausted.[57]

Under such conditions, it was hardly surprising that soldiers were susceptible to disease. The cumulative effects of malnourishment and cold took their toll. Colonel Israel Angell, whose Rhode Island regiment was at Valley Forge, returned to camp after a week away and "found all the officers well but the Soldiers very Sickly." Sleeping in huts and local homes offered the officer corps a standard of living that gave them some protection. This, of course, did not give them immunity, and some did get sick and die from disease. However, they generally did avoid the scale of suffering that affected the soldiers, who were debilitated and defenseless in the face of disease and unsanitary conditions.[58]

Slowly, the health of the army improved as soldiers and officers learned what was required of them, and as a result, camps became healthier places. Smallpox and other camp diseases took their worst toll in the early years of the war. In the winter of 1776 and 1777, there were periods when more than 30 percent of the available troops were on the sick list, and the number of sick stayed high, over 20 percent, in the summers of 1777 and 1778. Later in the war, these numbers were much improved. Apart from a brief sickly time early in 1782, the sick usually averaged about 10 percent of total strength. However, these relatively low averages mask a wide range of experiences. After the war moved to the South, most troops that remained in the North largely avoided periods of epidemic sickness. In the South, malaria and yellow fever continued to add to the miseries of camp life. For example, in April 1780, while some troops in New Jersey had around 10 percent of their number sick, some regiments in South Carolina around Charleston had over 20 percent. However, overall the army ended the war in a significantly healthier state than it had begun it.[59]

Over the years, a more experienced officer corps emerged. Judged by the health of their men, a few officers stand out as particularly able. One of those was "Light-Horse Harry" Lee. James Tilton observed that Lee was "distinguished in our Revolutionary Army, for the health and vigor of his corp. *I never saw one of his men* in the general hospitals." It is helpful to take a closer look at the qualities of this man who accomplished such a stunning victory over disease.[60]

Henry Lee, in the words of General Charles Lee, seemed "to have come out of his mother's womb a soldier." In December 1778, General Lee (who was no relation) recommended the twenty-two-year-old Henry to command a new "Body of Light Troops," that is, a unit of combined cavalry and infantry unburdened by heavy arms and equipment that could be highly mobile. "Light-Horse Harry" seemed to understand intuitively not only the practical aspects of military life and leadership but also the importance of what we would now call morale. Years later, Tilton, writing on the health of soldiers, perceived that a soldier's sense of honor could be used to instill good health. He observed that officers could accomplish more when they treated their soldiers with respect. He wrote that a "soldier with self-esteem and ambitious prospects before him, will not only be neat and clean, but prompt in all his duties." This was something Henry Lee knew without being taught.[61]

In Lee's legion of light troops, he was able to foster a heightened esprit de corps among his men. They were all volunteers who had signed on for long terms, and there were no substitutes. He promised them action and recognition. One of the reasons they were confident was because they were healthy, well fed, and well clothed. Sometimes Lee accomplished this by purchasing goods out of his own pocket and sometimes by being aggressive about getting his troops their share of captured enemy stores, especially if they had done the capturing. Lee had an understanding of soldiering that encompassed Rush's litany of dress, diet, cleanliness, and encampments and merged it with equipment, horses, and tactics for a holistic view of his profession.[62]

His humanitarianism and thoughtfulness did not extend much beyond his "band of brothers." The spirit of community that kept his own men alive and well could sometimes make them see themselves as too separate from the rest of the world. He recommended brutal discipline for deserters. In March 1781, he and his men tortured a loyalist prisoner. The month before, they had been involved in one of the worst atrocities of the war when they massacred 100 loyalist militiamen and wounded most of the remaining 200. One patriot North Carolina militiaman, who was with Lee, remembered that after the attack, he "felt such a horror as I never did before nor have since." Lee kept his men healthy by making them feel special, but to the detriment of anyone who resisted them.[63]

Francis Marion was another Revolutionary officer whose leadership boded well for the health of his men. Known as the "Swamp Fox" for his favored hiding places in the Georgia swamps, he, like Lee, practiced guerrilla warfare, raiding and harassing the enemy. A generation older than Lee, he had gained military experience in 1761 fighting the Cherokee. His bravery and leadership ability then brought him patronage, and he subsequently rose from modest circumstances to become a respected member of his community and a plantation owner. During the Revolutionary War, Marion achieved high rank serving with the militia before becoming a lieutenant colonel in the Continental army and then returning to the militia as a brigadier general.[64]

Marion had similar qualities to Henry Lee. Marion, too, paid close attention to camp sanitation and to clothing in a manner that would have made Monro proud. As soon as his militia regiment mustered, he instructed the quartermaster "to provide some pails & a wheel Barrow for the Regiment, to keep the Barracks Clean." In September 1775, he ordered that "[t]hey that have long trowzers to have them made into Breeches." He did not lessen his attention to this kind of detail. In June 1777, he ordered each man in his regiment to be supplied with a pair of "liggens."[65]

Like Lee, he combined humanity and compassion with tough discipline. When Marion's regiment was leaving Charleston by sea for Georgia, he instructed all officers to extend the "greatest humanity" to sick soldiers during the transportation. Yet, there were also occasions when he failed to honor flags of truce. When his own state troops and then Continental soldiers were raw recruits, he literally whipped them into shape. After the war, Nathanael Greene wrote to him that "[w]hen I consider how much you have done and sufferd and under what disadvantages you have maintained your ground, I am at a loss which to admire most[:] your courage & fortitude or your address and management."[66]

Apart from their commitment to discipline and sanitation, these two officers had another important factor in their favor when it came to keeping their soldiers healthy: their units were often on the move. Troops on the move were usually healthier than those in camp for a prolonged period, provided supplies and adequate rest were available, as they continually moved away from their own waste. Both Lee and Marion led mobile detachments fighting guerrilla actions and moved camp frequently. Marion's orderly book from 1781–82 shows that there were periods when they were moving almost every day. While Lee had access to captured enemy stores, Marion's forces in the South were able to capture stores and purchase or gather supplies from the surrounding countryside to such an extent that he was able to send desperately needed corn, rice, hogs, and cattle to General Greene's army. Marion's men lacked adequate tents, clothing, and, he noted, rum, but despite these inconveniences, they were well fed and stayed "remarkably healthy."[67]

Both Marion and Lee saw military life in broad terms that included both the camp and the battlefield. Many other officers, who were talented in tactics, were sometimes unable to tackle the larger and more deadly problems of camp organization. Colonel William Barton of the Rhode Island militia, for example, gained fame in 1777 after he meticulously planned and executed a daring raid on the western shore of Rhode Island with forty volunteers from his regiment. The raid resulted in the capture of a British general and his aide, who were then exchanged for the American general Charles Lee, whom the British held prisoner. A grateful Continental Congress awarded Barton honors and promotion. Yet a year earlier, Barton, along with another officer, had been in command of another group of militiamen who were not so fortunate. With "no rations except one-half a sea biscuit, and fresh mutton without a particle of salt," the soldiers weakened, a "camp distemper" broke out, "and many of them died."[68]

Just as in civilian life, to fall ill away from the comforts and caring of home was a distressing experience. Before the discovery of modern antibiotics, a fever or dysentery, if it did not kill you quickly, could drag on for weeks or months, leaving the victim horribly debilitated. Some veterans felt they never completely recovered from the various illnesses they endured during their service. In addition to the distress of their physical condition was the added sadness at being so far from a caring family. A Connecticut Continental chaplain, Benjamin Trumbull, expressed the despondency that was surely in the minds of many: "I am unwell and between three and four Hundred miles from Home."[69]

As many did when life seemed overwhelming, Trumbull put his trust in God and offered prayers of thanks when he found himself in good health. Another man, Ezra Tilden, tried to strike a deal with God when he became ill. He made "a solemn Vow unto God, that if ye Lord would be Pleased to Spare my Life, & Restore my health & Strength, unto me, again, I would by his Grace Assisting, Lead a better Life, th[a]n I had formerly done." Others enjoyed occasional visits from regimental chaplains, such as Ebenezer David, who led in prayer those who needed comfort or desired spiritual solace.[70]

Sometimes the social gap between ministers and soldiers made such visiting a chore for the minister. After calling upon sick soldiers, David wrote to a friend that "[n]otwithstanding their great distress [I] found them in general as stupid as the beasts that pearish." Yet, there were some who wanted to speak to him after prayers; these, he thought, he could minister to effectively. But as he was leaving, he heard a man say, *"Oh how I do love to hear Ministers talk,"* leaving David feeling that the men had enjoyed the form but had not received the content of his words. David, a young gentleman of education, wrote movingly about the soldiers' collective suffering, yet he was deeply aware of the gap in social rank and education between himself and them.[71]

David and other chaplains visited officers, too, but in very different circumstances. As in civilian life, when no gentleman would ever consider going to a hospital, so gentlemen officers would not enter one either for their own care. The nature of army organization, and the courtesy that one gentleman owed any other, meant that officers were never without a friend, associate, or subordinate to attend to their needs and arrange care appropriate to their rank. In sickness, or if they were wounded in battle, they sought the best comfort and care they could afford, and others went out of their way to provide for them accordingly.

On the battlefield, soldiers and officers came to the aid of wounded friends when possible. During an advance, soldiers were not permitted to stop on their own initiative for any reason. They could and did try to take wounded friends to relative safety. When Ebenezer Fletcher received a musket ball in the small of his back during the Battle of Hubbardton in July 1777, his uncle serving with him and another man immediately came to help the sixteen-year-old Continental. They carried him some distance and laid him behind a tree with another wounded man in the hope that he would be safe there while the battle raged. Unfortunately, the men were not able to return for him as the Americans began retreating, and Fletcher found that he was too far forward on the battlefield to be picked up by his comrades on their way back. He ended up a British prisoner. Some Massachusetts militiamen on the Quebec expedition went to extraordinary lengths to aid one of their group who was wounded. The man, injured in a skirmish with the British, was carried by his comrades for more than two weeks "slung in a blanket." The men were on a "hard march," fleeing the British and short of provisions, but years later one of them proudly remembered that they had saved their friend's life.[72]

At all times, officers could assign such tasks to soldiers as helping remove a wounded officer from the field if circumstances permitted. Wounded officers also had priority on the journey to safety in the rear. Only defeat or being too far forward for a retreating army to collect would prevent a wounded officer from being carried off. In that case, all the wounded were trusted to the hands of the enemy for their future care. After the Battle of Eutaw Springs in 1781, for example, a confused action after which both sides claimed victory, each had collected wounded from the other. Afterward, the British commander, Alexander Stewart, wrote to General Nathanael Greene advising him that he, Stewart, had had to leave behind fifty-four of his wounded men with a surgeon, and he requested particular care for a wounded officer, Lieutenant Douglas Hamilton, also in American hands. Stewart also informed Greene that a senior Continental officer he had captured, Colonel William Washington, a relative of the commander in chief, was "in no Danger from the Wound he received" in the battle. In reply, Greene assured Stewart that Hamilton would "have every attention paid him." The others would not be so fortunate. Greene said he would do what he could but that a "scarcity of spirits" meant that he would not be able to do all "as we could wish."[73]

Gentlemen had obligations to other gentlemen to offer protection in such circumstances, no matter how difficult it might be to carry out. Doctor Jonathan Potts was director general of the Northern Hospital Department at Fort George in the summer of 1776 when a gentleman of his acquaintance, Major Henry Sherburne of the Rhode Island Continentals, asked a "Singular favor": he wanted Potts to help his sick cousin, Caleb Gardner, a young militia officer. Sherburne wrote that Gardner was "much reduced" with fever, and since his regiment lacked medicines, Sherburne was sending him to Potts. Gardner's young age and "tender Manner of being Brot up induces me to send him to Fort George, particularly directed to your Care and friendly inspection." But Sherburne did not want Potts just to give the young man special care within the hospital; rather, he wanted Potts to "give Him a Birth [sic] in Your house as it is impossible for him to be taken that Care of in the General Hospital that his Tender Years Require."[74]

It was surely a request that was neither easy nor convenient for Potts to fulfill. He was overwhelmed by work at the hospital. He and a small staff were caring for "upward of one thousand sick, crowded into the sheds, and laboring under the various and cruel disorders of Dysentery, Bilious, Putrid Fevers, and the effects of a Confluent Small Pox." The soldiers were all in a "distressing situation." Into this setting came Gardner. We do not know Potts's response, but given the conventions of the time, Sherburne's request was reasonable for one gentleman to ask of another. Potts would have been obligated to respond with due courtesy.[75]

When illness or a wound permitted, officers arranged for their own care. Lieutenant Dudley Colman found himself at Fort Constitution in 1776 sick for seventeen days with a "slow, Dull, lingering Fever." He was pleased to tell his wife that he had secured "a good Room in a House to stay in & a good Bed" during that time. Lieutenant John Bell Tilden in South Carolina in 1782, suffering from a bad fever, referred in his journal to being taken by chair to hospital. In fact, he was installed in "an old coast house" near the hospital where he could be waited on by the doctor. Depressed by his continued ill health, his "boy brought my flute and music to me." Colonel Israel Angell, in camp in Rhode Island, his home territory, found himself "much unwell" in the fall of 1778 and asked General James Varnum for permission to travel to his home for one or two days. Permission was granted, and Angell went home, taking the regimental surgeon with him to care for him on the journey (leaving the regiment, of course, briefly without a surgeon).[76]

Angell, like his fellow officers, would not have dreamt of going to a hospital. Status alone would have made it unthinkable, but he was also well aware of the conditions that existed there. In December 1777, he noted that, at the hospital at Bethlehem, Pennsylvania, one of the hospitals to which the sick from Valley Forge were taken, two Virginia soldiers had died "froze to death" due to the "negligence of the Quartermaster not providing wood" for the fire. That would never be Angell's fate. As an officer, his options were taking lodging locally and hiring local help to care for him, or, as he was able to do, returning to the care of his family.[77]

The conditions in hospitals were sometimes so awful that neither officers nor soldiers, nor any others associated with the army, could find the words to describe adequately what they saw or experienced. The sight of the hospital at Ticonderoga appalled Ebenezer David. "When I came to where the large sheds called Hospitals were erected," he wrote, "I stood still and beheld with Admiration & sympathetic anguish what neither Tounge nor Pen can describe." A Pennsylvania regimental chaplain at Paulus Hook was moved by the sight of the sick on their way to the hospital left overnight "in the open air." Witnessing their distress the next morning gave him "a livelier idea of the horrours of war than anything I ever met with before." Doctor Lewis Beebe found words inadequate as he recorded the sight of the sick as he did his rounds at St. Johns, north of Lake Champlain, in June of that year. He simply wrote, "Language cannot describe nor imagination paint, the scenes of misery and distress the Soldiery endure." The same month, Bayze Wells, a Connecticut militiaman, was also overwhelmed when his camp became a collection point for the sick going to the general hospital. He wrote: "[O]h the Groans of the Sick What they undergo I Cant Expres[.] Nither is it in the Power of man to Give any Idea of the Distresses of them laying on the Ground nothing to cover them but the Heavens and Wet Cool weather."[78]

Many soldiers were too ill to influence their fate and had no option but to be removed from their friends and taken to whatever hospital was available, regimental or general, where they were at the mercy of strangers. Their grim experience began with the journey there. Soldiers must have despaired as they lay for long periods in carts like the one driven by a Continental teamster in the summer of 1777 who "took Some Sick Soldiers" to the hospital. The journey took two days, which meant that the sick spent the night lying in the wagon in the rain before being unloaded the next day at their destination. Similarly, in late December the same year, soldiers en route to a military hospital in Ephrata, Pennsylvania, were brought in open wagons "almost naked," without blankets, and unattended.[79]

Once at the hospital, conditions were grim, especially during periods of epidemics. Army surgeon James Tilton attested that during the sickly winter of 1777–78, the soldiers in hospitals "SUFFERED AND DYED IN A MANNER THAT WAS TRULY SHOCKING TO HUMANITY." Lewis Beebe thought the hospital at Mount Independence where he tended to the sick in September 1776 was similarly shocking. He bemoaned his workload and was exhausted at having to treat so many sick men at once. But, he conceded life was "harder for those who are sick to be crowded into a dirty, Lousy, stinking hospital, enough to kill well men." Some must have shared his feeling that they were enduring the wrath of the Almighty. "God seems to be greatly angry with us, he appears to be incensed against us, for our abominable wickedness," wrote Beebe after he had "[b]uried 4 this day."[80]

Many soldiers did whatever was in their power to keep themselves and friends out of hospital or to help in any way they could. When Thomas Hale and his friend Samuel Bowers got sick in the fall of 1776, they had "the luck to go to the hospital." More importantly for their health, they also had the luck to still be close enough to John Bowers (Samuel's brother?), who "took good care" of them both during their illness. Later the same year, when Solomon Nash and a friend both got sick, they had to walk fifteen miles to the hospital but were pleased that they managed instead to find care in "a private house." When Alexander Logan's messmates were dying in the hospital at Ticonderoga in 1776, he "would not consent" to go himself when he became ill and stayed in his tent with only a thin blanket for covering. Despite this discomfort, he survived, but the sick who went to the hospital all died. And when eighteen-year-old John Allgood was wounded at the Battle of Monmouth in 1778, he preferred to stay with his unit rather than go to the hospital, even though his commanding officer had advised him to go. He declined because it was where "there were many sick of various disorders," and he did not want to be among them.[81]

Soldiers used whatever financial resources they had to stay in private homes if possible. In South Carolina in 1779, the young militiaman James Fergus was taken ill and carried to the baggage wagons. Fergus must have had some money, because he sent word to Doctor David Ramsay of the Charleston hospital for medicine. Ramsay replied that he should be brought into the hospital, but Fergus answered, "I had seen the hospitals in Philadelphia, Princeton, and Newark and would prefer dying in the open air of the woods rather [than] be stifled to death in a crowded hospital." Fergus was lucky. He "had a relative in the city who, hearing of me, sent for me to be brought to his house to lie there." Either Fergus or his relative had resources enough to pay for Ramsay to attend him there, where he was grateful to Ramsay for his "humane and kindhearted care." A young Continental, Samuel Larrabee, also used money to provide for his care after he was taken ill with smallpox. His regiment had marched without him to Ticonderoga in 1776. There was no hospital available to him and no one he knew to take care of him. He stayed at the "Widow Dimond's" and sold his watch to pay her.[82]

At their most desperate, soldiers used whatever family resources they could draw on, and their families willingly responded. Family aid seems to have been particularly called on and given when the soldier was very young. Joseph Rundel was about seventeen years old when he became sick at West Point in December 1779. His brother-in-law, also a soldier, wrote home, and Joseph's father in New Fairfield, Connecticut, arranged a discharge and came to West Point to get him. When eighteen-year-old John Almy was taken ill in White Plains, New York, he wrote to his father in Tiverton, Rhode Island, for help. He had little hope that the letter would get to him and even less expectation that his father would be able to find him, as the young soldier had become separated from his company. His father came down right away and after a "diligent search" found John and took him home. Even fathers estranged from their sons rescued their teenagers in trouble. Thomas Gilmore at eighteen had lived away from home for more than eight years due to his father's "intemperate habits." But when Thomas became very sick, it was his father who traveled to bring him home. This generosity involved some risk for families. For example, when the three Davis brothers returned home from having served in the Virginia Continentals, all were sick with camp fever. They recovered, but their mother contracted it and died shortly afterward.[83]

Soldiers were glad to see family from home when they were sick, no matter what age they were. Benjamin Gilbert was a twenty-three-year-old sergeant when his father traveled to visit him. Gilbert gratefully "recd. a Chese and Two pair of Cotton stockings that my Dady brought me" and was pleased to have news from home.[84]

In sickness, soldiers called on family, friends, messmates, and townspeople. The transient, poor, or immigrant men who came to make up more of the army as the war progressed probably also drew on friends and comrades in arms. Not surprisingly, it is the actions of siblings serving together that are most apparent in the records. In 1775, Phineas Ingalls, a Massachusetts soldier, was serving with his brother Isaiah, who fell sick and was sent to the hospital. Phineas was anxious about his care and "staid at his hospital to take care of him." The following year, Obadiah Brown and his brother (or brother-in-law?) Waldo helped each other during a period of great hardship. Obadiah was wounded in the arm and went to the hospital where he "felt prity hard" as his bone had shattered. During the next few days, when he "thot my arm must be Cut of but Livd in hopes," Waldo visited him to comfort him. The following month, Obadiah was recovering from his wound, but now Waldo was sick. Obadiah visited Waldo and found him "very poor & Discouraged that he never wood git well," and Obadiah was "Concerned about him." He visited Waldo as often as he could, and he was soon pleased to note that "Waldo recovers."[85]

Sometimes, even attentive care from a loving brother could not alter a soldier's fate. In 1782, David Burrows and his brother Jonathan were serving in the Massachusetts Continentals when David came down with smallpox. Jonathan worried about his brother and visited him in the hospital "about every day." But Jonathan's attentiveness could not save David. Jonathan was profoundly saddened by David's death and wrote home from the camp at West Point to tell his family the bad news:

> Honoured father and Mother, brothers and Sisters. . . . I have wrote one letter to you for David when we was in Boston then he was well and hearty but now it is with great greif that I must wright to you that he is dead which news must be very terraf[y]ing to all at home as well as the awful sight was to me present, and I hope that his death may be sanctified to you all. . . . Time would fail me to write the thousand part of what is fresh in my mind at this time, but you must needs think that my comfort is verry little here, since I am left alone and intirely comfortless—But I hope God will

support and obhold me in al my troubles and trials in this present world
that they may be for my everlasting good.

At the time, Jonathan was about a year into a second three-year term in the Continentals, but now he lost heart. He hired a substitute to serve out his time and
returned home. During the year that Jonathan had been away on this period of
service, his new bride had given birth to a son that, in her husband's absence,
she had named Jonathan. However, even though the baby was seven months
old when Jonathan returned, he renamed him David in his brother's memory.[86]

Some soldiers were particularly attentive to those who had been their townsmen and friends before the war. David How of Methuen, Massachusetts, visited
his friend Stephen Barker when Stephen was in the hospital "Sick of a feavour."
Elisha James of Scituate, Massachusetts, wrote to his wife, Sarah, regularly with
news of "the Scituate men." He told her that one friend, "Benjamin Colleman
Juner," had been wounded badly and was not expected to live. "I have Ben to
See him Severall times," Elisha told Sarah, and "he told me he was not Long for
this world[.] the Last time I Saw him I askd him if he thought he could Resign
his will To God's holy will he said if it was God's will he was willing to Dye."
The attention of the Scituate men did not end with visiting. On the death of a
young townsman, another took responsibility for collecting and selling the dead
man's clothes so that "his Aged parents [might] Be Supported under this Severe
Stroke of Providence."[87]

Messmates, townsmen, and relatives made up an important source of aid in
time of need, but the system of centralized general hospitals isolated sick soldiers from these potential advocates and comforters. The distance of the general
hospital from the camp limited opportunities for friendly contact and worsened
a sick soldier's situation. Officers were also supposed to visit their sick soldiers
regularly, but again, the distance made the journey hard for even the few officers
who were inclined to exert themselves on their men's behalf. The evidence of the
rarity of these visits was that other people commented on it when it happened.
One young officer, remembering Captain Nathan Hale, a Continental officer
executed by the British for spying in September 1776, particularly recalled that
Hale visited and prayed with his sick soldiers, but he was an exception. While distance from the general hospital may have deterred some, fear of contagion restrained others. Whatever the reason, visiting did not happen often despite Washington's regulars orders reminding officers of their duty to attend sick soldiers.
Washington's orders were not motivated purely by compassion; he needed the

officers to look in on their sick troops so he could get accurate returns of available manpower. A visit by an officer would also inhibit soldiers considering desertion. However, few officers traveled the distance to brave the filth and sickness of the hospital to provide assistance.[88]

Soldiers in the hospital were, for the most part, out of sight and out of mind. Benjamin Rush wrote to John Adams from Reading, Pennsylvania, in October 1777 that the hospital conditions "grow worse and worse." He lamented that "[t]here are several hundred wounded soldiers in this place who would have perished had they not been supported by the voluntary and benevolent contributions of some pious whigs." The care of soldiers occasionally resembled that of the indigent poor in the cities where hospitals were the stepchild of local government and sustained by local philanthropy.[89]

There was, however, another option for those not too sick to do anything other than submit to their fate: they could try to cure themselves or have friends or officers treat them. In doing so, all were acting firmly in the tradition of the self-help medical culture. When surgeons or doctors were not available, officers sometimes tried their hand at medical care. Some did this more willingly than others. In January 1777, two young officers, Captain Thomas Rodney of the Continentals and Charles Willson Peale, at the time a militia lieutenant, each had the opportunity to tend to men in need following the Battle of Princeton. Peale warmed to the task of treating a sick ensign and decided that vomiting would make the young man feel better. He tried first with sugar, then "a puke of Doctor Crochwin." Finally he gave "a double portion of Tartar emetic" (potassium antimony tartrate), which also had little effect, then discovered that he needed to add some vinegar to make it work well. Peale seemed to enjoy the opportunity for empirical study in his medical treatment and gave no indication that he resented having to perform the duty. In contrast, Rodney, who was forced to dress a wound for a sergeant, did it with very poor grace. It was the day after the Battle of Princeton, and there were no surgeons available to deal with this accidental shooting. Rodney was clearly irritated by the circumstances. The sergeant had been shot by one of his own men "who had fired off his musket to light a fire." Rodney took care of the emergency and dressed the wound but "the next day got one of the prisoners to do it." While their attitudes differed greatly in having to doctor their sick, each man knew what to do.[90]

Soldiers, too, felt confident making potions and medicating themselves. Elihu Marvin, who kept an orderly book for Colonel John Durkee of the Connecticut Continentals, recorded in it thirty-one useful recipes for medicines. Some of these were in Latin and some in English with the notation "Buchan" beneath, referring to William Buchan. Private Zebulon Vaughan noted a recipe "for Curen aney kind of Camp dstempers" in his journal. The mixture of "Ocam jarusalem and one half pound of Buternot Bark" had to be boiled until it thickened. This proved "a good Cuer." Lemuel Roberts, when he was sick, used his own teas and other remedies. Even when he was in the hospital, he preferred his own cures to those of the physicians.[91]

Some doctors, when they were sick, preferred to let their diseases run their course rather than treat them at all. Doctor Isaac Senter observed that one "young gentleman," Matthew Irvine, a surgeon's mate from Philadelphia "brought up a physician in that city," was "tormented by disentery, for which he never paid any medical attention." It developed into a "violent rheumatism." Irvine's friend and another surgeon's mate were all afflicted the same way. Yet all three refused medicine, "[f]lattered as they were that nature would relieve them, yet they were *for once* mistaken." Irvine was left behind in great pain with someone to turn him and keep a fire going, but he still declined treatment. Even those "brought up a physician" could embrace commonsense healing.[92]

When the opportunity presented itself, soldiers tried to control their care and treatment. However, eighteenth-century patterns of social deference may have made it hard for them to exercise their wishes, especially if the doctor or surgeon was a college-educated gentleman. There is some evidence that they might have tried. Tilton, writing on the lessons of the war, noted that "the only observation that occurs to me worth mentioning is, that the longer we continued in service, amputation and cutting generally became less fashionable. From obstinacy in the patients and other contingencies, we had frequent opportunities of observing, that limbs might be saved, which the best authorities had directed to be cut off." We do not know the rank of those who were obstinate.[93]

Smallpox was another enemy against which the soldiers sought to defend themselves whenever possible and showed an inclination to make their own decisions. In the eighteenth century, inoculation was added to isolation as a primary means of protecting against the disease in North America. Colonists had first become aware of inoculation after the Reverend Cotton Mather of Massachusetts learned of it from his slave, Onesimus, in 1716 and wrote about it. Inoculation involved inserting material from a fresh lesion of smallpox from an infected person into a healthy individual by means of scarification or puncture in order to induce a mild case of the disease. By such means, Onesimus told Mather, he had had a little of the smallpox but would never get it again.[94]

When the next smallpox outbreak raged in Boston in 1721, Mather managed to convince others to have the procedure. Since the illness had a mortality rate of about 15 percent, it was natural that some would be afraid of introducing the disease deliberately to themselves or their families. Still, some brave souls began to be inoculated. To prevent contagion and to facilitate a quick recovery, they were isolated and encouraged to eat well for some time before and after the treatment and to get plenty of rest. Some of those inoculated did develop full-blown cases of the disease and die, but they were few in number. Later, Doctor Zabdiel Boylston, a friend of Mather's, calculated that only 2 percent of those who had been inoculated had died.[95]

Steadily, the practice gained acceptance. It was used increasingly in the British army before the Revolutionary War and had also been used in some of the American colonies. Some still perceived the process as too risky, and Virginia, Maryland, and some other colonies either prohibited or controlled the practice. Elsewhere, it was widely used. In New Jersey, John Cochran, Washington's surgeon, had a medical practice before the war that specialized in smallpox inoculation.[96]

At the beginning of the war, Washington thought the procedure too risky. When smallpox broke out in Boston in 1775 and among the troops marching to Canada, he prohibited inoculation, believing it would only spread the disorder. A year later, he still felt the same way. He assured soldiers that any discovered getting inoculated "will be most severely punished — As it is at present of the utmost importance, that the spreading of that distemper, in the Army and City, should be prevented." His reluctance was not entirely medically based. He could not afford the long systematic process of having his troops inoculated, which required them to be isolated and rested. He also could not afford for the British to know that part of his army was on enforced rest, as they would certainly take advantage of that situation. A few days later, a vigorous warning was sent to the officer corps that any among them who got inoculated "will be cashiered and turned out of the army, and have his name published in the News papers throughout the Continent, as an Enemy and Traitor to his country."[97]

By 1777, however, Washington changed his mind, and the army began to inoculate soldiers. The ravages of the disease had taken a terrible toll on the army. The northern army attacking Quebec had been devastated by it. Observers had been horrified by the conditions in the hospitals. Captain John Lacey described men crowded into hospitals with fevers and smallpox, with lice and maggots "creeping in Millions over the Victims" with only the "Sick to wate on one another." The disease not only depleted the army but also hurt recruitment, as accounts of the terrible suffering circulated. Troops who were not inoculated were also vulnerable to British attempts to spread the disease to the Continental army deliberately as an early form of biological warfare. It is unclear whether the Brit-

ish ever seriously intended such a thing, but the Americans certainly suspected
them of it. Washington's change of heart in 1777 led to the mass inoculation of
the troops, which resulted in the army becoming almost smallpox-free within a
year, a stunning success. The civilian population was not so fortunate. Smallpox
thrived on the movement and chaos of war, and the disease migrated with the
British and Continental armies into the South in 1780 where local people, slave
and free, suffered from the disease.[98]

In the early years of the war, many soldiers and officers disagreed with Washington's prohibition of inoculation. One of these was Captain Henry Dearborn,
a militia and later Continental officer taken prisoner by the British at Quebec.
Shortly after his capture, smallpox broke out and "[s]ixteen of us Concluded to
apply to some physician to inoculate us." Although one of that group later died,
Dearborn recovered fully. Josiah Sabin, a private and one of Colonel Seth Warner's
Green Mountain Boys, decided to take action, too. Having recently had smallpox himself, Sabin now inoculated troops, "but as this was against orders, they
were sent into his room blindfolded." Sabin acted with Warner's blessing. Indeed, Warner's son recalled that it was his father who recommended that the
men receive the smallpox inoculation in the thigh in order that they might escape detection. Sabin believed that many "lives were saved by this measure, as
none thus inoculated died, while three out of four who took it the natural way
died." Sabin's activities were discovered, and he was brought before General Benedict Arnold. However, Warner fully supported Sabin's actions and defended him
to Arnold. Sabin "was set at liberty without punishment." Arnold himself may
well have had mixed feelings about it. According to Lewis Beebe, Arnold finally
gave orders permitting inoculation, although these were reversed shortly afterward when General John Thomas arrived and announced "that it should be
death for any person to inoculate."[99]

Officers were not the only ones who held divided opinions on the efficacy of
inoculation; medical men did, too. James Thacher, while still a surgeon's mate
in Cambridge in 1776, chose to be inoculated despite the standing order against
it and had it done by a doctor friend. John Morgan tried to encourage general
acceptance of inoculation and argued that the existing evidence of its success
should be enough to overcome "the fears and prejudices of weak minded persons."
However, General Thomas, who had practiced medicine for many years in Massachusetts before the war, opposed it. It is a sad irony that Thomas himself died
of the disease within weeks of giving his order prohibiting inoculation.[100]

Given this divided opinion among officers, medical practitioners, and colonial governments, it is hardly surprising that some soldiers felt free to act. When

Washington finally approved inoculation, he brought under institutional control a practice that was already in widespread use by servicemen. However, done as it was in a haphazard way by soldiers who were already malnourished, unable to isolate themselves, and had little prospect of a week's rest and relaxation to fight off the infection, it was probably not as effective a strategy for the men as it might have been. Whatever the real statistical outcome, anecdotal evidence from the men supports their view that inoculation was lifesaving. Even Sabin, who contracted his smallpox after inoculation, continued to have faith in the procedure and attributed his full-blown attack to the debilitating conditions of the hospital. In all these situations, soldiers themselves assessing risks in their efforts to navigate the medical crises that confronted them was in keeping with self-help medical culture.[101]

Many soldiers who left journals, diaries, memoirs, or pension applications viewed the hospital as a place to be avoided at all costs, and many, if they had actually been in one, had nothing good to say about the experience. Outside of epidemic periods, Washington complained that hospitals allowed drunkenness and provided opportunities for desertion. He worried that soldiers stayed there too long when they were really fit for duty and feared that surgeons conspired with men to fake illnesses to get them out of duty. Yet, he was torn between this view and compassion for the sick men he saw around him. Ideally, he wanted to act in ways that served both good "policy and Humanity." As early as 1776, he identified the "constant bickering" between the regimental and general hospital surgeons as a central problem in the hospital system. At that time, he was not sure what the solution should be, but he did know that the situation "tends greatly to the Injury of the Sick."[102]

Indeed it did. The college-educated gentlemen physicians who were in charge of organizing the Hospital Department were determined to centralize their authority and limit the autonomy of the generally less well-educated regimental surgeons. As part of that strategy, regimental hospitals themselves were subordinate to general ones in the department's hierarchy, and the surgeons at regimental hospitals had to struggle to get adequate supplies. This organizational framework went against the teaching of fifty years of military medicine, well known to senior doctors in the department, which argued that local regimental hospitals were healthier places for soldiers regardless of the skill level of the attendants. However, given the views that John Morgan and others had of the future of the medical profession, it was hardly surprising that they worked so vigorously to subordinate the regimental surgeons and their hospitals.

Initially, high standards were set for all the army's medical practitioners. The first weeks of the war had been chaotic, and individual medical men with any skill were used wherever their services were needed. They simply sent their bills to the Massachusetts Provincial Congress. Then, that body instructed one of its members, Doctor Benjamin Church, to head up the hospital and, with three colleagues, form an examining board to screen applicants for positions. Of course, key appointments were reserved for college-educated physicians. Men with some training were first to come forward, believing, as Morgan had twenty years earlier, that military service was a good opportunity to develop professional skills. The examinations for appointments were rigorous. James Thacher, who was appointed as a surgeon's mate, remembered the pressure of studying for it. The exam covered anatomy, physiology, surgery, and medicine and "was in a considerable degree close and severe, which occasioned not a little agitation in our ranks." Of the sixteen men in the group who were examined the same day as Thacher, six were rejected.[103]

Such standards were not sustainable as the army's need for surgeons increased dramatically. At the outbreak of the Revolutionary War, there were probably about 3,500 medical practitioners in the colonies, of whom less than 400 either had bachelor's degrees or were doctors of medicine. Consequently, there were soon men with a large range of medical skills attending to the needs of the army.[104]

When Congress organized the Continental Hospital Department, headed by Benjamin Church, it concerned itself only with providing general hospitals. It did not include any consideration of regimental hospitals that might exist in the field. It also failed to mention regimental surgeons at all, much less what their relationship should be to the better educated and more rigorously screened staff of the general hospitals.

While regimental hospitals and surgeons were not considered at the time, they quickly became an issue. Church, whose tenure as director lasted only a few months before he was found guilty of treason, and John Morgan, the second director, both college-educated physicians, found themselves immediately and then continuously at loggerheads with the regimental surgeons. Church and Morgan insisted on the subordination of the regimental staff. They discovered that the regimental surgeons not only resented efforts to examine them to confirm their level of expertise but also stubbornly hung on to their autonomous hospitals and their right to draw on the stores of the general hospital.[105]

Not all regimental surgeons lacked a formal education. A few were able and dynamic doctors. However, even they, like their less well-trained colleagues, found themselves fighting for supplies and respect. In a 1778 report to Congress, Washington observed that the "continual jealousies and altercations" between the regimental and general hospital surgeons had "a very pernicious influence" on the care for soldiers. General hospital physicians had been refusing to release medicines and other supplies to the regimental hospitals, claiming they did not have enough themselves. Washington came down on the side of the regimental surgeons, noting that it made sense for the general hospitals to provide medicines to the regimental ones because they could be resupplied more easily. Also, while having neither "leisure nor opportunity" to examine the situation fully, Washington could see the good sense in smaller local hospitals, even though he was more swayed by military than medical advantages. He believed the local hospitals limited the loss of clothing and arms, curbed the opportunity for desertion, and enabled men to be treated quickly with the least loss of manpower to the service.[106]

The Hospital Department never became a happy, efficient organization, but things did improve. The dominance of Pennsylvania medicine continued when William Shippen, who had taught with Morgan at the College of Philadelphia, replaced Morgan in 1777. Despite this connection, there was no love lost between them. Morgan thought Shippen had engineered his removal, and he was probably right. Shippen, accused of financial irregularities, was later court-martialed but was acquitted. Despite all the petty intrigue, name-calling, and public denunciations of this period, some reorganizations that Shippen proposed with his fellow physician, John Cochran, brought new efficiencies. Cochran himself took the helm in 1781. Even though he saw an important role for general hospitals in the hospital system, he was not hostile to the regimental ones. He was also able to work with regimental surgeons, especially those who were college-educated, and to resolve some of the inefficiencies he himself had struggled against for so long.[107]

College-educated regimental surgeons, who objected to the inefficiency of the Hospital Department generally and the subordination of their hospitals particularly, kept up a barrage of criticism. They knew that Pringle and Brocklesby had also encountered entrenched resistance to the idea of redistributing resources to regimental hospitals. Tilton tried to argue to Congress that the new American political society should be more open to change. Brocklesby had been limited in what he could accomplish in the British army because "the good doctor lived under a monarchical government, where it was dangerous to give the least offence to favorites." Tilton wrote that he, in contrast, could "rejoice in the advantage I have over Brocklesby *in time and place*. I write under a republican government where the first principle of my education, the love of my country, teaches me to banish every fear, as well as every selfish consideration, that can come in competition with public good." But years later, Tilton conceded that it had been "impossible to overcome entirely the influence of interested individuals" in the new republic.[108]

Physicians such as Church and Morgan believed their subordination of regimental surgeons was perfectly justifiable. After all, they were the men with knowledge, education, and skill far superior to the great majority of regimental surgeons. However, in their determination to weaken the position of the regimental surgeons and their hospitals, these men were going against the significant body of evidence that regimental hospitals were far healthier than general hospitals by virtue of their smaller size and less crowded conditions, not their skilled attendants.

As head of the army Hospital Department, Morgan was ambitious for himself and his profession. He wanted to secure the place of physicians as honorable gentlemen, untainted by lesser crafts. Tilton and others did share some of his views. They were as sensitive as any gentlemen to perceived slights. Tilton, when considering an appointment in the Hospital Department in 1781, was concerned about the terms. He wanted "to be employed in a place of duty; but I wished that duty to become a Gentleman & a man master of his profession." When John Warren, a senior Continental surgeon, believed he had been passed over for promotion in 1777 and denied the opportunity to work with his friend Jonathan Potts, he felt his honor had been slighted and threatened to resign. He wrote to Potts that he was "not obliged to sacrifice my honor, even if it were to save a kingdom from destruction. I never will remain in any post a single moment longer than I can do it with honor and reputation."[109]

While many physicians agreed with Morgan on that point, they did not all share his view that there should be a rigid medical hierarchy. Tilton, who had been a student of Morgan's, believed that the British separation of the physician and surgeon into two specialties came from their "high degree of civilization and luxury" and was not applicable to the American situation. John Jones thought that the European division between physician and surgeon was an "invidious distinction." Jones was ambitious for his profession, but he was patient and recognized a need for flexibility. He realized that "[i]n new settled countries however, where opportunities for improvement are not within the reach of every student, many gentlemen are obliged to set out in practice, with such a stock of knowledge as they are able to acquire under the tuition of a single master, who may himself too often stand in need of instruction." Jones realized that many men would have to be self-taught and recommended them to a "diligent, attentive, and repeated perusal of the best English practical writers."[110]

Morgan's feelings about medical hierarchy made him inflexible in circumstances that required flexibility. He resorted to a strict adherence to the rules to deal with practitioners who lacked formal education, which only made him appear unreasonable. In 1779, Nathanael Greene told Morgan, after Morgan had been removed as director, that "great complaints were brought against you for withholding Medicine from the Regimental Surgeons." Morgan had claimed that providing such medicines would have left the general hospitals short. But as Greene noted, "However just your remarks, they were unsatisfactory to the army and gave rise to a great deal of censure and furnished a handle to insinuate that you were content so the sick did but die by rule."[111]

Meanwhile, other college-educated physicians serving in the department tried to navigate their way through the political morass in order to provide effective care. The most famous of these, Benjamin Rush, resigned from the department early in 1778, unable to tolerate any longer working for Shippen, whom Rush regarded as incompetent. In and out of the service, Rush kept up a barrage of provocative criticism. Indeed, his pamphlet, *Directions for Preserving the Health of Soldiers*, was part of that campaign, as was his agitation against Shippen, and later George Washington, whom he also considered unsatisfactory, though he later changed his mind about Washington. John Cochran, who ultimately succeeded Shippen, also added a voice of criticism while toiling at numerous hospitals. In a letter to Andrew Craigie, the apothecary general, in the summer of 1778, he begged, "[S]end us on a supply of Medicines & dressings, particularly lint otherwise we are ruined." He railed that "there never was so shameful a piece of conduct" as this neglect of soldiers.[112]

Perhaps the most innovative response came from Tilton. After he himself narrowly escaped death from a hospital fever, he began to pay close attention to the overcrowded conditions in the general hospitals. "It would be shocking to humanity," he wrote in 1781, "to relate the history of our general hospital, in the years 1777 and 1778." It was "a fatal tendency in the system to throw all the sick of the army" into such hospitals. Now, he said, "we should be able to learn from experience, to contract our plan to greater simplicity." Tilton did apply his experience, and under the supervision of his superior, John Cochran, he put his theories into practice at the encampment at Morristown in the winter of 1779–80. Tilton constructed a building laid out "in the style of an Indian hut" that inhibited cross-infection by segregating wounded patients from those with other illnesses and had an innovative ventilation system. His mortality statistics soon confirmed the value of his ideas.[113]

Tilton's actions were entirely in the spirit of Pringle. The British surgeon wrote in the introduction to his *Observations* that he hoped his book would "serve as

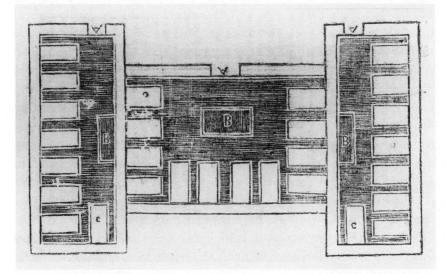

James Tilton's design for a hospital that segregated patients with different conditions and limited cross-infection. Courtesy American Antiquarian Society.

a foundation for others to go upon; who by making improvements on this subject, will concur with me, in attempting to draw from the calamities of war something that may be useful to the public." Tilton had found the conditions of the general hospitals in 1777–78 "shocking to humanity" and had felt compelled to act. The sight of the suffering soldiers that same winter also struck Rush, and he kept up vigorous attacks against the department. He wrote in a letter to Horatio Gates in 1778 that he had felt forced to resign because to continue to go along "with ignorance, negligence, and prodigality of the property and blood of freemen, is in my opinion high treason against the United States." His rage and public criticism never let up. He felt that the British army showed more human-ity "towards their *sweepings of the jails of Europe* than we possess for the sons of the virtuous farmers of America."[114]

Few at the beginning of the war imagined how bad conditions were going to get. On the day Captain Rodney, then of the Delaware militia, first mustered his men and marched to Wilmington in 1776, their baggage wagons did not catch up with them for many hours. His men, he noted, "were a little uneasy about their blankets." In hindsight, their anxiety is almost unbearably naive. When they were sick, the men of the Continental army and the militia must have often felt forgotten. They and their officers did what they could in the light of what Ebe-nezer Huntington, now a lieutenant colonel, called "[t]he Rascally stupidity which now prevails in the Country." A few rare individuals, like Henry Lee and Charles Willson Peale, knew how to master the situation and offer their soldiers some protection in an indifferent world. Other officers had to learn from expe-rience or from teachers like Steuben and Rush how to organize their camps in the healthiest way. As discipline improved, soldiers became more responsive to officers' instructions, and camp health improved. Throughout, the soldiers did not suffer passively if action was at all possible. Many were too sick or without resources to alter their fate, but those who had options exercised them whenever they could; in either case, it was never easy. As one Connecticut private wrote to his friend, "[I]t is trublesum times for us all but wors for the Solders."[115]

Officers and soldiers of the Continental army negotiated the medical crises they faced during the war using the resources available to them. In their own re-sponses and in the organization of institutional military medicine, the respective status of each was reflected and reinforced. Despite these differences, officers and soldiers shared some common experiences in dealing with sickness. Both groups had to face the fear of being sick away from the affectionate, caring sup-port of family and friends. They had to share the pain and horror of illness and their confrontations with death. After the horrors of battle or struggling with disease, death was "the *last* enemy" that soldiers and officers had to face. As the Reverend Samuel Stillman preached, death was a universal experience that all men faced. After death, there was one final rite of passage in which society af-firmed the honor and value it gave the deceased. In arranging for the funeral cer-emonies and the disposition of its dead, the Continental army gave its final and most unequivocal affirmation of military hierarchy.[116]

CHAPTER FIVE

The Last Duty to the Dead

Death and Burial in the Continental Army

There are some of them who have left a name,
So that men declare their praise.
And there are some who have no memorial,
who have perished as though they have not lived.

ECCLESIASTICUS 44:8, 9

ON SEPTEMBER 12, 1777, the day after the Americans were defeated at the Battle of Brandywine, Private Elisha Stevens looked at the bodies of the dead. The "Dolfful Sight" would, he felt, "Greave the Heardist of Hearts." Sad as the sight was, the bodies had to be buried, and someone had to do it. Invariably, that job fell to the "melancholy lot" of private soldiers, either Continental or militia, whichever could be most easily spared for the task. After a battle, the victors usually took responsibility for burying the dead, since they controlled the field. The defeated army carried off all the wounded who could be reached and the dead of the highest rank; everyone else was left to the enemy with the hope that they would respect warriors fallen on the field of battle and bury them with the appropriate "honors of war."[1]

Exactly what the "honors of war" were was widely understood by people in and out of the army. They involved a range of graveside rituals that varied according to the rank of the deceased and conformed to centuries-old western European military traditions. They were so well known that when Shakespeare wrote his plays, he needed only to refer to them in shorthand to be understood. At the end of *Hamlet*, Fortenbras instructs his men to bury the hero in military style:

> Let four captains
> Bear Hamlet like a soldier to the stage,
> For he was likely, had he been put on,
> To have prov'd most royal; and for his passage,
> The soldiers' music and the rites of war
> Speak loudly for him.

Fortenbras's last instructions are "Go bid the soldiers shoot," meaning that they should fire a volley as a mark of honor. So the "rites of war" for funerals included men of appropriate rank carrying the corpse, a parade, music, and volley fire.[2]

With all these elements, military funerals could be impressive. One young American thought that "[n]o scene can exceed in grandeur and solemnity a military funeral." That was indeed the case for the funerals of the highest ranking officers. At their interments, whole battalions made up the procession; any weapons the soldiers carried were reversed; a band played solemn music; black crepe decorated the coffin; assembled dignitaries wore black armbands; and cannons rather than muskets fired the volley.[3]

Neither the Americans, the British, nor any other European army made any distinction in their ceremonies between men who had fallen in battle and those who had died of disease. Rather, the most important factor determining funeral rites was the rank of the deceased. Any other variable that might influence the ceremony, such as the pressing circumstances of the battlefield or epidemics sweeping hospital or camp, played a secondary role. Burial rituals reinforced the divisions of rank that existed everywhere else in military life. Officers and soldiers were buried separately, with officers' interments accompanied by ceremony and elaborate ritual, while those of soldiers were mostly done in a perfunctory manner.

Funeral practices were the most visible, public way in which military communities honored their dead, but that was not the only way. The dead were also honored privately when officers and men recorded the names of dead comrades in their letters, orderly books, and journals. However, in this practice, too, the distinctions of rank governed who honored whom. Officers, doctors, surgeons, and ministers rarely recorded the names of dead soldiers in their private papers, even when circumstances indicated that they must have known them. On the other hand, they frequently recorded the names of dead officers, whether they knew them personally or not. Soldiers' diaries generally recorded the names of both dead soldiers and officers if they knew them. Even in official returns, any officers who had died were noted by name, but dead soldiers rarely were.[4]

Of course, on a whole variety of social and practical subjects, officers wrote a lot in their diaries about themselves and hardly at all about their men, which emphasized the two very different social worlds in which they and their men lived. Death rarely broke down that social barrier. Neither the political values of the military struggle, the shared experience of danger, nor regular confrontations with death broke through these conventions. They were followed as routinely by American officers as they were by their British counterparts. There were a few rare occasions when American officers named the dead soldiers around them, but it required extraordinary circumstances for them to do so.

In developing special traditions, public and private, to cope with death, military communities behaved just like the larger societies from which they were drawn. All societies develop rituals to manage the disruption caused by death. Everyone's life has meaning and value in his or her community, so a person's death requires a ritual that has meaning for those who remain. Funeral rituals, then, are done not just to fulfill the community's spiritual obligations to the dead but also to help a society deal with loss and separation and to affirm its values.[5]

Burial rituals take on a special importance when the deceased is particularly socially or economically valuable. The death of such a person leaves a community vulnerable, especially if the death was unexpected. Rituals can become even more critical when the society itself is unsettled or unstable. At such times, the rites become more pointedly about reaffirming the importance of the community. For armies in wartime, then, funerals take on an even greater importance than usual. Armies are continuously coping with unexpected and premature death, and while not all wars occur in socially or politically unstable environments, many do.[6]

The American military community during the Revolution was operating in such unstable circumstances. The society was engaged in a struggle against the most powerful nation in the world. It was also trying to digest the social implications of a political struggle that emphasized personal liberty and to cope with the daily disruptions of war fought on its home territory. The army frequently felt itself to be a vulnerable community. It was underfunded by Congress and state governments and shown little respect by civilians. It is hardly surprising that with all these factors in place, the whole panoply of military parades and ceremonies were, as discussed in chapter 2, an important part of military culture. There were many occasions found for a military ceremony, for example, the meeting and greeting of important figures or the celebration of a victory. How-

ever, given the army's mortality statistics, funerals were probably the most frequent ceremonial occasion.

Military funerals, like civilian ones, not only showed respect for the dead but
also reinforced the values of the military community. A core value of the military
community was respect for rank. The "rites of war" emphasized respect for rank
generally, the differences in rank among officers themselves and the gulf between officers and men. In life, officers separated themselves from those they
perceived as lesser. In death, their comrades affirmed that status. Soldiers, from
the earliest days of the war, were buried in ways that confirmed their low status,
often receiving treatment that matched that of the most degraded members of
colonial society. However, soldiers' letters and diaries show that, while they
could do little to change burial practices, they gave what respect they could to
dead friends. Even when circumstances prohibited them from showing respect,
their papers indicated the kinds of practices they found distressing or egregious.

The ways in which men recorded the deaths of others, the physical treatment
of corpses, and the rituals of funerals reflected the status of officers and men and
their social relations with each other. In camp life, corporal punishment, and
medical care, the individual himself was an important agent in shaping his fate.
His actions, resourcefulness, relations with family or friends, and his own freedom of choice — by acquiescence, desertion, or avoiding reenlistment — all affected his experience. In death, the social status of soldiers and officers was
confirmed by the world around them.

PRIVATE JAMES BATES was serving with North Carolina troops when they engaged the British at Eutaw Springs in September 1781. Among the American
dead in that battle was Major James Rutherford, the son of General Griffith
Rutherford. Bates and another soldier took the body of the young man to the
general, who was forty miles away. For this duty, Bates's commander, Captain
Cook, rewarded him with a furlough, and the grateful general gave him an additional reward: General Rutherford "would not let him return to the army
again but sent a man to Capt. Cook in his place."[7]

General Rutherford's gratitude was understandable. It was a desire common
to many cultures for families to want to have the bodies of their loved ones to
prepare and inter at death. However, for the families of soldiers in wartime, it
was almost impossible to have that desire fulfilled. Later, in the nineteenth century, after the development of modern embalming techniques, families could

pay for the dead body to be preserved and sent home for burial. However, this was an expensive procedure that few could afford. By the twentieth century, the development of refrigeration gave modern armies a more efficient and cheaper way of bringing the dead home from distant battlefields. With a rising importance of the individual and his sacrifice, and a greater insistence by the state on the military obligations of male citizens, great effort began to be made to collect the dead and ship them home. Prior to all these changes, death under any circumstances usually meant that bodies were buried quickly, close to where the death had occurred. Only General Rutherford's rank and his proximity brought him the gift of his son's body.

Still, Rutherford was not spared the fact that his son, like most other military men, died far away from the care and support of home and family. In civilian life in the eighteenth century, death was usually an intimate, domestic, family affair. Not only would most people have died in their own beds, but they would have done so with immediate family, distant relations, neighbors, and friends on the scene, if not actually present at the last moment. There were few undertakers in the eighteenth century. Usually, family and friends handled every part of the rituals of death. Only the building of the coffin and the digging of the grave were occasionally consigned to others. Washing the body of the deceased, wrapping it in a sheet, and laying it in the coffin were private rituals common all over colonial North America.[8]

While private rituals were widely shared, the public rituals varied enormously. These varied over time, from region to region, and by religious denomination. However, there was a range of practices colonists would have found familiar wherever they went. In every colony, the dead were buried on family plots on farms and estates, in neighborhood burial grounds when a few homes might be clustered together, in churchyards, or, in larger urban areas, public graveyards. The bodies of some wealthy families went into family tombs in coffins made of fine wood. The poorest of the urban poor went into public graveyards wrapped with only a winding sheet, the grave dug so carelessly that the earth barely covered the body. The community selectmen, parish council or other authority, or a local minister was responsible for hiring a sexton to supervise public or church graveyards. This person in turn hired men to dig graves and was responsible for maintaining the graveyard in healthy and neat conditions. While gravestones were used in urban areas, they remained relatively rare. In rural areas, wooden markers were more common, and graves in family plots would often be unmarked, the disposition of bodies simply remembered by the family.[9]

There were also variations determined by religious custom and geography. For example, Moravians in Bethlehem, Pennsylvania, had funerals in which the coffin was taken to the grave in a parade led by four trumpeters and accompanied by church members. A white sheet covered "the Coffin Embrordered all round with needle work," and the people assembled at the grave site and sang hymns. Climate greatly shaped rituals in places with harsh winters. There, communities adapted their traditional practices to the conditions. The bodies of the dead froze quickly outside in the cold. They were then put in "dead houses," small structures near their churches, where they were kept frozen until the ground thawed enough to permit burial.[10]

Public rituals were also shaped by factors such as population density and access to churches. For example, in the South, the more isolated nature of rural life meant that funerals often became occasions for both grief and hospitality for all social classes. The Anglican minister Hugh Jones noted that Virginians preferred to have funeral sermons not in churches but rather in their homes where "assembled a great congregation of neighbours and friends." The body itself was disposed of "in gardens or orchards, where whole families lye interred together, in a spot generally handsomely enclosed, planted with evergreens, and the graves kept decently."[11]

Among black slaves in the South, burials, like those for whites, were an opportunity for both grief and socializing. Blacks and whites occasionally attended the funerals of the other, and some plantations had graveyards that contained the remains of both races, although segregated. More commonly, slaves, many of whom at this time were African-born, struggled to hang on to the traditions of their homelands. Work patterns and white supervision restricted chances for a full celebration, but slaves did what they could. Sometimes a burial might take place weeks before an opportunity presented itself for a full community event that celebrated the deceased's journey home with singing and dancing.[12]

Another way to honor the dead was to acknowledge the death in private letters, diaries, or public announcements. There was surprising consistency between public and private statements about the dead, and they reveal the subtle ways in which social distinctions were played out in colonial society.

Key to recognizing someone's social value in the written record was whether at his or her death, the deceased was acknowledged by name. This was a convention carried over from other aspects of British and colonial life in which the way people wrote about others reflected their relative social status. In private letters and public documents alike, apprentices and servants were frequently mentioned or listed by their given name only. Slaves sometimes were listed by a given name and on other occasions simply as, for example, a negro man. A last name was given to free men and women as a mark of respect. The further addition of a title, such as Miss, Mister, or Esquire, was an indication of even higher social status. In writing about the dead, this same pattern was followed.

Another social convention was that one rarely wrote down one's emotions concerning death or loss in letters or diaries. This came partly from religious culture, in which excessive grief could be seen as a lack of faith. One should both be resigned to God's will and have faith that the deceased had gone to a better place. But this restraint also came from the fact that the gentry, who have left us the most written records, preferred to keep their emotions under wraps. Since being a gentleman meant not making others feel uncomfortable, it was simply good manners to avoid discussing emotionally tumultuous events. Letters then appear to be dismissive of events that were life-altering. When one Virginian wrote to his brother in 1765 on the death of his infant daughter, he imparted the news and then quickly moved on, saying, "[E]nough of that melancholy subject." Whether he was in fact able to dismiss his grief so readily we shall never know, but gentlemen did not invite discussion on emotional subjects. New York merchant John Watts was equally brisk when imparting devastating news. In a letter to a business associate, John Erving, he had to notify Erving that one of his sons had died in Cuba. Having done that duty, Watts reflected that "these are the Afflictions almost every parent suffers that has a number of children," and he quickly moved on to discuss their business interests.[13]

Diaries, too, could be matter-of-fact. John Boyle, a Boston printer, amidst details of the upheavals in his city in the spring of 1775, noted briefly the death of his son, Martin, "aged 9 Months and 9 days." The following spring his wife, "my affectionate consort," died. He did note some of the details of the sequence of her illness and her virtues but nothing of his own feelings, and there was no further reference to her other than on the day of her death.[14]

Military records, public and private, continued these social conventions. Unemotional comments, brevity, and honoring the dead with their full names if they were worthy of it were all conventions used by American military men during the war. In doing so, they were following not only general social conventions but also a long-standing military one. Shakespeare, again, demonstrated how deeply entrenched this convention was. For example, at the end of *Henry V*, the King asks the number of the English dead in battle. Handed the information on a piece of paper, he reads aloud:

Edward the Duke of York, the Earl of Suffolk,
Sir Richard Ketly, Davy Gam, esquire;
None else of name; and of all other men
But five and twenty.

The men named in this speech were ordered by social rank from nobleman to gentleman. Those beneath that rank were nameless.[15]

The division of the war dead into the named and the nameless as a mark of social value was as valid in military life during the American Revolution as it had been for the England of Shakespeare's day. In their journals and diaries, officers, doctors, surgeons, and ministers, when noting a death, rarely recorded the names of dead soldiers, even when they knew them. There were certainly factors other than status that influenced whether ordinary men were named or not. A name was more likely to be recorded if an individual's death had a profound personal impact on the writer. This might be the case if the deceased was from the same community and known outside of a military context. The deceased might be named if the death was particularly gruesome or unusual in some way. Proximity may also have been a factor, for example, if the death occurred near at hand, whether on the battlefield or in camp. Such a death would have had a greater impact on the person recording the event than a death removed from the writer by place or time. Another factor influencing whether the dead were named would be the writer's intended audience. In the case of a letter, if it was being sent to someone who did not know the deceased, there was less reason to record the name. A diary might be intended to be either private or shown to others, and that, too, would influence whether a writer named the dead.

However, no matter what the document or who its intended audience was, no matter how gruesome the death or its location, no matter what the relationship to the men with whom they served, men of rank frequently recorded the names of other men of rank who died but rarely recorded the names of private soldiers, even in circumstances when they must have known them. Officers rarely mentioned anything at all about the deaths of their own or any other soldiers in their journals or letters. When deaths were recorded, it was most frequently in connection with a military action. In this instance, an officer might record simply "four men kill'd." However, since deaths from disease significantly outnumbered those on the battlefield, most deaths would have occurred out of sight of officers in hospitals or tents and often went unrecorded in any correspondence or journals.[16]

On the other hand, officers frequently recorded the names of dead officers, whether they were known personally to them or not and regardless of the circumstances of their death. In addition, if the writer was acquainted with the deceased, not only would his name be recorded but also a few words honoring his character as an officer and a gentleman. One Captain Nott, who was murdered in 1781, was honored as "an active, spirited officer." When Captain John Speer died of a fever in February 1778, a brother officer wrote that he was "a gentleman possessed not only of a patriotic spirit, but also of a large degree of fortitude."[17]

Death in action would generally elicit more effusive descriptions. Colonel Otto Williams lamented the battlefield deaths of "many a brave man" at Eutaw Springs in 1781 but particularly "the gallant Campbell." When Captain Jacob Cheesman died at the assault on Quebec, he was described as "brave and heroick a spirit as ever animated the breast of an *Alexander*." With Colonel Thomas Knowlton's death in 1776 in a much-celebrated bold and successful assault at Harlem Heights, the patriots lost a particularly talented and daring officer. Colonel Joseph Reed wrote to his wife with the sad news and said that Knowlton's "name and spirit ought to be immortal."[18]

In their journals, doctors of the army also made a point of naming dead officers, their social equals, and omitting the names of soldiers. Doctor Lewis Beebe, though deeply moved by the suffering of the soldiers from disease on the expedition to Quebec, did not record the names of any soldiers who died. Overworked in the general hospital, he observed a steady stream of deaths. Those who were probably known to him were indicated by the notation that they had buried someone "belonging to *our* Regt" or that "one of *our* sick died." The names of officers known to him who died from disease were consistently recorded. This did not necessarily come from his high personal regard; rather, it came from his sense of whose position required his recognition.[19]

Soldiers' diaries, on the other hand, made no such distinction. Soldiers recorded the names of both dead soldiers and officers, if they knew them. In recording the names of dead soldiers, men were not only giving respect but also responding to the intimacy, both social and physical, of their confrontations with death. When the deceased was an acquaintance or townsman, the death did not need to happen at close quarters to be recorded. Private Samuel Bixby noted in July 1775 the death of his townsman named Stockwell "at the horspittle with the camp distemper . . . belonging to capt daggats company in the twentieth year of his age." When Private Zebulon Vaughan wrote down the name of the dead he knew, he provided some additional information. The added descriptions spoke to his own physically close encounters with death in the winter of 1777–78. While the men were freezing in a camp, his messmate "William Baley diyed in this Room He Beying weak and so he cold [could] not stanet [stand it] Bured today." Eleven days later, "Samuel Bennett diyed and he has Been heard praying thes 3 days past."[20]

Some soldiers' diaries had respectful comments about dead officers and men, whether they knew them personally or not. Bixby noted the accidental death of an officer in 1775 whose name he did not know but who had a connection to his own world. He was careful to record the death and the relationship; the dead man "was a lieut. in col. cottons rigt[.] he was brother to Surgt townsin in capt harwoods company in col larneds rigt." Bixby was in a different company in Colonel Ebenezer Learned's regiment. Private David How included in his diary the names of all he knew who died, officers and fellow soldiers. He added one additional mark of respect to all: next to the entry, he marked the page with a thick, black ink line, about an inch long, as a sort of literary mourning ribbon.[21]

When officers and others of gentlemanly status omitted the names of ordinary soldiers they knew who died, they affirmed the social distance between themselves and those beneath them. Not naming soldiers did not mean that an officer was uncaring about his men. There were a number of officers who worked hard on behalf of their men but whose language in their journals reflected their understanding of social value. Charles Willson Peale, a resourceful and energetic officer, never mentioned the funerals of any soldiers but did note those he attended of brother officers. Ebenezer Huntington, a young lieutenant in 1776, was also attentive to the needs of the soldiers under his command but never recorded names of the dead or noted that he attended any observance for them. On one occasion, he reported to his brother the effects of a recent exchange of shells after the Battle of Long Island. The shells, he wrote, "do little or no damage[.] they have killed but one man, at the place, and him a Poor Sick Man, that the Doctors despaird of." Huntington probably did not know the name of the dead man, and although there is some sympathy in his language, he did not appear to consider it a great loss.[22]

On the occasions when a few officers did name the dead from their companies, they appear to have been not only deeply moved by their suffering but also frightened. That seemed to be the case when Colonel Israel Angell and his Rhode Island regiment were in the midst of a camp epidemic in January 1778. One day he noted the names of some men who had just died of disease. His subsequent comment indicated his anxiety: "[I]t is a very allarming time amongst us[.] the troops are very Sickly. and die fast." The next morning, he awoke to find that yet another of his men had died and that he was obliged "to give one more mallencully order" to have a coffin made. He lamented, "[W]hat an allarm this must be to us, a Small Handfull of poor Naked Soles, dist[it]ute of Money and Every Necesary of Life, to See how we are Struck of off [sic] the List of time." When Angell felt alone and helpless, he was moved to name his men, but at other times he did not.[23]

Another circumstance that sometimes prompted an officer to give the name of a dead soldier was when he had a connection to him outside of military service or if the death was bizarre or noteworthy. Both of these were the case when Captain Persifor Frazer wrote to his wife about the death of his corporal, Joshua Davis, in the summer of 1776. He helped his wife place the young man by telling her that he had "liv'd near Colonel Waynes." Frazer had thought Davis "a fine young fellow in every respect" and was particularly distressed when the young man drowned after falling overboard from a transport vessel. However, despite these examples, for an officer to recognize by name anyone other than a fellow officer was highly unusual.[24]

Naming the dead, whether from disease or battle, was one way in which the writer showed respect and acknowledged the value of the sacrifice. The sacrifice of soldiers was occasionally recognized but not with a name. A British officer, Lieutenant William Digby, found a good example of the juxtaposition of patriotic rhetoric with soldiers' anonymity in death in the summer of 1776 at Isle aux Noix. He came across a single grave that contained the bodies of two American officers and two privates who had been scalped by "our Indians" (that was, those allied with the British). The unarmed Americans had been killed while out foraging. Digby noted down an inscription that had been written "on an old board at the head of the grave, which is no bad ruff production":

> Beneath this humble sod
> Lie
> Capn Adams, Lieut Culbertson & 2 privates of
> the 2d Pensilvanian regiment.
> Not Hirelings but Patriots
> Who fell —— not in battle
> but unarmed,
> Who were barbarously murdered and inhumanly
> scalped by the emissaries of the once just but
> now abandoned Kingdom of Britain.
> *Sons of America rest in quiet here,*

Britannia blush, Burgoyne let fall a tear,
And tremble Europe's Sons with savage race
Death and revenge await you with disgrace.

The inscription of the names of the officers and the omission of those of the privates on the grave marker was in keeping with their relative social standing. The soldiers may well have been patriots and not hirelings, but that distinction did not bring them the honor of being named.[25]

One unusual thing about this burial site was that the bodies of all four were deposited in a single grave. This probably indicates that the grave was dug in haste, perhaps in fear of further Indian attack or because the bodies were in an advanced state of decomposition when they were buried. Only this type of extenuating circumstance would lead to such a breach of etiquette, for that was what it was for the corpse of an officer to be buried in the same grave as that of an enlisted man.

That officers and men had to be buried separately was one of the most important guiding principles of military funerals. Men of all ranks might have shared their confrontation with death, which, as one minister noted, was "like fire which consumes without distinction." However, after meeting their common last enemy, the bodies of the officers and men of the army were interred in ways that emphasized the gap between them as well as among officers of different rank.[26]

In civilian life in colonial America, public burial rituals also made clear distinctions in social rank. That had not always been the case. For example, in New England in the earliest years of English settlement, burial practices had started out simply. Bodies had been interred by "all the neighbourhood, or a good company of them, [who] come together by tolling of the bell" to carry the dead to the grave "and there stand by him while he is buried." In those early years, no prayers or sermons were offered at the grave site, as that would have indicated a lack of faith. Years later, prayers were added, as was a social gathering after the interment. Funeral sermons, given later in church, also became part of the New England conventions.[27]

However, by the end of the seventeenth century, families used the occasion to display their wealth and status and to add to the honor and recognition of the deceased. Mourners might drape fabric on the coffin and have a decorated, horse-drawn cart to carry it. Gloves could be sent to friends and acquaintances to invite people to the grave site. Special mourning ribbons, scarves, cloaks, and rings all became part of the ritual. The cost of all this, and a large social gathering afterward, sometimes consumed up to 20 percent of the deceased's estate.[28]

As the eighteenth century progressed, there was a reaction against this excess, and it went out of fashion for all but the wealthiest families. The Massachusetts legislature tried to pass laws to curb the extravagance. Others were concerned that the "luxury" of the funerals of those from the upper levels of society set a bad example. Wealthy men, such as William Livingston, worried that "[p]eople in the inferior Stations of Life . . . [were] extremely apt to imitate those who move in the more elevated Sphere." He thought that families such as his should set a more modest example for the lower sort to follow.[29]

But elaborate funerals as a display of rank were not so easily abandoned. When a prosperous Rhode Island merchant died in 1766, the bill, which included charges for black taffeta, silk, and buckles; payments to "6 Men bearing the Corps to the Grave"; and a charge of £64 for the coffin, came to over £234. In the South, firing guns, drinking liquor, parading, and feasting sometimes marked public funerals for important individuals. When the governor of Virginia was buried in 1770 in Williamsburg, the procession to the church included members of the council and House of Burgesses, clergymen, and aldermen. The coffin, "with a cover of crimson velvet, [and] adorned with large silver handles," was "deposited in a vault, the militia firing three vollies at the interment."[30]

Few people were interred with such ceremony. Families made the small gestures that they could afford. The family of Nathaniel Loring of Boston arranged a modest funeral but paid six shillings for "5 Bells tolling" to mark his passing. When Paul Revere's mother died in 1777, the sexton's bill was less than three pounds, most of which went to the pallbearers and to the sexton himself for arranging and supervising the burial. In towns, church committees came up with fee schedules to help families make these decisions. St. George's church in Schenectady, New York, was prepared to take on the task of "[i]nviting the whole town" to a funeral for a fee of sixteen shillings and offered reduced rates for the burial of children under fifteen years old.[31]

The connection between the trappings of burial and status was stark when it came to the interment of the urban poor. In life they received little respect; in death they did no better. As early as the end of the seventeenth century in New York, the assembly had to pass legislation requiring the community to take an interest in the last journey of its poorest residents. The law required "three or four of the Neighbours" to be called in when "servants and others" died to make sure they had not been murdered. These neighbors had also, in accordance with "the desent Custom of Christendom," to see the body to a grave. In Boston, by the second half of the eighteenth century, the selectmen had to appoint individuals with the responsibility to "carry Bodies of the Dead to the Graves" and had to badger the sexton to make sure graves were properly covered. Even in South Carolina, the growing town of Charleston had to make provisions by 1768 to bury "strangers and transient white persons" who "happen to die" in town. Such people were certainly interred without ceremony.[32]

The bodies of slaves were also sometimes treated disrespectfully. There is no greater way of dishonoring a person or a community than by disallowing burial. Refusing burial appears to have been a way that some masters used to punish slaves who resisted white authority and to intimidate the remaining slave community. In 1769, the governor of South Carolina issued a proclamation prohibiting masters from throwing the bodies of "dead negroes" into the river. The proclamation did call the practice "inhuman and unchristian"; however, it prohibited it on the grounds that the smell arising from the "putrefaction may become dangerous to the health of the inhabitants of the province."[33]

Another way a person was denigrated in death was by the mutilation of the decedent's body. In colonial America, this took place in three different circumstances. The first was in frontier struggles involving native peoples in which some native groups took the scalps of their dead enemies. The next was when slaves had been executed for rebellion or conspiracy to rebel. Then, bodies or severed heads were sometimes displayed after death as a deterrent to others. While these occasions were rare, they were done with an awareness of the shock value and the insult that would be received. The third circumstance was when the bodies of dead slaves, the impoverished, or executed felons were handed over to doctors to be dissected for medical research.[34]

Through their years of working with native peoples, experienced fur traders and diplomats such as Sir William Johnston understood the broad cultural significance of scalping. They knew that it was one of a panoply of rituals concerning warfare and death in a number of native communities. Most colonists, however, simply thought it was evidence of Indian savagery. A few colonists knew of the practice through frontier life and military service. Most others knew about it through newspaper accounts and popular captivity narratives, accounts written by Europeans who had been held captive by native peoples. Based on the number of publications and their multiple editions, they enjoyed a wide popularity. Captivity narratives were an important part of a genre of adventure stories that included firsthand accounts of shipwrecks, piracy, and pestilence. Since a key part of the genre was sensation, horror, and excitement, the writer often emphasized the gory or terrifying. Consequently, what was perceived as unusual or brutal was sure to be featured.[35]

Some colonists were horrified when they saw evidence of scalping firsthand in wartime, and the fear of the possibility of the practice deterred some recruits from joining colonial forces. Sir William Johnson, who was leading a body of provincial troops and Indian allies in 1755, had difficulty recruiting colonial back-woodsmen for ranger companies to be used for scouting and raiding. The rangers were organized separately from provincial or regular troops. Even when men were raised for ranger companies, some scouting groups became nervous out in the field. One large group of scouts quickly abandoned an expedition when one of its sentries was found dead and scalped.[36]

However, there were occasions in wartime when colonists scalped Indians. For colonists, it did not fit into a recognized range of rituals of war; rather, it fit with long-held views that native peoples were less worthy of respect than Euro-peans and that the normal rules of war did not apply. Goldsbrow Banyar, the sec-retary to the governor of New York, felt that since the Indians did it, colonists could too. Such Indian action "pleads an Excuse for following so inhuman an Example," he wrote to Sir William. Banyar advised that "we should deal exactly with them as they do by us, destroy and scalp as they do." Some rangers and Brit-ish regulars shared the sentiment and scalped enemy Indians. Indeed, the British general James Wolfe himself sanctioned it. Although he forbade scalping gener-ally, he allowed it when the "enemy are Indians, or Canad[ian]s dressed like In-dians." Usual respect for the bodies of the dead could be suspended when the deceased was not, or did not appear to be, European.[37]

For colonists, then, violation of a body was tolerated only if the body was of someone who was perceived to be of low status, such as an Indian, a person of African descent, a convicted felon, or a person who was indigent. Otherwise, such violence toward the deceased not only offended colonial sensibilities but also distressed people, because any kind of violation of the body after death seemed to jeopardize the possibility of eternal rest.

The belief that death should be a peaceful state was one shared by many cul-tures in the world, but for Europeans, it was rooted in the Christian tradition. For Christians at the time, the potential of a peaceful eternity required the phys-ical body to be intact so that the body could be resurrected after death. This be-lief continued even though theologians of many Christian denominations had come to think that it was only the soul that mattered. The belief in a physical resurrection rather than a purely spiritual one was centuries old. The Old Tes-tament stated that after "worms destroy this body, yet in my flesh shall I see God." However, the idea that the soul was more important than the body gained currency from the thirteenth century onward, and, especially after the Reforma-tion, the body became less and less important. For Puritans and other Protestants, the soul of a dead person had already gone to its destiny and the physical corpse had become meaningless. As one Puritan writer noted, "[W]hen the soule departs this life, it carries nothing away with it, but grace, Gods favour, and a good conscience."[38]

But, old beliefs and traditions died hard. Whatever theologians said, colonial Americans still felt it necessary to place the body in the ground intact and whole in a position of peaceful repose, washed and laid out, carefully prepared for the Resurrection. This widely held cultural value makes even more disrespectful the casual treatment of the urban poor, criminals, or slaves who were disposed of in a perfunctory manner. Only the most friendless and destitute of the dead were simply tossed carelessly into graves unwashed.

Dissection was seen as yet another way that the peace of the dead was violated. In the seventeenth and eighteenth centuries, with the rise of medical interest in anatomy, surgeons who wanted to experiment or teach needed dead bodies. However, families preferred to have a "Care of the Body for Christian burial," that is, an assurance that their loved ones were interred whole. Surgeons then took cadavers from places where families were not around to protest, such as the poorhouse, public hospitals, or graves at night. When Doctor William Shippen dissected bodies for his anatomy classes in Philadelphia, the bodies were those of suicides, executed felons, or "now and then one from the Potter's field," the burial ground for the indigent.[39]

The bodies, then, were invariably those of men and women of low status. In 1764, Doctor Samuel Clossy, who taught anatomy at King's College, was frustrated because, having dissected a black woman, he needed another "young subject." However, he and his assistants "were so known in the place that we could not venture to meddle with a white subject and a black or Mulatto I could not procure." However, he later "dissected a Male Black for the sake of the Skeleton" to complete his research. So, the bodies acquired for dissection appear to have been those of the most powerless people in the community.[40]

Despite these clandestine activities, public authority was sensitive, officially at least, to showing respect to the remains of the dead from a somewhat higher social status. In Boston, in 1771, a local stonemason requested permission to build more tombs in the common burying ground. The selectmen granted it "provided that it can be done without disturbing the Bones of the dead." So concerned were they about the enterprise that they assigned a committee to look at the proposed place to make sure that the "Bones of the dead" would remain undisturbed.[41]

That the body be laid peacefully to rest was a vital element in the proper interment of the dead. However, spiritual peace was also important. The most desirable kind of death allowed one time for spiritual preparation. For this there were two important sources of guidance, instruction manuals and local ministers. One of these manuals was *The Friendly Instructor*. This guide, in addition to offering advice on manners, advised readers that through careful spiritual preparation, they could "submit with Cheerfulness to the Will of God whatever it shall be." Of course, assisting with this preparation was an important part of a minister's duties. Throughout his long career, Henry Muhlenberg regularly went out to visit those of his Lutheran congregation who were dying. He was pleased when his parishioners were able to pray with him and take communion and were thus spiritually "armed to meet the last enemy," and he was distressed when others died unprepared.[42]

All of these anxieties about being at peace, physically and spiritually, were intensified by the experience of war. Death in combat, even if the sacrifice were celebrated, would deny a person any chance to prepare spiritually, and the physical body would likely be disfigured in some way. The glory of death in battle offered some "sweet consolation." However, men who died from disease were denied even that solace. Worse still, they died away from the emotional and moral support of family, without a "parent, wife or sister, to wipe the tear of anguish from their eyes, or to soothe the pillow of death."[43]

The Continental army used elaborate funeral rituals, with all the details specified according to rank, to honor its dead and to navigate this confusing territory. The rituals it adopted closely followed British and European military practice. The army had observed British military funerals for years before the Revolution in wartime and peacetime and did so even during the Revolutionary War itself. Colonists also noted how the British buried American officers and reciprocated in the same style. In addition, they read British military manuals reproduced in the colonies at the beginning of the war. By these means, the colonists knew how to conduct a military funeral that was appropriately imposing and as dignified as the officer's rank required.[44]

In military manuals, such as Thomas Simes's *Military Guide for Young Officers*, published in London in 1772 and in Philadelphia in 1776, the burial rituals for officers were prescribed in detail, but they provided no rules for how the bodies of soldiers were to be buried. It was simply understood that soldiers were going to be buried in whatever way the circumstances of camp or battlefield allowed. Consequently, soldiers' interments had a wide range of practices. There were occasions when soldiers were buried in coffins, with friends or messmates accompanying it to the grave. More commonly, soldiers' bodies were treated in ways similar to those of the urban poor, and sometimes much worse. Friends and townsmen did what they could to offer respect to their comrades in arms. However, the exigencies of war frequently interfered with their ability to perform adequately their "Last Duty to the Dead."[45]

The commotions of war rarely interfered with the "Last Duty" owed to officers. In death, the lines of distinction between officers and soldiers had to be maintained wherever possible, and officers could get upset at honors being given where they were not due. Colonel Lewis Nicola, a stickler for the distinctions of rank on any and all occasions, was irate when one day he saw a sergeant being buried, accompanied by a drum and fifer playing the dead march. He was angry because music at a funeral was an honor that should only "be paid to a commissioned officer." He immediately fired off a letter of complaint to General Edward Hand, the adjutant general. It may seem like "a matter of no great consequence," Nicola wrote; however, he felt that anything "that breaks through the distinctions of ranks is prejudicial to the service."[46]

The meaning and importance of burial rituals with all their distinctions of rank that the American military community used were reinforced by continuous interaction with the British, Hessian, and French armies. Americans observed what their allies and enemies did and were obliged by military (and gentlemanly) convention to pay appropriate respect not only to dead officers who were allies but also to those who were foes who died while in their custody. After all, one of the central tenets of gentlemanly conduct, according to Lord Chesterfield, was that one should exhibit gracious and generous conduct to others *with a view to obtain the same indulgence from them.* So, each party had a motive to extend this courtesy to the others. While there were some small details of difference among the rituals each nation practiced, they were minimal compared to their similarities.[47]

Simes's *Military Guide for Young Officers* spelled out the details of what was required for noncommissioned officers and officers of every rank. Simes was concerned with public ritual, not private preparation of the body. That officers were interred in coffins, with the body appropriately prepared, was a requirement so basic he did not spell it out. Indeed, those courtesies were always paid to deceased officers if time and circumstances permitted. Even if circumstances prevented them, the kind of graveside ceremonies he laid out were rarely omitted entirely, though they might be abridged.

The parade to the burial place and graveside rituals were where the distinctions of rank were elaborately displayed. For example, a general went to his eternal rest accompanied by three rounds fired from eleven pieces of cannon with,

Simes instructed, eleven battalions and six squadrons. Assembled musicians had to play the dead march with drums muffled. A lowly lieutenant, in contrast, was supposed to be carried to the grave escorted only by a sergeant, one drummer and one fifer, and thirty-six soldiers, about half his company. His rank allowed him the honor of having three rounds of small arms fire as a volley.[48]

For Bostonians, the years of British military presence gave them ample opportunity to observe some grand military rites. When General Thomas Gage's secretary died in 1774, a huge procession attended the corpse to the grave. It was arranged as follows:

> First part of the 4th Regiment Under Arms
> then the Band & Musick
> then the Clergy—then the Corps[e]
> then the Generall & his Family
> then the 4th Regiment without Arms
> then the Officers of the Army & afterwards the
> Gentlemen of the Town.

The same year, there was a large funeral for a "Serjeant of the 47th Regiment." This was unusual because a sergeant would not normally have commanded an elaborate funeral. In fact, according to Simes, a sergeant only required an accompanying sergeant, eighteen soldiers, and three rounds of small arms fire. However, the funeral was large because the sergeant was a Mason and "there were 152 Brethren [that] followed the Corps & the whole 47th Regimt." Usually such public honors were reserved only for commissioned officers.[49]

Only the direst circumstances prevented the British from carrying out the honors due their dead officers of high rank. One of these occasions was during the Seven Years' War when a force of French and Indians routed the British and provincial troops led by General Edward Braddock in 1755. British officers killed or wounded numbered 63 out of 86, as were 914 out of 1,373 soldiers. The rattled remnants of this force fled, believing the enemy to be in hot pursuit. Braddock, mortally wounded, was one of the few who was carried away with the fleeing troops. At his death, his officers feared his body might be discovered and desecrated by the enemy. The young Lieutenant Colonel George Washington chose a site in the middle of the road for the general's grave so that the troops and wagons would march over it, preventing the enemy from locating the spot. There, Braddock was buried without ceremony, wrapped only in blankets. Of course, the army had little time to offer this courtesy to any other of its dead or wounded, many of whom were left to the enemy, officers and men alike.[50]

When the British did abridge ceremonies for more junior officers, it was usu-ally the pressing exigencies of war, the scale of the destruction, or advanced pu-trefaction of bodies that prompted them to do so. Colonel James Grant was act-ing in great haste when he disposed of his dead in June 1760 in the midst of a campaign against the Cherokee on the Carolina frontier. Grant was commander of the British and provincial forces in South Carolina, and he was intent on attack-ing Cherokee towns when Cherokee warriors launched a surprise attack. Grant's forces were able to drive off their attackers, but the commander was anxious to give chase. He gave his exhausted troops a brief rest and time to see to the wounded and to "sink the dead in the river" before the pursuit began. The next day, an en-sign died of wounds he had received in the battle, and he was buried under a house in an abandoned Cherokee town. The house was then pulled down and torched to prevent the junior officer's grave from being discovered.[51]

In one case during the Revolutionary War, it was the high death toll the British suffered at their pyrrhic victory at Freeman's Farm in September 1777 that forced them to give dead officers only the most basic attention. Lieutenant Thomas Anburey was in charge of a burial party there, which was, he wrote, "as unpleas-ant a duty as can fall to the lot of an officer." His men buried the soldiers in a per-functory way, "fifteen, sixteen, and twenty" to a hole. The only distinctions of rank his party had time to pay to dead officers was that they were buried alone. However, Anburey did note an exception even to this. They buried three very young junior officers together, "the eldest not exceeding seventeen." Usually, this would be a serious violation of military practice. His language suggested that, in this case, he was moved by the youthfulness of the dead officers and that keeping the boys together was an act of kindness. He described his actions as this "friendly office to the dead." On another occasion, it was advanced putrefac-tion of a body that forced cursory interment. British lieutenant William Digby came across a dead officer of another regiment at Fort Anne, near Skenesboro, New York, in July 1777, about two weeks after the battle there. He was forced to pay no honor to the corpse other than to have his men cover the dead man with leaves. The body was already decayed and gave off a "violent stench."[52]

However, the exigencies of war did not necessarily diminish the pageantry as-sociated with military funerals, especially those of high-ranking officers. When the British brigadier general Simon Fraser fell during the battle at Saratoga in 1777, his dying wish was to be buried at six o'clock on the top of a nearby hill. Despite the fact that the battle was raging around them, General John Burgoyne honored Fraser's dying wish. Baronness von Riedesel, the wife of the Hessian commander, saw the interment where "the entire body of generals with their retinues [were] on the hill assisting at the obsequies." During the service, performed by a chaplain in full view of the American artillery, "cannon balls flew continually around and over the party." Later, after Burgoyne's surrender, the American general Horatio Gates was apologetic. He said that if he had realized there was a funeral in progress, "he would not have allowed any firing in that direction."[53]

Americans observed a wide range of European military practices by friend and foe. When Hessian general Johann von Huyn died of disease in New York in 1780, he was buried "with great military service." The French were no less meticulous. One woman wrote to her father in August 1779 from Lancaster, Pennsylvania, that she had attended the funeral of a French colonel who had been buried with the "Honors of war." In fact, this was his second burial. He had been interred the day before, "but It was not regular." His comrades "took him up again" and reburied him with funeral rites that were appropriate to his rank. The British and Europeans, then, provided models for appropriate burial rituals for men of rank.[54]

As in the other areas of physical treatment, the difference among officers of various ranks pales beside the gap between the treatment of officers and soldiers. While British officers could count on a funeral commensurate with rank in most circumstances, the disposition of soldiers' bodies was dependent on the number of men who died at the same time. If there were very few concurrent deaths, either on the battlefield or in the hospital, a man might be placed in a coffin, usually without any preparation of the corpse.

In periods of high mortality, whether from disease or on the battlefield, the kind of respect shown to troops' bodies was minimal. At those times, any preparation of the body was quickly dispensed with; a coffin was also deemed a luxury. On the battlefield, a soldier might simply have a shallow grave dug beside where he had fallen so that he could easily be flipped over into it. Of course, that would happen after his body had been stripped of any salable or useful items, a long-standing perk of burial parties everywhere. Sometimes, if a group of men fell near each other, they would be buried in a single hole, as Lieutenant Anburey described above. Anburey felt badly about burying the dead collectively in these pits. However, he and his burial party had been more meticulous than some others "who left heads, legs and arms above ground." The bodies in mass graves were sometimes covered with quicklime, that is, pure lime or calcium oxide, if it were available. This facilitated putrefaction and neutralized the soil. This was done following the Battle of Bunker Hill in 1775, for example. After that battle, dead privates were buried in a pit and covered with quicklime. In contrast, British officers who had been killed in that battle were buried in local Boston churchyards.[55]

British soldiers were vulnerable to an even greater degradation. His Majesty's soldiers joined that list of dishonored individuals whose bodies were used by surgeons for dissection. Garrisoned in the remote outposts of the empire, soldiers died a great distance from the watchful eyes of their families. George Cleghorn, a surgeon with the army in Minorca in 1736, used soldiers' bodies to do important anatomical research, and his success inspired other ambitious surgeons to join the army to do the same.[56]

British military surgeons tried to acquire bodies whenever they could. In July 1775, after the Battle of Bunker Hill, General William Howe had to issue orders to prevent soldiers from grave-robbing. The incentive for soldiers was collecting a surgeon's bounty. Howe warned that "[a]ny Soldier convicted of opening the Tombs or Graves in the burying Ground at Charlestown will be severely punish'd. . . . Added to the meanness of such a practice a pestilence from the Infection of the Putrify'd Bodys might reach the camp." The record is vague about whose bodies were the target. It could have been either the bodies of British soldiers or the local transient poor. If, as Howe believed, soldiers were the culprits and, as also seems likely, soldiers were the victims, it tells us something of the pragmatism with which British soldiers dealt with the harsh realities of their lives. It is worth noting that General Howe's concern was centered on sanitation and not respect.[57]

The British example continuously reinforced American conceptions of appropriate behavior for disposing of officers and men. Early in the war, when the British had to bury the American dead, they faced a dilemma. If they acknowledged the rank of Continental army officers, then they recognized the new army's legitimacy. This was a problem the British confronted in other interactions. For example, in 1776, when General Howe sent a message addressed to "George Washington Esq." rather than "His Excellency, General Washington," Washington's aide refused to accept it. Both sides then were sensitive to actions that had symbolic importance in the political struggle. Treating the American dead with the respect of their rank, then, had important political implications.[58]

However, the traditions of European warfare and gentlemanly conduct were powerful cultural standards, and the British disposed of American dead in accordance with a system of rank that they understood. One event that helped commit the British to this path early in the war was that one of the highest-ranking American officers whose body fell to them for burial after battle had, only a few

years before, been one of their own. The Continental general Richard Montgomery, who died in the assault on Quebec, was an Anglo-Irishman. He had
been a captain in the British army and a friend of General Guy Carleton, the
British commander at Quebec. Montgomery had only resigned his commission
and immigrated to New York in 1773. On arriving in the colonies, he quickly
embraced their cause. He accepted a commission in the Continental army at its
inception and was second in command to General Philip Schuyler on the Cana-
dian expedition. After the American defeat at Quebec, the British found and removed his body from the battlefield and buried him with full military honors.[59]

Americans of every rank in the expedition were pleased to know that Montgomery was given this appropriate recognition and respect. Captain Henry Dearborn, held as a British prisoner in Quebec, noted that Montgomery was interred
by order of General Carleton "in a very decent manner." Benedict Arnold, a
colonel at the time, wrote that "[e]very possible mark of distinction was shown
to the corpse." Private John Joseph Henry, also a prisoner, remembered being
awed by the "coffin, covered with a pall, surmounted by transverse swords. . . .
The [British] regular troops, with reversed arms, and scarves on the left elbow,
accompanied the corpse to the grave." Even those some distance away, hearing
of it later, were delighted to know that "Montgomery was buried with all the
Honours due to his Rank." The recognition did exactly what the British had
wanted to avoid: legitimized his rank and status as an honorable enemy.[60]

However, some American officers went into that battle not quite certain
whether they would receive the appropriate honor from their enemy if they were
to die. Just before the assault at Quebec began, Captain Jacob Cheesman of
New York, aware of the great day ahead of him, dressed carefully and put "five
half joes in his pocket," saying that he hoped that would be enough to tempt the
burial party "to bury him with decency." It was insurance Cheesman would need
as he was killed in battle later that day.[61]

The British interred those whom convention required that they should, and
Americans returned the compliment. When the British captain William Leslie
was killed at the Battle of Princeton in January 1777, Benjamin Rush recognized
his body. Leslie was the son of the Earl of Leven, who had been kind to Rush
during his time in Edinburgh. Washington ordered due respect to be shown.
He instructed "40 of our light Infantry to attend the funeral" and that Leslie be
buried "with the honors of war." Despite Washington's orders and gentlemanly
standards for appropriate conduct, one American officer was not gracious about
complying. Captain Thomas Rodney of the Delaware line was supposed to offi-
ciate at the funeral, but he claimed that since he "had not paid any attention to

Military Funeral Ceremonies I requested Captain Humphries to conduct it." Despite his claim to ignorance, Rodney was able to perform a ceremony for a brother officer a few days later.[62]

Hessian officers also received similar attentions when they died. Colonel Carl von Donop received full military honors from the Americans when they buried him after the attack on Fort Mercer in October 1777. A number of Americans recorded Donop's death and burial in letters and journals. One American soldier, Samuel Smith, years later recalled carrying Donop, mortally wounded, from the field. Donop was brought in and buried the day before the other Hessian dead. Smith remembered because, the day after Donop's funeral, he and "the whole regiment was employed . . . digging a trench and burying the dead. Here we buried between four and five hundred." The real number was probably under four hundred, but that correction to Smith's memory does not alter his recollection of the courtesy shown to Donop in comparison to the treatment of the Hessian soldiers.[63]

Americans, like their European counterparts, found that practical circumstances led to considerable variation in burial practices. In the spring of 1776, a shortage of ammunition led Washington to order that in the future, there was "to be no expence of ammun[i]tion at the Interment of any officer, or soldier, of the Continental army" unless by his order. For officers, his orders were regularly contravened. And although he specifically mentioned soldiers in this order, volleys were rarely fired at a soldier's burial.[64]

Everyone understood and accepted that the burial of officers took priority. On June 29, 1778, the day after the grueling Battle of Monmouth, Washington ordered burial parties to go and bury the dead of all ranks of both armies. In case any might forget the need to respect rank, Washington ordered that the "officers of the American Army are to be buried with military honors due to men who have nobly fought and died in the Cause of Liberty and their Country." To the soldiers who fought and died in the same cause and on the same field, there was no respect paid. Soldiers set about the task of digging the graves and probably felt, as one young militiaman had the previous year at Freeman's Farm, that it was "a sad and laborious day's work."[65]

Years later, in pension applications, soldiers often remembered and noted when they had done burial duty after a major battle. Two militiamen, William Gilmore and Austin Wells, recalled burying the dead after the Battle of Bennington in August 1777. The day had special significance for them as it had been the occasion when the two had met, beginning a lifelong friendship. Sixty-four years later,

Gilmore, then ninety-one years old, in his support of Wells's pension application, was able to recall in detail their participation in the grim duty, even the names of the officers they buried.[66]

Like other veterans, they made no comment about the distinction of rank, even though it often caused them a great deal of work. James Fergus, when he was a Pennsylvania militiaman, had to dig officers' graves in the frozen ground after the Battle of Princeton. The ground was so hard that they did not attempt to bury dead soldiers. Instead, they were thrown "in the trenches of the redoubts 'till the ground thawed in the spring." However, Fergus and other soldiers did have to dig through the frozen ground to inter two officers, one from Delaware and the other from Virginia, who were buried "with the honors of war."[67]

If any ceremony took place at soldiers' burials, officers did not record it. They did, of course, note the funeral rites paid to officers. In July 1782, Lieutenant William McDowell recalled the death in the hospital "this morning at five o'clock" of Lieutenant McCullough, a fellow Pennsylvanian. The next evening, McCullough was buried with the honors of war, and McDowell wrote that he "commanded the party consisting of one sergt, one corporal, & 24 privates." Two days later, his diary had the brief observation, "[T]his day we buried a soldier of our batt'n," with no other information. His scant notation does not mean that there was no ceremony. His mentioning it at all implies that at least a group of the deceased's friends or messmates followed the coffin to its rest.[68]

When time allowed and rank required it, American officers' funerals were as impressive as those of British officers. The burial of Colonel William Bond at Mount Independence in September 1776 was, according to one observer, "conducted in a manner suitable to the occasion." Ebenezer David, an army chaplain, delivered the funeral oration and said a prayer. Then "the corpse was interred and the Colonel's character honoured by the discharge of three twenty-four-pounders from the Fort, and the usual volley from the musketry."[69]

This was modest compared to the interment of Lieutenant Colonel Barnard Elliott, a Continental artillery officer and an important figure in South Carolina society, after he died of disease in October 1778. General William Moultrie ordered that his corpse was to be borne by the "Field officers of the Corps of Artillery and other Field-Officers of Similar Rank." All the South Carolina regiments in the vicinity attended, with the colors of Elliott's Second South Carolina Regiment draped over the shoulders of the ensigns. As the parade approached the church, the troops formed rows through which the corpse was carried. The troops reversed their arms while the corpse passed. The accompanying band played a dead march composed especially "for this mournful occasion." Bringing up the rear of this procession were members of the legislature and all the important officeholders of the state.[70]

Even so, Elliott's funeral failed to match the grandeur of the one for General Enoch Poor, who died in September 1780 of a "putrid fever." One observer was awed by that funeral procession. It included "a regiment of light infantry, in uniform with arms reversed; four field pieces [artillery]; Major Lee's regiment of light horse; General Hand and his brigade." Also in the procession was "the horse of the deceased, with his boots and spurs suspended from the saddle." Washington, other generals, and the brigade that Poor had commanded followed the mahogany coffin, decorated with "a pair of pistols and two swords, crossing each other and tied with black crepe." The scene and the "melancholy dirge" had a great impact on the crowd, one of whom agreed that Poor was justly honored as he had been "a truly brave Judicious diserving Gentleman."[71]

Some officers were careful about whose funerals they honored with their presence. Captain Thomas Rodney not only delegated the funeral ceremony for the British captain Leslie but also avoided leading a ceremony "to bury Col. Ford with the honors of war" after the battle at Trenton. Rodney had been asked to command it, but since Ford was an officer with the New Jersey militia, he "put a Younger officer to do the Service." The next day, "[T]he infantry were ordered to bury General Hitchcock with the honors of war and as he was a Continental officer I took the command myself." Rodney made this distinction between Hitchcock and Ford even though, in a letter to his brother, Rodney acknowledged that Ford was the "owner of the house where we are & an elegant one it is." Rodney was unabashed that he had delegated Ford's funeral. After all, he wrote, "I have had the Command of a Light Infantry Battalion since the Battle of Prince Town being the Eldest Captain." Rodney treated the deceased militia officer with disdain. However, there is little evidence that many other Continental officers took their sense of superiority to this degree.[72]

Funerals, such as those for Hitchcock and Poor, were both a confirmation of rank and an occasion to instill awe in the crowd. Sometimes, the individual was important enough that an elaborate funeral had to be stage-managed after the fact, such as for Joseph Warren, after his death at the Battle of Bunker Hill. However, this was not the only occasion when someone was reinterred to restore order. On General John Sullivan's campaign in the west in the summer of 1779, the Reverend William Rogers recounted how the troops came to some rough graves "where Captain Davis and Lieutenant Jones, with a corporal and four privates were scalped, tomahawked, and speared by the savages." Rogers was concerned about this as a final resting place for "worthy departed friends and brethren." Their burial was troubling on two counts: it had been hasty, and the men's bodies had been mutilated. Rogers referred to the officers as brethren because they were not only brother officers but also fellow Masons. The Masonic brothers duly arranged for the bodies to be more properly interred. Consequently, Davis and Jones were later moved "to the proper burying ground. The brotherhood met at five o'clock, and marching by the general's marque, had the pleasure of his company. Colonel Proctor's and Hubley's regiments, with drums, fifes and the band of music accompanied them." At the grave site, "a short prayer was made, the bodies were interred in Masonic form, and three volleys of small arms fired." Order had been restored. The Masons and the other officers did not extend these courtesies to the soldiers and NCO who had been killed with the officers; they were left where they had originally been buried.[73]

Few ordinary soldiers or NCOs were buried with the full honors of war. One NCO who did receive these honors was Sergeant Robert Dixon, who died early in the war near Quebec in November 1775. A Pennsylvanian, Dixon did not serve as a commissioned officer, even though one of his soldiers described him as "a gentleman of good property and education" and "intuitively a captain." His wealth, education, and the personal respect he commanded, together with the fact that his death "was the first oblation made upon the alter of liberty at Quebec," probably caused others to bury him with "the usual military honors."[74]

Not surprisingly, soldiers made the greatest efforts to bury friends with dignity in the first campaigns of the war. This was the period before they became inured to death and while men were still mostly serving with others from their communities. Jeremiah Greenman, still a private at the time of the expedition to Quebec, wrote that when Josiah Carr, a soldier "belonging to our Company," died, the whole company attended his funeral. A chaplain said a prayer over the corpse, and then Greenman and his friends "carried him" two miles to a burying ground where they had permission to bury him.[75]

Also on the Quebec expedition, Private Henry was pleased to hear that a friend had been decently buried. The "friend" he referred to was a young first lieutenant he had probably known before the war. The young officer and his men were living in desperate circumstances, reduced to chewing leather after days without food. Henry had been anxious about the young man's fate because he had taken him to a private house where he was forced to leave him to the kindness of strangers when the company marched on. Henry certainly did not expect the young officer to receive the generous treatment he did. He heard a month later of his friend's death and that "his corpse received a due respect from the inhabitants of the vicinage." This touched Henry. "This real Catholicism towards the remains of one we loved, made a deep and wide breach upon my early prejudices."[76]

Henry had been glad of kind strangers to attend to the last duty to his friend. However, for some, trusting "the hands of a stranger to perform the last mournful duties" was by itself a traumatic departure from domestic life. Some soldiers were anxious to perform that service for friends when circumstances permitted. That was true for Elisha James of Scituate, Massachusetts. When one of his townsmen, Samuel Nickols, died in the late summer of 1777, the men "made a Coffin & had the Scituate people & the Cheif of the Company to Attend his funirall[.] I helpd Bury him [and] his body was Desently Lodged in the grave." Some soldiers showed concern for the bodies of strangers, too. Bayze Wells was disturbed when the body of a man accidentally hit by a cannon ball was blown into the river and was not recovered for three days. Then "he Rose and floted [and] we took him up and Buried him Decently."[77]

Joseph Plumb Martin and his friends were also anxious to do the right thing by a fallen soldier whose body they had brought off from the field after the Battle of Harlem Heights in 1776. They dug a grave near a gentleman's house and began to "commit the poor man, then far from friends and relatives, to the bosom of his Mother Earth." They were interrupted by two young women who came from the house to see what was happening. As they looked into the grave at the dead man, the two women were upset when they realized that the men intended to throw the earth on the man's "naked face." One of the women gave the men her handkerchief to be spread over the dead man's face that he might be spared that indignity. The grave was filled and the women left. Martin had worried that the dead man was being interred by strangers, "for there were none at his funeral who knew him." But Martin was pleased that, as a compensation, they had been able to offer the man "mourners and females too."[78]

In periods of great mortality, standards for the treatment of officers' and soldiers' bodies at death declined precipitously, though officers were still usually buried apart from their men in separate graves and in coffins. Such was the case at the hospital in Bethlehem, Pennsylvania, during the deadly winter of 1777–78. At first, Moravian carpenters made the coffins and dug the graves for the dead. However, when the death rate soared from a variety of "putrid fevers," these tasks were delegated to soldiers of the hospital guard. The bodies of officers, medical men, and their relatives were buried in the "Strangers' Row" of the Moravian cemetery. The soldiers' bodies were buried wherever space could be found. As hundreds of men died in the hospital at Bethlehem that winter, it is

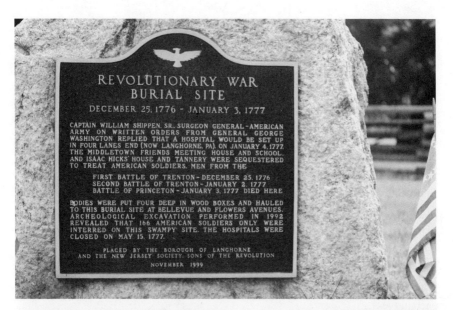

Many solders' burial sites are lost to us. In Langhorne, Pennsylvania, one has recently
been located and its existence researched and recorded. Photographs by Florence
Wharton, member, Revolutionary War Burial Site, Langhorne, Pennsylvania;
courtesy Revolutionary War Site Commemoration
Committee, Langhorne, Pennsylvania.

hardly surprising that an alternative to the churchyard had to be found, and under the social conditions, there could be no question as to who would occupy it.[79]

Hospitals buried their dead where and as they could. After the Battle of Trenton in December 1776, the army went to Attleboro (now Langhorne, Pennsylvania), just across the Delaware River from Trenton, and "took possession of Hicks' house and made a hospital of it." It was a sickly time. Probably 160 men died and were buried in a vacant lot in the southern part of the village. Years later, an elderly woman, who had lived in that community as a child, remembered the carpenter making coffins out of rough boards. She recalled that when she got up in the mornings, a cart would already be outside the makeshift hospital. It waited until it was laden with four coffins, then it went to the grave site. The dead were placed in individual coffins but not in individual graves. Pits were dug and the coffins stacked four deep. She also recalled that the pits had been so shallow that the following spring, rain washed the topsoil off, exposing the coffins. Then "the neighbors joined together and hauled dirt in carts and made mounds over each grave."[80]

It is unlikely, under these conditions, that any preparations were made to the bodies before interment. Certainly we know that shortages of supplies would have meant that many soldiers would have been interred naked and unwrapped. In 1778, Philip Turner, surgeon general in the Eastern Hospital Department, ordered that when a soldier died, his "arms and accoutrements" had to be turned in to the commissary. Turner declared it was the responsibility of those in charge of the wards to make sure that "no blankets or cloathing [were] expended in burying any that die in Hospital."[81]

When possible, such as when the army was in winter quarters in Pennsylvania, hospital doctors worked with local ministers and public officials to arrange burying places and put carpenters to work making coffins. If the army was further afield when epidemics swept through a camp, there were often not the resources available to dig graves or make coffins. Different camps recorded the deterioration of the quality of burials for soldiers in epidemic conditions. At Ticonderoga in 1776, Private Ezra Tilden was distressed by the small size of a soldier's funeral. Only four men were available to carry a coffin, with "none to Spell ym [them] no mourners; nor no. attendants: not but only 4 poor men, at ye funeral: . . . Such a Sight, I never Saw in my Life, before." Without mourners, the event seemed disrespectful.[82]

However, even this would have seemed like respect indeed to the men on Lake Champlain that summer. There, smallpox raged through the army and death had "now become a daily visitant in the camps." Doctor Lewis Beebe saw a man interred "without so much as a Coffin, and with little or no ceremony." By the end of the month, the dead were buried wherever a place might be found. Beebe recorded that "nine were buried this day on the point [probably Crown Point], sundry on chimney point." Two days later, he wrote that "[a] number are employed the other side, almost the whole of the day to dig graves & bury the dead." In early July, the men were still employed that way as "[d]eath visits us almost every hour." In these conditions, ceremony went by the wayside.[83]

Captain John Lacey, also on Lake Champlain in the summer of 1776, was deeply disturbed by the sight of the dead and dying. En route for Isle aux Noix, he recorded the death of eleven soldiers and two officers, "having only a Blanket each for his Coffin, and all consigned to one grave." The number of dead and the fact that the troops were in transit probably accounted for this breach of etiquette.

But Lacey had not yet seen the worst. He visited two camps on Isle aux Noix, one of New England and New York troops, the other of Jersey and Pennsylvania troops. He had heard that, in each camp, fifteen to twenty died daily, and he went to examine the burying grounds. There he found

two large holes dug in the Earth, one for each Camp — while there I saw several Corps[es] brought, carried by four Soldiers in a blanket, one holt of each corner. On their ariving at the pit or Grave, those next to it let go of the blanket, the other two giving a Hoist rolled the dead body into the pit where lay several bodies already deposited in the same way, with no other covering but the Rags in which they dyed, heads and points as they happened to come to the place. In this manner the burial continued all day, as soon as the breeth had left the unfortunate Victim, the body was thus laid on a dirty Blanket and toted off to the silent Toom, without a sie from a Friend or relative, or a single morner to follow it. In the evening the dirt in front of this General Grave, or deposit of the dead, was thrown over the Dead bodies leaving a new space open for the next Day.[84]

Lacey appeared to be distressed by this, though not unaware of its necessity. He had difficulty thinking of this "toom" as a grave. Each time he used the word "grave," he qualified it by calling it a "pit" or "deposit of the dead." His observation of the lack of ceremony or of a "single morner to follow" the corpse indicated that this method of disposition was not only a significant departure from the norm but also disturbing.

Sometimes high mortality combined with climate to create burial practices that observers found distressing. After the siege of Quebec, the dead from both sides were removed from the battlefield. Private Henry, now a prisoner of war after the American defeat, saw that many "carioles [carts] repeatedly, one after the other, passed our dwelling loaded with the dead, whether of the assailants or of the garrison, to a place emphatically called the 'dead house.'" This was the structure where bodies were kept until the ground thawed and they could be buried. General Montgomery and the other officers who had been killed had been buried the day before in the frozen ground. This had involved considerable labor. One British officer noted that, on another occasion when his men had to dig a grave in the region in wintertime, it had taken "near a days labor" and the men had found the ground "froze above six feet deep." Under these conditions, burial of the dead soldiers was not considered an option. However, the effort was made for officers of both sides.[85]

Like Lacey, Henry was disturbed by the disorderly way that bodies were gathered and piled. He saw that the bodies of dead soldiers had frozen in the position of their final death throes. He recalled that he and his friends felt "horror of the sight" when they saw their dead friends "borne to interment uncoffined, and in the very clothes they had worn in battle; their limbs distorted in various directions." He recognized a friend "on top of half a dozen other bodies — his arms extended beyond his head, as if in the act of prayer, and one knee crooked and raised, seemingly when he last gasped in the agonies of death." Henry absolved General Carleton of any inhumanity. He recognized this as a dictate of climate and rank. However, the sight of his "unhappy and lost brethren, though in humble station," with whom he had been through so much, "forced melancholy sensations."[86]

The sight of disordered bodies even on the battlefield distressed others. Elisha Bostwick, at the battle at White Plains in October 1776, exclaimed "[O]h! what a Sight that was to See within a distance of Six rods those men with their legs & arms & guns & packs all in a heap." After the Battle of Saratoga a year later, Ezra Tilden recorded in his diary a sight that "was Shocking, indeed." He watched the dead and wounded being brought into headquarters the night of the battle and the next day. He saw "[s]ev'ral Dead, & naked men" who were "lying dead in ye woods close by, or Even where ye battle was fought." Tilden was so moved that he wrote down a prayer in his journal and signed and dated it. From the "fates of war," he wrote, "good L'd, Deliver me!"[87]

The distress of all these men reflected the common cultural concern that death should bring peace, symbolized by a body laid in quiet repose. Bodies tumbled about in disorderly piles was bad enough. However, once a body was in a grave, further disruption was still possible. Some of these disturbances were more upsetting than others. For example, British and American troops were distressed when, after fighting in remote areas, wolves came down to feed off the dead.

After the battles at Hubbardton in Vermont in July 1777 and at Freeman's Farm two months later, the British buried the dead of both sides in shallow graves. Wolves, drawn by "the great stench thro the country," came down "to devour the dead." The animals "tore out of the earth" the dead who had been only slightly covered. The sight of the scratched-up graves was disturbing enough. The noise of the howling during the night was something troops found equally unsettling. Animals devouring human corpses was certainly beyond the pale of what everyone considered acceptable, but it did not lead either side to dig deeper graves.[88]

While everyone found this kind of disturbance distressing, there were other desecrations they were more cavalier about. For example, disturbing the graves of men or violating the bodies of those perceived to be lesser or different was acceptable. One such incident took place after the Battle of Newtown, New York, in August 1779, part of General Sullivan's expedition to the west against British, loyalist, and Iroquois Indian forces. Afterward, Major Daniel Piatt of the New Jersey line sent out a party specifically to search for Indian dead. The party found a few bodies and desecrated two of them. Lieutenant William Barton wrote that the party "skinned two of them from their hips down for boot legs; one pair for the major the other for myself." Both soldiers and officers participated in this incident.[89]

Also on Sullivan's expedition, soldiers opened and disturbed Indian graves searching for a warrior's weapons or other artifacts. Commanding officers had mixed feelings about it. One, Major James Norris, was not too concerned about it. Norris wrote simply that soldiers did it "[w]hether through principles of avarice or curiosity" and found inside such graves "a good many laughable relics." Lieutenant Colonel Francis Barber, on the other hand, forbade his troops "to open Indian graves." He shared the sanitation concerns of British general William Howe. He warned his troops that there had been "repeated instances of the most fatal disorders being occasioned by [grave-robbing]." He was not concerned with the violation of the bodies, disrespect, or theft.[90]

However, there were times in the war when white Americans disturbed the burial place of other white Americans, and there is no record of anyone finding it distressing or unacceptable. One occasion was when patriot leaders wanted to exhume Joseph Warren's body and give it a ceremonial interment. First they had to find his body amongst the other dead. Joseph's brother, John, described the area on which there were "a great number of rude hillocks, under which were deposited the remains, in clusters, of those deathless heroes who fell in the field of battle." Several days passed before his body was identified by his two artificial teeth. No one on the scene at the time noted how many other bodies were disturbed and exhumed before the searchers found him. His removal from the other "deathless heroes" established the social distance between the gentleman patriot and the soldiers.[91]

It had only been a few years earlier in 1771 that the Boston selectmen had been concerned that the work of a local stonemason in the common burial ground might disturb the remains of the dead nearby. As noted above, they had been so concerned that they appointed a committee to police the work to make sure nothing inappropriate happened. Now, on this occasion in 1776, the dead from Bunker Hill were not in an official city burial ground, and so the selectmen would have had no responsibility to supervise or comment on it. If anyone objected to the fact that the searchers disturbed the remains of others in order to find Warren, no record of it exists.

While there seems to have been no objections to the remains of dead soldiers being disturbed in this case, there was another kind of violation to which there was a swift response. Soldiers appear to have resisted attempts by surgeons to use the bodies of dead soldiers for dissection. American surgeons tested the limits of social acceptance in their quest for bodies to be used for teaching and research. In November 1775, James Thacher noted that "[t]he body of a soldier has been taken from the grave, for the purpose, probably of dissection, and the empty coffin left exposed." In the ensuing excitement, "both resentment and grief are manifested." Thacher identified status as the key element in the outraged response. The theft served to "impress the idea that a soldier's body is held in no estimation after death. Such a practice, if countenanced, might be attended with serious consequences as it respects our soldiers." It would appear that George Washington also feared the consequences, and he acted to stave off further problems. Thacher noted that "the practice in future is strictly prohibited by the commander in chief." No further incidents were recorded, and soldiers appear to have drawn the line successfully at this kind of violation.[92]

Wary of the attitudes of soldiers and the larger society to the sanctity of the body after death, Washington resisted any attempts by officers to use the mutilation of bodies after death as a form of punishment. Usually, at a military execution, the body would simply be deposited and put, unwrapped and sometimes without a coffin, in a grave prepared at the site. As discussed in chapter 3, "Light-Horse Harry" Lee thought that it would be good for discipline if the heads of executed deserters were cut off and publicly displayed. Washington was horrified at the suggestion, but his response came too late to prevent one incident in which a deserter was beheaded. Washington was concerned about the soldiers' and the public's response, should it become widely known, and ordered that the body be quickly buried. Most soldiers probably never heard anything about the incident.[93]

Soldiers, then, appear to have objected, or were assumed to object, to desecration of bodies as a matter of policy. They wanted public policy to stand against bodies being used for dissection, and Washington, certainly correctly, understood that they would want policy to stand opposed to desecration as a punishment. Soldiers did not object to the policy and practice of careless interment, either dictated by the necessities of war or by the distinctions of rank, even though they found it distressing. There is also no evidence that they objected to having soldiers' remains disturbed to find those of a more famous man.

These small but sharp delineations indicate that soldiers held their status to be above that of the most dishonored members of the civilian community and their British counterparts. As soldiers serving for short terms, unlike slaves or British soldiers, they were not prepared to depart completely from the practices and standards of civilian life. Their status in society may have been low, but they resisted the kind of treatment dealt out to society's most friendless and powerless individuals.

However, just as the physical remains of soldiers were treated with little respect, so too was their sacrifice. Dead officers were honored in general orders, newspapers, and public oratory. The sacrifice of soldiers was only occasionally acknowledged or remembered. In Philadelphia in 1779, Charles Willson Peale and two other men were instrumental in organizing a public "eulogium in honor of the brave men who have fallen in the contest." The three men noted that their invitation to city, state, and national leaders was "in behalf of a number of citizens." A report of the service, "an elegant Oration . . . in the Dutch Calvinistic Church," appeared in the *Pennsylvania Gazette*. The service was followed, according to the paper, by an entertainment thrown by the Congress for various foreign dignitaries, "several Continental officers, civil and military, and many strangers of distinction." During the evening there were thirteen volleys fired by the militia and thirteen toasts drunk. The eighth of these was a toast to "[t]he memories of those heroes who have nobly died in defending the rights of their country." Although soldiers were not singled out in this and other events like it, they were not specifically excluded.[94]

Neither were they named. Peale, early in the war, wrote "that those who do not enter [the] fight with us are against us." Two years later, he felt the same way. He scribbled a poem in his account book challenging those who sought to "[c]rush this vast design" of independence. He promised them that "[o]blivion shall entomb thy Name" for staying out of, or working against, the struggle. Of course, he was thinking of men of his own social rank, for soldiers' names were lost, whichever side of the struggle they took.[95]

Whether men died from disease or in battle, bodies were interred according to rank. Rush, in speaking of high death rates from disease, lamented the loss of "worthy citizens" who died. Yet despite their worth and usefulness to the cause of liberty, dead American soldiers fared only slightly better than their British counterparts. While American soldiers were spared the violation of dissection, any mark of respect at the grave was quickly dispensed with if circumstances required it or if friends were not able or willing to exert themselves. Officers, in contrast, were usually accorded the respect due their rank regardless of whether friends were present to act in their interests. In this, the soldiers acquiesced. They had no more expectation of equal treatment in death than they had in life. The officers and men of the Continental army were united in a common cause but divided by social value. Washington honored American soldiers for being "willing at all hazards, to defend their invaluable rights and privileges." That willingness, however, brought them no new recognition at death.[96]

CHAPTER SIX

Onspeakable Sufrings Such As No Man Can Tell

Status and the Treatment of Prisoners of War

Take courage, my children, cry to God,
and he will deliver you from the
power and hand of the enemy.

BARUCH 4:21

BY 1778, PHILIP FRENEAU, the young American poet and man of letters, had
served a stint in the Pennsylvania militia. He was not yet able to make a living as
a writer, so he was prepared to work, as he had done before the war, as master
and supercargo on a merchant ship. Before renewing that employment, he traveled as a passenger on the vessel *Aurora*, though he was mistakenly listed as its
third mate. The error cost him dearly. The British captured the ship and imprisoned its crew, including Freneau. The crew was sent to one of the notorious British prison ships anchored in shallow waters off New York, not far from Brooklyn. These were old British naval vessels, stripped of their guns, masts, and any
trimmings, with only their hulks remaining. In these, the British held American
seamen and those of many other nations captured off the North American
coast. They also held American soldiers.[1]

Freneau was fortunate. He was captive for less than two months before being
released, but the horrific experience compelled him to speak out. He had already
published prose and poetry supporting the patriot cause; after his imprisonment, he used the power of his pen to publicize the conditions in which he and

others had been held. In 1781, he published a broadside with a long poem, "The British Prison-Ship," in which he recounted how he had

> found, at length, too late,
> That Death was better than the prisoner's fate;
> There doomed to famine, shackles and despair
> Condemn'd to breathe a foul, infected air
> In sickly hulks, devoted while we lay,
> Successive funerals gloom'd each dismal day.

Even his short prison experiences had been enough to convince Freneau of British brutality. He chided "ungenerous Britain, you / Conspire to murder those you cannot subdue."[2]

From the distance of the twenty-first century, it is tempting to see his long, florid poem as an exaggerated account of prison life. It could have been propaganda that promoted the patriot cause. However, his descriptions are corroborated by the testimony of many other survivors. War memoirs recounted at length details of "wormmy" bread, shocking filth, and death from a variety of terrible diseases that swept the holds of the ships and other confined spaces where prisoners were held. Some veterans found that, even in old age, they struggled to find language to talk about it. One felt it was "impossible to conceive, much less to describe" the horror he had witnessed.[3]

And horrific it had been. At least 8,500 American prisoners of war died of disease. Additionally, seamen of other nations were also captured and held, so the total number of prisoner deaths was probably close to 11,000, matching the estimates of those present at the time. Soldiers later remembered the morning cry of the British guards, "Rebels, bring out your dead," or "How many are dead now?" The prisoners then duly passed out the bodies to be buried. It is impossible now to calculate mortality rates, as we do not know the total number of prisoners held at any one time. However, the sketchy information available indicates that being a prisoner was much more dangerous than either combat or camp life and possibly more dangerous than the two combined.[4]

In addition to the prison ships, the British used a variety of buildings including barns, jails, and sugar houses as makeshift prisons in North America. Indeed, they used any large structure that could be made secure. Ships were used primarily in New York and South Carolina where the British found themselves with more prisoners than they knew what to do with.

Usually, only soldiers were held in these facilities. Most of the time, imprisoned officers were housed separately, generally billeted in private homes, apart

The British Prifon-Ship:

A

P O E M,

IN FOUR CANTOES.----

Viz. CANTO {
1. *The Capture,*
2. *The Prifon-Ship,*
3. *The Prifon-Ship, continued,*
4. *The Hofpital-Prifon-Ship.*

To which is added,

A POEM on the Death of Capt. N. B I D D L E,
who was blown up, in an Engagement with the
Yarmouth, near Barbadoes.

------------*Immediately a place*
Before his eyes appear'd, fad, noifom, dark
A Lazar houfe it feem'd, wherein were laid
Numbers of all difeas'd : all maladies
Of ghaftly fpafm, or racking torture, qualms
Of heart fick agony ; all feverous kinds
Convulfions ------
Demoniac phrenzy, moping melancholy
And moonftruck madnefs ------
Dire was the toffing, deep the groans; defpair
Tended the fick, bufied from couch to couch
And over them triumphant death his dart
Shook, nor delay'd to ftrike. ------
Mliton, Par. loft. Lib. XI. 477.

P H I L A D E L P H I A :
PRINTED BY F. BAILEY, IN MARKET-STREET.
M.DCC.LXXXI.

Frontispiece to the 1781 edition of *The British Prison-Ship: A Poem, in Four
Cantoes*, attributed to Philip Freneau. Courtesy Collection of
The New-York Historical Society, #76048D.

from soldiers just as they were in camp. This did not mean that their lives were always easy or comfortable, but they were spared the greater miseries of their men. Colonel Samuel Miles, who was held with some other officers in New York, felt that they had "been treated as genteely by the Hessian & Hig[h]land Officers as we could expect or have wished so far as they had it in their power to oblige us." They lacked only "sugar & some necessaries of that kind." However, Miles had to petition British general William Howe on behalf of the noncommissioned officers and privates held captive. They were, he wrote, "suffering the most extreme Misery" and "must all inevitably Perish unless Speedily relieved." Unfortunately, relief was not given and many did die.[5]

American officers expected their rank to be recognized because, just like British officers, they were gentlemen. As such, they should be able to trust that gentry values would govern their treatment. The central tenet of gentlemanly conduct was that one should treat others well in the hope and expectation that they would extend the same courtesy. One British officer reminded Colonel Ethan Allen, a fastidious colonial gentleman, of this truth. Allen had been captured by the British and was being shipped to Halifax, Nova Scotia, and then on to Britain. He had trouble consistently receiving the respect he wanted from British officers, but finally he found one who shared his high standards of conduct, a Captain Smith. Allen was touched by the courtesy with which Smith treated him and hoped that he might somehow be able to return the favor. Smith assured him it was not necessary since "this is a mutable world, and one gentleman never knows but it may be in his part to help another." Allen was so moved by this thought that when some of his fellow captive American officers hatched a plan to seize control of the ship by killing Smith, Allen not only declined to join them but talked them out of it.[6]

Like many prisoners taken in the eighteenth century by European armies, Allen could be reasonably certain that his condition would not last for the duration of the war. It was common for prisoners of each side to be exchanged in complex bargaining arrangements known as cartels. Under these cartels, men of each rank had a particular value. Usually the exchanges involved men of a similar rank; however, at times there were complex packages. It was usually easier for an officer to be exchanged under this system, because he need only wait for the other side to have a prisoner of his rank for an exchange to take place. For ordinary soldiers, there was a long wait for large groups to be batched together.[7]

No matter what rank American men were, many of them wrote of their wartime captivity with sadness. Apart from the terrible things that some men had witnessed, many also keenly felt their isolation from family and community. Officers too expressed this isolation, even though they often had considerable freedom to move around and socialize in the communities in which they were held. One young ensign, held at Quebec, felt especially lonely after the death of a "Brother Officer . . . with whom I had form'd a firm friendship." He wrote to his wife that he now felt "like a lone bird in a cage."[8]

For soldiers, the conditions of their confinement, the discipline under which they were held, the medical care they received, and the ways in which they were buried all reflected the low esteem in which they were held by the British. Most of the time, men were helpless in the face of their captors' treatment. However, the resourceful ways in which men of all ranks responded and conducted themselves under these conditions tell us something about how they felt about themselves and their place in their own society. While imprisoned, a man's honor and his sense of his place in his community guided his conduct. The value he placed on his own life relative to the lives of others sometimes determined survival itself.

IT IS NOT SURPRISING that when colonial Americans launched themselves headlong into a war, they forgot to think about some of the details. As we have seen, they seemed surprised by the medical needs of their army. Soldiers went through clothing and shoes faster than they anticipated. And the cost of fighting for liberty was something they found continually shocking. So, it is also hardly surprising that they gave little thought to what they might do with any prisoners taken, either loyalist or British, or how they would act when their own troops were seized. What is perhaps surprising is that the British seemed equally unprepared for the phenomenon of taking captives and of being captured. This should not have been something that caught them unaware. Taking and exchanging prisoners were central parts of European and imperial wars, and they were already familiar with the niceties of exchange negotiations.[9]

However, despite this lack of preparedness, both sides quickly began to formulate policies to deal with captives. When, in the fall of 1775, the colonists stopped to think about the treatment of prisoners, both those they held and their own taken, many assumed that it would be governed by the informal conventions under which all European armies at the time operated. Under those, officers were treated in a way that honored and recognized their rank, and soldiers were treated in ways dictated by conditions. Both were exchanged as speedily as possible.

Despite these conventions, neither the colonists nor the British could be sanguine about the fate of their prisoners for several reasons. History showed that there were a great many variables in addition to rank that governed the treatment of prisoners. Some of these were philosophical, others practical. Struggles involving Indian allies changed the possibilities again. Additionally, in wars of rebellion, that is, domestic struggles against constituted authority, history had shown that less gentlemanly rules applied for both sides.

Even when war took place between nations who engaged in prisoner exchanges, the practice was far from fixed and immutable. It was a relatively recent phenomenon, and its philosophical and practical underpinnings were themselves in a state of flux. Philosophically, from the seventeenth century onward, two ideas had been undergoing exposition and revision: one was the idea of humanitarian treatment, and the other was ransom. Since ancient times, men of any rank held as prisoners of war could ransom themselves if they could come up with the money. By the late seventeenth century, this was becoming formalized. International agreements set ransom prices for men of each rank. Not surprisingly, these prices reflected the social value of the person involved. One French agreement set the ransom for a general at 50,000 livres. The ransom for a private soldier was set at 7.[10]

At the same time that ransom arrangements were becoming formal, others were thinking about the problem of prisoners in humanistic terms. Hugo Grotius, a Dutch scholar who had been imprisoned for four years for his political associations and beliefs, thought that captured soldiers and officers had need of humanitarian protection. His book, *The Rights of War and Peace*, was published in 1625. In it, he wrote that men had natural rights "so purely personal" they could not "be lost even in captivity." His influential book did not immediately transform international relations, but it did cause people to think in new ways about the problem. There was a turning point in 1648 when, under the Treaty of Westphalia that ended the Thirty Years' War, prisoners of all ranks were not ransomed; they were simply exchanged.[11]

In the eighteenth century, philosophers developed these ideas further. Montesquieu, in *The Spirit of Laws*, published in 1748, argued that nations should conduct wars inflicting "as little harm as possible." He rejected outright the execution or enslavement of prisoners. Rather, all nations had to conduct war in accordance with "the laws relative to their mutual intercourse, which is what we call the *law of nations*." This law required "strict justice" in their relations, and that extended to the treatment of prisoners. Another Frenchman, Emmerich Vattel, asserted in *The Law of Nations* that as soon as an enemy had surrendered, the captors had "no further right over his life." He cautioned a victorious army to remember that its prisoners "are men, and unfortunate."[12]

While these philosophical ideas were evolving, there were practical considerations that encouraged nations to be friendly to the possibility of exchange. Neither side wanted the burden of feeding or caring for prisoners. It was also easier for armies to recruit soldiers and officers if they had some assurance that attempts would be made to retrieve them in the event of capture.

These practical considerations outweighed the two main advantages of having prisoners. The obvious one was that the enemy lost the service of those held. The other was that captives might be coerced or enticed into changing allegiance and join the enemy. Since, at the time, many men serving in European armies had been born in a country other than the one in whose army they served, they often felt no particular emotional attachment to it. Also, some rulers simply hired out their soldiers. In such cases, the men serving often resented being sent far from home. Both sides, then, had reasons for wanting their own troops back. Whatever the exchange agreement, it could take months, and sometimes years, to be reached. As Simeon Moulton, a New Hampshire private, remembered, this could result in "onspeakable sufrings Such as no man can tell without undergoing the Same."[13]

By the second half of the eighteenth century, informal conventions were common. Some of these showed the flexible, pragmatic ways in which philosophy and expediency were mixed together. For example, the fate of the prisoners taken by the British at Fort Frontenac in 1758 during the Seven Years' War shows the ways in which commanders altered exchange practices to suit their own needs. During that war, the British and the French enacted a series of cartels to exchange prisoners. In this case, the British lieutenant colonel John Bradstreet and his troops had overwhelmed the French fort after a short siege. When the French commander, Major Pierre-Jacques Noyen, ran up a flag of truce, Bradstreet proposed terms for accepting the French force's surrender. One of these was that they would all be marched immediately to Albany. Once there, arrangements would be made for their exchange for British and provincial prisoners held by the French. Noyen quickly consented to this transaction.[14]

However, inside the fort, the British found a depleted garrison of only 110 soldiers, many of whom were wounded, and a large number of women and children. The next day Bradstreet gave the French an even better deal: he told them they could go directly to Montreal unescorted and exchange themselves. Noyen gave his word that he would send back the British and colonial prisoners in compliance with the terms of the agreement. Bradstreet was being pragmatic. He did not want to be burdened by the wounded, women, and children, preferring instead that his troops make a dash back to Albany unencumbered. Gentry and military conventions of the time meant that he could make this arrangement with a European ally, certain that the agreement would be honored.[15]

Sometimes commanders exacted a more compelling guarantee than a gentleman's word, taking hostages as an extra incentive to assure compliance with the terms. This happened when the young George Washington surrendered to the French at Fort Necessity in 1754. Again the victorious commander wanted the return of his own imprisoned men held by the enemy, but, not wanting to be burdened with prisoners himself, he had them exchange themselves. The French, however, took two provincial Virginia officers with them as an insurance policy. It is a testimony to the acceptance of the practice of exchange and its utilitarian value that such a deal could be negotiated without war even having been officially declared between the two sides.[16]

Commanders expected men on each side to respect the terms of their surrender, but this was especially true for officers. Since officers on both sides were gentlemen, all felt bound by any promise they made. Soldiers could make no such promises. This was partly because their low status meant that their word did not count for much; it was also because others governed their actions. Soldiers had to do whatever they were told to do. Consequently, only officers truly had responsibility for their actions. By the eighteenth century, this had come to mean that officers could give their word of honor to stay out of the fighting, not attempt to escape, and live quietly as gentlemen until their exchange. Soldiers could not be trusted to do so and therefore had to be confined.

Having given his word to not attempt to escape, an officer was referred to as being on parole. While on parole, he usually had to live in a community designated by the captor but was allowed to live in whatever style he could afford and even send for his family if he wished. This system worked because an officer's honor was at stake, and it was understood that a gentleman would never do anything to compromise it. Consequently, as Vattel observed, a captor releasing an officer on parole felt "as secure of him as if it had detained him in the closest prison."[17]

Some officers during their captivity enjoyed living in the same high style they did at home. Certainly the two Virginia provincial officers taken at Fort Necessity did. After a brief stay in Fort Duquesne, they were taken to Quebec where they enjoyed the pleasures of that city's society. One of them, Captain Robert Stobo, even entered into a business arrangement with a leading merchant there. The men had freedom of movement in a wide area around the city until the French discovered that Stobo had secretly supplied the British with a map of

Fort Duquesne. This violated the terms of his parole. He was convicted of spying and sentenced to death. However, a spy was typically someone out of uniform pretending to be an innocent civilian. Stobo was recognized to be a military officer but one who had violated the trust placed in him. That was a shameful act, but not a death penalty offense. The French government chose caution and suspended his sentence. From then on, Stobo's movement was more restricted, but he still lived in conditions of some comfort. He also could receive guests. Even his repeated attempts to escape did not make his captors treat him as anything less than a gentleman.[18]

Not every officer held in captivity enjoyed the comforts that Stobo found in Quebec, but neither did they suffer the hardships their soldiers endured while in captivity. The adventures of one young Massachusetts provincial in the Seven Years' War reveal the range of soldiers' experiences and the complications that came from large international conflicts. Stephen Cross was one of eighteen men, all experienced boat builders, recruited from the town of Newbury to build boats for the British and provincial troops on Lake Ontario in 1756. The hapless Newbury men were captured after the French and their Indian allies besieged Forts Ontario and Oswego. Under the terms of the surrender, they had to go to Montreal, then Quebec, escorted by French soldiers.[19]

Once in Quebec, it was clear that the prisoners faced varied futures. One group was sent to England, probably to be part of an exchange. Other prisoners were offered a chance for freedom of movement if they went to work in the countryside of New France, which a number of them volunteered to do. The Newbury men were sent to France to be held awaiting a cartel. The journey to France marked the beginning of their real misery. Trapped in close confinement below deck for much of the day, the men could do little to alleviate their suffering. Bad food, a terrible storm at sea, and poor ventilation all made them feel "benighted and Distressed." The men were philosophical about the fact that their officers not only did not suffer with them but also did nothing to aid them. The officers had freedom to move around the quarterdeck and dine with the French officers, and the men saw that as a fact of their relative positions in life. They also realized that if the officers were to help them, it would jeopardize the freedom they enjoyed, if not their lives. So, as Cross reflected, "[W]e Could not Blame them for our close Confinement."[20]

Winter found the imprisoned soldiers in Brest, France. After a period there, they were marched to a castle over 100 miles away to wait for a cartel. As part of an international group being held, the Newbury men and other provincials joined Dutch, Swedish, and Guernsey seamen, around 1,400 prisoners altogether, Cross estimated. For all of them, their conditions would have been truly pitiful had it not been for the provisions of the will of a local wealthy widow. Over the years, she had taken pity on the men she had seen held at the castle. After her death, she provided for money to be paid to each "cloas confined" prisoner so he could buy food. She had also donated an acre of land to be used as a burying ground. Both were resources the prisoners would need as winter approached.[21]

Despite better food, close confinement and cold took a terrible toll. Cross reported that by the end of their time there, the widow's acre had been "almost Dug over." When sick, the men were moved to hospital quarters. Some tried to stay out of it as long as possible as the typical report of conditions there "[s]trikes a terror to us." When illness forced Cross to the hospital, he entered with "verry Gloomy Aprehensions." As he walked in, he fully expected to "Joyn the happy Company of Saints which Surrounds the throne of God." Fortunately, Cross recovered.[22]

Cross's odyssey soon came to an end. He was exchanged, returned to Newbury, and led a long and productive life, but many of his friends had not been so lucky. They had been buried along the way, often interred in the most cursory way. Cross's adventure reveals the harsh realities of soldiers' experiences as prisoners of war. It also shows that the more delays that were involved and the more complex the international exchanges were, the greater the hardship that befell soldiers.

The ways in which agreements were negotiated between European armies were always fluid. When native allies were involved, things became even more uncertain. This was because Indian allies were frequently not consulted about the terms of any surrender, nor were their goals or interests considered. They therefore did not regard themselves party to any agreement European or colonial officers made. This was a recipe for confusion and occasionally disaster.

Native peoples had their own conventions surrounding prisoners. Some of these were particular to their communities; others they shared with Europeans. Taking captives had been central to war in the region long before the arrival of Europeans. Prisoners were part of the spoils of war and were sought for ransom, sacrifice, or adoption. The last was part of those communities whose culture required dead warriors to be replaced. After Europeans arrived on the continent, the taking of captives by both sides became a source of tension between them. Both parties quickly discovered that ransom was a practice they shared. Throughout the colonial period, British and French colonial authorities and private individuals paid ransoms to redeem captives taken by different groups of native peoples.[23]

European or colonial principals were hardly unaware of Indian needs; 150 years of intermittent warfare had educated them. In the Seven Years' War, Indian allies were not paid, individually or collectively, for their support of either side. The traditional spoils of war were to be their reward. So when European or colonial officers ignored Indian desires, it was more commonly due to their sense of cultural or racial superiority and a desire to hold to European conventions rather than to lack of knowledge. For example, when Cross and others were first taken prisoner, they were held for a night in Fort Ontario under French guard. The guard, Cross remembered, was to prevent the prisoners from escaping and "to Prevent the Indians from Murthering us." The French knew their Indian allies operated with different conventions.[24]

Newbury men such as Cross knew it, too. On this occasion, while Cross and his fellows were being protected, they heard that the Indians had taken others prisoner, especially the sick. Also, among the Indians they passed along the way to Quebec, Cross noticed several former provincial soldiers "Picked off, from us in times Passed" who were now "Dressed and Painted" in Indian fashion. Cross gave no indication that he and his friends saw these men as deserters. Presumably they had been adopted.[25]

When European commanders completely ignored native needs, the results could be disastrous. One such occasion was when the British lieutenant colonel George Monro surrendered to the Marquis de Montcalm, the French commander, at Fort William Henry in 1757. Each man assumed both sides would honor the terms of the surrender, which were generous. Montcalm allowed the British to keep their possessions; he assumed responsibility for caring for the British sick and wounded and agreed to repatriate them when they recovered; and he let the defeated British leave to go to the British-held Fort Edward. All he required in exchange was that the British troops stay out of military action for a year and a half and that they return French prisoners held by the British.[26]

However, Montcalm had not consulted his Indian allies on this issue. They had been expecting the victory to bring rewards to them, too. Now, the Indians, disgusted at the way the French had treated them, decided to take matters into their own hands. They attacked the British, the provincial troops, and their dependents as they departed the fort, leaving about sixty-nine dead and many more missing. The French, horrified by what had happened and feeling the slight to their honor in the eyes of the British, tried to retrieve as many of the prisoners as they could from their allies. They did this mostly by paying a ransom themselves to get the prisoners back.[27]

This was by far the most egregious breach of European wartime etiquette of the Seven Years' War. Not surprisingly, it made British commanders reluctant to go along with the conventions of honorable surrender in the future, not only because native allies introduced uncertainty into the equation but also because the British desired revenge. They did not completely depart from familiar conventions, but they drew back from the spirit of trust and generosity that had characterized them before.[28]

Making the British stance more complicated was their relationship with their own native allies. The British and provincials themselves had not insisted on following European conventions with their own allies from the earliest days of the war. One of their first compromises was in the summer of 1755, when a provincial army under Sir William Johnson and his Mohawk allies defeated the French, under Baron de Dieskau, and his native allies at Lake George. The provincials captured the wounded Dieskau and twenty other French soldiers. Johnson, who had long-standing relations with the Mohawk through diplomacy, trade, and marriage, knew well the needs of his Indian allies. The Mohawk needed captives to replace their fallen warriors in order to meet the demands of their ritual mourning war. Johnson, acknowledging his most important obligation under the demands of European honor, held onto the aristocratic commander, Dieskau. However, he handed over some of the other wounded to the Mohawk and kept that information from the governor of Massachusetts, to whom he reported.[29]

Throughout the Seven Years' War, when the British and colonial Americans were fighting native peoples, multiple factors affected the possibility of exchanging prisoners, not the least of which was a lack of mutual trust. In May 1760, William Bull, the governor of South Carolina, had observed in connection with prisoners that faith was "sacred between Enemies" but that, in the case of native peoples, faith was hard for both sides to sustain. A good example of the complications that resulted from that lack of faith occurred when the British officer Paul Demere surrendered his garrison at Fort Loudoun to the Cherokee in August 1760. Things did not go as planned. Under the terms negotiated, the British troops and their dependents were supposed to have been escorted on their way to safety, but they were attacked shortly after they left. The ambush left 29 dead and 120 prisoners. It is unclear whether this had been the Cherokee's intent all along, or if the moderates among the Cherokee were unable to restrain those who wanted revenge for earlier wrongs, or if the British provoked the attack by violating the terms of their departure somehow. What is clear is that resolving the fate of the remaining prisoners became tangled in divisions within each side as well as between them. Moderate Cherokee leaders had to restrain extreme elements in their own communities and tried to stave off any British revenge attacks by quickly opening negotiations. Some Cherokee leaders hoped these could be part of a larger peace negotiation. James Grant, the British commander sent again to fight the Cherokee in the Carolinas, was also inclined to be pragmatic and look for a compromise. However, doing so openly became politically impossible. Governor Bull found he could not pursue a peace plan while the public clamored for revenge for the attack. Grant's pragmatism was also opposed by Sir Jeffrey Amherst, overall commander of the British forces in North America. He thought the Cherokee "feign a Repentance" and that they had to be "punished . . . and that severely." Still, Grant was on the scene and was inclined to be practical given continued Cherokee strength, and even Governor Bull sought quietly to ransom the prisoners with trade goods. By these means, individual prisoners were slowly ransomed, and by spring the following year, most had been redeemed. The lack of trust between the two sides and the fact that each sought to gain the maximum amount from those held complicated any negotiations.[30]

So, the conventions of European war, fluid for intellectual and practical reasons, were flexible, and they were adjusted as the occasion required. However, the American Revolution did not begin as a war between two rival nations; rather, it began as a war between an imperial power and its colonial dependents. The colonists knew that was the situation, but they expected that, since they were fighting in the manner and style of European armies, European conventions would apply. As Washington reminded British general Thomas Gage in August 1775 when he inquired about prisoners held, "Obligations arising from the Rights of Humanity, & Claims of Rank, are universally binding and extensive." Since all the principals were gentlemen, surely they could agree to do the gentlemanly thing.[31]

Of course, this was an easier position for the colonists to take than it was for the British. Just as in determining how the enemy dead should be buried or how communications should be addressed, the British were reluctant to do anything that appeared to recognize formally the Continental army or any other colonial soldiers. For them, this was not a war against an external enemy but against domestic rebels. They saw their captives as traitors who should be tried for treason and not as prisoners subject to exchange.

However, this was also a situation with which the British had had some experience. This was not the first war of recent times in which the state had been involved in a conflict with an internal enemy. In the previous century, it had been embroiled in a bloody civil war in which the forces of Parliament had triumphed over those of the king. At the outbreak of the war in 1642, the king had declared that all who opposed him should be hanged as traitors, and certainly some prisoners taken were executed. The Parliamentarians were, on occasion, equally ruth-less. However, a more pragmatic approach to those taken captive soon evolved, especially because the two sides were well matched and each held significant numbers of the other's soldiers. This did not necessarily lead to good treatment. Prisoners of both sides could count on being robbed of any item remotely valu-able by their captors. They could count on rough treatment, hunger, confinement in unsanitary places, and pressure to come over to fight on the captor's side. But as the war progressed, they could also usually count on being exchanged for men of equivalent rank or being sent home on their word that they would stay out of the fighting in the future. In the winter of 1643–44, the Royalist Sir George Goring and Sir William Waller of the Parliamentary forces were able to negoti-ate a large prisoner exchange. Sir William's "droll" greeting to Sir George in his letter proposing negotiations appears to have swung Goring's sentiments in favor of the exchange. "Noble Lord," Sir William began, "God's blessing be upon your heart, you are the jolliest Neighbour I ever met with." Most cartel arrange-ments probably did not begin so cordially, but, despite some very bloody excep-tions and great hardship experienced by soldiers, exchange and parole became commonplace.[32]

A century later, during the Scottish Highland rebellion of 1745, the British again had to find a way to deal with prisoners whom they saw as traitors rather than as prisoners of war. In the beginning, the government had ruled that there was to be no "cartel for the exchange of prisoners." The bloody rebellion was one that the British army put down without officially changing that policy. How-ever, in practice, the policy created enormous complications.[33]

The first of these complications was the question of what the British army should do with the prisoners it captured during the rebellion. In the middle of the struggle, some British commanders were not inclined to wait for the process of law, and sometimes captives were executed without a trial. However, the Brit-ish commander, the Duke of Cumberland, was occasionally cautious about do-ing that. In December 1745, he "did not care" to put the prisoners he held to death when the enemy "have so many of our Prisoners in their Hands." He was not opposed to prisoners being killed; he just did not want to be seen to do it. So, he "encouraged the Country People to do it, as they may fall in their way." The army also did not want to be burdened by supplying and guarding prison-ers until they might be tried. So, they deposited prisoners in convenient town jails so that the towns bore the burden of care instead. However, in such jails, se-curity was sometimes lax, and a number of men escaped from them.[34]

At the end of the rebellion, the British had hundreds of prisoners that they were determined to try for treason as quickly as possible. A particularly large number were in Carlisle, where a Jacobite (rebel) garrison had surrendered at the end of 1745 and prisoners from other locations were sent. The numbers involved made the legal process enormously complicated. The government resorted to processing the prisoners by lots, sifting through each batch to find those who might easily be shown leniency, for example, the sick, those who might bear witness against others, or those who were very young.[35]

This was just the beginning of their problems. Carlisle quickly became overcrowded with prisoners, dependents, witnesses, clerks, prosecutors, and their servants. Crown prosecutors struggled to find witnesses to testify and identify reliably each of the accused. Even when they could bring witnesses in, the town had become so crowded that some of them "had not a bed to lye on" and threatened to leave. Once in the courtroom, prosecutors had difficulty finding sympathetic juries. Even when some prisoners avoided a trial by pleading guilty to treason in exchange for a sentence of transportation to the colonies, the problems did not end. Many men had been taken prisoner with their dependent wives and children, who also wanted to be transported, even though they had not been tried and convicted. It is hardly surprising, then, that when King George II read the report of the last trial connected to the rebellion, he scribbled on a minute attached to it, "I am glad this tedious affair is over."[36]

Apart from the legal and logistical issues connected to prisoners taken during a rebellion, the no-exchange policy had another unforeseen side effect: it made British allies nervous. The British had recruited Hessian mercenaries to help them put down the uprising, and the Hessians were uncomfortable with the rule that prohibited cartels. This meant that the Duke of Cumberland was hesitant to put any of the Hessian soldiers into situations where they would be at risk of capture. Consequently, he held the Hessians back from action, though he did so secretly at the time.[37]

As war broke out in the colonies in 1775, the same problem reared its head. In September of that year, Sir Joseph Yorke, a British diplomat in The Hague working to recruit Hessian troops to help the British, quickly made the connection between the circumstances of 1745 and 1775. He asked the government not to repeat the "very embarrassing" situation of the earlier conflict in which prisoners could not be exchanged. He was afraid that if the Hessian soldiers got to America and discovered this policy a second time, the British would not find them "pliable." The British secretary of state, Lord Germain, in turn encouraged

General William Howe, occupying Boston, to figure out a way to exchange prisoners with the patriots because of "possible difficulties" involving "foreign troops."[38]

Future Hessian recruits and their commanders were not the only ones concerned about this; both the British and colonial forces in North America were, too. By the end of 1775, British and colonial troops imprisoned by the other were languishing in each other's jails. The British, tied to the point of honor concerning rebel troops and forgetting for the moment the practical problems involved, were in a difficult position. They refused to accord colonial soldiers the status of prisoners of war, but they wanted back their own men held captive. The colonists wanted their men given appropriate military status.

The British became creative. In February 1776, Lord Germain reminded Howe that he could not "enter into any treaty or agreement with the Rebels for a regular cartel." However, Germain suggested that Howe's "own discretion will suggest to you the means of effecting such exchange, without the King's dignity and honour being committed, or His Majesty's name used in any negotiations for the purpose." In other words, Howe had to arrange cartels but call them by another name. Germain encouraged him to do it on the grounds of "expediency."[39]

This willingness to exchange on the grounds of expediency did not immediately make all matters easy; it simply began a whole other round of complications. The exact powers and responsibilities of the Continental Congress to negotiate for, support, and try to protect its soldiers held by others were not enumerated anywhere. The thirteen colonies, each of which raised its own troops and militia in addition to its Continental regiments, wanted to retain a voice in the treatment and exchange of their own men. The Congressional resolution on exchanges in 1776 left things vague. It specified that exchanges should be on a rank-for-like-rank basis but gave the commanders in each department of the Continental army the power to negotiate. It also gave the states the "right to make any exchange they think proper for prisoners taken from them or by them." And if this left Americans unclear as to who had authority at any time, the British certainly were unsure with whom they should be negotiating.[40]

This problem was just the beginning. Maneuvering by each side to gain the best advantage from the negotiations further complicated matters. The British might be tempted to delay an exchange when the American prisoners held were men serving for short terms. Delay meant that soldiers could be held until almost the end of their service contracts. This denied Washington the men's service not only while they were in confinement but also afterward. Of course, this maneuvering also worked against the British as it delayed the return of their own troops; they, too, suffered from manpower losses due to desertion and disease and lacked much needed reinforcements. Also the prisoners' conditions could become part of the discussion. In the spring of 1777, Washington chided Howe that men who had been healthy when they were seized were returned to him in poor physical condition. He claimed that the men were "reduced to such extremity" that they effectively "continued as your prisoners." True as this claim was, such charges and countercharges were grist for the mill of exchange negotiations.[41]

Similarly, tensions surrounding the imprisonment of important figures from either side delayed the exchange process and shifted focus away from men of lesser rank. For example, concern over the imprisonment of General Charles Lee, captured by the British in December of 1776, was a great distraction. It was unclear how he was ever to be exchanged as the Americans held no British officer of exchangeable rank. The situation was resolved when the Americans finally captured an appropriate British officer six months later, and Washington then prepared "immediately" to make a deal with Howe. Additionally, focus on the trials and executions of officers of each side as spies stalled other exchange discussions. Officers faced charges of spying if they were captured out of uniform. The trials of Continental captain Nathan Hale and British major John André were particularly notorious. Cases that were sensational or involved high-ranking men complicated exchange discussions as each side considered the possibilities of retaliation.[42]

Despite this chaotic situation, some conventions did emerge. Informal cartels took place with each rank exchanged for like rank, one to one, and soldiers exchanged in batches. While throughout the war, each side probably took about the same number of prisoners, it was rare for them each to have the same number at any one time, and so exchanges were intermittent. Many were like the exchanges that Washington and Howe negotiated between July and September 1776. With the plan confirmed by Congress of exchanges of rank for like rank, the two men began working out the details. Both sides were most concerned about the men of highest rank. In September, Howe was very specific about the exchange of General William Alexander (Lord Stirling, captured near New York) on the American side and Montfort Browne (governor of Nassau in the Bahamas, captured in a naval action) on the British side. Howe gave Washington a list of the British officers of lesser rank that Howe believed were held prisoner. He made it clear that if there were any errors or omissions from the list, Washington should add the officers' names and "just put opposite to their names such of your officers of equal rank as you would have in exchange for them." The names of British NCOs and privates believed held were not sent, "being unnecessary," but he assured Washington that he would "redeem them by a like number of those [prisoners] in my possession." Howe and Washington had arranged a formal cartel, though Howe was not allowed to call it such.[43]

For the British, the legal issues of exchange altered when the war became an international conflict in 1778. They formally acknowledged prisoners from other nations as bone fide prisoners of war. Finally in 1782, Parliament relented and allowed formal cartels for Americans "according to the custom and usage of war and the law of nations." This decision simply gave formal authority to a system that had been working more or less effectively during the whole war.[44]

Of course, the system did not work, and was never intended to work, with native allies and enemies. During the American Revolution, just as in the Seven Years' War, relations with native peoples changed the nature of prisoner exchanges. Whenever war raged on the frontier, exchanges were rare and were complicated by entrenched racial attitudes and social tensions.

Shortly after the Revolutionary War began, South Carolina was quick to formalize this different state of affairs. In the summer of 1776, the newly independent state was facing increasing conflict with the Cherokee nation on its western frontier. The Cherokee were joined by loyalists, and both were encouraged and supplied by the British. By early fall, the South Carolina assembly had to come up with a policy to deal with prisoners from groups not considered to be worthy of the usual conventions. The issue was a pressing one. Prisoners were already in the hands of each side. In considering legislation, the assembly was trying to bring order to a situation threatening to escalate out of control.[45]

Tensions ran high in the west. Some patriot soldiers had long-standing tensions with the Cherokee, but many also had grievances with their white neighbors. Old scores played out as neighbors divided into patriot or loyalist affiliations. Reports from the west already indicated that patriot soldiers were "exasperated" and wanted to give "no quarter." In other words, they wanted to take no prisoners and simply kill those who fell into their hands, Indian or loyalist. Indeed, when thirteen loyalist soldiers were seized, a couple of whom were "painted as Indians," the chief justice of South Carolina himself lamented privately that it would have been a public service "had they been all instantly hanged." He also told a correspondent that there were many other influential people who agreed with him. The chief justice was not content just to deny loyalists treatment as either prisoners of war or citizens subject to trial by jury; he also had a suggestion for the Cherokee: he wanted all their towns burnt and all prisoners taken to be held as slaves, becoming the "property of the taker." Patriot soldiers agreed. One officer whose troops had captured three Cherokee prisoners tried to hold them until he had formal instructions. However, he was pressured by his men to give in. They insisted that the prisoners had to be either sold for slaves or killed.[46]

Fortunately, cooler heads prevailed in the Carolina legislature. It never considered moving to European-style exchanges in its frontier wars; however, it did see the problems with outright slaughter or enslavement of its enemies. Even apart from the legal issues involved, the legislature realized such practices would lead to many difficulties. They would "obstruct and impede a future peace, give the *Indians* a precedent that may be fatal to those of our own people who may unfortunately fall into their hands, and prevent a mutual exchange of prisoners—an object of too much consequence to be put out of our power."[47]

The South Carolina assembly sought to find some middle ground. It completely rejected enslavement but came nowhere close to European conventions. In September 1776, it resolved instead to pay a reward of £75 for every Indian man killed. This required a certificate of verification from a commanding officer and the scalp produced as evidence in Charleston. It offered a £100 reward for taking an Indian man prisoner, the extra money presumably an incentive not to kill. It also offered an £80 reward for "every other prisoner," a reference to loyalists. The assembly had tried to satisfy the various social pressures and exigencies of war. Soldiers got a financial reward as if the prisoner had become property to be sold. Indians would either be killed or held prisoner. Loyalists and Indians held would give the patriots men to exchange to get their own back. And patriot officers now had incentives to offer their men to encourage restraint.[48]

It was not only on the southern frontier that the war became more brutal and exchanges less frequent; it happened wherever Indians and colonists fought. On General John Sullivan's campaign against the Iroquois in 1779, few prisoners were taken on either side. Records from the expedition note few Indian captives taken. After one skirmish that left seventeen of the enemy dead, the patriots took only two prisoners: "a Tory & a Negro." One occasion, referred to by many officers who kept journals, involved the seizing of a junior officer and a soldier by the Indians. The officer, Lieutenant Thomas Boyd, and his party of twenty-six men had attacked some Indians and then found themselves attacked in turn. A few survivors made it back to camp to tell the tale, and a burial party went out to do its duty. However, the bodies of Boyd and one soldier were missing. Later, the advancing expedition came across their bodies, horribly mutilated. Prisoners in the frontier war were few and far between.[49]

The problems surrounding the legal status of the American prisoners and the logistical problems of cartels and maneuvering by each side, compounded by the racial and social dimensions of the frontier war, meant long delays in exchanges. These delays contributed greatly to the sufferings of soldiers held by both sides. Even when the legal status of prisoners was clear, such as that of the British and Hessian, confusion about who was to have custody, who was to pay to support them, and how they were to be exchanged added to the misery of their experiences. For patriot troops of any branch of the service, the uncertainties that surrounded their status and support meant that standards of treatment varied widely. Even once regular exchanges were carried out, the numbers held captive at any one place or time, the personality of individual commanders, and the resources available to them had a great impact on the kinds of conditions in which prisoners found themselves. Neither side in the war could claim the moral high ground in their treatment of prisoners.[50]

The first contentious issue of the war for patriot leaders was ensuring the appropriate treatment of their officers held by the British. They wanted to be sure that they would be treated according to their status as gentlemen. Colonial officers, given the uncertainty about their legal status, wanted to be clear at least about their social status. Washington responded quickly to perceived slights to his officers' honor. A brief exchange between Washington and General Gage in the summer of 1775 saw each man defending his position. Washington accused Gage of holding colonial officers "indiscriminately," that was, holding them with soldiers without any distinctions of rank. Washington felt that respect for the honors of rank was a requirement so basic that any political disagreements between the two parties or legal niceties were "foreign to this Point." Gage, in response, conceded that he had held colonial prisoners without regard to rank because "I acknowledge no Rank that is not derived from the King." However, Washington countered that a rank derived from the "uncorrupted Choice of a brave and free People" was equally worthy of respect. The fact that Washington held some British officers prisoners gave him leverage in this discussion.[51]

American officers held "indiscriminately" railed against the insult. From the moment of his captivity in September 1775, Colonel Ethan Allen challenged British officers to show him "gentleman-like" treatment. Some responded as he hoped; others did not. His captors had orders to treat Allen roughly and held him in chains for a brief period alongside private soldiers. Later, freed from his leg irons, some British officers treated him with kindness and invited him to dine with them. One commander sent Allen "a fine breakfast and dinner from his own table, and a bottle of good wine." Still, there were occasional insults.

One time, he was barred from taking the air on deck because "it was a place for gentlemen." This comment, of course, was a red rag to a bull. As a gentleman, Allen asserted his right to walk on the deck. However, finally being ordered off by the captain, he went below, not because he conceded the point but "to set an example to the ship's crew, who ought to obey him." In true gentlemanly fashion, Allen understood the need for the captain's rank to be respected even by his enemies.[52]

Other officers were sensitive to perceived slights even when they were held separately and in much better conditions than their soldiers. In January 1777, Colonel Samuel Miles, held in New York, wrote to Joseph Reed, the adjutant general, complaining of his and his colleagues' suffering while confined with the British. He wrote that he would not "in the least Murmer" at being a prisoner had he and the others been treated in a manner that their "Caractor as Officers . . . call'd for." Additionally, Miles charged that Congress also was slighting them. It had been delinquent in both negotiating an exchange and in getting their pay to them, which left them "destitute of cash."[53]

The last was a critical issue for all imprisoned men. Each side was supposed to augment the prison rations by providing its imprisoned soldiers and officers with their pay or an allowance so they could purchase additional necessities. This was done through an agent. The best known American agent was Elias Boudinot. He used his own money and borrowed "on my own private Security" to provide necessities for American prisoners held while Congress contemplated how much it might commit. The longest serving British agent was a former British army officer and New England loyalist, Joshua Loring.[54]

When allocating resources to prisoners, Boudinot and Congress knew that officers needed more than soldiers. Congress had agreed to provide money for prisoners held "according to their ranks and pay in the continental service." The money was to be paid to an agent whose mandate was to provide the prisoners with "proper provisions and cloathing." Boudinot, the first appointed agent, was energetic. He provided much needed cash and goods to officers. However, since Congress was usually providing money to Boudinot after the fact, reimbursing him for his expenses, he rarely passed on money directly to soldiers. He functioned more as a quartermaster, making large purchases for distribution.[55]

This did not mean that Boudinot's compassionate aid to soldiers was trivial. It was significant and brought some relief. Indeed, even when Congress was dragging its feet about reimbursing his expenses, he continued to supply prisoners when he heard "of the death of several more than had been usual." However, he knew that the distinctions of rank, social and military, had to be maintained.

In 1780, Boudinot provided 300 officers held in New York with a "handsome suit of Cloathes" and 1,100 soldiers "with a plain suit." For soldiers he tried to augment their rations from the British by supplying "Bread & Beef."[56]

Congress also believed that officers needed more compensation than their pay to assist them. For example, when allocating cash for prisoners in 1780, it designated over $45,000 for officers. This was to provide for food, clothing, and lodging to all officers regardless of rank and to help them meet their expenses. Additionally, a portion of it had to be distributed to those who had been held the longest. At the same time, Congress provided just over $6,000 for all sick soldiers and seamen held. The money was for necessaries and "contingent expences." While we do not have an accurate total of the number of officers and men held at this or any other time, we can be sure that the number of soldiers and seamen held was much greater than the number of officers held. Without being able to do an exact calculation, it appears that the relative allocation of resources at least mirrored the pay differential and possibly increased it.[57]

Officers, and society at large, knew that gentlemen needed more financial support than soldiers because they were expected to live at a different level, even in confinement. Although a few officers were held "indiscriminately" early in the war, later practice reinforced the social and military distinctions of rank. The conditions in which officers were held varied. When large numbers of officers were taken at one time, they were sometimes required temporarily to sleep in a confined space. Even so, they were separate from their men and usually had freedom to move around the town in which they were held. After a brief period of this kind of confinement, officers typically were on parole, living in designated communities and lodging in private homes.[58]

All this took money. If an officer had resources, that is, either access to cash or credit, his standard of living was greatly improved. He was usually free to board wherever he might afford. Such resources greatly added to his comfort and his chances of staying in good health. So, for an officer, receiving his pay or any additional financial support transformed his experience of captivity.

Soldiers, with little access to money and kept in close confinement, had little opportunity to alter their circumstances. I noted in chapter 2 how the difference between the financial resources of officers and soldiers had an impact on health and welfare under normal conditions. Then, low pay made it hard for soldiers to purchase food to supplement the ration allocated to them. Low pay also tempted them to sell their clothing. This often left the men cold and poorly nourished. However, we also saw that soldiers were resourceful. They were able to forage for food, hunt, or steal to augment their rations. In winter, when firewood and food was in short supply, a local farmer's fencing or poultry provided a usable if illegal resource that kept body and soul together.

If this standard of living was severe in normal conditions, it became catastrophic in captivity. Soldiers were often held in cramped, poorly ventilated spaces and had little freedom of movement. The British provided a meager allowance of food, often of bad quality if not contaminated, and there was no means of supplementing it. Food vendors occasionally came by the prison ships or jails to try to sell food to those who had some ready cash. More commonly, low pay, unreliably delivered, left soldiers without the means of saving themselves. Few had the resources to purchase food supplements. Some were reduced to selling any good clothing they had, "[s]uch as buckskin briches or good coats," in order to buy food.[59]

The multiple accounts of prisoners tell the same story of ghastly captivity when they were held in large numbers on prison ships and in improvised jails. They told of long periods held in "confinement and starvation." One recounted a thirty-day period on a British prison ship in South Carolina in 1780 with only a pint of rice per day. A Connecticut militiaman, Levi Hanford, held in New York in the Sugar House Prison in 1777, remembered eating biscuits that were "full of worms and very mouldy." He and his friends found an ingenious way of combining this with the "old and unsavory" pork. They boiled water in a camp kettle, broke up the biscuit into it, which enabled them to skim off the worms, and then added the pork to make a stew. Sometimes they lacked the fuel to do even this. Hungry as they were, they ate it anyway as "there was nothing in the shape of food that was rejected, or that was unpalatable."[60]

The combination of cold and hunger was sometimes unbearable. Simeon Moulton, a Continental private, was taken prisoner with two others in January 1781 and sent to New York. There, they were kept in a loft with no source of heat, no covering on the windows, and ice already formed on the floor. Here is his account:

> We were vary thinly clothed & neither blankets nor straw but lay our bones on the cold frozen floor. . . . [H]ere we were locked in fast & not a spark of fier[.] our lownce was Six ounces of bread & three ounces of old meet rotten with rust & condemned by thair Stores [i.e., condemned as unfit for consumption by British soldiers] So thay gave it to us & the water was almost Poisen[.] we could not drink one Swolar without gaging . . . here we

were Parshing with cold threw the winter & in a State of Starvation the hool time[.] here I lost my nature & health for life[.] we were so much parished that it was Judged that we had not one Pound of flash on one of our frames.

He and his friends survived and were exchanged nine months later.[61]

The separate exchanges done by the Continental army and the states were part of the reason it took months for the men to be freed. The British had thought of exchanging Moulton and his companions as soon as they were seized. A British officer asked them if they were "nine months men or reglar," and they answered honestly that they were regulars, in the Continental army for three years or more. The British officer was disappointed. If they had been short-term soldiers, he could have exchanged them quickly for some of his own men held by the state. Since they were not, they had to go to city jails and wait there for a Continental exchange.[62]

In the grim conditions of captivity, some could not survive long enough to be exchanged. Held in close confinement, disease ran rampant. Thomas Boyd, a former prisoner, attributed their sickness to "the too great proximity of the excrements." Between foul air and inadequate food of bad quality, "it was not strange that disease and pestilence should prevail." Outbreaks of smallpox added to the misery. In these circumstances, men longed to be exchanged. For many, it was too late. As one militiaman remembered, they had "already been exchanged by that Being who has the power to set the captive free." God had liberated them through death.[63]

Compounding the problems of imprisoned soldiers was the fact that they suffered not only away from public view but also in circumstances where it was hard for their officers to offer any assistance. In normal camp life, soldiers' conditions could be improved by the efforts of active, energetic officers. In imprisonment, officers were often living some distance away from their confined men, and even if they could have contact and knew of their circumstances, there was little they could do to alleviate their suffering. Some officers did try. As noted above, Colonel Miles petitioned British officers on behalf of his men. However, these efforts were few and far between and had little impact.

In this circumstance, even compassionate and caring officers were often more concerned with their own problems. Lieutenant Henry Bedinger, a Virginian, worried about his soldiers even though dealing with his own distress and hardship took most of his time. Imprisoned after the surrender of Fort Washington at the end of 1776, he and his fellow officers were billeted in empty houses without fuel or provisions. They were not allowed a servant, and so, taking turns at the duty, they had to get coal and food, cook it as they could, and "tr[y] to keep from starving." His own problems consumed his time, though he knew his circumstances were comfortable compared to that of his men. His "poor Soldiers," he wrote, "fared most wretchedly different." One junior officer held in New York for two years after his capture at the Battle of Long Island in 1776 was shocked to see his men dressed in "Rotten Raggs close beset with unwelcome vermin," but he had no money to relieve them. Indeed, his time was taken up with getting assistance for his own sudden poverty. Lieutenant Jabez Fitch, who was also in New York at the same time, occasionally did go and visit his soldiers. He had been "Inform'd that the Prisoners in Genll: grow Remarkably sick & Die very fast." But for the most part, his diary was filled with his own struggles. He had to spend one day mending his clothes that were becoming ragged. He needed money and was able to borrow some from a fellow officer. This enabled him to buy good dinners supplied to him and his fellow officers by a local woman, Mrs. Archer. Indeed, it was Mrs. Archer who was initially the source of his information about the state of his soldiers. So, officers had little opportunity or means to help their men, even if they were motivated to do so.[64]

On the few occasions when officers and men were held together, officers were still unable to do very much to help. When Ethan Allen was held with his soldiers, they were all very short of food. He insisted that what little they had, had to be shared equally, even though his men offered him more. He felt it was important to set an "example of virtue and fortitude to our little commonwealth." He was active, badgering British officers with complaints and requests on behalf of himself and his men, particularly trying to get medical care for the sick, but with little success.[65]

Junior officers from privateers or merchant ships more commonly found themselves held with their men, and although they had a few extra comforts, they also felt helpless observing the misery around them. That was Thomas Dring's experience when he was held prisoner. He was a master's mate on board a privateer when he was captured and held for five months on the notorious *Jersey* prison ship in 1782. Dring had enough cash about him to buy some food from an enterprising woman who rowed out to the ship. He felt badly about being able to buy food when others were hungry, but he did not possess "the means of generosity, nor had any power to afford them relief." Still, he did not enjoy eating "in the presence of so many needy wretches."[66]

Imprisoned officers, for the most part, lived in a significantly different world. Even so, their welfare was very dependent on having access to money. Apart from a man's personal resources, having friends or family within striking distance or the kindness of their fellow officers could transform a man's experience in captivity. One Major Williams, while captive in New York in 1777, received forty silver dollars from a friend. He then lent three of his fellow officers ten dollars each so they could be provided with shoes, clothing, "and some other small matters." One young Connecticut officer was aided during his New York imprisonment in 1776 by "a Masonic brother." A colonel was able to arrange parole for a young ensign who had worked for him before the war. Major John Habersham, held in Charleston in 1780, got his brother to send him barrels of flour, clothes, and twenty pounds in cash. His brother told him he would have sent more money except there was a shortage of specie in Richmond, Virginia, where he lived, due to so many people sending it to "their friends in Captivity."[67]

Sometimes officers received cash in unanticipated ways. One young private was held with his company captain in New York, to be his servant. Even though they were free to walk around the city, they lacked "food, fuel and other necessaries." The captain was lucky because his servant was a tailor in civilian life. The private was able to work at his trade and earn "something to support himself and his Captain with, or otherwise they might both Starve to death, as they had no hard money." By this means, the private kept them both healthy. The private left no information about how this changed their relationship, if at all.[68]

When officers of the highest rank were imprisoned, they usually had no difficulty in gaining access to cash or credit and living in the style to which they were accustomed. When General Charles Lee was imprisoned, Washington at first feared that he was being badly treated for a man of his rank. However, Boudinot was able to report that Lee was confined to a "handsome House" and kept a "genteel table" while in captivity.[69]

In captivity, no pressure was put on gentlemen to change sides and join the enemy. No one would presume that he might compromise his honor by doing so. Soldiers, on the other hand, men without that kind of delicate honor, might be coerced. And indeed, they were continuously pressured to enlist in the British army. Some of the accounts of soldiers' enlisting with the enemy reveal the different perceptions of soldiers' honor. Some of them were contradictory. These contradictions came not only from officers and men about each other but also from men themselves. Kept in miserable conditions, a soldier could at any time remove himself from them by going over to the enemy. That so many died rather than do so is surely a testament to the fact that they understood on every level, personal and political, the meaning of going over to the other side and saw their honor at stake.[70]

In their public testimony during the war, soldiers adamantly proclaimed their reluctance to be coerced by the British. In their sworn affidavits to Congress, newly exchanged prisoners testified to the pressure that they had resisted and to their loyalty to the cause. They described occasions when the British, having met with little success in getting recruits, treated prisoners much more harshly. The prisoners, subject to the British articles of war in their confinement, were now flogged for "imaginary fault." One deponent conceded that a few took up the British offer of "pardons & protection; and money," but he described their actions as "dastardly." Most, he said, refused "to prostitute their *confinement to serve the Emissaries of the Prince of Darkness*." Decades later, another remembered that prisoners were so attached to their principles, their country, and "their honor" that men chose "the horrors of their dungeon, and in fact, even death itself" rather than enlist.[71]

But the reality was much more complicated. Some men did choose to enlist with the British, and despite the words above, few blamed them for it. When they wrote about it later in memoirs or declared it in their pension applications, they made no apologies. The veterans presented their British service as simply an extension of their imprisonment and their suffering. Provided there was some evidence that enlistment was coerced or done purely to relieve immediate suffering and was followed by attempts to escape from British service, the men were rarely censured.[72]

We have few glimpses into the thinking of the men as they wrestled with this decision. One was recorded by Colonel Ethan Allen. Allen, imprisoned himself, spoke to soldiers to hear their complaints. One young Pennsylvanian approached him who, Allen observed, was "reduced to a mere skeleton." The young man said that he and his brother had resolved to die before enlisting with the British, and indeed, his brother had died the night before. The young man himself, frail and weak, expected to die himself very soon. Allen was horrified at the young man's condition, and when they were alone, he whispered to the young man that he should enlist with the British to save himself and then desert at the first opportunity. Allen recounted that the young man "then asked, whether it was right in the sight of God! I assured him that it was." He told the private that it was a "duty to himself." The young man was delighted and agreed to do it. Allen's scruples about this action were not in encouraging the young man to enlist; it was in encouraging him to desert. He feared that his advice "should get air, and I should be closely confined in consequence of it." Allen was sure he had done the right thing. He was moved by the young man's willingness to die. He remembered later that "[t]he integrity of the suffering prisoners is hardly credible."[73]

Allen's narrative, first published during the war in 1779, revealed some of the different ways in which soldiers and officers perceived their honor. A gentleman's conduct always had to be above reproach. Allen never acted in any way that put his own reputation as a gentleman in doubt, even when that caused him hardship and inconvenience. As noted earlier, he even refused to be involved in an attempt to seize control of a ship on which he was held prisoner on the grounds of honor. Elias Boudinot felt similarly compromised when the imprisoned General Lee asked him to carry a secret letter to Congress. Unwilling to betray or compromise his reputation with the British, Boudinot refused.[74]

There was a rare occasion when an officer broke his parole and escaped. Lieutenant William "Long Bill" Scott of Peterborough, New Hampshire, did so in the summer of 1776, making his getaway from Halifax, Nova Scotia. In March 1777, Joshua Loring, the British commissary for prisoners, sent Washington a list of some officers who had "deserted from their paroles" and demanded their return. Loring was sure that Washington would not "Countenance" such actions. But these events were rare. Escape was ungentlemanly and jeopardized the whole system of parole and exchange.[75]

Allen's advice to the young Pennsylvanian indicated that he perceived the soldiers' honor as a more flexible thing than his own. It was all right for private soldiers to practice deception, pursuing a greater good. They could enlist to free themselves and then desert. This act required taking a new oath and contravening it, something a gentleman could not do. This particular soldier had some misgivings. His brother had, after all, died rather than enlist. Would enlistment now both dishonor his brother and himself? Would it be "right in the sight of God"? Allen told him that doing so to save himself and to plan to desert made it honorable. Allen would not consider doing it himself and even felt compromised recommending it.

Allen published this account during the war without damaging his high reputation. However, when rumors circulated that another officer held captive by the British had been trying to get soldiers to enlist, without encouraging later desertion, senior Continental officers felt very differently about the matter. In 1777, General Gates advised Washington that a Pennsylvanian officer might be guilty of that kind of "insidious Conduct." The officer had now been exchanged, and Gates wanted to bring the man to trial. Washington encouraged him to give the matter his "attention." However, Gates had no opportunity. The officer went over to the enemy himself and his commission was rescinded, a highly dishonorable end.[76]

Young men who went from being soldiers to officers had to rethink their own sense of honor in captivity. One socially ambitious private, Lemuel Roberts, had very clear ideas on the subject. He and some others had been offered commissions but had not yet formally received them when the British captured them. They were dressed as officers but told the British that since they had not received their commissions, they did not "conceive our paroles to be binding." However, the British did not want the burden of confining them and let them live in lodgings. The young men felt free to run away without compromising their honor. Recaptured, they were chastised for thinking so little of their honor that they would act as private soldiers. They gave their word a second time not to escape, and this time, when tempted, they did not want "the imputation of dishonorable procedure" and stayed put.[77]

Escape was one way that soldiers could avoid the hardships of imprisonment. However, many private soldiers, confined as they were largely in conditions of great privation, had little opportunity to shape their destiny that way. The decision to enlist in the service of their captors was one of the few choices open to them. Many chose death or died without ever making a conscious decision. As men became sick, the decisions they made about how to treat their illness presented them with some of the small ways they had to alter their fate. Of course, those who have left us memoirs or pension applications are among those whose efforts to treat themselves succeeded. Undoubtedly, many more tried to alter their destiny, but those efforts came to nothing.

In prison, as in camp, it did not take men too long to notice that those who went to the hospital did not come back. The hospitals could be as crowded as the prisons themselves and no healthier. One Continental veteran remembered that in New York in 1781, prisoners were sent from the jail where they were held to the hospital when they were too weak to walk. He could not remember anyone who had lived for "twenty four hours after they got thare." The young Connecticut militiaman Levi Hanford wrote to his father from prison that he had been sick but "would not go to the Hospital for all manner of diseases prevail there." He also asked his father if he would send money to help him.[78]

Wherever possible, men tried to effect their own cures. At Halifax, a soldier imprisoned with Ethan Allen on board a British sloop used his initiative to cure himself of scurvy. The British had not allowed any doctors to visit the prisoners, and the men were "pinched with hunger." The sick man was laid on the side of the ship, "almost dead," when some Indians passed in a canoe. The man bought two quarts of strawberries from them, using the last "money he had in the world." These almost brought about a complete cure. In this matter, the soldier's knowledge (or intuition) served him better than Allen's. After watching scurvy spread through the crew of the ship, Allen had been convinced the disease was infectious.[79]

Soldiers were not the only ones who took such initiatives. Thomas Dring, the master's mate held on the *Jersey* prison ship, decided that he should be inoculated against smallpox after it broke out among the prisoners. Since there was no "proper" person on board who might do it for him, he "concluded to act as my own physician." He found someone who was at the proper point of the disease to provide "the matter for the purpose." Dring was determined. Even though the only tool he could find to carry out the process was a "common pin," he went ahead, using the pin both to cut himself and to remove infected material. The procedure was a success. He took the disease "lightly" and recovered quickly. Following his example, some of his men were also inoculated in the same way.[80]

As with captivity itself, there was no uniform experience in sickness. Soldiers who fell ill on the prison ships or while confined in jails generally ended up in hospitals in conditions similar to that of their prison. Prisoners who were already sick or wounded when they were taken occasionally managed to avoid these horrors. Benjamin Rush, who, under a flag of truce, went to visit the wounded held by the British after the Battle of Brandywine, was impressed by the standards of care he observed. Indeed, he believed that the wounded taken to American hospitals "were not half so well treated as those whom we left in General Howe's hands." Rush was writing to John Adams in Congress, anxious to make a case for American delinquency in order to secure a reorganization of the Continental hospital establishment. Still, his comments probably had some truth and reflected the better preparation of British "flying" hospitals, that is, those that traveled with an army into battle.[81]

Soldiers themselves had mixed reports. Even individual soldiers experienced inconsistent treatment. One was Ebenezer Fletcher. Badly wounded in July 1777, he was picked up by the British and taken to a field hospital. While there, he was "stripped of everything valuable" and found "[s]ome of the enemy very kind; while others were very spiteful and malicious." Yet, Fletcher felt he was "treated as well as I could expect." In fact, he found the doctor who attended him very kind and attentive, even though he did occasionally try to get him to enlist with the British.[82]

The British were also willing to extend paroles to wounded soldiers to be spared the burden of care. Frederick Padget, who suffered multiple wounds when the British seized Charleston in 1780, never ended up in the awful prison ships or overcrowded hospitals. He, along with other American wounded, was first taken to a hospital in a barn and from there to one in a church. He stayed there a month until he was paroled, free to return home, providing he served no more. Hamlin Cole had a similar experience. In 1781, the British captured him and fifty-four others. However, some of the men, including Cole, had been badly wounded in the skirmish and were going to need care. The healthy men were marched off to prison ships. The wounded who were incapable of marching anywhere were immediately paroled. Cole was free to go home, but for a while he was not able to go anywhere as he was dangerously ill. The British were acting efficiently. For Cole, difficult as his situation was, he was probably better off than his healthy comrades.[83]

For the most part, American prisoners taken sick in confinement languished without even cursory attention from British surgeons. American surgeons or physicians taken prisoner were of course eligible for parole as officers and so were not available to them. Occasionally, American doctors received permission from the British to visit prisoners on board the prison ships to offer care, but this was rare. In Charleston, where the British confined American prisoners on ships after they seized the town in 1780, Doctor Peter Fayssoux did take an interest in prisoners' welfare. He immediately realized that he could do little in the face of "putrid fevers" that arose from the crowded "human miasma." The overcrowding did not last too long, however. He noted that death from disease and enlistments in the British army took care of the overcrowding issue, and conditions then improved. In New York, the prisoners were not so fortunate as there was a steady influx of new prisoners to replace the dead and enlistees.[84]

Fayssoux had a curious mind and was eager to find out something about the exact cause of death of the soldiers. He asked the hospital to hold two bodies for his inspection. There is no indication that he performed a dissection on the men. He simply made a very careful observation of the state of their bodies at death, particularly noting "the marks of a highly septic state." Having made his observations, Fayssoux made no comment as to what happened to the bodies when he was finished with them.[85]

Fayssoux, an outside observer and not a captive himself, stayed silent on the subject of burial, but few men held on the ships did. Many soldiers' memoirs and those of officers held "indiscriminately" with their men even for the shortest time at least touched on the subject. Few of them could comment exactly on the final disposition of the bodies. For the most part, they did not get to see it. They usually were able to observe only the death itself and the passing of naked or scantily clad bodies out of ships onto boats or out of buildings onto carts. The disorder and lack of respect in the way in which even that was done was an important part of the degradation of confinement, and men felt it deeply.

If burial could be observed, it was done from a distance. In New York, the men on the prison ships were a few hundred yards from the shore. The dead were piled on boats for removal to a sandy beach for burial. One seaman imprisoned on the *Jersey* in the summer of 1781 remembered that he used to stand on deck in the morning and watch the interments in the distance. He would "count the number of times the shovel was filled with sand to cover a dead body; and certain I am that a few high tides, or torrents of rain, must have disinterred them."[86]

Indeed, the few prisoners who were part of burial parties noticed that their efforts on the beaches did not last too long. It was not often that prisoners had to do this duty, as burial parties provided too easy an opportunity for escape. However, when the order was given, most did not mind doing it. They did not join burial parties because they were a chance to pay respect to dead friends. In fact, Dring remembered that the men had become numb to that thought. Rather, they enjoyed it because it was an opportunity to be outside and on land. Also, their participation did not necessarily mean better treatment of the dead. They had to work quickly, and one party noticed that they could already see body parts exposed from those buried a few days earlier.[87]

Burial on land was no better. It took place anywhere that was convenient. Ethan Allen noted that bodies were only "slightly buried." As on other occasions, it was unlikely that dead soldiers from a large prisoner population were ever buried in churchyards. In New York, some prisoners were buried in the trenches that had been dug by the Americans when they had tried to fortify the city in 1776 prior to evacuating it (present day Grand Street). Others were probably buried either in the Negro burying ground (Broadway and Chambers Street) or in the Jewish burial ground (Chatham Square). While soldiers were a diverse group, the majority were white and Christian. So, the latter two sites would have been intended to be not only disrespectful treatment to dead soldiers but also an insult to the dead already buried there.[88]

Many on prison ships remembered the sight in the morning of a boat moving from ship to ship collecting the dead. One recalled the boat, already laden with dead, on its way to shore as the sight that greeted him as he emerged on deck in the morning. Thomas Dring left us an account of the daily ritual of moving the bodies piled on deck to the boats. This was done by strapping the bodies to boards. The process was complicated by the fact that the bodies were often not yet cold and so rigor mortis had not set in, which made lowering the bodies more cumbersome. The prisoners themselves did this duty, and if there were several waiting to be lowered, they did it one at a time "for the sake of decency." The prisoners knew that the bodies' fate was a mass grave, but at least in the part they controlled, men would be treated as individuals.[89]

The speed with which the recently dead were buried led to stories of men being buried alive. The dread of this added to the horror of captivity and the fear of becoming ill. Whether it actually happened or not is inconsequential, because the men believed that it had. Prisoners were sure the British wanted to be rid of them. They thought the British were in such a rush "that some, while yet alive were thrown with the dead on the Cart, and then thrown with the dead into the open pit." One recounted with certainty that a man who had been thrown in a pit with the dead had revived. The man "with help got out" and seemed likely to make a full recovery.[90]

Under these conditions, there was little chance that the body would receive any preparation and little respect. Certainly no coffin was provided. The best and last kindness the dead could hope for was to be wrapped in a blanket. Men could pay their last respects to dead friends by sewing up a blanket around them. There was little else they could offer.[91]

Men were also disturbed by the disorder of such a death. They remembered the dead being carried off "in heaps." Levi Hanford described the scene he encountered when he saw the dead buried in New York in 1777. Bodies were loaded onto a cart and

> driven off to the fortifications, where they were hastily covered, I cannot say interred.
>
> On one occasion, I was permitted to go with the guard to the place of interment, and never shall I forget the scene that I there beheld. They tumbled the bodies promiscuously into the ditch, sometimes even dumping them from the cart, then threw upon them a little dirt and away they went. I could see a hand here, a foot there, and there again a part of a head, washed bare by the rain, and all swollen, blubbering, and falling to decay. I need not add that the stench was anything but tolerable.[92]

As noted in chapter 5, the descriptive language showed people's distress when friends, or even strangers, were denied peace in death. Hanford objected to the "tumbling" of bodies and the casual way they were placed in the grave. He also felt unable to use the word "grave" or call what was happening an "interment." The bodies were simply covered, not buried.

Officers who died in captivity faced a different fate. They could not be buried with full honors, but their fellow officers did what they could. Lieutenant Jabez

Fitch and other officers held in New York in 1776 were able to attend the burial of their captain. At his death, the officers notified the British, who arranged to have a grave and coffin prepared. Fitch was pleased that he and others were able to attend the "Corpse to the Grave." The captain was buried in an orchard near the house where he had died. When a colonel died, he was buried in a church-yard "with as much Deacence[y] as our circumstances would Admit." The dignity of a coffin and the accompaniment of friends were the only courtesies the officers could offer, but they were important ones for all concerned.[93]

Fitch's diary contains the stark contrasts between the world of the soldiers and himself. He was a caring officer and was one of the few who visited his men. He became steadily more enraged about the sad conditions in which he saw them. However, he moved between their world and his, and he gave no indication that the contrast bothered him. For example, one day, after a good breakfast, he and his fellow officers received a visit from Ethan Allen, just arrived in New York and still a prisoner. Then Fitch went down to visit his sergeant and some of his men, whom he found in "a very Pityful cituation, both on acct: of Sickness & Accomodation." Then he returned to his own quarters to find his fellow officers "Zealously Engaged at Card playing." Later that day, he went to the burial ground and saw four men placed in a single grave, then went on to have "a very good dinner with the Frenchmen," and afterward he went on for an evening cup of tea with other friends. If Fitch ever carried any food or material aid to his men, he never recorded it. The contrast in their lives was just the way things were.[94]

Although a few officers were willing and able to visit their men, it did not necessarily bridge the social gap that separated them. Few ever mentioned their soldiers by name. Ethan Allen, caring and energetic as he was on behalf of the suffering soldiers he saw, never once did so. He honored every officer he encountered, British or American, by making a point of remembering their names, and when he could not, he made a point of noting his lapse.[95]

However, at times unusual horror did break through this barrier, and officers named their soldiers who died. After a while, Fitch started to name the NCO he was visiting and the soldiers he knew who died. His diary became much more emotional as his captivity progressed. He was a longtime diarist who rarely made mention of anything personal and never anything emotional. Even his marriage was noted in a few words. However, Fitch was a caring officer, and despite his hectic social activities, his men's suffering moved him. The strongest language in his diary was reserved for criticism of the British. They were the "powers of

Earth & Hell" who denied his men comforts. After a few months of observing his men's condition, he began to name those who died.[96]

Another officer who named his soldiers at their death seemed to be overwhelmed by his own responsibility for bringing them to that end. For Lieutenant Henry Bedinger, a list of names of his dead soldiers was a burden he carried his whole life. In the summer of 1776, Bedinger and another lieutenant had been sent out recruiting to Berkeley County, Virginia. They recruited seventeen men and rejoined their regiment. In November 1776, the regiment was part of the garrison that surrendered to the British at Fort Washington. All were taken prisoner. Separated from his men, Bedinger only heard of the terrible conditions they endured. Of the seventy-nine privates and NCOs of his company, fifty-two died in captivity.[97]

Bedinger appears to have felt deeply the burden of his responsibility as a recruiter who had brought men to that place. He wrote down a list of the seventeen men he had recruited that fateful summer, and beside their names he wrote their fates. Only one man of the seventeen, a sergeant, lived to be exchanged. Beside each of the other names he carefully recorded the date of death. At the end of the list he added the few personal items of information he knew about them. For example, he wrote that William Seaman, who died July 8, 1777, "was the son of Jonah Seaman of Darkesville. Isaac Price [died February 5, 1777] was an orphan living with James Campbell's father." Bedinger lived to old age, and when he died, the list of his recruits' names and their dates of death was among his papers.[98]

On another occasion when an officer named men beneath him, he was responding to a variety of terrible circumstances. Thomas Dring named three people, members of his own ship's crew and fellow townsmen, who had died. He felt particularly shocked at the deaths of two of the men. He knew that they had died only when he came across their bodies at the last moment before they were removed for burial. He and others had just enough time to get some blankets to wrap around them before they were taken away. Dring felt terrible that he had not even known they were ill, but he admitted that the reality of their situation was that they scattered among a "great mass" of prisoners, each living in a "little world of concentrated misery."[99]

One of these three deaths particularly moved Dring for a variety of reasons. The seaman who died, named Palmer, was only about twelve years old. He had been a waiter to the officers before captivity and continued to serve them while imprisoned. He died of smallpox that he contracted while undergoing inoculation, a practice that Dring himself had initiated on board the prison ship. Dring felt close to the boy as he "had always looked up to me as a protector, and particularly so during his sickness." During the boy's last night, Dring had a distressing time "holding him during his convulsions" and found it "heart-rending" to listen to the boy as he screamed for his mother. Dring remembered that in "the midnight gloom of our dungeon, I could not see him die; but I knew by placing my hand over his mouth, that his breathings were becoming shorter; and thus felt the last breath as it quit his frame." Dring found there was only "one more kind office" he could give the dead boy: he assisted in sewing the blanket around the corpse before it was removed for burial. It was hardly surprising in these circumstances that Dring should name the dead child.[100]

Dring wrote his memoir in 1829, almost fifty years after the events themselves took place, yet the details of the horror of his captivity stayed with him. As a seaman serving with men from his town and continuing to live in the same community after the war, he was never removed from his past. Whenever he saw a descendant or relative of one of his shipmates who had died on the prison ship, the "recollection comes fresh to my mind." He was not alone in remembering his imprisonment. The evidence of memoirs and pension applications is that, no matter whether one served the new nation on sea or land, the memories of captivity did not easily fade.[101]

For the Revolutionary generation, the names of the British prison ships became symbols of heroic suffering, immortalized in memoirs and in works of writers such as Freneau. He gave the terrible litany of names:

> There, the black SCORPION at her mooring rides;
> There, STROMBOLO swings, yielding to the tides;
> Here, bulky JERSEY fills a larger space,
> And HUNTER, to all hospitals disgrace —.

The names became symbols for the sufferings of all men who had been held and particularly of those who had died in captivity.[102]

But suffering had been borne most heavily by the ordinary American soldiers and seamen, and not only the British could be blamed. The Revolutionaries treated men as in a world apart from their officers. Congress and the states came to prisoners' aid but only in ways that sustained the existing separations of rank. They did so despite the much greater need of the men at the lowest level of military life and the desperate nature of their circumstances in captivity.

Caring officers exerted themselves in the few ways that were available to them. Soldiers did what they could to alter their fate. In captivity, as much as on the battlefield, a man's honor guided his actions. Some felt that the honorable thing to do was to choose death rather than serve with the British. Others thought that honor was satisfied by choosing survival. Whatever their choice, it went unacknowledged by the larger society. It would be thirty years before there was a proposal in New York to build a memorial to the dead from the prison ships.

CONCLUSION

Let us now praise famous men,
And our fathers in their generations.

ECCLESIASTICUS 44:1

JOSEPH PLUMB MARTIN, a veteran of seven years of Continental service, lamented in his 1830 memoir that the soldiers' hard labor and sacrifice would always go unrecognized. "Great men get great praise, little men nothing. But it
was always so and always will be." He was not the only veteran who felt unap-
preciated. An old militiaman in his memoirs felt that "old soldiers," if they were
remembered at all, were remembered too late. They stayed "forgotten, until they
have nearly all gone to their graves."[1]

As these writers indicate, the soldiers of the Revolution, like many other eighteenth-century soldiers, did not quickly receive the thanks of a grateful nation.
In speeches that marked the anniversaries of already-important Revolutionary
occasions such as the Boston Massacre, Independence Day, and the battle at
Lexington, orators pushed aside the accomplishments of the professional soldiers and lauded instead the virtuous citizens, the soldiers of the militia. Zabdiel
Adams, in a speech in April 1783 on the Lexington anniversary, argued that the
militia not only had protected citizens in peacetime but also had been responsible for some of the great victories of the war. However, in the printed version of
his remarks, Adams qualified his comments in a footnote to add that he meant
no disrespect to the troops of the standing army. He acknowledged their "toils
and labors, their patience and perseverance under peculiar discouragements." But
he was quite clear that no matter that their fortitude was "unexampled in history," it was important that they now "cheerfully return to the peaceful walks of
life." The militia was to be at the center of the military stage in the national myth
of the Revolution.[2]

As a number of modern historians have argued, national mythmaking is an essential part of nation building. The rituals of public life, its ceremonies and celebrations, both those invented and those that have evolved, all play key roles in the evolution of the nation state, which one historian has called an "imagined political community." At moments of great transition in any nation or society, traditions are used and appropriated in a variety of ways as the community reinvents itself. Thus, the traditional rituals and symbols of a society, such as flags, bell-ringing, salutes, toasts, speeches, fasting, days of prayer, or days of playful social inversion, such as when servants would play masters and masters servants, continue but with new variations and content.[3]

Consequently, historians have studied the national mythmaking of the new United States for what it reveals of continuities between the colonial world and the new republic and the ways in which the new United States was inventing itself as a nation. The British North American colonial world was one already rich in public rituals. Life was filled with the traditions listed above and many more. In the years before the Revolution, colonists in urban areas had used some of these to express their hatred of British policies and added some new rituals and symbols of their own, such as the liberty tree. Even before the war, the anniversary of the Boston Massacre of 1770 had been marked with parades, speeches, and sermons. While the war was going on, the anniversaries of the first bloodshed at Lexington, the day the British evacuated Boston in 1776, and, of course, Independence Day had become important days on the calendar of the new nation to be marked with as much pomp and ceremony as could be mustered.[4]

Some of these new traditions emerged as spontaneous outpourings of sentiment, and others were created quite self-consciously by the Continental Congress. Joseph Warren of Boston, who was killed at Bunker Hill in 1775, was one of the first people to be celebrated for his heroism and sacrifice in large public ceremonies. Next was General Richard Montgomery, following his death at the assault on Quebec. As news of his death spread, there were private and public expressions of sadness. People wrote about the event in letters and diaries, and Montgomery was quickly immortalized in songs that honored him as a "valliant Heroe" and that mourned the country's "Boundless loss." In one song, he even became something of a savior, a Christ-like figure, who had "fought and Dide that you / Might Live and yet be free"; the song hailed "The Spirit of the truly brave / From thy obscure Sequestered grave / Montgomery arise."[5]

Some of those who celebrated Montgomery's life and sacrifice did so spontaneously, but others acted with specific purpose. As soon as news of his death reached Congress in January 1776, there was a resolution to build a monument to him. This was done not only as a "just tribute of gratitude" to his service and his memory but also "to inspire posterity" to emulate him and to pass on "to future ages, . . . his patriotism, conduct, boldness of enterprise, insuperable perseverance, and contempt for danger and death."[6]

While Warren and Montgomery stand out as heroic martyrs of the Revolution, they were not the only fallen officers honored. In celebratory speeches and toasts, a pantheon of senior officers' names was recited. Occasions such as the Fourth of July celebrations in White Plains, New York, in 1778 included a toast to the "immortal memory" of fallen generals. Continental army general Hugh Mercer, who had died a few days after being wounded in the Battle of Princeton in January 1777, was included, as was General Francis Nash of North Carolina. Nash had been mortally wounded at Germantown in October 1777. General David Wooster, who had died of wounds received in the British raid on Danbury, Connecticut, in April of the same year, was also listed. The heroic remembrance of Wooster's death was not affected by the fact that he had earlier been recalled from the Quebec campaign for incompetence and was, in the words of one historian, "dull and uninspired."[7]

A number of senior officers were celebrated in their lifetimes, with George Washington himself achieving mythic status. In receiving Washington's resignation in December 1783, Congress hailed him as the man who had "defended the standard of liberty in this new world" and thanked him for "invariably regarding the rights of the civil power." He was duly the subject of speeches, sermons, toasts, and parades on a wide variety of occasions and anniversaries, including his own birthday. Even during and after his presidency, when he was strongly identified with Federalism—strong national government—those who stood in opposition could and did still celebrate him as a military hero of the Revolution.[8]

As the war was ending, the accomplishments of the soldiers of the Continental army were becoming a footnote to the new national myth of the war. Washington and other general officers, the political rhetoric went, had led citizen soldiers in the defense of their liberties. Indeed, as Congress told Washington, his leadership enabled his "fellow-citizens . . . to display their martial genius and transmit their fame to posterity." Increasingly in postwar speeches, public speakers were already remembering the war as one fought by outraged citizens who picked up their arms when the situation demanded it. Speakers such as William Jackson in his Independence Day speech in 1786 lauded the nation's military accomplishments and claimed that the new United States was a "happy country! whose sons are at once citizens and soldiers." Even during the war, in a 1779 Fourth of July eulogy to the war dead, those who had died were hailed not as men who were professional soldiers but as those who had given up the "simplicity and innocence of country life, the philosophic ease of academic leisure, and the sweets of rural life." The speaker, Hugh Henry Brackenridge, gave an accurate account of the soldiers' hard life and celebrated men felled by "the fever of the camp" and "the wasting hunger of the prison ship." But he celebrated the dead as citizens rushing to arms to defend *"the cause of Liberty,"* men who were "not the vassals of a proud chieftain" but rather "chieftains of their own cause," motivated by the "best principles of patriotism." Brackenridge and others were able to overlook the fact that the army included draftees and substitutes as well as volunteers and that steadily more lucrative bounty payments were required to get recruits of any kind.[9]

Still, the soldiers who served in the Continental army were, as Brackenridge observed, "the chieftains of their own cause." Many of them served voluntarily. For some, their own cause might have been the political cause itself. For others, their cause was financial opportunity when the bounty or a substitution fee might satisfy pressing financial needs for themselves or their families. For others, their cause may have been to be free from supervision of a master or parent, or to pursue adventure and excitement, or to be with friends. None of them need have enlisted. Even draftees or those who served as a punishment for another crime could desert. So, even those who served by compulsion did so, to some degree, as "the chieftains of their own cause."

Yet, no matter how soldiers came to be in the army and no matter whether they were from the lowest levels of society or not, all men, when they served, had to be prepared to live as the lowest members of society and to be viewed with contempt by others. Few at the time — soldiers, officers, patriot leaders, or colonists at large — thought that the status of soldiers could or should be anything else. With the exception of the radicals in Philadelphia at the heart of the Associators, few could consider how an army might be made differently. As noted earlier, this meant soldiers had to endure, and accept, physical treatment worse than that of free men in the society. For some, there would have been little distinction between their military status and their civilian one. For others, it may have been a sacrifice worth making, no matter how difficult an adjustment, for one's own cause, whatever it might be.

Whatever the reasons for enlisting initially, the reasons for staying probably changed over time. As disease and hardship took their toll, soldiers probably found things other than their own cause to sustain them. As time wore on, even being paid for one's service would not have seemed such a grand inducement to stay and risk one's life. A few perhaps had little to go home to. Some may have stayed, having been politicized through their service. Perhaps another key element that sustained them as the war passed was esprit de corps. Men, from a disparate range of experiences and backgrounds — some who were young and eager for adventure, some who had lived on the margins of communities, some who were recent immigrants, some who had moved often, some who were unskilled, some who had been convicted of crimes, some who had been enslaved or indentured — all came to feel part of something larger than themselves. The army became disciplined and militarily successful. It succeeded in driving out a larger and more experienced enemy. By the end of the war, the men had become good soldiers. They had shared and survived the experiences of war, its occasional excitement and terror and its prolonged drudgery. They had shared harsh treatment, the hardships of camp life, and resentment when the larger community neglected them. They had become professional soldiers.[10]

Yet, whatever sense of comradeship or professionalism had developed within the army, only officers appear to have transferred it to civilian life. When the war ended, soldiers drifted back home. They formed no clubs or associations. It was not until the first half of the nineteenth century that ordinary working men generally began to associate and form clubs, and American ex-soldiers did not associate around their service until after the Civil War. In the eighteenth century, veterans of the Revolution divided in peacetime along the same lines of rank that had divided them in wartime. It would take more than 130 years for veterans to celebrate the universal qualities of military service and the triumph of comradeship in the face of adversity. When the veterans' organization the American Legion was formed after World War I, it committed itself "to consecrate and sanctify our comradeship by our devotion to mutual helpfulness," making no distinctions of rank.[11]

After the American Revolution, officers immediately acknowledged their separate and distinct comradeship in arms. They formed a group that celebrated their own sacrifice and accomplishments. Called the Society of the Cincinnati, it was founded by General Henry Knox and other high-ranking officers, with Washington as its first president. The Society of the Cincinnati embraced ideals of comradeship and fellowship but saw those sentiments as limited to gentlemen such as themselves. Indeed, it restricted eligibility for membership to those officers who had served at least three years in the Continental army. Members committed themselves to "cordial affection," "brotherly friendship," and "acts of beneficence." Some in political life feared the organization because of its conservatism. It celebrated the virtues of an ordered society and, some suspected, even monarchy. However, what it mostly celebrated was itself. It was one of the first secular, national pressure groups, and its central mission was to protect the interests of its members in terms of pensions and national recognition.[12]

Soldiers slipped back into a very different world. There is little indication that any formal effort was made to associate with former comrades in arms. Forty-five years after the war, when Congress finally awarded pensions on the basis of service rather than of pressing financial need, a large number of applicants no longer knew a single person who could bear witness to their service. Phrases such as "reputed to be" or "had the reputation of a Revolutionary War soldier" are sprinkled through the pension records. Occasionally, men raised in the same town, still living there decades later, could testify on each other's behalf. In those cases, others in the community hint at local fellowship. For example, in the pension testimony of the widow of Joshua Dean, neighbors were able to confirm that at Dean's death in 1799, he was "buried in a war-like manner by some of the Revolutionary soldiers." But such references were few and far between. By the 1830s, family, work, and other associations had taken precedence over the experiences of early manhood.[13]

With no organization to advocate for their interests and with their vital contribution to Revolutionary victory having slipped from the national consciousness, Continental army soldiers became a relatively forgotten group. Throughout the war, soldiers had been reminded constantly of their honor. It was an incentive for them to act diligently and behave well. They were told that good conduct would "procure them the most glorious of all characters—that of being esteemed good soldiers." Being thought of as good soldiers, however, had not elevated their standard of treatment either during the war or after. For those soldiers, decades passed before the laurels of victory, rhetorical or practical, were awarded to them.[14]

Of course, adequate financial resources, administrative ability, and national confidence were all important prerequisites for a nation to engage in large-scale pension distributions. However, as the Society of the Cincinnati showed, lobbying and high social status could help shape national policy. Although pensions for soldiers had existed from an earlier date, they were on a very limited scale. During the war, as detailed in chapter 2, postwar payments had been offered as an incentive for service. Officers secured generous postservice financial rewards, initially set at seven years of half pay, which was later changed to five years of full pay. Soldiers were awarded a parting gratuity and land warrants. Initially, the state or national government offered pensions to dependents for wartime death or permanent disability, based on with which regiment a soldier had served. The fact that soldiers were not rewarded sooner with pensions was another testament to the way in which their low status and their absence from the national myth of the Revolution were mutually reinforcing and left the soldiers without material recognition.[15]

It took nearly forty years, another major war (the War of 1812), and a large budget surplus for the national government to begin to take a more active interest in its Revolutionary veterans. In 1818, when the first pension legislation was passed, it was in response to claims that many veterans were destitute. Congress initiated need-based pensions for those who had served at least nine months in the Continental army as a reward for service. In 1820, Congress amended the program to require veterans to pass a means test to qualify. It did so because costs were escalating dramatically, and it suspected that some applicants might be feigning poverty. Ten years later, the law changed again. Veterans no longer had to show need; service alone now qualified them. In 1832, the terms of eligibility were further broadened. Most veterans received pensions just when, as the militiaman above noted, they had "nearly all gone to their graves."[16]

This pension legislation represented a dramatic turning point in the lives of veterans and in the political culture itself, changing the picture of the Continentals in the public mind. By the end of Jefferson's administration in 1808, Continental soldiers began to reappear in public rhetoric, and by 1818, the image of their suffering, both during the Revolutionary War and after, became a popular symbol of the willingness of individuals to sacrifice for the republic.

This shift was part of a number of social, cultural, and political changes. At the beginning of the nineteenth century, there was a rising tide of sentimentality about the Revolution. As Federalists and Democratic Republicans, the two main political parties of the era, battled for the hearts and minds of voters, they each appropriated images and myths of the Revolution and celebrated them and the Revolutionary generation from many angles. The sentimental picture of the suffering soldier appealed to both as a symbol of virtue, honor, and commitment. As Europe was engulfed in the Napoleonic Wars and the United States experienced repeated crises in its relationship with Britain, American political rhetoric increasingly celebrated the nation's virtues, and the figure of the heroic, suffering veteran became central to that. In the light of some military failures of the War of 1812, Revolutionary accomplishments seemed even more heroic. The pension legislation itself is a testament to the power of the image of the Revolutionary veterans' service and sacrifice. The proponents of the legislation were able to overcome traditional hostility toward the payment of any kind of national pension, which was seen as creating an aristocracy or a body of men in the pocket of the government, both being detrimental to a republic. By 1818, Fourth of July speakers, such as Austin Denny in Massachusetts, were celebrating the Continental army as a "band of heroes" who had showed great "fortitude in suffering" during the war.[17]

The image embodied both wartime and present suffering, and a great many of the veterans were indeed presently suffering. From the inception of the pension program through the decades of expanded eligibility, a total of about 88,000 veterans or their widows applied for pensions or bounty lands. Of these, 30,000 applied on the basis of need in response to the act of 1818 and its amendments of 1820 and 1823. The evidence the veterans produced to support their claims confirmed the popular picture of them as impoverished and suffering. John Resch's wonderful study of a randomly selected statistical sample of the Revolutionary veterans' need-based pension records sheds light on these, the most luckless of the Continental veterans. More than 13 percent of them were completely penniless, and another 46 percent had assets of less than fifty dollars. Many reported few household possessions. Those from New York had per capita wealth that was only a fraction of that of the average state resident. Many applicants reported ill health connected to their wartime experiences (indeed, less than 1 percent described themselves as healthy), and a number reported already having received public or private charity.[18]

Additionally, Resch studied all the veterans of Peterborough, New Hampshire, who applied for pensions at any time. His study indicates that the number of elderly, destitute veterans was disproportionately large relative to their age cohort in town who did not serve in the war. His study also indicates that the veterans, collectively, fared less well economically in the postwar years than those who did not serve. This held true no matter what their economic starting point. Those who began lower did not rise as some of their contemporaries did. Others slipped "farther and faster down the economic ladder" than their cohort. This could be a statistical aberration in a small town, a reflection of some bad luck, or, as Resch speculates, part of a wider problem of alienation felt by veterans.[19]

It had taken decades for Continental army soldiers to receive recognition, either rhetorical or practical, for their service. However, whatever the changes wrought by shifting sentiment about Revolutionary veterans, very few of those new sentiments trickled down to soldiers who were serving in the regular army in the decades after the Revolution. Continued antipathy toward a standing army was reflected in the Constitutional requirement that any appropriations to "raise and support Armies" could only last for two years, so the matter of funding would have to be regularly revisited. Congress initially created a very small army, the bare minimum necessary for frontier security. But, as violence flared against Indians in the Northwest Territory after 1790 and tensions rose again with the British, Congress haltingly moved toward establishing a small professional army. By 1800, Congress had established a policy of keeping the regular army small and using militia and federal volunteers to augment it in wartime or other emergencies. That policy would last for the next hundred years.[20]

The establishment of a regular army in the new republic resulted in little change in the status and relationship of officers and men or soldiers' physical treatment. In 1802, with Jefferson's support, a new military academy was established at West Point, New York, which further separated officers from soldiers. However, after an initial burst of enthusiasm, the institution was floundering. Only a small number of officers was trained there, and among the officers it graduated, social connections mattered much more than ability. Failures and inefficiencies of the officer corps in the War of 1812 (1812–15) showed just how costly poorly trained officers could be to the army and the country. After that war, President James Monroe used the consensus of the era to support turning West Point into a military academy that would produce a knowledgeable, professional corps. West Point served its purpose and turned out steadily more and more of the army's officers, from less than 15 percent in 1817 to 76 percent in 1860.[21]

Soldiers were still drawn from the lowest levels of society. At the outbreak of the War of 1812, army pay for a private, at five dollars a month, was about half of what an unskilled laborer could make. However, during the war, a desperate shortage of recruits and high mortality rates caused Congress again to tempt potential soldiers with cash. Pay went to eight dollars a month, still less than that of most laborers, but Congress made the first three months payable in advance, so new recruits had some cash in their pockets for themselves or their families. Bounties were also used and went from $31 and 160 acres of land at the beginning of the war to $124 and 320 acres, the cash portion now equivalent to a year's pay for a laborer. Unfortunately, after the initial cash payment, the country was frequently late in paying its troops, sometimes by as much as a year, but even the promise of it tempted more than a few.[22]

The delays in pay, combined with continued problems in administration and distribution of supplies, left soldiers suffering. Supply was as much of a problem as it had been in the Revolution. There had been little improvement in the infrastructure of the nation. Roads of poor quality and inadequate numbers of wagons and teamsters continued to limit the abilities of even able administrators, of which there were perilously few. The army began the war with no general staff, and the new appointments at the outbreak of war reflected political interests and not abilities. That, combined with poorly thought-out lines of authority and jurisdiction, led to administrative chaos. Additionally, food for the army was to be supplied by independent contractors who had been selected by competitive bidding. One officer, Thomas Jesup, called the system "madness in the extreme." Since the contractor's profits were greater if he bought low-quality food, many chose to do so and supplied the army with tainted food. In the fall of 1813, Doctor W. M. Ross discovered bread contaminated with excrement, and a food inspector found the quality of flour so bad he sarcastically observed that it would kill a horse. Transportation problems meant that even this poor quality food often did not reach soldiers in a timely manner.[23]

Punishment stayed brutal relative to civilian society. Slowly, the larger society was moving away from any kind of public corporal punishments. Citizens of the new republic felt themselves to be part of a bold new political experiment, and that encouraged them to explore new ideas in criminal justice. Some community leaders, especially those in eastern cities, increasingly began to believe that they should lead the way in implementing the ideas of Cesare Beccaria and other Enlightenment reformers, as discussed in chapter 3, who recommended moving away from harsh punishments. In 1801, Thomas Eddy, advocating change in New York, wrote that "barbarous usages" had no place in a republican society. From the earliest years of the new republic, states had begun to build prisons to incarcerate offenders, and by the 1820s, a few eastern states were experimenting with penitentiaries, which were prisons specially thought out and designed to reform criminals, not just confine them. The death penalty began to be used almost exclusively for first-degree murder. However, despite these shifting sentiments and bold experimentation, in much of the country, particularly in the West, corporal punishment continued to be used in sentencing. For southern slaves, of course, corporal punishment remained the cornerstone of social control.[24]

The army was not immune to these ideas, but their impact was limited. The army continued to use varieties of noncorporal punishments such as fining, docking pay, and stopping the whiskey ration. As to corporal punishment, the revised articles of war in 1806 set a new lash limit at fifty lashes—beyond civilian practice but less than that used in the Revolutionary War—but they left other corporal punishments open to the court's discretion. There was no thought yet of long prison sentences for soldiers. Indeed, it was unclear whether imprisoning a soldier, thus removing him from the daily unpleasantness of service, was punishment at all. Corporal punishment was considered essential to the exigencies of war and had to be swift and shocking to be a deterrent to others. But Congress's shifting sentiment over the use of the lash was reflected in an amendment to the articles in 1812 as war broke out. The amendment prohibited lash sentences entirely for two years, but it did nothing to curb other kinds of punishment. Creative courts-martial got around the prohibition on the lash by using "cobbing," that is, paddling. Cobbing did not cut the flesh the way the lash did; it only resulted in bruising. Even so, when the sentence was fifty "cobs," the pain inflicted would not have been significantly different from that doled out by the lash. Additionally, courts-martial continued to use "picketing" and riding the wooden horse. For desertion, they practiced cropping and branding, which had not been used by the Continental army.[25]

Courts-martial did edge toward confinement or restricted movement rather than corporal punishment. Still, the army preferred to have a soldier's manpower, and so these periods of restriction tended to be short but brutal. Soldiers were confined in "the black hole," meaning they were to be kept in darkness in solitary confinement in a specially dug hole for a period of days. Some men were sentenced to hard labor. John Stockland got six months' hard labor for disobeying orders, and Moses Williams was sentenced to one month of hard labor and to a period in the black hole and also had his liquor ration stopped for leaving his post and threatening to kick the corporal who caught him. Some soldiers were sentenced to drag around a ball and chain, day and night. The ball usually weighed about six pounds.[26]

The death penalty was used continuously during the war. A firing squad usually carried out the sentence, which was almost exclusively handed down for desertion. That crime was a particular problem in 1814, due to soldiers' bounty-jumping. This was when soldiers deserted in order to reenlist in another regiment to collect a second bounty. Compared to the Continental army during the Revolution, execution rates for the War of 1812 were high. Overall, about 79 percent of those sentenced were executed, with only 21 percent being reprieved. However, in 1814, 90 percent of death sentences were carried out, which some thought was absolutely necessary to "put a stop to this growing evil." During the Revolution, Washington had pardoned regularly, both because he felt that courts-martial had too few sentencing options and because he wanted to avoid any appearance of brutality. Civil authorities did so for the same reasons. That the army during this war executed so many of those sentenced probably reflected the increased confidence and power of the state. It also served to emphasize the continued subordination of the army and the low status of the soldiers who served.[27]

Medical treatment for soldiers continued to be terrible, even by the standards of the time. Indeed, one historian has referred to the period between the Revolution and the War of 1812 as "a low point in the history of the medical service of the U.S. Army." In the civilian world, some newly established medical schools created hospitals for the "worthy poor," that is, those whose morals and conduct met the community's approval. However, the primary function of these hospitals was to provide clinical practice for medical students, so hospital care remained the last hope of the destitute and friendless. As for the army, its medical establishment had effectively ceased to exist at the end of the Revolutionary War. For the next two decades or more, there was no centralized authority, no surgeon general, no coordination, and no system of supplying medicines to regimental surgeons. Soldiers suffered accordingly. When war broke out in 1812, Congress seemed to forget the medical needs of an army and did not get around to appointing a surgeon general or other medical executives until nine months after the declaration of war. Not only did the inadequate supply of food and clothing jeopardize the health of the army but also, as in the Revolution, soldiers and officers came to their service with little knowledge of hygiene and camp discipline. The soldiers, accordingly, died in large numbers. Probably 17,500 died of disease compared to the 2,260 who died on the battlefield. Dysentery, typhus, and measles were the big killers of this war.[28]

The only good news was that doctors who served in this war, among them James Tilton, who was now surgeon general, learned a great deal from it. Some wrote numerous scientific papers with their observations, and positive changes were later made to the medical department. In print, doctors considered the many problems of diet, environment, and the spread of disease. Some of what they learned was reiterating what Sir John Pringle and Donald Monro and many other eighteenth-century military surgeons had discovered long ago. The thoughtful Doctor James Mann, in charge of the medical care for the troops in upstate New York, considered, just as Monro had, that the key to the health of soldiers lay in a good supply of appropriate clothing, for example, woolen shirts. Joseph Lovell agreed, but also thought that men sitting with wet, cold feet for long periods of time had "a deleterious effect upon the constitution." Mann also thought that the quality of recruits might be the cause of sickness in the army. After all, he noted, the young and healthy did not join. Another doctor agreed and referred to the new recruits in 1814 as "the miserable refuse of society who never had energy to demonstrate that they lived." The medical lessons of the Revolution and subsequent years had never really sunk in, partly due to the low status of those whose lives were most effected. However, a more prosperous, confident nation listened now to its doctors, who were also more confident as their professional authority increased. More medical schools had been established since the Revolution, and college-trained physicians were now lobbying to require state licensing exams as a means of excluding less well-educated medical practitioners. As a result, military doctors were able to use the experience of the War of 1812 finally to bring home the importance of a permanent military medical establishment, and one was duly formed in 1818.[29]

In death, soldiers' bodies continued to be treated carelessly, and their deaths occurred with little written acknowledgement from their officers. Not unexpectedly, burial practices declined precipitously when mortality rates were high. For example, the bodies of soldiers who died of measles near Buffalo in December 1812 waited several days to be buried while coffins were being built. A war such as this one that involved Indian enemies led to desecration of bodies by both sides. One soldier, Tarrance Kirby, reported that he had participated in killing Tecumseh, the Shawnee leader, in 1813. He wrote that he had helped "*Skin him* and brot Two pieces of his yellow hide home with me to my Mother & Sweet Harts." As before, soldiers' deaths went largely unrecorded by name. In private correspondence and official returns, officers' deaths were recorded in honorable language, such as that of the luckless Major Daniel Beasley who "fell gallantly," while soldiers, unnamed, were simply noted as "killed."[30]

Soldiers continued to suffer disproportionately when they were prisoners of war. In the War of 1812, the British and United States quickly entered into an exchange agreement. Officers, as usual, were allowed freedom of movement upon offering their "parole of honour." The British confined soldiers mostly on prison ships and jails throughout its empire. Wherever they were held, soldiers suffered just as men in the Revolution had from wormy bread, bad meat, and cold. There was a brief crisis over the treatment of prisoners when the British threatened to treat American prisoners of war who were of Irish birth as traitors. However, after much public name-calling, restraint and diplomacy triumphed, and there were no treason charges or retaliatory actions. No matter what dynamic political changes had occurred in the larger society since the Revolution, little had changed for the men of the regular army.[31]

Revolutionary soldiers had lived in a world of deference and strict hierarchy. For a few, the army provided opportunities by offering social mobility, eye-opening experiences, and increasing literacy. Ambitious young men of modest means used the army as a vehicle for advancement. For the vast majority of men who served, however, the army confirmed their low social status. In considering burial practices, punishment, medical care, and camp life, they did take small steps to protect and defend a more refined sense of dignity and honor than the world would allow them. Although hard to detect, small and limited in scope, the fact that soldiers took these steps at all indicates that they were occasionally able to value themselves more than they were valued by others.

This book began with examples of the ways in which physical treatment, burial in particular, reflects social value and reveals some of the complexities of political and social life. It ends with a similar story, set this time in early nineteenth-century New York. It concerns a social and political organization and how it used the remains of dead Revolutionary War soldiers to alter its own political fortunes.

After the Revolution, the Tammany Society was founded in New York as a social club. By 1808, it was making its political presence felt in the state. It was officially a philanthropic organization, but its real influence lay in its ability to manipulate public opinion for political gain. After some early missteps, the Tammany Society, led by Matthew Davis, was becoming a large-scale political machine. It was a strong supporter of the Democratic Republican party, and both it and the Society were beginning to sound the drumbeat for a war against Britain. However, the Society's political influence was in jeopardy. Recent public disclosures had revealed possible corruption within the organization. Davis persuaded Tammany leaders to do something that would remind citizens of the club's patriotism and associate it not with corruption but with liberty.[32]

They decided to reinter the remains of American servicemen who had died while prisoners of war on British prison ships during the Revolution. The ships had been moored off Brooklyn, and the men's bodies had originally been interred along the shoreline. Their bones began to come to light as construction began on the Brooklyn Navy Yard in 1802. Tammany's plan was to move the remains to a nearby piece of property, conveniently owned by a Tammany leader. They organized a very public campaign to collect the remains, reinter them, and place a monument on the site.

For a moment, it seemed that the bodies of ordinary men of the Revolution were finally to be treated with some dignity. Two big public ceremonies were involved in the event. The first in April 1808 laid the cornerstone of the vault that was to house the remains and involved a parade with a company of marines, citizens, and Tammany officials. The state legislature was so moved that it voted to give Tammany $1,000 to build the planned monument. The ceremonial reinterment was carried out a month later with drama and pomp. Thirteen open boats (representing the original thirteen states), each carrying a single symbolic coffin, traveled to Brooklyn. Each coffin was covered with black crepe. Tammany members accompanied the coffins in solemn procession, as did military officers, congressmen, and the governor of New York. As a Tammany account of the events proudly stated, the nation's debt to the war dead was finally to be discharged.[33]

The event was more successful in restoring the reputation of the Tammany Society than it was in providing lasting honor for the war dead. From Tammany's point of view, it garnered just the kind of publicity it was looking for, even though its political opponents saw it all as just election year maneuvering. As to the war dead, after the parade, their remains languished in what was later described as a "temporary wooden structure." Indeed, over the following decades, the tomb became so dilapidated that "the sacred remains were again exposed to the gaze of the multitude." The monument was not built, and there is no record of what became of the $1,000.[34]

Decades passed before there was renewed interest in securing the remains safely in a crypt and building a memorial. In 1873, the city of Brooklyn arranged for another reinterment in a permanent tomb in Washington Park, today Fort Greene Park, and with that move, the dead from the prison ships at last reached a final resting place. In 1888, the Society of Old Brooklynites, an organization of long-standing Brooklyn residents, petitioned Congress for a $100,000 appropriation to build a monument over the crypt. With those funds, money from the state and city of New York, and private donations, a grand memorial column was built and finally dedicated by President William Taft in a well-attended public ceremony in 1908. The men of ordinary rank from the Revolution were finally collectively honored.[35]

Their journey had taken more than one hundred years.

NOTES

Abbreviations

The following abbreviations are used throughout the notes.

AAS   American Antiquarian Society, Worcester, Mass.
APS   American Philosophical Society, Philadelphia, Pa.
DLAR   David Library of the American Revolution, Washington Crossing, Pa.
HL   Huntington Library, San Marino, Calif.
HSD   Historical Society of Delaware, Wilmington, Del.
HSP   Historical Society of Pennsylvania, Philadelphia, Pa.
MHS   Massachusetts Historical Society, Boston, Mass.
NAB   National Archives Building, Washington, D.C.
NEHGS New England Historic Genealogical Society, Boston, Mass.
SCHS   South Carolina Historical Society, Charleston, S.C.

Preface

1. John Warren, *Journal*, quoted in Frothingham, *Life and Times of Joseph Warren*, 522; *New England Chronicle*, ibid., 523; Daniel Richardson Diary, April 8, 1776, U.S. Revolution Collection, AAS.

2. *New York Times*, July 12, 1998, sec. 7, p. 14, col. 2; *Oakland Tribune*, July 12, 1998, p. 1, col. 5.

3. Waldstreicher, *Perpetual Fêtes*, 1.

4. F. Barker, *Tremulous Private Body*, 24.

5. George Osborne, *Subjection to Principalities, Powers, and Magistrates, Explained and Enforced* (London, 1735), 12–13, quoted in McGowen, "Body and Punishment," 653; ibid., 654.

6. W. Frank Craven, "Why Military History?," in *The Harmon Memorial Lectures in Military History, 1959–1987*, ed. Harry R. Borowski (Washington D.C.: Office of Air Force History, 1988), 12, quoted in Paret, *Understanding War*, 220; Middlekauff, "Why Men Fought," 143–45. My thanks to Robert Middlekauff for many provocative discussions on this subject.

7. William Tudor, "Remarks on the Rules and Articles for the Government of the Continental Troops," ca. August 1775, vol. 1, p. 1, item 41, Papers of the Continental Congress, RG 11, M247, roll 38, NAB.

8. "Hearing on Uniform Code of Military Justice," House Armed Services Committee, March 7, 1949, *Index and Legislative History*, 597, 663, 664.

9. Cremin, *American Education*, 181–82, 479–509.

10. Revolutionary War Pension Files, RG 15, NAB.

11. Purcell, *Sealed with Blood*; Summers, ed., "Obituary Notices," 445, 449. For important discussions on the use of the war in public rhetoric in the Early Republic, see Waldstreicher, *Perpetual Fêtes*, and Resch, *Suffering Soldiers*.

12. Neimeyer, *America Goes to War*, xiv–xv; J. K. Martin, "A 'Most Undisciplined Profligate Crew,'" 119–40; George Washington to The Committee of Congress with the Army, January 29, 1778, in Washington, *Writings of George Washington*, 10:396.

13. Evelyn, *Memoirs and Letters*, 68–69.

14. Martin and Lender, *Respectable Army*, xii, 69–77; Papenfuse and Stiverson, "General Smallwood's Recruits"; Lender, "New Jersey Brigade"; Neimeyer, *America Goes to War*, xiv–xv; Resch, *Suffering Soldiers*, 10; Royster, *Revolutionary People at War*, 373–78.

15. Samuel Man Diary, March 1777, AAS. This diary is written around the pages of an almanac for 1777; the entry is written on the page for March. Neimeyer, *America Goes to War*, xiv–xv; Middlekauff, "Why Men Fought"; Zuckerman et al., "Deference and Defiance"; G. Wood, *Radicalism of the American Revolution*. Wood's book emphasizes the social and political transformations of the Revolution.

16. Mayer, *Belonging to the Army*, 1–2.

17. J. Laurens, "Correspondence between Henry Laurens and His Son, John," 50.

Chapter One

1. Royster, *Revolutionary People at War*, 25.

2. Williams, "Journal," October 6, 1775, 8.

3. Martin and Lender, *Respectable Army*, 70; Benjamin Rush, "Directions for Preserving the Health of Solders [*sic*]," *Pennsylvania Packet and Daily Advertiser*, April 22, 1777; Charles Lee to Benjamin Rush, October 10, 1775, in C. Lee, *Lee Papers*, 4:212; Testimony of Susan Bateman, widow's pension claim for William Asberry, Pension File W2988, in Dorman, *Virginia Revolutionary Pension Applications*, 3:16–7.

4. Samuel Bixby Diary, July 3, 1775, AAS.

5. Joseph Reed, quoted in Kaplan, "Rank and Status," 321.

6. Shy, "A New Look at Colonial Militia," 176–77; Royster, *Revolutionary People at War*, 85.

7. Martin and Lender, *Respectable Army*, 71, 89–91.

8. Elliott, "Barnard Elliott's Recruiting Journal," 98; Graydon, *Memoirs*, 120.

9. My own research indicates that most soldiers' diaries and letters that are extant

were written in the early years of the war when men of higher social status were still participating in the soldiers' ranks.

10. Revolutionary War Pension Files, RG 15, NAB. These pension records are on microfilm, organized alphabetically by the last name of the applicant and allocated a serial number depending on the type of claim made, for example, whether it was made by a veteran or a widow. Genealogists have done the most work to date collecting or transcribing the information within this extensive collection; see, for example, Sherrill's *Revolutionary War Pension Applications from Franklin County, Tennessee*. John Frederick Dorman's lifelong work gives an indication of the size and scope of the collection. In his multivolume work, *Virginia Revolutionary Pension Applications*, which he began in 1958, he has listed Virginia veterans alphabetically and transcribed all the application information. In 2003, he published the fifty-first volume and is still less than halfway through the alphabet. Historian John Dann has collected some of the most engaging applications that include detailed narratives in his book *The Revolution Remembered*.

11. Jesse Lukens to John Shaw Jr., September 15, 1775, in Lukens, "Incidents of the Siege of Boston," 548; King, *Two Tracts*, 31.

12. Houlding, *Fit for Service*, 117–21; Bowen, *War and British Society*, 15; Childs, *Armies and Warfare in Europe*, 61–63; James Wolfe, quoted in Childs, *Armies and Warfare in Europe*, 61; C. Duffy, *Army of Frederick the Great*, 55–57; Frey, *British Soldier in America*, 6–16; Shy, *Toward Lexington*, 391–92.

13. Trenchard, *Standing Armies in England*, 5. My thanks to the Society of the Cincinnati Library, Washington, D.C., for making this book available to me. J. R. Jones, *Country and Court*, 234–55; Schwoerer, *"No Standing Armies!"* 139–42, 146.

14. Schwoerer, *"No Standing Armies!"* 188. For colonial objections to a standing army, see, for example, Martin and Lender, *Respectable Army*, 6–9, and Royster, *Revolutionary People at War*, 35–38.

15. Shy, "New Look at Colonial Militia," 181–82.

16. Georgia General Assembly, "An Act for the better ordering and regulating the militia of this state," November 15, 1778, in Vollmer, *Military Obligation*, vol. 2, pt. 4, p. 139; Shy, "A New Look at Colonial Militia," 182–84.

17. Titus, *Old Dominion at War*, ix; Selesky, *War and Society in Colonial Connecticut*, 149–59.

18. Selesky, *War and Society in Colonial Connecticut*, 159.

19. North Carolina Assembly, "An Act facilitating the raising Recruits to serve his Majesty," December 12, 1754, in Vollmer, *Military Obligation*, vol. 2, pt. 10, p. 24; Titus, *Old Dominion at War*, 59–60; *Statutes at Large of Virginia*, 7:70.

20. Robert Dinwiddie to Lord Holdernesse, March 12, 1754, in *Dinwiddie Papers* 1:94, quoted in Titus, *Old Dominion at War*, 38; Titus, *Old Dominion at War*, 63, 81, 88; George Washington to Robert Dinwiddie, March 9, 1754, in Washington, *Papers: Colonial Series*, 1:73. For further reading on racial attitudes in Virginia, see E. Morgan, *American Slavery, American Freedom*.

21. "An Act for the Speedy Levying of Soldiers," March 1759, in *Acts and Resolves,* 4:193; General Abercromby, August 10, 1756, quoted in Pargellis, *Lord Loudoun in North America,* 99; Governor Thomas Pownell to William Pitt, September 10, 1758, quoted in F. Anderson, *People's Army,* 62.

22. Leach, *Roots of Conflict,* 83; Philadelphia Municipal Archives, Common Council Minutes, August 16, 1755, ibid., 179 n. 23.

23. Leach, *Roots of Conflict,* 93; Colonel Henry Bouquet, ibid., 87.

24. Wright, *Continental Army,* 436. At full complement, companies in the British and Continental army consisted of about 100 men, including officers and noncommissioned officers, but sometimes they were significantly understrength. Martin and Lender, *Respectable Army,* 88; Henry Bedinger, "Part of a Letter from Major Henry Bedinger to a Son of General Samuel Finley," quoted in Dandridge, *American Prisoners,* 11–12.

25. Painter, *Autobiography of Thomas Painter,* 9; J. P. Martin, *Ordinary Courage,* 12.

26. J. P. Martin, *Ordinary Courage,* 12–13; George Bedinger, Pension File W2992, Jonathan Burrows, Pension File W15615, Austin Wells, Pension File S32054, Israel Ide, Pension File W21431, RG 15, NAB.

27. Israel Trask in Dann, ed., *Revolution Remembered,* 406–7; Alexander Milliner, quoted in Hillard, *Last Men of the Revolution,* 67–71.

28. Henry Bedinger, quoted in Dandridge, *American Prisoners,* 13; *Connecticut Courant,* June 30, 1777.

29. Martin and Lender, *Respectable Army,* 71, 89–91.

30. Gross, *Minutemen and Their World,* 151–52; Lender, "New Jersey Brigade," 31, 33; Sellers, "Common Soldier," 154–55.

31. Quarles, *Negro in the American Revolution,* 59.

32. J. P. Martin, *Ordinary Courage,* 38, 39.

33. Barnabas Hailey, Pension File S30477, in Dorman, *Virginia Revolutionary Pension Applications,* 49:39.

34. Papenfuse and Stiverson, "General Smallwood's Recruits," 117–32; Colonel Pinckney's After Orders, March 16, 1778, in Roger P. Saunders Orderly Books, SCHS.

35. Resch, *Suffering Soldiers,* 10, 22–25.

36. Wright, *Continental Army,* 92; *Laws of Maryland,* October 31, 1777, chap. 8, sec. 4, and July 22, 1779, chap. 15, sec. 9; North Carolina Assembly, "An Act for raising Men to compleat the Continental Battalions belonging to this State," April 17, 1780, in Vollmer, *Military Obligation,* vol. 2, pt. 10, p. 91; Papenfuse and Stiverson, "General Smallwood's Recruits," 124.

37. *Laws of Maryland,* October 31, 1777, chap. 8, sec. 7; *Votes and Proceedings of the House of Delegates,* March 26, 1778; Ramsay, *Revolution of South Carolina,* 103.

38. North Carolina Assembly, "An Act to Regulate and Establish a Militia in this State," April 14, 1778, in Vollmer, *Military Obligation,* vol. 2, pt. 10, p. 70; North Carolina Assembly, "An Act for raising Men to complete the Continental Battalions belonging to this State," April 14, 1778, ibid., vol. 2, pt. 10, p. 80; South Carolina General

Assembly, "An Act for Completing the Quota of Troops to be raised by the State for the Continental Service," March 28, 1778, ibid., vol. 2, pt. 13, p. 59; Maryland General Assembly, "An Act to procure recruits," October 1780, ibid., vol. 2, pt. 5, p. 130.

39. General Lachlan McIntosh, Recruiting Orders to Capt. Wal[ton], December 21, 1776, in McIntosh, "Letter Book of Lachlan McIntosh," 258; Charles Lee to Benjamin Rush, October 10, 1775, in C. Lee, *Lee Papers*, 4:212; William Tudor to Stephen Collins, September 9, 1775, Sol Feinstone Collection, DLAR, on deposit APS.

40. Quarles, *Negro in the American Revolution*, ix; George Washington, General Orders, October 31, December 30, 1775, in Washington, *Papers: Revolutionary War Series*, 2:269, 620.

41. Neimeyer, *America Goes to War*, 72–84; Quarles, *Negro in the American Revolution*, viii–ix, 54–57. The literature on the contradictions of slavery in the Revolutionary era is extensive. For further reading, see Davis, *The Problem of Slavery in the Age of Revolution*, and Frey, *Water from the Rock*.

42. Council of War, October 8, 1775, in Washington, *Papers: Revolutionary War Series*, 2:125. Officers present were Washington, Ward, Lee, Putnam, Thomas, Spencer, Heath, Sullivan, Greene, and Gates. Quarles, *Negro in the American Revolution*, 14–15; Graydon, *Memoirs*, 131.

43. Quarles, *Negro in the American Revolution*, xi–xii; Neimeyer, *America Goes to War*, 73–74; John Sweet, private communication. Sweet is the author of *Bodies Politic: Colonialism, Race and the Emergence of the American North: Rhode Island, 1741–1831* (Baltimore: Johns Hopkins University Press, 2003).

44. General Greene's Opinion on Washington's Queries of October 5, October 6–7, 1775, in Greene, *Papers of General Nathanael Greene*, 1:132.

45. P. Wood, *Black Majority*; Quincy, "Journal of Josiah Quincy," 454.

46. Charles Lee, General Orders, June 19, 1776, in C. Lee, *Lee Papers*, 2:74. Charleston was not the only place where white soldiers felt this way. A militiaman in Virginia also objected to doing "servile labor" (Joseph French, Pension File W79, in Dorman, *Virginia Revolutionary Pension Applications*, 40:62).

47. "An Act for the more Effectual Prevention of the Desertion of the Soldiers and Sailors in the Service of this Colony," April 1776, in *Statutes at Large of South Carolina*, 4:340–41; "An Act for the Better Ordering and Governing of Negroes and other slaves in this province," April 1740, in *Public Laws of the State of South Carolina*, 163–64.

48. Colonel Pinckney's Orders, April 8, 1778, in Roger P. Saunders Orderly Books, SCHS.

49. "An Act for the Better Ordering and Governing of Negroes and other slaves in this province," April 1740, sec. 3, in *Public Laws of the State of South Carolina*, 163–64.

50. William Asberry, Pension File W2988, in Dorman, *Virginia Revolutionary Pension Applications*, 3:16.

51. Anon., August 4, 1776, Sol Feinstone Collection, DLAR, on deposit APS. This is a draft of a letter to George Washington. An abridged version is included in Washington, *Papers: Revolutionary War Series*, 5:557. There, the editor notes there is no record of

the letter being received. Samuel Carpenter, Pension File W6631, in Dorman, *Virginia Revolutionary Pension Applications*, 15:92–93.

52. Linn, *Military Discourse*, 10, 19–21.

53. Ibid., 18–19.

54. British Articles of War, 1765, sec. 15, art. 22, in W. Winthrop, *Military Law and Precedents*, 2:1466; Massachusetts Articles of War, art. 46, April 5, 1775, ibid., 2:1476; Articles of War, art. 47, June 30, 1775, ibid., 2:1483; Articles of War, sec. 14, art. 21, September 20, 1776, ibid., 2:1500; U.S. Code: title 10, sec. 933, art. 133, Uniform Code of Military Justice, ‹http://uscode.house.gov›.

55. Royster, *Revolutionary People at War*, 85–86; Colonel Lewis Nicola to General Edward Hand, May 26, 1781, Sol Feinstone Collection, DLAR, on deposit APS; George Washington to John Hancock, September 25, 1776, in Washington, *Papers: Revolutionary War Series*, 6:396.

56. Kaplan, "Rank and Status," 323; *Pennsylvania Packet and General Advertiser*, January 28, 1778; John Adams to Nathanael Greene, August 4, 1776, in Greene, *Papers of General Nathanael Greene*, 1:274; George Washington to John Hancock, September 25, 1776, in Washington, *Papers: Revolutionary War Series*, 6:395. See also Kollmann, "Reflections on the Army."

57. James Sullivan to General Sullivan, December 6, 1775, in Force, ed., *American Archives*, 4th ser., 4:206.

58. Royster, *Revolutionary People at War*, 86–94; Kollmann, "Reflections on the Army," 160; Middlekauff, "Why Men Fought," 147.

59. Selesky, *War and Society in Colonial Connecticut*, 206; Robert Orme, quoted in Titus, *Old Dominion at War*, 66.

60. Selesky, *War and Society in Colonial Connecticut*, 207; F. Anderson, *People's Army*, 112–15.

61. Selesky, *War and Society in Colonial Connecticut*, 212. The total number of Connecticut officers was 541.

62. Ibid., 213.

63. Kaplan, "Rank and Status," 323; George Washington to John Hancock, September 25, 1776, in Washington, *Papers: Revolutionary War Series*, 6:395–96.

64. Bushman, *Refinement of America*, xii–xv.

65. Ibid., 61; Greven, *Protestant Temperament*, 309–10; J. Lewis, "Domestic Tranquility," 136, 149.

66. Chesterfield, *Letters*, 154, 163, 170.

67. Bushman, *Refinement of America*, 31–38; Hawkins, *Youth's Behaviour*.

68. Bushman, *Refinement of America*, 36; Lyngard, *Letter of Advice*, 3–4, 6–9; Moody, *School of Good Manners*. For further reading on this subject, apart from Bushman, see Elias, *History of Manners*; Aresty, *Best Behavior*; and Jaeger, *Origins of Courtliness*.

69. Williams, "Journal," October 9, 10, 1775, 11.

70. Washington, *Rules of Civility*, rules 26, 85, and 106.

71. Bushman, *Refinement of America*, 43.

72. Burr, "Honor," 558; Wiebe, *Opening of American Society*, 15.

73. Grose, *Advice to the Officers of the Army*, 2.

74. Houlding, *Fit for Service*, 104–6.

75. Ibid., 100–103; Guy, *Regimental Agency*, 40–41.

76. Wright, *Continental Army*, 98–99; Rossie, *Politics of Command*, 26–27, 138–39.

77. Wright, *Continental Army*, 81.

78. Ibid., 77–78; Lender, "New Jersey Brigade," 35.

79. James Lovell to John Trumbull, March 22, 1777, quoted in Rossie, *Politics of Command*, 140–42.

80. Light horse regiments were cavalry regiments unburdened by heavy equipment; they were thus more mobile. George Washington to Colonel George Baylor, January 9, 1777, in Washington, *Papers: Revolutionary War Series*, 8:17.

81. Isaac Bangs Journal, April 1776, MHS; Graydon, *Memoirs*, 113–14.

82. Francis Marion to Isaac Harleston, March 4, 1780, SCHS; John Lacey to the State and Council of Pennsylvania, April 15, 1777, HSP.

83. Lacey, "Memoirs," 3, 4; Posey, *General Thomas Posey*, 14–30, 31.

84. Royster, *Revolutionary People at War*, 86.

85. Vaughan, "Journal," September 9, 1779, 325.

86. Lender, "New Jersey Brigade," 36.

87. Greenman, *Diary*, xiv–xvi, 61, 105, 199.

88. B. Gilbert, *Citizen-Soldier*, 12; *Winding Down*, 11; and *Citizen-Soldier*, January 8, 13-28, 1778, July–December 1779, February 21, 1780. Benjamin Gilbert spent three days with Rufus Putnam in 1784 on his way to settling near Otswego, a sign of Gilbert's improving status.

89. Lacey, "Memoirs," 3; Greenman, *Diary*, 206, 210, 214. Greenman was referring to Henry Fielding's *Tom Jones*, John Trenchard and Thomas Gordon's *Cato's Letters*, and Alain-Rene Le Sage's *Adventures of Gil Blas of Santilane*. B. Gilbert, *Winding Down*, 17; Gilbert to Daniel Gould, February 3, 1783, in B. Gilbert, *Winding Down*, 84.

90. George Washington, "Address," January 8, 1756, in Washington, *Papers: Colonial Series*, 2:257.

Chapter Two

1. Lieutenant Samuel Armstrong Diary, March 11, 1778, Mss C 1058, R. Stanton Avery Special Collections Department, NEHGS.

2. "The Soldier's Fortune," in Thomas Fanning Notebook, AAS; "The Soldiers Adieu," in Lieutenant George Bush Journal, HSD. For more information on the history of all the songs in George Bush's journal, see Keller, "Fiddle, Dance, and Sing," 47–49.

3. General Orders, August 23, 1776, in Washington, *Papers: Revolutionary War Series*, 6:109–10.

4. *Oxford English Dictionary*, 2nd ed., s.v. "honor"; *Washington, Rules of Civility*, rule 32.

5. Vaughan, "Journal," October 18, 1777, 104; Daniel Morgan to Nathanael Greene, January 19, 1781, in Greene, *Papers of General Nathanael Greene*, 7:155; *New York Gazette*, undated, in Force, ed., *American Archives*, 4th ser., 4:708.

6. E. Anderson, "Personal Recollections," 57–58.

7. George Washington to Patrick Henry, October 5, 1776, in Washington, *Papers: Revolutionary War Series*, 6:482.

8. Wyatt-Brown, *Southern Honor*, 88; Anon., *Happy man*; George Washington to Patrick Henry, October 5, 1776, in Washington, *Papers: Revolutionary War Series*, 6:482.

9. Articles of War, sec. 18, art. 5, September 20, 1776, in W. Winthrop, *Military Law and Precedents*, 2:1503.

10. Childs, *Armies and Warfare in Europe*, 92–93.

11. "Museum of the Royal Regiment of Artillery," Royal Arsenal, Woolwich, ‹http://www.firepower.org.uk›; Childs, *Armies and Warfare in Europe*, 90–91; Vauban, *De L'Attaque*; Frederick II, *Instructions of Frederick the Great*, 301–400; British Army Adjutant General's Office, *Manual of Exercise*; Wolfe, *Instructions to Young Officers*.

12. Stevenson, *Military Instructions for Officers*; Clairac, *L'Ingénieur de campagne*; Grandmaison, *Light Horse and Light Infantry*; Nicola, *Treatise of Military Exercise*; George Washington, General Orders, March 28, 1778, in Washington, *Writings of George Washington*, 11:163; von Steuben, *Regulations*.

13. Simes, *Military Guide for Young Officers*, 358; Stevenson, *Military Instructions for Officers*, 53; von Steuben, *Regulations*, 102–3.

14. Lachlan McIntosh to George Walton, December 15, 1776, "Letter Book of Lachlan McIntosh," 256; George Washington, "General Instructions for the Colonels and Commanding Officers of Regiments in the Continental Service," December 1777, in Washington, *Writings of George Washington*, 10:238; John Adams to William Tudor, October 12, 1775, and Tudor to Adams, October 28, 1775, in J. Adams, *Papers of John Adams*, 3:194–95, 261. De Saxe's *Thoughts on the Art of War* and Le Blond's *Treatise of Artillery* were translated into English in 1759 and 1746 respectively. Greenman, *Diary*, 210; Ewald, *Diary of the American War*, 108. This last claim by Ewald was almost certainly an exaggeration, as Frederick's *Instructions* to his officers was not translated into English until 1797.

15. Charles Lee to Benjamin Rush, October 10, 1775, in C. Lee, *Lee Papers*, 4:212; Nathanael Greene to Governor Nicholas Cooke of Rhode Island, November 29, 1775, in Greene, *Papers of General Nathanael Greene*, 1:155; *Connecticut Courant*, January 29, 1776.

16. *Journals of the Continental Congress*, November 4, 1775, 3:323; A. Young, "George Robert Twelve Hewes," 602–3; George Washington to John Hancock, September 25, 1776, in Washington, *Papers: Revolutionary War Series*, 6:394.

17. George Washington to John Hancock, September 25, 1776, in Washington, *Papers: Revolutionary War Series*, 6:395.

18. Ibid.; Neagles, *Summer Soldiers*, 26 and s.v. "Parker"; George Washington, General Orders, August 2, 1775, in Washington, *Papers: Revolutionary War Series*, 1:212.

19. *Resolutions, Laws, and Ordinances*, 7–8.

20. Ibid., 8–9. For comparison, in the U.S. Army in the present day, the pay of the most junior officer is two times that of a new enlistee and that of a newly appointed colonel is nearly nine times that of a new enlistee ("U.S. Army Defense Finance and Accounting Service," ‹http://www.dfas.mil/money/milpay/pay/bp-1.htm›).

21. Royster, *Revolutionary People at War*, 295–99; Martin and Lender, *Respectable Army*, 148–52.

22. Brereton, *British Soldier*, 23–24. See Brewer, *Sinews of Power*, for a discussion of how the British harnessed financial resources and administrative skill in the eighteenth century in order to fight wars more effectively.

23. Joseph Nichols, August 8, 1758, in F. Anderson, *People's Army*, 102; Sweat, "Personal Diary," September 1758, 52.

24. Glasier, "French and Indian War Diary," May 29–31, 1760, 91; Governor Dinwiddie to John Carlyle, September 11, 1754, *Dinwiddie Papers*, 1:318–19, quoted in Titus, *Old Dominion at War*, 56–57.

25. Shy, "Logistical Crisis and the American Revolution," 163, 174; Carp, *To Starve the Army at Pleasure*, 219–20.

26. Nathanael Greene to Christopher Greene, January 5, 1778, in Greene, *Papers of General Nathanael Greene*, 2:247.

27. John Williams to Elisha Porter, July 21, 1776, Elisha Porter Papers, MHS; Doctor Samuel Adams to Sally Preston Adams, August 11, 1779, Sol Feinstone Collection, DLAR, on deposit APS.

28. Tilden, "Journal of John Bell Tilden," January 7, 1782, 218; Frazer, "Papers of General Persifor Frazer," 141; Doctor Samuel Adams to Sally Preston Adams, October 18, 1776, October 31, 1778, Sol Feinstone Collection, DLAR, on deposit APS.

29. Israel Trask, in Dann, ed., *Revolution Remembered*, 407; Joseph Rundel, ibid., 65–66.

30. Tilden, "Journal of John Bell Tilden," January 10, 1782, 218; Isaac Bangs Journal, July 7, 1776, MHS.

31. Greenman, *Diary*, 145; Moses Greenleaf Diary, July 8, 1777, MHS; Brooks, "Letter," January 5, 1778, 243–45.

32. Joanna Eliot to Joseph Eliot, November 1, 1776, Joseph and Joanna Elliot Correspondence, Ella Florence Elliot Papers, Mss 46, II/C, R. Stanton Avery Special Collections Department, NEHGS; J. P. Martin, *Ordinary Courage*, 50–53; Sergeant Moses Moody Journal, January 1777, MHS; Thomas Bailey, Pension File W2991, in Dorman, *Virginia Revolutionary Pension Applications*, 3:97–99.

33. J. P. Martin, *Ordinary Courage*, 43.

34. Ibid., 46; L. Roberts, *Memoirs*, 38–40.

35. Joseph Eliot to Joanna Eliot, October 25, 1776, Joseph and Joanna Elliot Correspondence, Ella Florence Elliot Papers, Mss 46, II/C, R. Stanton Avery Special Collections Department, NEHGS; Vaughan, "Journal," January 1, 1780, July 22, June 9, 1779, 329, 323–24, 322.

36. Vaughan, "Journal," October 27, 1778, July 22, November 2, 1779, III, 323–24, 328. In his pension application in 1820, Vaughan declared that he was a house carpenter, though too old to work, in debt, and owned only household articles valued at $8.50 (ibid., 47).

37. Ebenezer Huntington to Andrew Huntington, July 7, 1780, HM3698, HL; Joslyn, "Teamster in the Continental Service," May 4, 1778, 355; White, "Narrative of Events," 75.

38. Anon., "Campaign from Philadelphia to Paulus Hook," 460.

39. McMichael, "Diary of Lt. James McMichael," May 27, 1776, January 12, 1777, 195, 204; Lieutenant Samuel Armstrong Diary, December 20, 1777, Mss C 1058, R. Stanton Avery Special Collections Department, NEHGS; Ebenezer Huntington to Andrew Huntington, July 7, 1780, HM3698, HL.

40. Greven, *Protestant Temperament*, 310. For a further discussion on the social meaning of clothing in colonial and Revolutionary society, see Baumgarten, *What Clothes Reveal*, and Prude, "To Look Upon the 'Lower Sort.'"

41. Childs, *Armies and Warfare in Europe*, 73–75.

42. Francis Marion Orderly Book, September 3, 1775, HM623, HL; Finke, "Insignia of Rank," 71–73; George Washington, General Orders, June 18, 1780, in Washington, *Writings of George Washington*, 19:21–22.

43. Kimmel, "Revolutionary War Uniform," 62. Tilghman's uniform is in the collections of the Maryland Historical Society in Baltimore.

44. Elting, ed., *Military Uniforms in America*, v; Haarman and Holst, "Friedrich von Germann Drawings," 8. The drawings that survive, which are in the New York Public Library, are almost certainly nineteenth-century copies of the von Germann originals. Haarman and Holst, "Friedrich von Germann Drawings," 1. Colonel Daniel Morgan, Regimental Orders, May 19, 1777, Orderly Book, Eleventh Virginia Regiment, May 15–June 9, 1777, in *Early American Orderly Books*, reel 4, item 45.

45. George Washington, General Orders, August 15, 1776, in Washington, *Papers: Revolutionary War Series*, 6:27.

46. McBarron, "Continental Army Uniforms and Specifications"; Nathanael Greene to Deputy Governor Nicholas Cooke of Rhode Island, July 9, 1775, in Greene, *Papers of General Nathanael Greene*, 1:98; J. P. Martin, *Ordinary Courage*, 117; General John Glover to Joseph Palmer, June 15, 1777, Joseph Palmer Papers, MHS.

47. Carp, *To Starve the Army at Pleasure*, 66–67; Royster, *Revolutionary People at War*, 192.

48. Francis Marion Orderly Book, December 2, 1775, May 21, 1777, HM623, HL.

49. Dorothy C. Barck, introduction to *Uniforms of the American, British, French and German Armies in the War of the American Revolution, 1775–1783*, by Charles M. Lefferts, 9–12; Trask, in Dann, ed., *Revolution Remembered*, 409; General Orders, July 24, 1776, in George Washington, *Papers: Revolutionary War Series*, 5:439.

50. E. Anderson, "Personal Recollections," 67.

51. Colonel Lewis Nicola to General Edward Hand, May 26, 1781, Sol Feinstone Col-

lection, DLAR, on deposit APS; General John Sullivan, Standing Orders, February 12, 1777, in J. Sullivan, *Letters and Papers of Major General John Sullivan*, 1:316.

52. General Orders, July 13, 1777, in George Washington, *Papers: Revolutionary War Series*, 10:263; Neagles, *Summer Soldiers*, s.v. "Daugherty."

53. George Washington to the Major Generals and Officers Commanding Brigades, January 22, 1780, in Washington, *Writings of George Washington*, 17:427; Lacey, "Memoirs," 503; Barnard Elliott Orderly Book, November 5, 1777, SCHS.

54. George Washington to Patrick Henry, October 5, 1776, in Washington, *Papers: Revolutionary War Series*, 6:482; Wiebe, *Opening of American Society*, 14–15.

55. Ramsay, *Revolution in South Carolina*, 2:143.

56. Boatner, *Encyclopedia*, s.v. "Montgomery"; Middlekauff, *Glorious Cause*, 307.

57. E. Anderson, "Personal Recollections," 7, 23. Holland had served with the British at the Battles of Dettington and Fontenoy. He had resigned his commission after trying and failing to get justice done for a young woman of his acquaintance who was seduced by two young noblemen who were the nephews of his colonel. Holland filed suit against them. They were acquitted but his colonel was outraged with Holland's action and demanded his resignation. Holland, recognizing the powerful forces against him and that he would never see justice, resigned and went to America (ibid., 46).

58. Von Riedesel, "Her Revolutionary War Journal," 346; Washington, *George Washington's Rules of Civility*, rules 22, 23.

59. Peter Wraxall to Henry Fox, September 27, 1755, in Pargellis, ed., *Military Affairs in North America*, 140; F. Anderson, *Crucible of War*, 125.

60. Boatner, *Encyclopedia* , s.v. "Donop"; Greenman, *Diary*, October 31, 1777, 83.

61. Captain Henry Bellew to Colonel Robert Howe, December 30, 1775, and Howe to Bellew, December 30, 1775, in Force, ed., *American Archives*, 4th ser., 4:477.

62. Royster, *Revolutionary People at War*, 43–44, 197–200. See also Wright, *Continental Army*.

63. Thomas Burke, "Abstract of Debates," February 12–19, 1777, in *Letters of the Members of the Continental Congress*, 2:262.

64. Colonel Return Jonathan Meigs to Anthony Wayne, August 22, 1779, and Lieutenant Colonel Sherman to Wayne, August 26, 1779, Coll. No. 699, Anthony Wayne Papers, HSP.

65. Anthony Wayne to Captain Thomas Posey, August 28, 1779, and Wayne to Colonel Meigs, August 23, 1779, Coll. No. 699, Anthony Wayne Papers, HSP; Nathanael Greene to Henry Lee, January 28, 1782, in Greene, *Papers of General Nathanael Greene*, 10:268–69; Nathanael Greene to Officers of the Pennsylvania Line, March 29, 1782, in Greene, *Papers of General Nathanael Greene*, 10:559.

66. *Orderly Book, Virginia Infantry 6th Regiment*, June 10, 1776, 48; Isaac DuBose Orderly Book, May 8, 1777, SCHS.

67. Isaac DuBose Orderly Book, June 10, 1777, SCHS; General Orders, January 18, 1778, in Washington, *Writings of George Washington*, 10:312.

68. Moses Greenleaf Diary, January 30, 1779, MHS; General Orders, June 13, 1780, in Washington, *Writings of George Washington*, 19:4–5.

69. General Persifor Frazer to Polly Frazer, May 23, 1776, in Frazer, "Papers of General Persifor Frazer," 139; Tilden, "Journal of John Bell Tilden," October 9, September 16, 1781, 61, 57. The importance of the cordial handshake remains part of military culture at the United States Military Academy at West Point where upper classes recognize plebes at the end of their first year with a handshake.

70. Beatty, "Journal of Lieut. Erkuries Beatty," August 1, 1779, 230.

71. Chesterfield, *Letters*, xvii.

72. Lacey, "Memoirs," 352; Beebe, "Journal," June 1, 1776, 331.

73. "Standing Regimental Orders to be Observed," in Roger P. Saunders Orderly Books, SCHS; von Steuben, *Regulations*, 115–16. See also Barber, "Order Book," 151–52.

74. Colonel Pinckney's Orders, December 21, 1777, in Roger P. Saunders Orderly Books, SCHS; Washington, *George Washington's Rules of Civility*, rules 30, 29.

75. General Orders, January 1, 1777, in Washington, *Papers: Revolutionary War Series*, 7:499; General Orders, May 23, 1777, Robert Kirkwood General Orders, HSD; Fogg, *Orderly Book of Jeremiah Fogg*, January 13, 1776; Ambrose Madison Orderly Book, January 10, 1778, Coll. No. 1884, Twelfth Virginia Regiment, HSP.

76. Stevens, *Fragments of Memoranda*, May 6, June 8, 1778.

77. Adlum, *Memoirs*, 24–36.

78. John Laurens to Henry Laurens, March 9, 1778, in J. Laurens, *Army Correspondence*; Ebenezer Huntington to Joshua Huntington, May 3, 1779, HM3694, HL.

79. Ebenezer Huntington to Joshua Huntington, December 21, 1778, HM3692, HL.

80. John Smith Diaries, September 29, 1776, AAS.

81. I. Putnam, *General Orders*, June 29, 1777, 16.

Chapter Three

1. Blatchford, "Narrative of John Blatchford," 2:26–30. Another fine adventurous war narrative is by Jacob Nagle, *The Nagle Journal: A Diary of the Life of Jacob Nagle, sailor, from the year 1775 to 1841*.

2. Colonel Lewis Nicola to George Washington, November 6, 1780, in Washington, *George Washington's Papers*, ser. 4, reel 72.

3. Martin and Lender, *Respectable Army*, 6–9; British Articles of War, 1765, sec. 15, art. 22, in W. Winthrop, *Military Law and Precedents*, 2:1448–69; Grose, *Military Antiquities*, 2:199.

4. New York General Assembly, "An Act for Regulating the Militia of this Colony," February 27, 1746, in Vollmer, *Military Obligation*, vol. 2, pt. 9, p. 162.

5. Trenchard, *Standing Armies in England*, v; Blackstone, *Commentaries on the Laws of England*, 1:572. This subordination of the standing army to the larger society is still part of British and indeed American law. In the earliest years of the new United States following the ratification of the Constitution in 1789, military courts and subsequent

legislative acts concurred that the Constitution did not apply to servicemen. The right
to due process is the only protection extended to military personnel from the Bill of
Rights. See Wiener, "Courts Martial and the Bill of Rights," 266–304.

6. Salmon, *New Geographical and Historical Grammar*, 223.

7. William Tudor, "Remarks on the Rules and Articles for the Government of the
Continental Troops," ca. August 1775, vol. 1, p. 1, item 41, Papers of the Continental
Congress, RG 11, M247, roll 38, NAB.

8. Rosswurm, *Arms, Country, and Class*, 49–53; G. Nash, *Urban Crucible*, 146, 168–
69.

9. "Articles of Association of Pennsylvania," Meeting of the Committee of Safety, August 15, 1775, *Pennsylvania Colonial Records*, 10:308, 310.

10. Ibid., 10:310–11.

11. Rosswurm, *Arms, Country, and Class*, 59–75. The reference to making "the world
over again" is to Paine, *Common Sense*, 120.

12. Martin and Lender, *Respectable Army*, 71; J. P. Martin, *Ordinary Courage*, 159.

13. Articles of War, September 20, 1776, in W. Winthrop, *Military Law and Precedents*,
2:1489–1503; "An Act Directing the Trial of Slaves," 1748, in *Statutes at Large of Virginia*,
6:111.

14. Rothman, *Discovery of the Asylum*, 48–50.

15. Spindel, "Criminal Justice," 154–57; Kealey, "Patterns of Punishment," 177–78;
Hay, "Property, Authority and the Criminal Law," 33–34.

16. Rothman, *Discovery of the Asylum*, 15, 18; Masur, *Rites of Execution*, 3; Hobart, *Excessive Wickedness*, 23; Cohen, *Pillars of Salt*, ix. It is not clear whether executions in the
southern colonies had the same religious context. With fewer ministers available, no
towns of great size, and a large slave population, public executions would certainly have
been different, but there is little information available. Recent histories have considered
the whole North American colonial experience of crime and punishment, but the sources
used were largely from the northern and middle colonies. Since those regions were the
birthplace of nineteenth-century reform movements, historical research has largely ignored the southern experience.

17. Gatrell, *Hanging Tree*, 29–31. The reference to going gently "into that good
night" is from the poem by Dylan Thomas, "Do Not Go Gentle into That Good Night"
(1952).

18. Romilly, *Observations on the Criminal Law*, 7–8; Masur, *Rites of Execution*, 3;
Printer's note to Goss, *Last Words and Dying Speech of Thomas Goss*.

19. Minutes of the Provincial Council, November 9, 1720, April 14, 1753, in *Pennsylvania Colonial Records*, 3:110, 5:612.

20. Fitzroy, "Punishment of Crime," 261.

21. Greenberg, "Crime, Law Enforcement, and Social Control," 293–325; Fede, "Le-
gitimized Violent Slave Abuse," 93–150; Goebel and Naughton, *Law Enforcement in
Colonial New York*, 703–05; Greenberg, "Effectiveness of Law Enforcement," 199; P.
Wood, *Black Majority*, 283–84.

22. Brown, *South Carolina Regulators*, 135–37, 50; W. Lee, *Crowds and Soldiers in Revolutionary North Carolina*; *South Carolina Gazette*, June 13, 1768.

23. Hindus, *Prison and Plantation*, 101; Greenberg, "Crime, Law Enforcement, and Social Control," 309–10; Preyer, "Penal Measures in the American Colonies," 330–31; Roeber, "Authority, Law, and Custom."

24. Beattie, *Crime and the Courts in England*; Hay, "Property, Authority and the Criminal Law"; Meranze, *Laboratories of Virtue*; McGowen, "Body and Punishment," 652–53; Foucault, *Discipline and Punish*; Eden, *Principles of Penal Law*; Blackstone, *Commentaries on the Laws of England*; Beccaria, *Essay on Crimes and Punishments*; Rush, *Essays, Literary, Moral and Philosophical*, 138, 39; Jefferson, *Papers of Thomas Jefferson*, 1:505, 663.

25. A. Gilbert, "Changing Face of British Military Justice," 80–84; Frey, "Courts and Cats," 5–11.

26. British Articles of War, 1765, Continental Articles of War, 1776, in W. Winthrop, *Military Law and Precedents*, 2:1448–69, 1489–1503. British and Americans were prepared, albeit reluctantly, to execute officers from the other side caught spying. Most famously, the Americans executed British major John André as a spy and for his role in Benedict Arnold's treason. However, both sides were very uncomfortable with doing so. The British army mourned his death, and Americans, deeply troubled by the execution, honored André's courage and sense of duty (Boatner, *Encyclopedia*, s.v. "André").

27. F. Anderson, *People's Army*, 122.

28. Hanford, "Narrative," 1:20–21. For the use of the gauntlet in the Continental army, see Neagles, *Summer Soldiers*, 36–37, 68–280.

29. Leach, *Roots of Conflict*, 188 n. 10. For use of piquet in the Continental army, see, for example, Francis Marion Orderly Book, October 8, 1778, HM625, HL; Isaac DuBose Orderly Book, October 3, 1777, SCHS; Neagles, *Summer Soldiers*, 68–280; and William Gipson, in Dann, ed., *Revolution Remembered*, 188–89. Grose, *Military Antiquities*, 2:200.

30. Childs, *Armies and Warfare in Europe*, 68; Brereton, *British Soldier*, 28–29; A. Gilbert, "Changing Face of British Military Justice," 81; Leach, *Roots of Conflict*, 112. Brereton records one extreme case in which a British soldier received a sentence of seven floggings of 1,800 lashes each. The first 1,800 were applied, which he barely survived. The remainder was remitted. His crime was killing his colonel's horse and selling the hide (29).

31. Clover, quoted in Brereton, *British Soldier*, 31; Andrews, "Letters of John Andrews," January 27, 1775, 397.

32. Adye, *Treatise on Courts Martial*, 112; Simes, *Military Guide for Young Officers*, 1:1–5; Stevenson, *Military Instructions for Officers*, 53.

33. Andrews, "Letters of John Andrews," 341.

34. Croswell, *Exposition of Paul's Journey*, 3, 10; ibid., 2nd edition, 1768, 2.

35. Croswell, *Exposition of Paul's Journey*, 2nd ed., 2; George Robert Twelve Hewes, quoted in A. Young, "George Robert Twelve Hewes," 586.

36. *Pennsylvania Journal*, August 28, 1766.

37. Perry, "Life of David Perry," 23.

38. F. Anderson, *People's Army*, 123.

39. One exception was South Carolina, which provided for a forty-lash sentence if the offender was an indentured servant (South Carolina General Assembly, "Acts Relating to the Militia," June 13, 1747, in Vollmer, *Military Obligation*, vol. 2, pt. 13, p. 48).

40. Titus, *Old Dominion at War*, 67; South Carolina General Assembly, "Acts Relating to the Militia," June 13, 1747, in Vollmer, *Military Obligation*, vol. 2, pt. 13, pp. 51–52.

41. Massachusetts Mutiny Act, quoted in F. Anderson, *People's Army*, 124; Selesky, *War and Society in Colonial Connecticut*, 186.

42. George Washington to Robert Dinwiddie, October 8, 1755, in Washington, *Papers: Colonial Series*, 2:84; *Statutes at Large of Virginia*, 6:559–64.

43. Titus, *Old Dominion at War*, 91; George Washington to Adam Stephen, November 18, 1755, in Washington, *Papers: Colonial Series*, 2:172.

44. Adam Stephen to George Washington, July 25, 1756, in Washington, *Papers: Colonial Series*, 3:294; Washington to Robert Dinwiddie, January 12, 1757, ibid., 4:93.

45. Titus, *Old Dominion at War*, 68.

46. George Washington to John Campbell, Earl of Loudoun, January 10, 1757, in Washington, *Papers: Colonial Series*, 4:84–85; Washington to Robert Dinwiddie, April 29, 1757, ibid., 4:144.

47. Massachusetts Mutiny Act, 1754, in F. Anderson, *People's Army*, 124–25. Anderson found only one illegal sentence of 100 lashes and that for the crimes of profanity and attempted sodomy. He thought that the outrage at the sodomy would have prompted the extreme punishment. Leach, *Roots of Conflict*, 111.

48. *Journals of Each Provincial Congress of Massachusetts*, April 5, 1775, 120–29; Massachusetts Articles of War, April 5, 1775, in W. Winthrop, *Military Law and Precedents*, 2:1470–77.

49. Massachusetts Articles of War, April 5, 1775, in W. Winthrop, *Military Law and Precedents*, 2:1470–77. Articles for Connecticut, Rhode Island, and New Hampshire are in Force, ed., *American Archives*, 4th ser., 2:565, 1153, 1180. For a general discussion of these, see Heller, "Military Law in the Continental Army"; Bernath, "George Washington"; Berlin, "Administration of Military Justice."

50. To George Washington, June 20, 1775, *Secret Journals of the Acts and Proceedings of Congress*, 1:18.

51. *Journals of the Continental Congress*, June 30, 1775, 2:120–32; W. Winthrop, *Military Law and Precedents*, 1:12.

52. William Tudor, "Remarks on the Rules and Articles for the Government of the Continental Troops," ca. August 1775, vol. 1, p. 4, item 41, Papers of the Continental Congress, RG 11, M247, roll 38, NAB.

53. *Journals of the Continental Congress*, June 14, 1776, 5:442. Thomas Jefferson (Va.), John Rutledge (S.C.), James Wilson (Pa.), and Robert Livingston (N.Y.) made up the "committee on spies" who were given the task of revising the articles. George Washing-

ton to the President of Congress, September 2[5], 1776, in Washington, *Papers: Revolutionary War Series*, 6:398; William Tudor to John Adams, July 7, 1776, in J. Adams, *Papers of John Adams*, 4:367; J. Adams, *Diary and Autobiography*, 3:409–10; Adams to Tudor, July 10, 1776, in J. Adams, *Papers of John Adams*, 4:377; *Journals of the Continental Congress*, September 20, 1776, 5:788–807; W. Winthrop, *Military Law and Precedents*, 1:13, 2:1486–1503.

54. Elbridge Gerry to Horatio Gates, June 25, 1776, in Gates, *Horatio Gates Papers*, reel 2, 1172; Charles Lee to Edmund Pendleton, May 25, 1776, in C. Lee, *Lee Papers*, 5:38; Colonel Joseph Reed to John Hancock, July 25, 1776, vol. 19, p. 41, item 78, Papers of the Continental Congress, RG 11, M247, roll 101, NAB.

55. J. Adams, *Diary and Autobiography*, 4:410, 434.

56. Wright, *Continental Army*, 91–93.

57. Ibid., 72–73.

58. Henry Laurens to John Laurens, June 23, 1775, in H. Laurens, *Papers of Henry Laurens*, 10:186; Francis Marion Orderly Book, April 21, August 16, 1776, HM623, HL.

59. For indications of the origin of the soldiers of South Carolina, see, for example, Colonel Pinckney's After Orders, March 16, 1778, in Roger P. Saunders Orderly Books, SCHS, and Charles Lee to Edmund Pendleton, May 25, 1776, in C. Lee, *Lee Papers*, 5:38. Henry Laurens to John Laurens, June 18, 1775, in H. Laurens, *Papers of Henry Laurens*, 10:181 and editor's note.

60. *Journals of the Continental Congress*, June 18, 1776, 5:462; "An Act for the more Effectual Prevention of the Desertion of the Soldiers and Sailors in the Service of this Colony," April 1776, in *Statutes at Large of South Carolina*, 4:340–41; "An Act for the Better Ordering and Governing of Negroes and other slaves in this province," April 1740, in *Public Laws of the State of South Carolina*, 163–64; Charles Lee to Edmund Pendleton, May 25, 1776, in C. Lee, *Lee Papers*, 5:38; General John Armstrong to Lee, May 8, 1776, in C. Lee, *Lee Papers*, 5:11.

61. William Tudor to John Adams, September 23, 1776, in J. Adams, *Papers of John Adams*, 5:36.

62. Samuel Bixby Diary, June 28, 1775, AAS; Fogg, *Orderly Book of Jeremiah Fogg*, November 3, 1775, 7.

63. Francis Marion Orderly Book, November 5, 1776, October 8, November 3, 1778, HM623, HL.

64. George Washington to Congress, February 3, 1781, in Washington, *Writings of Washington*, 21:178–79; *Journals of the Continental Congress*, 20:657–58. The congressional committee consisted of Joseph Jones, Alexander McDougall, and John Sullivan. John Sullivan to George Washington, July 2, 1781, *Letters of Delegates to Congress*, 17:368–69; Boatner, *Encyclopedia*, s.v. "Sherman."

65. All new state constitutions are in *Federal and State Constitutions*. Quoted here are "Constitution of North Carolina—1776," 5:2788; "Constitution of Pennsylvania—1776," 5:3090; and "Constitution of South Carolina—1778," 6:3267. Voting on the resolution

to amend the articles of war, June 16, 1781, to change the lash limit to 500 lashes from 100 was as follows: New Hampshire—Sullivan (Y), Livermore (N); Rhode Island—Varnum (N); Connecticut—Huntington (N), Ellsworth (N), Sherman (N); Massachusetts—Partridge (N), Osgood (N); Pennsylvania—Montgomery (Y), Atlee (Y), Clymer (Y), Smith (Y); Delaware—Rodney (N), McKean (N); Maryland—Jennifer (N), Carroll (Y), Potts (Y); Virginia—Madison (Y), Bland (N), Smith (N); North Carolina—Sharpe (N), Johnston (Y); South Carolina—Mathews (Y), Motte (Y), Eveleigh (Y); Georgia—Walton (Y), Howly (N). The delegate vote was fourteen to thirteen against, and by state, six to three with three tied (*Journals of the Continental Congress*, 20:657–58).

66. Articles of War, 1776, sec. 17, art. 1, in W. Winthrop, *Military Law and Precedents*, 2:1501; Neagles, *Summer Soldiers*, 68–280; Peter Dago, "a transient negro," in Neagles, *Summer Soldiers*, s.v. "Dago"; Colonel Peter Simmons Orderly Book, South Carolina Militia, June 13, 1776–August 1, 1776, in Neagles, *Summer Soldiers*, 68–280.

67. George Washington to the President of Congress, September 25, 1776, in Washington, *Papers: Revolutionary War Series*, 6:398–99; General John Armstrong to Charles Lee, May 8, 1776, in C. Lee, *Lee Papers*, 5:10; Greenman, *Diary*, 73.

68. John Smith Diaries, September 13, 1778, AAS; Neagles, *Summer Soldiers*, s.v. "Ricky"; Benjamin Beal Journal, July 6, 1776, AAS.

69. *Pennsylvania Evening Post*, March 11, 1777; *Independent Chronicle and the Universal Advertiser*, July 2, 1778.

70. Thomas James to Elisha James, October 3, 1777, and Sarah James to Elisha James, October 5, 1777, Elisha James Letters, MHS.

71. "Capt. Bingham's Order Book, 8th CT Regiment," December 31, 1779, in *Record of the Service of Connecticut Men in the War of the Revolution*, 135; "Records of the South Carolina Line," 89.

72. Higginbotham, *Daniel Morgan*, 92–95.

73. Articles of War, 1776, in W. Winthrop, *Military Law and Precedents*, 2:1489–1503.

74. Moses Greenleaf Diary, May 26, 1777, MHS; Littell, "Revolutionary Journal and Orderly Book," January 29, 1779, 162.

75. Francis Marion Orderly Book, October 8, 1778, HM625, HL; Isaac DuBose Orderly Book, October 3, 1777, SCHS; Neagles, *Summer Soldiers*, 68–280. William Gipson, a South Carolinian militiaman, told in his pension application of his company carrying out an impromptu court martial of a loyalist and sentencing him "to be spicketed." In this case, the unfortunate man was not only impaled on the spike but also twisted by his captors so that the spike went through his foot (Dann, ed., *Revolution Remembered*, 188–89).

76. A. Lewis, *The orderly book*, 72; Colonel Francis Johnson, "Orderly Book, 5th Pennsylvania June 6, 1779–July 7, 1779," June 10, 1779, in *Early American Orderly Books*, reel 8, item 88; Colonel John Lamb Orderly Book, 2nd Regiment of Continental Artillery, June 26, 1780–December 30, 1780, in *Early American Orderly Books*, reel 12, item 118.1;

Greene, Orders, August 11, 1775, in Greene, *Papers of General Nathanael Greene*, 1:108; Neagles, *Summer Soldiers*, 68–280 (see, for example, s.v. "Samuel Woods," "John Themes," "Thomas Smith," and "Cicero Sweat").

77. Judith Stevens (née Sargent) to Winthrop Sargent, July 20, 1781, quoted in Skemp, *Judith Sargent Murray*, 40; J. Thacher, *Military Journal*, 224.

78. Morton, "Diary of Robert Morton," 23, 10.

79. Major Pinckney's Orders, December 28, 1775, "Extracts from the Order Book of Charles Lining," in Gibbes, ed., *Documentary History of the American Revolution*, 1:245; George Washington to Marquis de Lafayette, November 6, 1780, in Washington, *Writings of George Washington*, 20:309.

80. Hamilton, ed., *Braddock's Defeat*; I. Putnam, *General Orders*, August 13, 1777, 55.

81. William Tudor to John Adams, September 23, 1776, in J. Adams, *Papers of John Adams*, 5:36; Henry Laurens to John Laurens, February 6, 1778, in J. Laurens, "Correspondence between Henry Laurens and His Son, John," 50.

82. Vaughan, "Journal," January 1, 1779, 113.

83. William Moultrie General Orders, August 7, 1779, SCHS.

84. George Washington to Colonel Thomas Hartley, May 29, 1778, and Washington's General Orders, May 29, 1778, in Washington, *Writings of George Washington*, 11:480, 487; Kirkwood, "Journal and Order Book," May 1, 1777, 4; Neagles, *Summer Soldiers*, 68–280; Grimke, "Journal of the Campaign to the Southward," July 14, 1778, 206.

85. Bloomfield, *Citizen Soldier*, 41, 103.

86. Moses Greenleaf Diary, January 18, 1779, MHS.

87. Barnard Elliott Orderly Book, June 9, 1776, SCHS; Barber, "Order Book," August 12, 1779, 199.

88. General St. Clair's Division Orders, July 4, 1779, "Colonel Francis Johnson's Orderly Book," in *Early American Orderly Books*.

89. Dabney Freeman, R3778, in Dorman, *Virginia Revolutionary Pension Applications*, 40:39; Israel Trask, in Dann, ed., *Revolution Remembered*, 411.

90. Kirkwood, "Journal and Order Book," July 2, 1777, 95.

91. Willcutt, *Revolutionary War Pension Applications*.

92. George Washington to the Council of General Officers, August 20, 1778, in Washington, *Writings of George Washington*, 12:344; Neagles, *Summer Soldiers*, 37; A. Bowman, *Morale of the American Revolutionary Army*, 89. Bowman calculated 40 out of 225 capital sentences completed. He cites Fitzpatrick (editor of Washington, *Writings of George Washington*) as counting 75 and admits that the data were incomplete. George Washington to Colonel Goose Van Schaick, October 27, 1778, in Washington, *Writings of George Washington*, 13:167.

93. Rogers, *Journal of a Brigade Chaplain*, 66–69.

94. Wild, "Journal of Ebenezer Wild," January 10, October 17, 1778, 106, 119.

95. Grimke, "Journal of the Campaign to the Southward," May 21, 1778, 64.

96. Ibid., May 24, June 6, 1778, 66–67, 121.

97. J. P. Martin, *Ordinary Courage*, 29; E. Anderson, "Personal Recollections," 23–24.

98. J. P. Martin, *Ordinary Courage*, 29. An angry Colonel Joseph Reed had accused Sergeant Leffingwell of deserting his post. The sergeant claimed he had been acting under the orders of another officer. After a court-martial sentenced him to death, Reed, now calmer, lobbied for his reprieve (ibid., n. 23).

99. E. Anderson, "Personal Recollections," 24; *Independent Chronicle and the Universal Advertiser*, July 9, 1778.

100. Seymour, "A Journal of the Southern Expedition," 22; George Washington to Henry Lee, July 9, 10, 1779, in Washington, *Writings of George Washington*, 15:388, 399; Royster, *Revolutionary People at War*, 81–82.

101. Tilden, "Journal of John Bell Tilden," 61; Neagles, *Summer Soldiers*, s.v. "Joseph Leaunden."

102. General John Armstrong to Charles Lee, May 8, 1776, in C. Lee, *Lee Papers*, 5:11.

103. Ambrose Madison Orderly Book, March 11, 1778, Coll. No. 1884, Twelfth Virginia Regiment, HSP; Neagles, *Summer Soldiers*, s.v. "Lambert"; Nicola, *Treatise of Military Exercise*, 90–91; Daniel Morgan Orderly Book, August 22, 1777, Coll. No. 973, Eleventh Virginia Regiment, HSP.

104. Wild, "Journal of Ebenezer Wild," March 15, 1778, 107.

105. Neagles, *Summer Soldiers*, 68–280. What follows are the data extracted from the orderly books of selected regiments from Neagles. Captain Robert Kirkwood, Delaware Regiment, March 1, 1777–December 21, 1777: officers tried, 18, acquitted 6 (33%); NCOs tried, 8, acquitted, 3 (38%); soldiers tried, 83, acquitted, 10 (12%). Orderly Book of the Sixth Maryland Regiment, August 15, 1779–December 24, 1779: officers tried, 14, acquitted, 4 (28.6%); NCOs tried, 1, acquitted, 0 (0%); soldiers tried, 9, acquitted, 0 (0%). Colonel Samuel Webb's Connecticut Regiment, September 9, 1778–October 8, 1783: officers tried, 10, acquitted, 7 (70%); NCOs tried, 7, acquitted, 4 (57%); soldiers tried, 119, acquitted, 24 (20.2%). General Heath, Massachusetts Regiment, May 23, 1777–October 20, 1778: officers tried, 13, acquitted, 6 (46%); NCOs tried, 1, acquitted, 0 (0%); soldiers tried, 53, acquitted, 13 (24.5%). Civilian comparisons are highly variable from region to region. The most complete records are in Massachusetts where Linda Kealey has calculated a total 17 percent acquittal rate during the eighteenth century. This is not broken down by social status (Kealey, "Patterns of Punishment," 170). Kealey notes wide variations in conviction rates for different kinds of crimes. There is similar inconsistency in the military world, and in both, the reasons behind variations in sentences or acquittals are mostly lost to us. My thanks to Sharlene Messer for her help in compiling the data from *Summer Soldiers*.

106. Barber, "Order Book," August 12, 1779, 199.

107. Phineas Ingalls Journal, July 15, 1775, MHS; John Smith Diaries, September 16, 1776, AAS.

108. Greenberg, "Effectiveness of Law Enforcement," 173–74.

Chapter Four

1. Barnard Elliott Orderly Book, August 18, 1776, SCHS.

2. Rush, *Directions for Preserving the Health of Soldiers*.

3. Charles Lee to General John Armstrong, July 14, 1776, in C. Lee, *Lee Papers*, 2:139; Nathanael Greene to George Washington, July 11, 1776, in Washington, *Papers: Revolutionary War Series*, 5:263–64; J. P. Martin, *Ordinary Courage*, 33.

4. There is a voluminous literature on the Hospital Department of the Continental army. See especially Saffron, *Surgeon to Washington*; Bell, *John Morgan*; Gillett, *Army Medical Department*; and Bayne-Jones, *Evolution of Preventive Medicine*.

5. McKeown and Brown, "Medical Evidence," 120; Saffron, "Tilton Affair," 67.

6. Zinsser, *Rats, Lice and History*, 152.

7. Howard, *War in European History*, 56–57.

8. C. Jones, *Charitable Imperative*, 220–22; "Articles of War of James II (1688)," art. 36, in W. Winthrop, *Military Law and Precedents*, 2:1440; Brereton, *British Soldier*, 16; Guy, *Regimental Agency*. These hospitals, the Royal Chelsea and the Royal Kilmainham, were pre-dated by the Hôtel des Invalides, established by the French in 1670. However, that institution was intended primarily as a home for older, impoverished veterans and not as a hospital (C. Jones, *Charitable Imperative*, 217–18).

9. "Articles of War of James II (1688)," art. 59, W. Winthrop, *Military Law and Precedents*, 2:1444; "British Articles of War of 1765," sec. 17, art. 2, ibid., 2:1467; "American Articles of War of 1776," sec. 15, ibid., 2:1501.

10. Zinsser, *Rats, Lice and History*, 152; *Journals of the Continental Congress*, July 27, 1775, 2:210–11.

11. Pringle, *Observations on the Diseases of the Army*; Brocklesby, *Oeconomical and Medical Observations*; Monro, *Account of the Diseases*, 315.

12. Pringle, *Observations on the Diseases of the Army*, viii; Selwyn, "Sir John Pringle," 266–74.

13. Selwyn, "Sir John Pringle," 266–74.

14. Monro, *An Account of the Diseases*, ix; Brocklesby, *Oeconomical and Medical Observations*, 28.

15. *Pennsylvania Gazette*, September 4, 1755; Bayne-Jones, *Evolution of Preventive Medicine*, 9, 41; Bell, *John Morgan*, 101–2.

16. Rosenberg, *Care of Strangers*, 4; Ulrich, *Midwife's Tale*, 11.

17. Risse, "Medical Care," 1:45–77; Starr, *Social Transformation of American Medicine*, 30–37; Joy, "Natural Bonesetters," 416–41; T. Thacher, *Brief Rule to the Common People*; Tennent, *Every Man His Own Doctor*; Tissot, *Advice to the People*; Buchan, *Domestic Medicine*.

18. Buchan, *Domestic Medicine*; Tennent, *Every Man His Own Doctor*, 3, 5; Tissot, *Advice to the People*.

19. Wesley, *Primitive Physick*; Rogal, "Pills for the Poor," 81–90.

20. Starr, *Social Transformation of American Medicine*, 33–35; Rogal, "Pills for the

Poor," 85; Muhlenberg, *Journals of Henry Melchior Muhlenberg*, February 2, 1780, 3:396, 423–24.

21. Starr, *Social Transformation of American Medicine*, 31–37; Buchan, quoted in Risse, "Medical Care," 1:63; Risse, "Medical Care," 1:62–63; Ulrich, *Midwife's Tale*, 254.

22. Gelfand, "History of the Medical Profession"; R. French, "Anatomical Tradition," 1:93–98; Lawrence, "Surgery (Traditional)," 2:978; Gillett, *Army Medical Department*, 14–18.

23. Bell, *John Morgan*, 155; Hindle, *Pursuit of Science*, 115.

24. Gelfand, "Modern Concept of Medical Specialization," 521–23; J. Morgan, *Institution of Medical Schools*, 43, xvii.

25. Samuel Bard Letter (to John Morgan), January 21, 1767, Autograph Case, Library, College of Physicians of Philadelphia.

26. Middleton, *Medical Discourse*, 52–53, 65–66.

27. Black, *European Warfare*, 39; Bell, *John Morgan*, 31–32.

28. F. Anderson, *People's Army*, 99, 101; Selesky, *War and Society in Colonial Connecticut*, 190–91; Greven, *Four Generations*, 196–97 n. 16; F. Anderson, *Crucible of War*, 500–501. Boston's mortality rate averaged between roughly 31 and 46 per 1,000 from the beginning of the century until the Revolution. Andover's annual mortality rates were usually below about 21 per 1,000 but had a high of 71 per 1,000 during a "throat distemper" (probably diphtheria) epidemic. In contrast, death rates for different units of Massachusetts provincials varied widely but ranged as high as 137.5 per 1,000 for a period of much less than a year. Connecticut troops in Havana experienced a mortality rate of 193 per 1,000 for a similarly short period. Data are from the works cited.

29. Sweat, "Personal Diary," September 1758, 49–51.

30. Bell, *John Morgan*, 32; Sweat, "Personal Diary," September 1758, 49–50.

31. Frey, *British Soldier in America*, 22–52; Benjamin Rush to John Adams, October 1, 1777, in Rush, *Letters of Benjamin Rush*, 1:155.

32. T. Sullivan, "Common British Soldier," 236; W. Howe, *Orderly Book*, May 18, 1776, 278; Donkin, *Military Collections and Remarks*, 116.

33. Bowen, *War and British Society*, 16; Hayter, "Army and the First British Empire," 111–32; J. Duffy, *Epidemics in Colonial America*, 214–15; Clodfelter, *Warfare and Armed Conflicts*, 1:99–100, 174.

34. Frey, *British Soldier in America*, 29, 42; Clodfelter, *Warfare and Armed Conflicts*, 1:198. So deadly were British naval adventures in the Tropics during the Revolution that personnel losses are calculated as 18,541 dead from disease versus 1,243 killed in action, a ratio of almost fifteen to one (Clodfelter, *Warfare and Armed Conflicts*, 1:198). For all statistics given, the numbers of men who died of wounds some time after the battle are included in the total for all disease fatalities, since many wounded men died from a cross-infection contracted in hospitals rather than from the wound itself. Consequently, records of the period rarely make the distinction. For a succinct discussion of the many variables and problems in calculating death rates, see Corvisier and Childs, "Losses of Life."

35. Benjamin Rush to John Adams, October 1, 1777, in Rush, *Letters of Benjamin Rush*, 1:156; J. Thacher, *Military Journal*, 426; Bayne-Jones, *Evolution of Preventive Medicine*, 55–56.

36. Peckham, *Toll of Independence*, 131–33. Peckham derived his number for deaths from disease from the data collected for the companion volume edited by Charles Lesser, *The Sinews of Independence*. Peckham describes James Thacher's estimate of 70,000 as "far wrong" (*Toll of Independence*, xi, 132). There has been some revision to Peckham's total of battle deaths as new analytical techniques emerge, but his data remain the best comprehensive examination of Revolutionary War mortality. For a revision for one battle and a detailed look at some of the problems in making the calculation, see Babits, *Devil of a Whipping*, 150–52.

37. Benjamin Rush to General Nathanael Greene, February 1, 1778, in Rush, *Letters of Benjamin Rush*, 1:195.

38. James Fergus, Pension File W25573, Alexander Logan, Pension File W2821, RG 15, NAB. Fergus noted that some of the men died after they had returned home, further complicating mortality data. It is impossible now to calculate meaningful rates of deaths per thousand, a standard measure of community mortality. The total number of men serving in Continental, militia, and state troops has been variously estimated at 200,000 to 250,000 over the whole war, but how many of these men served at one time is not clear. Since the pattern of mortality from disease cannot be reconstructed other than for a few weeks at a time, it is hard to arrive at even suggestive data. Peckham calculates the death toll as a percentage of total population as 0.9 percent, making it second only to the Civil War in this measure of American wartime experience (Peckham, *Toll of Independence*, 132).

39. *Journals of the Continental Congress*, 2:210–11, 5:568–71, 7:231–37, 10:128–31, 18:878–88. For a detailed account of the sequence and politics of the legislation, see Gillett, *Army Medical Department*.

40. Carp, *To Starve the Army at Pleasure*, 219–20; John Cochran to Jonathan Potts, March 18, 1780, in Saffron, *Surgeon to Washington*, 227.

41. For studies of age distributions of the different forces, see, for example, Lender, "New Jersey Brigade," 29; Papenfuse and Stiverson, "General Smallwood's Recruits," 121; and Frey, *British Soldier in America*, 23–24.

42. Lesser, *Sinews of Independence*, xxx–xxxi; Tilton, *Economical Observations*, 44–45.

43. J. Thacher, *Military Journal*, 385; Van Swieten, *Diseases Incident to Armies*. The Dutch-born Van Swieten was the director of army medical services for Empress Marie Theresa of Austria.

44. Rush, "Directions for Preserving the Health of Solders [*sic*]," in *Pennsylvania Packet and Daily Advertiser*, April 22, 1777; Rush, *Directions for Preserving the Health of Soldiers*, in Rush, *Letters of Benjamin Rush*, 1:140–47; Nathanael Greene to Benjamin Rush, May 3, 1777, in Greene, *Papers of General Nathanael Greene*, 2:68.

45. Von Steuben, *Regulations*, 83, 89.

46. George Washington, General Orders, May 4, 1776, in Washington, *Papers: Rev-*

olutionary War Series, 4:198-99; Colonel Daniel Morgan Orderly Book, Eleventh Virginia Regiment, May 22, 1777, in *Early American Orderly Books*, reel 4, item 45.

47. Bayne-Jones, *Evolution of Preventive Medicine*, 34-35.

48. John Irwin Orderly Book, August 12, 1777, HM939, HL; "Francis Marion's Orderly Book," General Orders, June 19, 1777, in Gibbes, ed., *Documentary History of the American Revolution*, 2:59.

49. Colonel Daniel Morgan Orderly Book, Eleventh Virginia Regiment, May 15-June 9, 1777, in *Early American Orderly Books*, reel 4, item 45; Francis Marion Orderly Book, September 7, 1775, HM623, HL; George Washington, General Orders, July 11, 1776, in Washington, *Papers: Revolutionary War Series*, 5:263.

50. John Smith Diaries, December 12, 1776, AAS.

51. Washington, (After) Orders, October 1, 1777, in Washington, *Writings of George Washington*, 9:298; Anon., draft of a letter to George Washington, August 4, 1776, Sol Feinstone Collection, DLAR, on deposit APS.

52. Norton, "Revolutionary Diary," 339-40.

53. John Irwin Orderly Book, August 12, 1777, HM939, HL; Washington, General Orders, January 7, 1778, in Washington, *Writings of George Washington*, 10:273.

54. Brigadier-General Lachlan McIntosh, quoted in Bodle and Thibaut, *Valley Forge Historical Research Report*, 153.

55. Mayer, *Belonging to the Army*, 1-22; Sarah Osborn, in Dann, ed., *Revolution Remembered*, 242, 244.

56. Charles Willson Peale Diary, January 1777, HM974, HL.

57. Greenman, *Diary*, 18; Grimke, "Journal of the Campaign to the Southward," 119.

58. Israel Angell Diary, February 26, 1778, MHS.

59. Lesser, *Sinews of Independence*, xxx-xxxi, 160-61. The average percentage of sick for 1779 was 10.47 percent; for 1780, 9.64 percent; for 1781, 10.79 percent (for the nine months for which data are available); for 1782, 14.11 percent; and for 1783, until the army was disbanded in the summer, 10.88 percent. Data from the work cited.

60. Tilton, *Economical Observations*, 45.

61. Charles Lee, "Proposals for the Formation of a Body of Light Troops Ready to be Detach'd on Emergent Occasions," 1778, in C. Lee, *Lee Papers*, 3:287; Tilton, *Economical Observations*, 44.

62. Royster, *Light-Horse Harry Lee*, 14, 18-19.

63. Henry Banks, *The Vindication of John Banks*, 61, quoted in Royster, *Light-Horse Harry Lee*, 19; Royster, *Light-Horse Harry Lee*, 37; Moses Hall, in Dann, ed., *Revolution Remembered*, 202.

64. Boatner, *Encyclopedia*, s.v. "Marion."

65. Francis Marion Orderly Book, June 30, September 3, 1775, June 19, 1777, HM623, HL.

66. Ibid., March 9, 1777; Bass, *Swamp Fox*, 4; Nathanael Greene to Francis Marion, April 24, 1781, in Greene, *Papers of General Nathanael Greene*, 8:144.

67. Francis Marion Orderly Book, February 1781-December 1782, HM622, HL;

Nathanael Greene to Francis Marion, January 16, 1781, Marion to Greene, January 20, 1781, Marion to Greene, January 1, 1781, in Greene, *Papers of General Nathanael Greene*, 7:131, 165, 36.

68. Boatner, *Encyclopedia*, s.v. "Barton"; Abel Potter, in Dann, ed., *Revolution Remembered*, 23.

69. Trumbull, "Concise Journal," 168.

70. Ibid.; Ezra Tilden Journal, September 25, 1776, MHS; Ebenezer David to Nicholas Brown, August 31, 1776, in David, *Rhode Island Chaplain*, 27.

71. Ebenezer David to Nicholas Brown, August 31, 1776, in David, *Rhode Island Chaplain*, 27.

72. Fletcher, "Narrative," 2:13; pension file of Benen Foster, in Sherman, *Dubrose Times*, 15.

73. Nathanael Greene to the President of Congress, September 11, 1781, in Greene, *Papers of General Nathanael Greene*, 9:332; Colonel Alexander Stewart to Greene, September 9, 1781, ibid., 9:310; Greene to Stewart, September 13, 1781, ibid., 9:343. The editor of the Greene papers suggests that perhaps Greene was annoyed that Stewart had destroyed stores of rum as he retreated from the field (ibid., 9:310). A brief biographical sketch of William Washington can be found in 8:389.

74. Henry Sherburne to Jonathan Potts, August 13, 1776, Coll. No. 521, Potts Papers, HSP; Heitman, ed., *Historical Register*, s.v. "Sherburne," "Gardner."

75. Doctor Jonathan Potts to John Morgan, August 10, 1776, Coll. No. 521, Potts Papers, HSP.

76. Dudley Colman to his wife, September 26, 1776, Dudley Colman Letters, MHS; Tilden, "Journal of John Bell Tilden," May 28, June 25, 1782, 226–27; Angell, *Diary of Colonel Israel Angell*, September 19, 20, 1778.

77. Angell, *Diary of Colonel Israel Angell*, December 31, 1778.

78. Ebenezer David to Nicholas Brown, August 31, 1776, in David, *Rhode Island Chaplain*, 26–27; anonymous chaplain of Colonel Durkee's Regiment (Pa.), "Extract from Journal," in Force, ed., *American Archives*, 5th ser., 2:460; Beebe, "Journal," 336; B. Wells, "Journal of Bayze Wells," 239.

79. Joslyn, "Teamster in the Continental Service," 320; Jacob Kimmel's testimony at the court-martial of William Shippen, as reported by John Morgan in *Pennsylvania Packet and Daily Advertiser*, October 21, 1780.

80. James Tilton testimony, *Pennsylvania Packet and Daily Advertiser*, October 14, 1780; Beebe, "Journal," 347, 338.

81. Thomas Hale to his parents, September 13, 1776, Sol Feinstone Collection, DLAR, on deposit APS; S. Nash, "Journal of Solomon Nash," August 19, 1776; Alexander Logan, Pension File W2821, RG 15, NAB; John Allgood, Pension File W1350, in Dorman, *Virginia Revolutionary Pension Applications*, 1:88–89.

82. James Fergus, in Dann, ed., *Revolution Remembered*, 184; Samuel Larrabee, ibid., 11.

83. Joseph Rundell, in Dann, ed., *Revolution Remembered*, 68; John Almy, Pension File W1531, in Dorman, *Virginia Revolutionary Pension Applications*, 1:97–98; Thomas

Gilmore, Pension File R4044, RG 15, NAB; Thomas Davis, Pension File R2755, in Dorman, *Virginia Revolutionary Pension Applications*, 28:26–27.

84. B. Gilbert, *Citizen-Soldier*, December 3, 1778. The editor of Gilbert's diary notes that, based on his symptoms, Gilbert was probably suffering from a vitamin deficiency such as pellagra or beriberi (ibid., xxx).

85. Phineas Ingalls Journal, August 19, 1775, MHS; Obadiah Brown Journal, September 16–October 31, 1776, MHS.

86. Jonathan Burrows, April 16, 1782, in Sherman, *Dubrose Times*, 9; Jonathan Burrows, Pension File W15615, RG 15, NAB.

87. How, *Diary of David How*, January 30, 1776, 4; Elisha James to Sarah James, October 19, September 2, 1777, Elisha James Letters, MHS. The evidence of this visiting is largely in the letters and diaries of New England servicemen. This is perhaps a reflection of the fact that there were more towns there or more men there enlisted in the company of others they knew.

88. Elisha Bostwick, Pension File S10376, RG 15, NAB.

89. Benjamin Rush to John Adams, October 21, 1777, in Rush, *Letters of Benjamin Rush*, 1:161.

90. Charles Willson Peale Diary, January 1777, HM974, HL; Middlekauff, *Glorious Cause*, 524; T. Rodney, "Diary of Captain Thomas Rodney," January 4, 1777, 39.

91. John Durkee Orderly Book, HM826, HL; Vaughan, "Journal," 110; L. Roberts, *Memoirs*, 26, 36.

92. Senter, "Journal of Isaac Senter," 21. Emphasis mine.

93. Tilton, *Economical Observations*, 62.

94. Fenn, *Pox Americana*, 32.

95. Ibid., 33; Douglass, *Inoculation of the Small Pox*, 23–24; Boylston, *Historical Account of the Small-Pox*, 34–35.

96. Ibid., 33–34; Bayne-Jones, *Evolution of Preventive Medicine*, 17; Saffron, *Surgeon to Washington*, 20.

97. General Orders, May 20, 26, 1776, in Washington, *Papers: Revolutionary War Series*, 4:343–44, 384–86; Fenn, *Pox Americana*, 47–48; Bayne-Jones, *Evolution of Preventive Medicine*, 53.

98. Lacey, "Memoirs," 203; Fenn, *Pox Americana*, 102–34.

99. Dearborn, *Revolutionary War Journals*, 77; Josiah Sabin, in Dann, ed., *Revolution Remembered*, 19; Israel Warner to Henry Stephens, January 15, 1846, quoted in Fenn, *Pox Americana*, 71; Beebe, "Journal," 328; Fenn, *Pox Americana*, 67–72.

100. J. Thacher, *Military Journal*, 53; Fenn, *Pox Americana*, 53, 71, 75; Bell, *John Morgan*, 188; J. Morgan, *Recommendation of Inoculation*, 6; Boatner, *Encyclopedia*, s.v. "Thomas."

101. Josiah Sabin, in Dann, ed., *Revolution Remembered*, 19.

102. George Washington to John Hancock, September 8, 1776, in Washington, *Papers: Revolutionary War Series*, 6:250; Washington to Hancock, September 25, 1776, ibid., 6:398.

103. Owen, *Medical Department*, 1–2; Journals of the Provincial Congress, May 8, 1775, ibid., 11; Doctor Samuel Adams to Sally Adams, November 9, 1776, Sol Feinstone Collection, DLAR, on deposit APS; J. Thacher, *Military Journal*, 34.

104. Cash, *Medical Men*, 1. Cash stated that this figure excluded women, whom he identified as mostly midwives. However, as Ulrich has since shown, many midwives were involved in a broad range of medical activities (*Midwife's Tale*).

105. Carp, *To Starve the Army at Pleasure*, 26.

106. George Washington to the Committee of Congress with the Army, January 29, 1778, in Washington, *Writings of George Washington*, 10:394–95.

107. Gillett, *Army Medical Department*, 22–49.

108. Tilton, *Economical Observations*, 9, vi.

109. James Tilton to Thomas Rodney, April 9, 1781, HSD; John Warren to Jonathan Potts, May 16, 1777, in Neill, ed., *Biographical Sketch of Doctor Jonathan Potts*; Boatner, *Encyclopedia*, s.v. "Warren."

110. Tilton, *Economical Observations*, 19; J. Jones, *Plain Concise Practical Remarks*, ii, vii.

111. Nathanael Greene to John Morgan, January 10, 1779, in Greene, *Papers of General Nathanael Greene*, 3:159.

112. Saffron, *Surgeon to Washington*, 47–48; John Cochran to Andrew Craigie, August 9, 1780, ibid., 228.

113. Saffron, "Tilton Affair," 67; Tilton, *Economical Observations*, 13–14.

114. Pringle, *Observations on the Diseases of the Army*, xiv; Benjamin Rush to Horatio Gates, February 4, 1778, in Rush, *Letters of Benjamin Rush*, 1:198; Rush to Gates, April 9, 1778, in Rush, *Letters of Benjamin Rush*, 1:208–9.

115. T. Rodney, "Diary of Captain Thomas Rodney," December 15, 1776, 12; Ebenezer Huntington to Andrew Huntington, July 7, 1780, HM3698, HL; Ichabod Ward to Abraham Pierson, January 19, 1778, in Bodle and Thibaut, *Valley Forge Historical Research Report*, 163.

116. Stillman, *Death the Last Enemy*.

Chapter Five

1. Stevens, *Fragments of Memoranda*, September 12, 1777; Anthony Crockett, Pension File S10492, in Dorman, *Virginia Revolutionary Pension Applications*, 25:2; James Fergus, Pension File W25573, RG 15, NAB.

2. *Hamlet*, 5.2.395–400.

3. J. Thacher, *Military Journal*, 254.

4. Laqueur, "Naming and Memory in the Great War," 150–52. My thanks to Thomas Laqueur for introducing to me the concept of naming in a seminar he taught on the Great War.

5. Blauner, "Death and Social Structure," 378–83; Huntington and Metcalf, *Celebrations of Death*, 2.

6. Blauner, "Death and Social Structure," 378–83; Stannard, *Puritan Way of Death*, 128; Huntington and Metcalf, *Celebrations of Death*, 5–17.

7. James Bates, Pension File S30850, in Dorman, *Virginia Revolutionary Pension Applications*, 5:35. Bates in his pension application says James Rutherford died in a skirmish with the British around the beginning of October, three weeks after the battle at Eutaw Springs. However, other sources indicate that the death occurred at Eutaw Springs (Heitman, ed., *Historical Register*, s.v. "James Rutherford"). My thanks to Craig Scott for his help on the genealogy of the Rutherford family.

8. Fritz, "Undertaking Trade in England," 241–53; Vinovskis, "Angels' Heads and Weeping Willows," 282–83; R. Wells, *Facing the King of Terrors*, 4–5.

9. Pike and Armstrong, *Time to Mourn*, 15–16; Stannard, *Puritan Way of Death*, 117, 156–57; Sloane, *Last Great Necessity*, 14–15.

10. Israel Angell Diary, January 4, 1778, MHS; Anburey, *Travels Through the Interior Parts of America*, 1:159–60.

11. Wilson and Ferris, eds., *Encyclopedia of Southern Culture*, 478; H. Jones, *Present State of Virginia*, 67–68.

12. Genovese, *Roll, Jordan, Roll*, 194; Sobel, *World They Made Together*, 218–22; Blassingame, *Slave Community*, 41–42.

13. Stannard, *Puritan Way of Death*, 103; Frederick Jones to Thomas Jones, January 10, 1765, Jones Family Papers, quoted in J. Lewis, "Domestic Tranquility," 145; J. Lewis, "Domestic Tranquility," 141, 146; John Watts to John Erving, November 29, 1762, in Watts, *Letterbook of John Watts*, 99.

14. Boyle, "Boyle's Journal," 85: 13, 121–22.

15. *Henry V*, 4.8.103–6; Laqueur, "Naming and Memory in the Great War," 150–52.

16. Israel Angell Diary, November 14, 1777, MHS.

17. Thomas Nelson Jr. to Colonel Josiah Parker, July 27, 1781, in Parker, "Revolutionary Correspondence," 264; McMichael, "Diary of Lt. James McMichael," February 8, 1778, 216.

18. Otto Williams, "Account furnished by Col. Otto Williams," in Gibbes, ed., *Documentary History of the American Revolution*, 3:151; anon., February 9, 1776, "Extract from a letter from Canada," in Force, ed., *American Archives*, 4th ser., 4:706–7; Colonel Joseph Reed to Mrs. Reed, September 22, 1776, in Force, ed., *American Archives*, 5th ser., 2:443–44.

19. Beebe, "Journal," 337–42. Emphasis mine.

20. Samuel Bixby Diary, July 13, 1775, AAS; Vaughan, "Journal," 106.

21. Samuel Bixby Diary, September 7, 1775, AAS; How, *Diary of David How*.

22. Charles Willson Peale Diary, 1776–77, HM974, HL; Ebenezer Huntington to Andrew Huntington, September 12, 1776, HM3670, HL.

23. Israel Angell Diary, January 25, 1778, MHS.

24. Persifor Frazer to Polly Frazer, July 9, 1776, in Frazer, "Papers of General Persifor Frazer," 143.

25. Digby, "Journal of Lieut. William Digby," 135–36.

26. Stillman, *Death the Last Enemy*, 7.

27. Lechford, *Plain Dealing*, 87–88.

28. Stannard, *Puritan Way of Death*, 110–13, 128.

29. Ibid., 115; Livingston, "Of the Extravagance of Our Funerals," 45.

30. Christopher Champlin, bill to the estate of Robert Jenkins, May 28, 1766, Wetmore Papers, MHS; *Virginia Gazette*, October 18, 1770 (supp.), quoted in Isaac, *Transformation of Virginia*, 326–27.

31. Joseph Edmunds, sexton of the North Burying Ground, Boston, bill to the estate of Nathaniel Loring, October 31, 1770, Nathaniel Loring Papers, MHS; Joseph Edmunds, bill dated May 27, 1777, Revere Papers, MHS; "Vestry of St. George's Chapel," March 26, 1768, quoted in Hanson, *History of St. George's Church*, 1:48–49.

32. "A Law Concerning Burialls," October 28, 1684, in *Colonial Laws of New York*, 1:152–53; *Annual Reports of the Record Commissioner*, April 5, 1786, June 13, 1781, 25:305, 149; Act 1081, April 1768, in *Public Laws of the State of South Carolina*.

33. Meaders, "South Carolina Fugitives," 301; *South Carolina Gazette*, June 13, 1769.

34. Goebel and Naughton, *Law Enforcement in Colonial New York*, 703–5; P. Wood, *Black Majority*, 283–84.

35. VanderBeets, *Held Captive By Indians*, xi, xx.

36. F. Anderson, *Crucible of War*, 768–69 n. 4; Steele, *Betrayals*, 71–72.

37. Goldsbrow Banyar to Sir William Johnson, in James Sullivan, ed., *The Papers of Sir William Johnson*, quoted in Steele, *Betrayals*, 206 n. 35; Steele, *Betrayals*, 64; General James Wolfe, *General Orders in Wolfe's Army* (Quebec, 1875), 29, quoted in F. Anderson, *Crucible of War*, 788–89 n. 1.

38. Job 19:26; Bynum, *Resurrection of the Body*, 10–11; Robert Bolton, *Mr. Boltons Last and Learned Works of the Foure Last Things* (London, 1635), quoted in Stannard, *Puritan Way of Death*, 100.

39. Linebaugh, "Tyburn Riots," 83; Gordon, *Aesculapius Comes to the Colonies*, 70, 158, 463; F. Lee, "School of Medicine," 308, 326.

40. Samuel Clossy to George Cleghorn, undated, 1764, in Clossy, *Samuel Clossy, M.D.*, xxx, xxxi.

41. *Report of the Record Commissioners*, August 28, 1771, 23:96.

42. Anon., *Friendly Instructor*, 36; Muhlenberg, *Journals of Henry Melchior Muhlenberg*, November 1751, April 14, 1764, 1:314, 2:66. For a discussion of attitudes toward death, see Houlbrooke, *Death, Religion and the Family in England*, 191–203; Ariès, *Western Attitudes toward Death*, 55–82; and Demos, "From This World to the Next."

43. Rush, "Directions for Preserving the Health of Soldiers," in Rush, *Letters of Benjamin Rush*, 1:140; J. Thacher, *Military Journal*, 135.

44. Simes, *Military Guide for Young Officers*.

45. Ibid., 1:358–60; Dring, *Recollections of the Jersey Prison Ship*, 60.

46. Louis Nicola to Edward Hand, May 26, 1781, Sol Feinstone Collection, DLAR, on deposit APS.

47. Chesterfield, *Letters*, 170.

48. Simes, *Military Guide for Young Officers*, 1:358–60.

49. Rowe, *Letters and Diary of John Rowe*, December 17, 18, 1774, 288.

50. F. Anderson, *Crucible of War*, 104; Washington, *Papers: Colonial Series*, 1:335.

51. Oliphant, *Peace and War*, 162.

52. Anburey, *Travels Through the Interior Parts of America*, 1:421–22; Digby, "Journal of Lieut. William Digby," 234.

53. Von Riedesel, "Her Revolutionary War Journal," 325–27.

54. Popp, "Popp's Journal, 1777–1783," July 25, 1780, 35; Rachel Gratz to Bernard Gratz, August 3, 1779, Sol Feinstone Collection, DLAR, on deposit APS.

55. Anburey, *Travels Through the Interior Parts of America*, 1:421; Cash, *Medical Men*, 62.

56. Kirkpatrick, *Medical Teaching in Trinity College*, 132–33; Clossy, *Samuel Clossy, M.D.*, xvii, xix; Saffron, "Influence of Dublin on American Medicine," 842. On the conditions of regiments stationed in distant posts for years, see Houlding, *Fit for Service*, 12–23.

57. W. Howe, *Orderly Book*, July 7, 1775, 44; Cash, *Medical Men*, 62; letter, June 19, 1775, in Willard, *Letters on the American Revolution*, 137.

58. Flexner, *Washington in the American Revolution*, 102.

59. Boatner, *Encyclopedia*, s.v. "Montgomery."

60. Dearborn, *Revolutionary War Journals*, 78; Benedict Arnold to General Wooster, January 2, 1776, in Arnold, "Colonel Arnold's Letters," 105; J. Henry, "Campaign against Quebec," 389; Lieutenant Dudley Colman to his wife, January 28, 1776, Dudley Colman Letters, MHS.

61. A half joe was half a Portuguese Johannes, a gold coin that circulated in the colonies (McCusker, *Money and Exchange in Europe and America*, 5–6). Anon., "Extract from a letter from Canada, February 9, 1776," in Force, ed., *American Archives*, 4th ser., 4:707.

62. T. Rodney, "Diary of Captain Thomas Rodney," January 5, 1777, 39–40.

63. Buettner, *Narrative of Johann Carl Buettner*, 53; S. Smith, "Memoirs," 1:9.

64. General Orders, May 16, 1776, in Washington, *Papers: Revolutionary War Series*, 4:310.

65. General Orders, June 29, 1778, in Washington, *Writings of George Washington*, 12:130–31; Samuel Woodruff, in Dann, ed., *Revolution Remembered*, 103.

66. William Gilmore, Pension File S8571, Austin Wells, Pension File S32054, RG 15, NAB.

67. James Fergus, Pension File W25573, RG 15, NAB.

68. McDowell, "Journal of Lieut. William McDowell," July 15, 16, 18, 1782, 326.

69. Anonymous letter to unknown recipient, September 4, 1776, Camp Mount Independence opposite Ticonderoga, in Force, ed., *American Archives*, 5th ser., 2:169; Ebenezer David to Nicholas Brown, August 31, 1776, in David, *Rhode Island Chaplain*, 27.

70. Grimke, "Order Book," 13:99–101.

71. J. Thacher, *Military Journal*, 253–54; Henry Marble to Breck Parkman, September 11, 1780, U.S. Revolution Collection, AAS.

72. T. Rodney, "Diary of Captain Thomas Rodney," January 13, 1777, 44; Thomas Rodney to Caesar Rodney, January 14, 1777, HSD.

73. Rogers, *Journal of a Brigade Chaplain*, June 23, July 29, 1779, 71–72.

74. J. Henry, *Arnold's Campaign Against Quebec*, 90; J. Henry, "Campaign against Quebec," 360.

75. Greenman, *Diary*, December 3, 1775, 22.

76. J. Henry, *Arnold's Campaign Against Quebec*, 75.

77. J. Thacher, *Military Journal*, 135; Elisha James to Sarah James, September 2, 1777, Elisha James Letters, MHS; B. Wells, "Journal of Bayze Wells," 268.

78. J. P. Martin, *Ordinary Courage*, 28.

79. Jordan, "Military Hospitals," 142–43, 148–49, 153.

80. Stewart, "Grave Site Delineation." I am grateful to Professor Stewart of the anthropology department at Temple University for making this report available to me. Joshua Richardson, "Record of Richardson House Written by Joshua Richardson, With the Recollections of his Aunt Jane Richardson, transcribed and owned by Middletown Friends Meeting at Langhorne, Pennsylvania." I am grateful to the clerk of the Religious Society of Friends at Middletown Meeting, Florence Wharton, member of the Revolutionary War Burial Site Commemoration Committee, Langhorne, and the Historic Langhorne Association for making this transcript available to me.

81. Philip Turner, "Rules and Directions for the Better Regulating the Military Hospitals of the United States," February 6, 1778, vol. 22, p. 567, item 78, Papers of the Continental Congress, RG 11, M247, roll 103, NAB.

82. Ezra Tilden Journal, September 27, 1776, MHS.

83. Beebe, "Journal," 332, 337–39.

84. Lacey, "Memoirs," 202–4.

85. J. Henry, *Campaign Against Quebec*, 389; Digby, "Journal of Lieut. William Digby," 183.

86. J. Henry, *Campaign Against Quebec*, 389–90.

87. Bostwick, "Connecticut Soldier under Washington," 101; Ezra Tilden Journal, October 8, 9, 1777, MHS.

88. Digby, *The British Invasion From the North*, 246; Anburey, *Travels Through the Interior Parts of America*, 1:432–33.

89. Mintz, *Seeds of Empire*, 128; Barton, "Journal," 8. Several diarists referred to this event and noted that soldiers performed the task, though they are unclear as to whether the boots were intended for soldiers or officers. One officer, perhaps out of haste, disgust, or embarrassment, resorted to oblique abbreviations to describe the incident. After noting, in full sentences, that the dead were collected, he observed the desecration simply by "Sm. Skn. by our S. fr. Bts." (Van Hovenburgh, "Journal," 284). See also Sergeant Thomas Roberts, "Journal," 244.

90. Major James Norris, A Journal of the West Expedition Commanded by the Hon-

ble Major General Sullivan, began at Easton, June 18, 1779, John Sullivan Papers, MHS; Barber, "Order Book," August 26, 1779, 159.

91. John Warren, *Journal*, quoted in Frothingham, *Life and Times of Joseph Warren*, 522; *New England Chronicle*, ibid., 523.

92. J. Thacher, *Military Journal*, 40–41.

93. George Washington to Henry Lee, July 9, 10, 1779, in Washington, *Writings of George Washington*, 15:388, 399; Royster, *Revolutionary People at War*, 81–82.

94. Petition to the President of Pennsylvania, July 1, 1779, signed by Charles Willson Peale, Edward Pole, and Francis Bailey, Charles Willson Peale Papers, BP31, APS; *Pennsylvania Gazette*, July 7, 1779.

95. Charles Willson Peale to Benjamin West, August 31, 1775, Charles Willson Peale Papers, BP31, APS; poem in the hand of Charles Willson Peale written in St. George Peale's account book, "Accounts with the Board of War, 1777," ibid.

96. Rush, "Directions for Preserving the Health of Soldiers," in Rush, *Papers of Benjamin Rush*, 1:140; General Orders, October 2, 1775, in Washington, *Papers: Revolutionary War Series*, 2:217.

Chapter Six

1. Marsh, ed., *Freneau Sampler*, 28.

2. Philip Freneau, "The British Prison-Ship," in Marsh, ed., *Freneau Sampler*, 87.

3. Thomas Boyd affidavit, February 27, 1777, p. 41, item 53, Papers of the Continental Congress, RG 11, M247, roll 66, NAB; Hanford, "Narrative," 1:23.

4. Peckham, *Toll of Independence*, 132; *Pennsylvania Packet or General Advertizer*, September 4, 1781; Thomas Boyd affidavit, February 27, 1777, p. 41, item 53, Papers of the Continental Congress, RG 11, M247, roll 66, NAB. Historians have calculated that 4,000 troops were captured in the summer and fall of 1776 in and around New York and 5,000 in Charleston in 1780. These were the two occasions when American troops were taken in large numbers. In addition, approximately 2,000 seamen were captured. Unknown are the number of foreign seamen held and the number of American soldiers captured in skirmishes or on other occasions. Commager and Morris, *The Spirit of 'Seventy-Six*, 2:844; Peckham, *Toll of Independence*, 132.

5. Samuel Miles to Joseph Reed, September 1, 1776, Miles to General Howe, undated, ca. early 1777, Samuel Miles Papers, BM589, APS.

6. E. Allen, *Ethan Allen's Narrative*, 30–31.

7. A. Barker, *Prisoners of War*, 7.

8. James Knowles to his wife, January 15, 1776, Sol Feinstone Collection, DLAR, on deposit APS.

9. Commager and Morris, *Spirit of 'Seventy-Six*, 2:844.

10. A. Barker, *Prisoners of War*, 6–7.

11. Grotius, *Rights of War and Peace*, 346; A. Barker, *Prisoners of War*, 7.

12. Montesquieu, *Spirit of Laws*, 103, 190; Vattel, *Law of Nations*, 3.8.527–28.

13. Simeon Moulton, in Sherman, *Dubrose Times*, 11–12.

14. F. Anderson, *Crucible of War*, 262.

15. Ibid., 264.

16. Alberts, *Adventures of Robert Stobo*, 78.

17. Vattel, *Law of Nations*, 3.8.528.

18. Alberts, *Adventures of Robert Stobo*, 135, 168–83; F. Anderson, *Crucible of War*, 351–52.

19. Cross, "Journal," 75:335, 76:16. I am grateful to Fred Anderson for introducing me to this narrative.

20. Cross, "Journal," 76:23, 26.

21. Ibid., 76:39.

22. Ibid., 76:39, 41.

23. Namias, *White Captives*, 3–5; Axtell, *European and the Indian*, 173–74; Steele, *Betrayals*, 14–15.

24. F. Anderson, *Crucible of War*, 196; Cross, "Journal," 76:16.

25. Cross, "Journal," 76:18.

26. F. Anderson, *Crucible of War*, 196.

27. Ibid., 187–88, 197–99; Steele, *Warpaths*, 204–5.

28. F. Anderson, *Crucible of War*, 255–56.

29. Ibid., 121; Steele, *Warpaths*, 113, 191–94. For a full discussion of the role of the Iroquois mourning war, see Richter, "War and Culture."

30. William Bull to Archibald Montgomery, May 23, 1760, quoted in Oliphant, *Peace and War*, 119; ibid., 137–45; Jeffrey Amherst to James Grant, February 13, 1761, ibid., 144; ibid., 150.

31. George Washington to Thomas Gage, August 11, 1775, in Washington, *Papers: Revolutionary War Series*, 1:289.

32. Carlton, *Going to the Wars*, 44, 240–45, 248.

33. Sir Joseph Yorke to Secretary Weymouth, September 5, 1775, quoted in Bancroft, *Letter on the Exchange of Prisoners*, 2–3.

34. Duke of Cumberland, quoted in Jarvis, *Jacobite Risings*, 1:256.

35. Jarvis, *Jacobite Risings*, 2:255–56, 264–65.

36. Ibid., 2:256, 269, 1:273, 2:273.

37. Sir Joseph Yorke to Secretary Weymouth, September 5, 1775, quoted in Bancroft, *Letter on the Exchange of Prisoners*, 2–3.

38. Ibid.; Lord George Germain to General William Howe, February 1, 1776, in Force, ed., *American Archives*, 4th ser., 4:903.

39. Lord George Germain to General William Howe, February 1, 1776, in Force, ed., *American Archives*, 4th ser., 4:903.

40. Bolton, *Private Soldier under Washington*, 192; Metzger, *Prisoner in the American Revolution*, viii; *Journals of the Continental Congress*, July 22, 1776, 5:599.

41. George Washington to General William Howe, April 9, 1777, in Washington, *Pa-*

pers: Revolutionary War Series, 9:103; Mackesy, *War for America*, 118; Middlekauff, *Glorious Cause*, 346, 368.

42. George Washington to John Hancock, July 16, 1777, in Washington, *Papers: Revolutionary War Series*, 10:294.

43. George Washington to General William Howe, July 30, 1776, in Washington, *Papers: Revolutionary War Series*, 5:521–22; Howe to Washington, September 21, 1776, ibid., 6:360–61.

44. O. Anderson, "Treatment of Prisoners of War," 66–67.

45. Nadelhaft, *Disorders of War*, 34.

46. William Drayton to Francis Salvador, July 24, 1776, in Gibbes, ed., *Documentary History of the American Revolution*, 3:28; Calloway, *American Revolution in Indian Country*, 48–49.

47. Proceedings of the General Assembly of the State of South Carolina, September 27, 1776, in Force, ed., *American Archives*, 5th ser., 3:31–33.

48. Ibid., 3:33.

49. Barton, "Journal," 11; Campfield, "Journal," 56.

50. Commager and Morris, *Spirit of 'Seventy-Six*, 844. For a thorough review of the experiences of each side, see Metzger, *Prisoner in the American Revolution*, and Sampson, *Escape in America*. For a full discussion of American prisoners held in Britain, see Metzger, *Prisoner in the American Revolution*, and Anderson, "Treatment of Prisoners of War."

51. George Washington to Thomas Gage, August 11, 1775, Gage to Washington, August 13, 1775, Washington to Gage, August 19, 1775, in Washington, *Papers: Revolutionary War Series*, 1:289, 302, 327.

52. E. Allen, "Narrative," 138–41.

53. Samuel Miles to Joseph Reed, January 25, 1777, in Washington, *Papers: Revolutionary War Series*, 8:329 n.

54. Boudinot, *Journal of Events*, 68; Boatner, *Encyclopedia*, s.v. "Loring."

55. *Journals of the Continental Congress*, April 22, 1777, 7:289.

56. Ibid., April 21, 1780, 16:381–83.

57. Boudinot, *Journal of Events*, 71.

58. L. Bowman, *Captive Americans*, 14.

59. William Darlington affidavit, February 27, 1777, p. 41, item 53, Papers of the Continental Congress, RG 11, M247, roll 66, NAB.

60. William Iddings, Pension File S22849, RG 15, NAB; Hamlin Cole, Pension File S39342, in Dorman, *Virginia Revolutionary Pension Applications*, 20:82; Hanford, "Narrative," 1:14.

61. Simeon Moulton, in Sherman, *Dubrose Times*, 12.

62. Ibid.

63. Thomas Boyd affidavit, February 27, 1777, p. 41, item 53, Papers of the Continental Congress, RG 11, M247, roll 66, NAB; Hanford, "Narrative," 1:14–16, 30.

64. Major Henry Bedinger, "Part of a Letter from Major Henry Bedinger to a Son of General Samuel Finley," in Dandridge, *American Prisoners*, 17; Lieutenant Jonathan Gillett, in Stiles, ed., *Letters from the Prisons and Prison Ships*, 10–12; Fitch, *New York Diary*, 56, 61, 99.

65. E. Allen, *Ethan Allen's Narrative*, 28.

66. Dring, *Recollections of the Jersey Prison Ship*, 74.

67. Bedinger, "Part of a Letter from Major Henry Bedinger to a Son of General Samuel Finley," in Dandridge, *American Prisoners*, 18; Lieutenant Jonathan Gillet, in Stiles, ed., *Letters from the Prisons and Prison Ships*, 1; Oliver Waldron, Pension File 11022, RG 15, NAB; James Habersham to John Habersham, December 6, 1780, Sol Feinstone Collection, DLAR, on deposit APS.

68. James Stuart deposition, February 27, 1777, p. 41, item 53, Papers of the Continental Congress, RG 11, M247, roll 66, NAB.

69. George Washington to General William Howe, April 9, 1777, in Washington, *Papers: Revolutionary War Series*, 9:103; Boudinot, *Journal of Events*, 73, 78.

70. Lemisch, "Listening to the 'Inarticulate,'" 14.

71. Thomas Boyd affidavit, February 27, 1777, p. 41, item 53, Papers of the Continental Congress, RG 11, M247, roll 66, NAB; Hanford, "Narrative," 1:16.

72. Blatchford, "Narrative of John Blatchford," 2:iv, 20–25; Joseph Parker, in Dann, ed., *Revolution Remembered*, 70; Dann, ed., *Revolution Remembered*, 68. See also Nagle, *Nagle Journal*.

73. E. Allen, *Ethan Allen's Narrative*, 35.

74. Boudinot, *Journal of Events*, 76.

75. Shy, *A People Numerous and Armed*, 169; Joshua Loring to George Washington, March 24, 1777, Sol Feinstone Collection, DLAR, on deposit APS. Note that this letter is not in Washington, *Papers: Revolutionary War Series*.

76. Horatio Gates to George Washington, February 15, 1777, in *Horatio Gates Papers*, reel 4, 461; Washington to Gates, March 1, 1777, in Washington, *Papers: Revolutionary War Series*, 8:471; Heitman, ed., *Historical Register*, s.v. "Nicholas Haussegger."

77. L. Roberts, *Memoirs*, 64–74.

78. Simeon Moulton, in Sherman, *Dubrose Times*, 12; Levi Hanford, in Stiles, ed., *Letters from the Prisons and Prison Ships*, 26.

79. E. Allen, "Narrative," 143–44.

80. Dring, *Recollections of the Jersey Prison Ship*, 20.

81. Benjamin Rush to John Adams, October 1, 1777, in Rush, *Letters of Benjamin Rush*, 1:155.

82. Fletcher, "Narrative," 2:16.

83. Frederick Padget, in Chilton, ed., *Revolutionary War Pensions*, 34; Hamlin Cole, Pension File S39342, in Dorman, *Virginia Revolutionary Pension Applications*, 20:81–82.

84. Peter Fayssoux to David Ramsay, March 26, 1785, in Gibbes, ed., *Documentary History of the American Revolution*, 2:119; Hanford, "Narrative," 1:13–14.

85. Peter Fayssoux to David Ramsay, March 26, 1785, in Gibbes, ed., *Documentary History of the American Revolution*, 2:119.

86. Andros, "Captivity of Thomas Andros," 197.

87. Dring, *Recollections of the Jersey Prison Ship*, 58, 60.

88. E. Allen, "Narrative," 147; editor's notes to Hanford, "Narrative," 1:67–69; Hanford, "Narrative," 1:28.

89. Andros, "Captivity of Thomas Andros," 197; Dring, *Recollections of the Jersey Prison Ship*, 58–59.

90. Thomas Boyd affidavit, February 27, 1777, p. 41, item 53, Papers of the Continental Congress, RG 11, M247, roll 66, NAB; James Stuart affidavit, February 27, 1777, ibid.

91. Hanford, "Narrative," 1:27.

92. Thomas Boyd affidavit, February 27, 1777, p. 41, item 53, Papers of the Continental Congress, RG 11, M247, roll 66, NAB; Hanford, "Narrative," 1:28.

93. Fitch, *New York Diary*, 35, 57.

94. Ibid., 75.

95. E. Allen, *Ethan Allen's Narrative*.

96. Fitch, *New York Diary*, 89.

97. Henry Bedinger, "Part of a Letter from Major Henry Bedinger to a Son of General Samuel Finley," in Dandridge, *American Prisoners*, 13.

98. Henry Bedinger, "List of Men Raised by Lieutenant Henry Bedinger, and That He Brought From New Town, Berkeley County, VA, August First, 1776," in Dandridge, *American Prisoners*, 80.

99. Dring, *Recollections of the Jersey Prison Ship*, 68.

100. Ibid., 65–66.

101. Ibid., 5.

102. Philip Freneau, "The British Prison-Ship," in Marsh, ed., *Freneau Sampler*, 88.

Conclusion

1. J. P. Martin, *Ordinary Courage*, 59; Sergeant R., "Battle of Princeton," 519.

2. Z. Adams, *Evil Designs of Men*, 28–29.

3. B. Anderson, *Imagined Communities*, 6; Hobsbawm, "Inventing Traditions," 4–6. The literature on this subject is extensive. See also Chase and Shaw, *Imagined Past*.

4. There has been a burst of scholarship on the subject. See Purcell, *Sealed with Blood*; Resch, *Suffering Soldiers*; Waldstreicher, *Perpetual Fêtes*; A. Young, *Shoemaker and the Tea Party*; and Rosenzweig and Thelen, *Presence of the Past*. Also see Craven, *Legend of the Founding Fathers*.

5. The popular song is taken here from Thomas Fanning Notebook, AAS.

6. *Journals of the Continental Congress*, January 25, 1776, 4:89–90.

7. Purcell, *Sealed with Blood*, 19, 99; Boatner, *Encyclopedia*, s.v. "Mercer," "Nash,"

"Wooster." The quote "dull and uninspired" is from Stanley Pargellis, quoted in Boat-ner, s.v. "Wooster."

8. *Journals of the Continental Congress*, December 23, 1783, 25:837–38; Purcell, *Sealed with Blood*, 98.

9. *Journals of the Continental Congress*, December 23, 1783, 25:838; W. Jackson, *Oration*, 28; Brackenridge, *Eulogium*, 8, 12–13.

10. Middlekauff, "Why Men Fought," 140–47.

11. *American Legion Weekly*, July 4, 1919, 10.

12. First Minute Book of the Society of the Cincinnati, May 10–13, 1783, Archives of the Society of the Cincinnati, Washington, D.C.; M. Myers, *Liberty without Anarchy*, ix.

13. Joshua Dean, R2810, in Dorman, *Virginia Revolutionary Pension Applications*, 28:65–66.

14. Major Pinckney's Orders, December 28, 1775, "Extract from the Orderly Book of Charles Lining," in Gibbes, ed., *Documentary History of the American Revolution*, 1:245.

15. Resolutions, Laws and Ordinances, introductory review to the Revolutionary War Pension Files on every reel, 11–15, RG 15, NAB.

16. Resch, *Suffering Soldiers*, ix; Dann, ed., *Revolution Remembered*, xv–xvi. See also *Resolutions, Laws and Ordinances*.

17. Resch, *Suffering Soldiers*, 3–6; Purcell, *Sealed with Blood*, 3, 161–70; Waldstreicher, *Perpetual Fêtes*, 3, 207; Austin Denny, *An Oration Delivered at Worcester, July 4, 1818* (Worcester, Mass.: William Manning, 1818), 8–10, in Resch, *Suffering Soldiers*, 4.

18. Resch, *Suffering Soldiers*, appendix A, 203, 179, appendix B, 220–21.

19. Ibid., 61–62. Resch tentatively but provocatively speculates that this lack of eco-nomic success is an early reflection of what became known in the last quarter of the twentieth century as post-traumatic stress disorder. He makes the case that the Peter-borough veterans experienced a host of social, economic, and family problems in much greater numbers than their non-serving cohort of the same age. He connects this phe-nomenon with the recent literature on the experiences of Vietnam War veterans (ibid., 62–64).

20. U.S. Constitution, art. 1, sec. 8; Millett and Maslowski, *For the Common Defense*, 92–103.

21. Millett and Maslowski, *For the Common Defense*, 134–35.

22. Hickey, *War of 1812*, 76–77, 111.

23. Quimby, *U.S. Army in the War of 1812*, 3; Thomas Jesup, September 8, 1814, in Hickey, *War of 1812*, 78; Doctor W. M. Ross, quoted in Hickey, *War of 1812*, 78.

24. Thomas Eddy, *An Account of the State Prison or Penitentiary House, in the City of New York* (New York, 1801), quoted in Rothman, *Discovery of the Asylum*, 60–61; ibid., 79–81; Hare, "Military Punishments in the War of 1812," 225.

25. Art. 87, "Articles of War of 1806," in W. Winthrop, *Military Law and Precedents*, 2:1520; Hare, "Military Punishments in the War of 1812," 225–39; W. Winthrop, *Military Law and Precedents*, 1:657–75.

26. Hare, "Military Punishments in the War of 1812," 228, 231.

27. Ibid., 238; Hickey, *War of 1812*, 222; William Jones to Arthur Sinclair, May 19, 1814, quoted in Hickey, *War of 1812*, 222. In total, in the War of 1812, 260 men were sentenced to death and 205 were executed. In 1814 alone, 160 were sentenced and 146 were executed. In contrast, during the Revolution, as noted in chapter 3, probably only 40 of 225 death sentences were carried out. Even allowing for the much shorter war and the much larger army in the War of 1812, the pace of sentencing and the low number of reprieves, in 1814 particularly, is surprising (Hare, "Military Punishments in the War of 1812," 238; A. Bowman, *Morale of the American Revolutionary Army*, 89).

28. Gillett, *Army Medical Department*, 129; Rosenberg, *Care of Strangers*, 20–21; Hickey, *War of 1812*, 302–3.

29. Gillett, *Army Medical Department*, 192–93, 157–61, 178, 197–98; Kett, *Formation of the American Medical Profession*, 14–29.

30. Gillett, *Army Medical Department*, 184; Tarrance Kirby, quoted in Clark, "Kentucky in the Northwest Campaign," 94; General F. L. Claiborne to General Thomas Flournoy, September 3, 1813, in Brannan, *Official Letters*, 203, 274.

31. Hickey, *War of 1812*, 176–77; Captain N. Heald to Adjutant General T. Cushing, October 23, 1812, in Brannan, *Official Letters*, 85; Abraham Walter affidavit, November 1818, in Brannan, *Official Letters*, 279–80.

32. O. Allen, *Tiger*, 1–21; Purcell, *Sealed with Blood*, 146–47; G. Myers, *History of Tammany Hall*, 27.

33. Anon., *Account of the Procession*; Tammany Society, *Historical Account of the Interment*; O. Allen, *Tiger*, 21; G. Myers, *History of Tammany Hall*, 26; Purcell, *Sealed with Blood*, 148; Cray, "Commemorating the Prison Ship Dead," 583–85.

34. Society of Old Brooklynites, *A Christmas Reminder*, 5.

35. Ibid., 4–5; *New York Times*, November 15, 1908, 2–3.

BIBLIOGRAPHY

Manuscript Collections

Boston, Massachusetts
  Massachusetts Historical Society
    Israel Angell Diary
    Isaac Bangs Journal
    Obadiah Brown Journal
    Dudley Colman Letters
    Moses Greenleaf Diary
    Phineas Ingalls Journal
    Elisha James Letters
    Nathaniel Loring Papers
    Moses Moody Journal
    Joseph Palmer Papers
    Elisha Porter Papers
    Revere Papers
    John Sullivan Papers
    Ezra Tilden Journal
    Wetmore Papers
  New England Historic Genealogical Society
    Samuel Armstrong Diary
    Ella Florence Elliot Papers
Charleston, South Carolina
  South Carolina Historical Society
    Isaac DuBose Orderly Book
    Barnard Elliott Orderly Book
    Francis Marion Letter
    William Moultrie General Orders
    Roger P. Saunders Orderly Books
Langhorne, Pennsylvania
  Middletown Friends Meeting at Langhorne

Philadelphia, Pennsylvania
  American Philosophical Society
    Samuel Miles Papers
    Charles Willson Peale Papers
  College of Physicians of Philadelphia
    Samuel Bard Letter
  Historical Society of Pennsylvania
    John Lacey Letters
    Ambrose Madison Orderly Book
    Daniel Morgan Orderly Book
    Potts Papers
    Anthony Wayne Papers
San Marino, California
  Huntington Library
    John Durkee Orderly Book, 1777
    Ebenezer Huntington Letters
    John Irwin Orderly Book, 1777
    Francis Marion Orderly Book, 1175–77, 1778, 1781
    Charles Willson Peale Diary
Washington, D.C.
  National Archives Building
    Papers of the Continental Congress
    Revolutionary War Pension Files
  The Society of the Cincinnati
    First Minute Book of the Society of the Cincinnati
Washington Crossing, Pennsylvania
  David Library of the American Revolution
    Sol Feinstone Collection
Wilmington, Delaware
  Historical Society of Delaware
    George Bush Journal
    Robert Kirkwood General Orders
    Thomas Rodney Letters
    James Tilton Letter
Worcester, Massachusetts
  American Antiquarian Society
    Benjamin Beal Journal
    Samuel Bixby Diary
    Thomas Fanning Notebook
    Samuel Man Diary
    John Smith Diaries
    U.S. Revolution Collection

Government Documents

Acts and Resolves, Public and Private, of the Province of Massachusetts Bay. 21 vols. Boston: Wright and Potter Printing Company, 1869–1922.

Annual Reports of the Record Commissioner of Boston. 39 vols. Boston: Rockwell and Churchill, 1876–1909.

Colonial Laws of New York from the Year 1664 to the Revolution. 5 vols. Albany, N.Y.: James B. Lyon, 1894.

Extracts from the Journals of the Provincial Congresses of South Carolina, 1775–1776. Edited by William E. Hemphill. Columbia: South Carolina Archives Department, 1960.

Federal and State Constitutions: Colonial Charters and Other Organic Laws of the States, Territories, and Colonies Now or Heretofore Forming the United States of America. 7 vols. Edited by Francis Newton Thorpe. Washington, D.C.: Government Printing Office, 1909.

Index and Legislative History: Uniform Code of Military Justice. Washington, D.C.: Government Printing Office, 1950.

Journals of Each Provincial Congress of Massachusetts in 1774 and 1775 and of the Committee of Safety. Boston: Dutton and Wentworth, 1838.

Journals of the Continental Congress, 1774–1789. 34 vols. Edited by Worthington Chauncey Ford. Washington, D.C.: Government Printing Office, 1907.

Laws of Maryland. Annapolis, 1777, 1779.

Letters of Delegates to Congress, 1774–1789. 25 vols. Edited by Paul H. Smith. Washington, D.C.: Government Printing Office, 1976–96.

Letters of the Members of the Continental Congress. 8 vols. Edited by Edmund C. Burnett. Washington: Carnegie Institute, 1921–34.

Pennsylvania Archives. 119 vols. Philadelphia: J. Severns & Company, 1852–1935.

Pennsylvania Colonial Records. 16 vols. Philadelphia: Theo Fenn Company, 1851–53.

Public Laws of the State of South Carolina from Its First Establishment as a British Province down to the Year 1790 Inclusive. Edited by John Faucheraud Grimke. Philadelphia: R. Aitken & Sons, 1790.

Records of the Federal Convention of 1787. 4 vols. Edited by Max Farrand. New Haven: Yale University Press, 1966.

Report of the Record Commissioners of the City of Boston. 28 vols. Boston: Rockwell and Churchill, 1893.

Secret Journals of the Acts and Proceedings of Congress. 4 vols. Boston: Thomas B. Wait, 1821.

Statutes at Large of South Carolina. 10 vols. Edited by Thomas Cooper and David J. McCord. Columbia, S.C.: A. S. Johnson, 1836–40.

Statutes at Large of Virginia from the First Session of the Legislature in the Year 1619. 18 vols. Edited by W. W. Hening. Richmond, Va.: Samuel Pleasants, 1809–23.

Votes and Proceedings of the House of Delegates, Maryland House Journals. Annapolis, 1778.

Newspapers

American Legion Weekly (Indianapolis)
Boston Gazette
Connecticut Courant (Hartford)
Independent Chronicle and the Universal Advertiser (Boston)
New England Chronicle (Boston)
New York Times
Oakland Tribune
Pennsylvania Evening Post (Philadelphia)
Pennsylvania Gazette (Philadelphia)
Pennsylvania Journal (Philadelphia)
Pennsylvania Packet and Daily Advertiser (Philadelphia)
Pennsylvania Packet and General Advertizer (Philadelphia)
South Carolina Gazette (Charleston)
Virginia Gazette (Williamsburg)

Electronic Sources

"Museum of the Royal Regiment of Artillery," Royal Arsenal, Woolwich, April 7,
    2003, ‹http://www.firepower.org.uk›. September 10, 2003.
"U.S. Army Defense Finance and Accounting Service," February 14, 2001,
    ‹http://www.dfas.mil/money/milpay/pay/bp-1.htm›. September 10, 2003.
U.S. Code: Title 10, Section 933, Article 133, Uniform Code of Military Justice, 2000,
    ‹http://uscode.house.gov›. September 12, 2003.

Published Primary Sources

Adams, John. *Diary and Autobiography of John Adams.* 4 vols. Edited by L. H. But-
    terfield. Cambridge: Belknap Press, 1961.
———. *The Papers of John Adams.* 8 vols. Edited by Robert J. Taylor. Cambridge: Belk-
    nap Press, 1979.
Adams, Zabdiel. *The Evil Designs of Men: Mr. Adams's Sermon Preached at Lexington,
    Nineteenth of April, 1783.* Boston: Benjamin Edes, 1783.
Adlum, John. *Memoirs of the Life of John Adlum in the Revolutionary War.* Edited by
    Howard Peckham. Chicago: William L. Clemens Library Associates, 1968.
Adye, Stephen Payne. *A Treatise on Courts Martial.* New York: H. Gaine, 1769.
Allen, Ethan. *Ethan Allen and His Kin: Correspondence, 1772–1819.* Edited by John J.
    Duffy. London: University Press of New England, 1998.
———. *Ethan Allen's Narrative of the Capture of Ticonderoga and of his Captivity and*

Treatment by the British Written by Himself. Philadelphia, 1779. 5th ed. Burlington, Vt.: C. Goodrich and S. B. Nichols, 1849.

———. "The Narrative of Colonel Ethan Allen." In *Life and Death on the Ocean: A Collection of Extraordinary Adventures in the Form of Personal Narratives*, edited by Henry Howe, 138–41. Cincinnati: Privately published, 1855.

Anburey, Thomas. *Travels Through the Interior Parts of America in a Series of Letters*. 2 vols. London: William Lane, 1789.

———. *With Burgoyne from Quebec: An Account of the Life at Quebec and of the Famous Battle at Saratoga*. Toronto: Macmillan, 1963.

Anderson, Enoch. "Personal Recollections of Captain Enoch Anderson . . . in the Revolutionary War." Edited by Henry Hobart Bellas. *Papers of the Historical Society of Delaware* 2 (1896): 3–78.

Andrews, John. "Letters of John Andrews, 1772–1776." *Proceedings of the Massachusetts Historical Society* 8 (1865): 316–412.

Andros, Thomas. "The Captivity of Thomas Andros." In *Life and Death on the Ocean: A Collection of Extraordinary Adventures in the Form of Personal Narratives*, edited by Henry Howe, 195–210. Cincinnati: Privately published, 1855.

Angell, Israel. *Diary of Colonel Israel Angell*. New York: Arno Press, 1971.

Anon. *An Account of the Procession together with Copious Extracts of the Oration Delivered at the Walla-bout, April 8, 1808*. New York: J. Low, 1808.

Anon. "A British Officer in Boston in 1775." *Magazine of History* 18 (1914): 1–15.

Anon. *The Friendly Instructor: or a Companion for Young Ladies and Gentlemen*. New York: J. Holt, 1769.

Anon. *The Happy man: or The true gentleman*. Salem, Mass.: J. Napier and Rogers, 1776.

Anon. "A Journal of a Campaign from Philadelphia to Paulus Hook." Edited by Algernon Roberts. *Pennsylvania Magazine of History and Biography* 7 (1883): 456–63.

Anon. "Journal of a Pennsylvania Soldier: July–December 1776." *Bulletin of the New York Public Library* 8 (1904): 547–49.

Anon. "Notes and Quotes." *Historical Magazine* 4 (October 1860): 313.

Arnold, Benedict. "Colonel Arnold's Letters." In *March to Quebec: Journals of the Members of Arnold's Expedition*, edited by Kenneth L. Roberts, 67–123. New York: Doubleday, Doran, 1938.

Asbury, Francis. *The Heart of Asbury's Journal*. Edited by Ezra Squier Tipple. New York: Eaton & Mains, 1904.

Baldwin, Jeduthan. *The Revolutionary Journal of Col. Jeduthan Baldwin, 1775–1778*. Bangor, Maine: Privately published, 1906.

Barber, Francis. "The Order Book of Lieut. Colonel Francis Barber, May 26, 1779–September 6, 1779." *Proceedings of the New Jersey Historical Society* 65–67 (1947–49).

Bard, Samuel. *A Discourse upon the Duties of a Physician*. New York: A. & J. Robertson, 1769.

——. *An Enquiry into the Nature, Cause and Cure, of the Angina Suffocativa or, Throat Distemper*. New York: S. Inslee and A. Car[r], 1771.

Barker, John. *The British in Boston Being the Diary of Lieutenant John Barker of the King's Own Regiment from November 15, 1774 to May 31, 1776*. Cambridge: Harvard University Press, 1924.

Barton, William. "Journal of Lieut. William Barton." In *Journals of the Military Expedition of Major General John Sullivan against the Six Nations of Indians in 1779*, edited by Frederick Cook, 3–14. Auburn, N.Y.: Knapp, Peck & Thomson, 1887.

Bauermeister, B. "Letters of Major B. Bauermeister During the Philadelphia Campaign, 1777–1778." Edited by Bernard A. Uhlendorf and Edna Vosper. *Pennsylvania Magazine of History and Biography* 59 (1935): 392–419.

Baxter, James Phinney, ed. *The British Invasion from the North: The Campaigns of Generals Carleton and Burgoyne, with the Journal of Lieut. William Digby*. Albany, N.Y.: Joel Munsell's Sons, 1887.

Beatty, Erkuries. "Journal of Lieut. Erkuries Beatty in the Expedition Against the Six Nations under Genl. Sullivan, 1779." In *Journals and Diaries of the War of Revolution with Lists of Officers and Soldiers, 1775–1783*, edited by William Henry Egle, 219–53. Harrisburg, Pa.: E. K. Meyers, 1893.

Beccaria, Cesare. *An Essay on Crimes and Punishments*. New York: James Rivington, 1773.

Beebe, Doctor Lewis. "Journal of a Physician on the Expedition against Canada, 1776." *Pennsylvania Magazine of History and Biography* 59 (1935): 321–61.

Belknap, Jeremy. "Extracts from Dr. Belknap's Note-books." *Proceedings of the Massachusetts Historical Society* 14 (1876): 91–98.

Blackstone, Sir William. *Commentaries on the Laws of England*. 2 vols. Edited by William Carey Jones. San Francisco: Bancroft-Whitney Company, 1915–16.

Blatchford, John. "The Narrative of John Blatchford, detailing his sufferings in the Revolutionary War, while a prisoner with the British." In *Crumbs for Antiquarians*, edited by Charles I. Bushnell, 2:1–116. New York: Privately published, 1864.

Bloomfield, Joseph. *Citizen Soldier: The Revolutionary War Journal of Joseph Bloomfield*. Edited by Mark E. Lender and James K. Martin. Newark: New Jersey Historical Society, 1982.

Bostwick, Elisha. "A Connecticut Soldier under Washington: Elisha Bostwick's Memoirs of the First Years of the Revolution." *William & Mary Quarterly*, 3rd ser., 6 (1949): 94–107.

Boudinot, Elias. *Journal of Events in the Revolution*. Philadelphia, 1894. Reprint. New York: Arno Press, 1968.

Boyle, John. "Boyle's Journal of Occurrences in Boston." *New England Historical and Genealogical Society* 84–85 (1930–31).

Boylston, Zabdiel. *A Historical Account of the Small-Pox*. Boston: Gerrish and Hancock, 1730.

Brackenridge, Hugh Henry. *An Eulogium of the Brave Men Who Have Fallen in the Contest with Great-Britain, Delivered July 5, 1779*. Philadelphia: F. Bailey, 1779.

Bradford, S. Sydney, ed. "A British Officer's Revolutionary War Journal, 1776–1778." *Maryland Historical Magazine* 56 (1961): 150–75.

Brannan, John. *Official Letters of the Military and Naval Officers of the United States During the War with Great Britain in the Years 1812, 13, 14, & 15*. Washington City: Wax and Gideon, 1823.

British Army Adjutant General's Office. *The Manual of Exercise as Ordered by His Majesty in 1764*. London: J. Millan, 1778.

Brocklesby, Richard. *Oeconomical and Medical Observations in two parts From the year 1758 to the Year 1763 inclusive tending to the improvement of Military Hospitals and to the Cure of Camp diseases incident to Soldiers*. London: T. Becket and P. A. De Hondt, 1764.

Bromfield, William. *Chirurgical Observations and Cases*. London: T. Cadell, 1773.

Brooks, John. "Letter." *Proceedings of the Massachusetts Historical Society* 13 (1873–75): 242–45.

Buchan, William. *Domestic Medicine or The Family Physician*. Philadelphia: Dunlap, 1772.

Buettner, Johann Carl. *Narrative of Johann Carl Buettner in the American Revolution*. New York: C. F. Heartman, 1915.

Burgoyne, John. *Orderly Book of General John Burgoyne from his entry into the state of New York until his surrender at Saratoga, 16th Oct. 1777*. Edited by E. B. O'Callaghan. Albany, N.Y.: Munsell, 1860.

Burr, Aaron. "Honor." Edited by William Eleroy Curtis. *Cosmopolitan* 21 (1896): 557–60.

Bushnell, Charles I., ed. *Crumbs for Antiquarians*. 2 vols. New York: Privately published, 1864–66.

Campfield, Jabez. "Journal of Dr. Jabez Campfield." In *Journals of the Military Expedition of Major General John Sullivan against the Six Nations of Indians in 1779*, edited by Frederick Cook, 52–61. Auburn, N.Y.: Knapp, Peck & Thomson, 1887.

Castiglione, Baldassare. *The Book of the Courtier*. New York: E. P. Dutton, 1944.

Chesterfield, Lord. *Lord Chesterfield Letters*. Edited by David Roberts. New York: Oxford University Press, 1992.

Chilton, Ann, ed. *Revolutionary War Pensions, Bedford Co., Virginia*. Signal Mountain, Tenn.: Mountain Press, 1988.

Clairac, Chevalier de. *L'Ingenieur de campagne or Field Engineer*. Translated by Lewis Nicola. Philadelphia: Robert Aitken, 1776.

Clossy, Samuel. *Samuel Clossy, M.D., Professor of Anatomy at King's College, New York: The Existing Works*. Edited by Morris Saffron. New York: Hafner Publishing Company, 1967.

Coit, William. "Orderly Book." *Collections of the Connecticut Historical Society* 7 (1899): 1–91.

Collignon, Charles. *Medicina Politica: Or Reflections on the Art of Physic, as Inseparably Connected with the Prosperity of a State*. Cambridge: J. Bentham, 1765.

Collins, James P. *Autobiography of a Revolutionary War Soldier*. New York: Arno Press, 1979.

Cornelius, Elias. *Journal of Elias Cornelius, M.D.: A Revolutionary Surgeon and Biographical Sketch*. N.p.: Privately published, Chester T. Sherman, 1775.

Cross, Stephen. "Journal of Stephen Cross of Newbury-Port, Entitled 'Up to Ontario': The Activities of Newburyport Shipbuilders in Canada in 1756." *Essex Institute Historical Collections* 75–76 (1939–40).

Croswell, Andrew. *Part of an Exposition of Paul's Journey to Damascus, Acts XXVI.x.* Boston: Kneeland & Adams, 1768.

Dandridge, Danske. *American Prisoners of the Revolution*. Charlottesville, Va.: Mitchie Company, 1911.

Dann, John, ed. *The Revolution Remembered: Eyewitness Accounts of the War for Independence*. Chicago: University of Chicago Press, 1980.

David, Ebenezer. *A Rhode Island Chaplain in the Revolution: Letters of Ebenezer David to Nicholas Brown*. New York: Kennikat Press, 1949.

Dearborn, Henry. *Revolutionary War Journals of Henry Dearborn, 1775–1783*. Edited by Lloyd A. Brown and Howard H. Peckham. Chicago: Caxton Club, 1939.

de Grandmaison, Major General. *A Treatise on the Military Service of Light Horse and Light Infantry*. Translated by Lewis Nicola. Philadelphia: Robert Bell, 1777.

De Lancey, Oliver. *De Lancey's Orderly Books of the Three Battalions of Loyalists, 1776–1778*. New York: New-York Historical Society, 1917.

de Saxe, Marshal Maurice. "My Reveries on the Art of War." In *Roots of Strategy*, translated and edited by Thomas R. Phillips, 177–300. Harrisburg, Pa.: Military Service Publishing Company, 1940.

de Vattel, Emmerich. *The Law of Nations (Les droits des gens)*. Paris, 1758. Reprint. New York: Berry and Rogers, 1787.

de Vauban, Sébastien Le Prestre. *De l'attaque et de la défense des places*. La Haye: Pierre De Hondt, 1737.

Digby, William. "The Journal of Lieut. William Digby." In *The British Invasion from the North: The Campaigns of General Carleton and Burgoyne from Canada, 1776–1777, with the Journal of Lieut. William Digby of the 53D or Shropshire Regiment of Foot*, edited by James Phinney Baxter, 77–253. New York: Joel Munsell's Sons, 1887.

Dohla, Johann Conrad. *A Hessian Diary of the American Revolution*. Translated and edited by Bruce E. Burgoyne. Norman: University of Oklahoma Press, 1990.

Donkin, Robert. *Military Collections and Remarks*. New York: H. Gaine, 1777.

Dorman, John Frederick. *Virginia Revolutionary Pension Applications*. 51 vols. to date. Washington, D.C.: Privately published, 1958.

Douglass, William. *A Dissertation Concerning Inoculation of the Small Pox*. Boston: Henchman and Hancock, 1730.

Douthat, Marilee. *Revolutionary War Pension Applications: Roane County, Tennessee.* Signal Mountain, Tenn.: Mountain Press, 1988.

Dring, Thomas. *Recollections of the Jersey Prison Ship from the Manuscript of Capt. Thomas Dring.* Edited by Albert Greene. Providence, R.I., 1829. Reprint. New York: Corinth Books, 1961.

Early American Orderly Books. 19 reels. New Haven: Research Publications, 1977.

Eden, William (Lord Auckland). *Principles of Penal Law.* London: E. B. White and T. Cadell, 1771.

Elbert, Samuel. "Order Book of Samuel Elbert, Colonel and Brigadier General in the Continental Army: October 1776–November 1778." *Collections of the Georgia Historical Society* 5 (1902): 5–191.

Elliott, Barnard. "Barnard Elliott's Recruiting Journal, 1775." *South Carolina Historical and Genealogical Magazine* 17 (1916): 95–100.

Enys, John. *The American Journals of Lt. John Enys.* Edited by Elizabeth Cometti. Blue Mountain Lake, N.Y.: Adirondack Museum, 1976.

Evelyn, W. Glanville. *Memoirs and Letters of Capt. W. Glanville Evelyn of the 4th Regiment ("King's Own") from North America, 1774–1776.* Edited by G. D. Scull. Oxford: James Parker & Company, 1879. Reprint. New York: Arno Press, 1971.

Ewald, Johann. *Diary of the American War: A Hessian Journal.* Translated and edited by Joseph P. Tustin. New Haven: Yale University Press, 1979.

Extract from the Proceedings of the New York State Society of the Cincinnati, convened on the 4th of July, 1786. New York, 1786.

Feltman, William. *The Journal of Lieut. William Feltman of the First Pennsylvania Regiment, 1781–82.* New York: Arno Press, 1969.

Fitch, Jabez. *The New York Diary of Lieutenant Jabez Fitch of the 17th (Connecticut) Regiment from August 22, 1776 to December 15, 1777.* Edited by W. H. W. Sabine. New York: Privately published, 1954.

Fletcher, Ebenezer. "Narrative of the Captivity and Suffering of Ebenezer Fletcher." In *Crumbs for Antiquarians,* edited by Charles I. Bushnell, 2:1–86. New York: Privately published, 1864.

Fogg, Jeremiah. *Orderly Book of Jeremiah Fogg.* Exeter, N.H.: Exeter News-Letter, 1903.

Force, Peter, ed. *American Archives.* 9 vols. Washington, D.C.: M. St. Clair Clarke and Peter Force, 1837–53.

Frasier, Isaac. *A Brief Account of the Life of Isaac Frasier who was Executed at Fairfield, September 7th, 1768, penned from his own mouth, and signed by him a few days before his execution.* New Haven: T. & S. Green, 1768.

Frazer, Persifor. "Some Extracts from the Papers of General Persifor Frazer." *Pennsylvania Magazine of History and Biography* 31 (1907): 129–44.

Frederick II, King of Prussia. *The Instructions of Frederick the Great for his Generals, 1747.* In *Roots of Strategy,* translated and edited by Thomas R. Phillips, 301–400. Harrisburg, Pa.: Military Service Publishing Company, 1940.

Gates, Horatio. *The Horatio Gates Papers, 1726–1828*. 20 reels. Edited by James Gregory
    and Thomas Dunnings. Sanford, N.C.: Microfilming Company of America, 1979.

Gibbes, R. W., ed. *Documentary History of the American Revolution*. 3 vols. New York:
    D. Appleton & Company, 1855. Reprint. Spartanburg, S.C.: Reprint Company, 1972.

Gilbert, Benjamin. *A Citizen-Soldier in the American Revolution: The Diary of Benjamin
    Gilbert in Massachusetts and New York*. Edited by Rebecca D. Symmes. New York:
    New York State Historical Association, 1980.

——. *Winding Down: The Revolutionary War Letters of Lieutenant Benjamin Gilbert of
    Massachusetts, 1780–1783*. Edited by John Shy. Ann Arbor: University of Michigan
    Press, 1989.

Glasier, Benjamin. "French and Indian War Diary of Benjamin Glasier of Ipswich,
    1758–1760." *Essex Institute Historical Collections* 86 (1950): 64–92.

Gore, Obadiah, Jr. "Diary of Lieut. Obadiah Gore, Jr., in the Sullivan-Clinton Cam-
    paign of 1779." Edited by R. W. G. Vail. *Bulletin of the New York Public Library* 33
    (1929): 711–42.

Goss, Thomas. *Last Words and Dying Speech of Thomas Goss in a Private Conference Pre-
    vious to His Execution*. Conn., 1778.

Graydon, Alexander. *Memoirs of a Life Chiefly Passed in Pennsylvania Within the Last
    Sixty Years*. Harrisburg, Pa.: John Wyeth, 1811.

Greene, Nathanael. *Papers of General Nathanael Greene*. 12 vols. to date. Various eds.
    Chapel Hill: University of North Carolina Press, 1976–2002.

Greenman, Jeremiah. *Diary of a Common Soldier in the American Revolution, 1775–1783:
    An Annotated Edition of the Military Journal of Jeremiah Greenman*. Edited by
    Robert C. Bray and Paul E. Bushnell. DeKalb: Northern Illinois University Press,
    1978.

Grimke, John Faucheraud. "Journal of the Campaign to the Southward, May 9th to
    July 14th, 1778." *South Carolina Historical and Genealogical Magazine* 12 (1911):
    60–69, 118–34, 190–206.

——. "Order Book of John Faucheraud Grimke." *South Carolina Historical and Ge-
    nealogical Magazine* 13–19 (1912–19).

Grose, Francis. *Advice to the Officers of the Army, to the Officers of the Ordnance, and to
    the Secretary at War with the Addition of some hints to the Drummer and Private
    Soldier*. Philadelphia: Matthew McConnel, Jr., 1813.

——. *Military Antiquities Respecting a History of the English Army from the Conquest to
    the Present Time*. 2 vols. London: S. Hooper, 1788.

Grotius, Hugo. *The Rights of War and Peace (De Jure Belli ac Pacis)*. Translated and ed-
    ited by A. C. Campbell. Frankfurt, 1625. Reprint. Washington, D.C.: M. Walter
    Dunne, 1901.

Hadden, James M. *Hadden's Journal and Orderly Books*. Edited by Horatio Rogers.
    Albany, N.Y.: Joel Munsell's Sons, 1884.

Hamilton, Charles, ed. *Braddock's Defeat: The Journal of Robert Cholmley's Batman, The*

Journal of a British Officer, Halkett's Orderly Book. Norman: University of Oklahoma Press, 1959.

Hanford, Levi. "A Narrative of the life and Adventures of Levi Hanford." In *Crumbs for Antiquarians*, edited by Charles I. Bushnell, 1:1–80. New York: Privately published, 1864.

Hawkins, Francis. *Youth's Behaviour, or Decency in Conversation among Men*. London: W. Wilson, 1651.

Hawks, John. *Orderly Book and Journal of Major John Hawks on the Ticonderoga–Crown Point Campaign Under General Jeffrey Amherst, 1759–1760*. New York: Society of Colonial Wars in the State of New York, 1911.

Henry, John Joseph. *Account of Arnold's Campaign Against Quebec and of the Hardships and Sufferings of that Band of Heroes who traversed the Wilderness of Maine from Cambridge to the St. Lawrence in the Autumn of 1775*. Albany, N.Y.: Joel Munsell's Sons, 1877.

———. "Campaign against Quebec." In *March to Quebec: Journals of the Members of Arnold's Expedition*, edited by Kenneth L. Roberts, 299–429. New York: Doubleday, Doran, 1938.

Henshaw, William. *The Orderly Books of Col. William Henshaw*. Worcester: Massachusetts Historical Society, 1948.

Hitchcock, Enos. "Diary of Enos Hitchcock, D.D., A Chaplain in the Revolutionary Army." *Publications of the Rhode Island Historical Society*, n.s., 7 (1899): 87–134.

Hobart, Noah. *Excessive Wickedness, the Way to an Untimely Death: A Sermon Preached at Fairfield in Connecticut, September 7th, 1768, at the execution of Isaac Fraiser*. New Haven: T. & S. Green, 1768.

Holyoke, E. A. "A Bill against the [Massachusetts] Bay Colony for Professional Services." *Historical Collections of the Essex Institute* 13 (1876): 233–35.

How, David. *Diary of David How, a private in Colonel Paul Dudley Sargent's regiment of the Massachusetts line, in the army of the American revolution*. Morrisania, N.Y.: H. D. Houghton and Company, 1865.

Howe, Henry, ed. *Life and Death on the Ocean: A Collection of Extraordinary Adventures in the Form of Personal Narratives*. Cincinnati: Privately published, 1855.

Howe, Sir William. "British Army Orders: Gen. Sir William Howe, 1775–1778." *Collections of the New-York Historical Society* 16 (1883): 251–585.

———. *General Sir William Howe's Orderly Book at Charleston, Boston and Halifax, June 17, 1775 to 1776, 26 May*. Edited by Edward Everett Hale. London: Benjamin Franklin Stevens, 1890.

Hughes, Thomas. *A Journal by Thomas Hughes for His Amusement, & Designed Only for His Perusal by the Time He Attains the Age of 50 if He Lives So Long, 1778–1789*. Edited by E. A. Benians. Cambridge: Cambridge University Press, 1947.

Huntington, Ebenezer. *Letters Written by Ebenezer Huntington during the American Revolution*. Edited by G. W. F. Blanchfield. New York: C. F. Heartman, 1914.

Jackson, William. *An Oration to Commemorate the Independence of the United States*. Philadelphia: Eleazar Oswald, 1786.

Jefferson, Thomas. *The Papers of Thomas Jefferson*. 28 vols. Edited by Julian P. Boyd. Princeton: Princeton University Press, 1950.

Johnson, Sir John. *Orderly Book of Sir John Johnson during the Oriskany Campaign, 1776–1777*. Albany, N.Y.: Joel Munsell's Sons, 1882.

Jones, Hugh. *The Present State of Virginia*. New York: Joseph Sabin, 1865.

Jones, John. *Plain Concise Practical Remarks on the Treatment of Wounds and Fractures*. Philadelphia: Robert Bell, 1776.

Joslyn, Joseph, Jr. "A Teamster in the Continental Service, March 1777–August 1778." *Collections of the Connecticut Historical Society* 7 (1899): 297–369.

Kennedy, Samuel. "Letters to his Wife." *Pennsylvania Magazine of History and Biography* 8 (1884): 111–16.

King, Gregory. *Two Tracts a) Natural and Political Observations and Conclusions upon the State and Condition on England b) Of the naval Trade in England Anno 1688 and the National Profit Then Arising Thereby*. London, 1698. Reprint. Baltimore: Johns Hopkins University Press, 1936.

Kirkwood, Robert. "Journal and Order Book of the Delaware Regiment of the Continental Line." *Papers of the Historical Society of Delaware* 6 (1910): 4–277.

Knox, Henry. *Life and Correspondence of Henry Knox, Major General in the American Revolutionary Army*. Edited by Francis S. Drake. Boston: Samuel G. Drake, 1873.

Lacey, John. "Memoirs of Brigadier-General John Lacey of Pennsylvania." *Pennsylvania Magazine of History and Biography* 25–26 (1901–2).

Lamb, Roger. *An Original and Authentic Journal of Occurrences During the Late American War from Its Commencement to the Year 1783*. Dublin, 1809. Reprint. New York: Arno Press, 1968.

Laurens, Henry. *The Papers of Henry Laurens*. 15 vols. Edited by David R. Chesnutt. Columbia: University of South Carolina Press, 1985.

Laurens, John. *The Army Correspondence of John Laurens*. Edited by William Simms. New York: Privately published, 1867.

——. "Correspondence between Henry Laurens and His Son, John, 1777–1780." *South Carolina Historical and Genealogical Magazine* 4 (1905): 47–52.

Lechford, Thomas. *Plain Dealing; or News From New England*. Boston: J. K. Wiggin & W. P. Lunt, 1867.

Le Dran, Henri Francois. *Observations in Surgery Containing One Hundred and Fifteen Different Cases with Particular Remarks on Each, for the Improvement of Young Students*. London: James Hodges, 1740.

Lee, Charles. *The Lee Papers. Collections of the New-York Historical Society* 4–7 (1871–74).

Lee, Henry. *Memoirs of the War in the Southern Department of the United States*. New York: Burt Franklin, 1920.

Leonard, Abiel. *Prayer Composed for the Benefit of the Soldiers in the American Army.* Cambridge: S. E. Hall, 1775.

Lewis, Andrew. *The orderly book of that Portion of the American Army stationed at or near Williamsburg, Virginia, under the Command of General Andrew Lewis from March 18, 1776 to August 28, 1776.* Edited by Charles Campbell. Richmond, Va.: Privately published, 1860.

Lewis, Morgan. "Addressed to the Newly Admitted Members." In *An Oration Delivered Before the Society of the Cincinnati of the State of New York, in Commemoration of the Fourth Day of July,* by Robert R. Livingston, 19–22. New York: Francis Childs, 1787.

Linn, William. *A Military Discourse, delivered in Carlisle March 17th, 1776 to Colonel Irvine's Battalion of Regulars and a very respectable number of the inhabitants.* Philadelphia, 1776.

Lister, Jeremy. "Jeremy Lister (Ensign) 10th Regiment, 1770–1783." *Journal of the Society for Army Historical Research* 41 (1963): 59–73.

Littell, James. "A Revolutionary Journal and Orderly Book of General Lachlan McIntosh's Expedition, 1778." *Western Pennsylvania Historical Magazine* 43 (1960): 162–63.

Livingston, William. "Of the Extravagance of Our Funerals." In *Passing: The Vision of Death in America,* edited by Charles O. Jackson, 42–47. Westport, Conn.: Greenwood Press, 1977.

Lukens, Jesse. "Incidents of the Siege of Boston, in 1775." *American Historical Record* 1 (1872): 546–50.

Lyngard, Richard. *A Letter of Advice to a Young Gentleman leaving the University Concerning his Behaviour and Conversation in the World.* New York: V. V. Bradford, 1696.

Mackenzie, Frederick. *Diary of Frederick Mackenzie.* 2 vols. Cambridge: Harvard University Press, 1930.

Marsh, Philip M., ed. *A Freneau Sampler.* New York: Scarecrow Press, 1963.

Marshall, Christopher. *Extracts from the Diary of Christopher Marshall, 1774–1781.* Edited by William Duane. Albany, N.Y.: Joel Munsell's Sons, 1877. Reprint. New York: Arno Press, 1969.

Martin, Joseph Plumb. *Ordinary Courage: The Revolutionary War Adventures of Joseph Plumb Martin.* Edited by James Kirby Martin. New York: Brandywine Press, 1993.

McCarty, Thomas. "The Revolutionary War Journal of Sergeant Thomas McCarty." *Proceedings of the New Jersey Historical Society* 82 (1964): 29–46.

McCready, Robert. "A Revolutionary War Journal and Orderly Book of General Lachlan McIntosh's Expedition, 1778." Edited by Edward G. Williams. *Western Pennsylvania Historical Magazine* 43 (1960): 7–17, 157–77, 267–88.

McDowell, William. "Journal of Lieut. William McDowell of the First Penn'a Regiment, in the Southern Campaign, 1781–1782." In *Journals and Diaries of the War of*

Revolution with Lists of Officers and Soldiers, 1775–1783, edited by William Henry Egle, 295–340. Harrisburg, Pa.: E. K. Meyers, 1893.

McIntosh, Lachlan. "Letter Book of Lachlan McIntosh, 1776–1777." *Georgia Historical Quarterly* 38 (1954): 148–69, 253–67, 356–68.

McMichael, James. "Diary of Lt. James McMichael." In *Journals and Diaries of the War of Revolution with Lists of Officers and Soldiers, 1775–1783*, edited by William Henry Egle, 193–218. Harrisburg, Pa.: E. K. Meyers, 1893.

Meigs, Return. "Major Return J. Meigs' Journal." In *March to Quebec: Journals of the Members of Arnold's Expedition*, edited by Kenneth L. Roberts, 171–92. New York: Doubleday, Doran, 1938.

Melvin, James. *The Journal of James Melvin, Private Soldier in Arnold's Expedition against Quebec in the Year 1775*. Portland, Maine: Hubbard Bryant, 1902.

Middleton, Peter. *A Medical Discourse, or an Historical Inquiry into the Ancient and Present State of Medicine*. New York: Hugh Gaine, 1769.

Monro, Donald. *An Account of the Diseases Which were most frequent in the British Military Hospitals in Germany from January 1761 to the Return of the Troops to England in March 1763*. London: A. Millar, D. Wilson, and T. Durham, 1764.

———. *Observations on the Means of Preserving the Health of Soldiers and of conducting military Hospitals*. 2nd ed. London: J. Murray, 1780.

Montesquieu. *The Spirit of Laws (De L'Esprit des Loix)*. Geneva, 1748. Reprint. Edited by David Wallace Carrithers. Berkeley: University of California Press, 1977.

Moody, Eleazar. *The School of Good Manners*. New London, Conn.: Timothy Green, 1715.

Moore, John. *A View of Society and Manners in France, Switzerland and Germany: With Anecdotes relating to some Eminent Characters by a Gentleman who has resided several years in those Countries*. London: W. Strachan and T. Cadell, 1779.

Morgan, John. *A Discourse upon the Institution of Medical Schools in America*. Philadelphia: William Bradford, 1765.

———. *A Recommendation of Inoculation according to Baron Dimsdale's Method*. Boston: J. Gill, 1776.

———. *A Vindication of his Public Character*. Boston: Powars & Willis, 1777.

Morton, Robert. "The Diary of Robert Morton." *Pennsylvania Magazine of History and Biography* 1 (1877): 1–39.

Muhlenberg, Henry Melchior. *The Journals of Henry Melchior Muhlenberg*. 3 vols. Edited by Theodore G. Tappert and John W. Doberstein. Camden, Maine: Picton Press, 1993.

Murray, Sir James. *Letters from America, 1773–1780, Being the Letters of a Scots Officer, Sir James Murray, to his Home during the War of American Independence*. Edited by Eric Robson. Manchester, Eng.: Manchester University Press, 1951.

Nagle, Jacob. *The Nagle Journal: A Diary of the Life of Jacob Nagle, Sailor, from the Year 1775 to 1841*. Edited by John C. Dann. New York: Weidenfeld & Nicholson, 1988.

Nash, Soloman. "Journal of Soloman Nash, A Soldier of the Revolution." In *Crumbs *for Antiquarians*, edited by Charles I. Bushnell, 1:1–65. New York: Privately published, 1864.

Newsome, A. R., ed. "A British Orderly Book, 1780–1781." *North Carolina Historical Review* 9 (1932): 366–92.

Nicola, Lewis. *A Treatise of Military Exercise, calculated for the use of the Americans.* Philadelphia: Styner and Cist, 1776.

Norton, George. "Revolutionary Diary Kept by George Norton of Ipswich, 1777–1778." *Essex Institute Historical Collections* 74 (1938): 337–49.

Orderly Book and Journals Kept By Connecticut Men While Taking Part in the American Revolution, 1775–1778. Collections of the Connecticut Historical Society 7 (1899).

Orderly Book, Virginia Infantry 6th Regiment. Richmond, Va.: Privately published, 1863.

Owen, William. *The Medical Department of the United States Army [Legislative and Administrative History] during the Period of the Revolution [1776–1786].* New York: Paul B. Hoeber, 1920.

Paine, Thomas. *Common Sense.* Edited by Isaac Kramnick. New York: Penguin Books, 1986.

Painter, Thomas. *Autobiography of Thomas Painter Relating His Experiences during the War of the Revolution.* N.p.: Privately published, 1910.

Paley, William. *Principles of Moral and Political Philosophy.* Boston: West and Richardson, 1818.

Pargellis, Stanley. *Lord Loudoun in North America.* New Haven: Yale University Press, 1933.

———, ed. *Military Affairs in North America, 1748–1765.* New York: D. Appleton-Century Company, 1936.

Parker, Josiah. "Revolutionary Correspondence of Col. Josiah Parker, of Isle of Wight County, Va." *Virginia Magazine of History and Biography* 22 (1914): 257–66.

Pattison, James. "A New York Diary of the Revolutionary War." Edited by Carson I. A. Ritchie. *New-York Historical Society Quarterly* 50 (1966): 221–80.

Perry, David. "Life of David Perry." *Magazine of History* 35 (1928): 7–137.

Pettengill, Ray W., ed. *Letters from America, 1776–1779, Being Letters of Brunswick, Hessian, and Waldeck Officers with the British Armies during the Revolution.* Port Washington, N.Y.: Kennikat Press, 1964.

Philips, George Morris, ed. *Historic Letters from the Collection of the West Chester State Normal School.* Philadelphia: J. B. Lippincott, 1898.

Popp, Stephen. "Popp's Journal, 1777–1783." *Pennsylvania Magazine of History and Biography* 26 (1902): 25–41, 245–54.

Pott, Percival. *A Treatise on Ruptures.* London: L. Hawes, W. Clarke, and R. Collins, 1763.

Pringle, Sir John. *Observations on the Diseases of the Army, in Camp and Garrison.* London: A. Millar, D. Wilson, T. Payne, 1752.

Putnam, Israel. *General Orders issued by Major General Israel Putnam when in Com-*

mand of the Highlands in the Summer and Fall of 1777. Edited by Worthington Chauncey Ford. Brooklyn: Brooklyn Historical Printing Club, 1893.

Putnam, Rufus. *Journal of General Rufus Putnam Kept in Northern New York During Four Campaigns of the old French and Indian War, 1757–1760*. Albany, N.Y.: J. Munsell's Sons, 1886.

Quincy, Josiah. "Journal of Josiah Quincy." *Proceedings of the Massachusetts Historical Society* 49 (1916): 424–81.

R., Sergeant. "Battle of Princeton." *Pennsylvania Magazine of History and Biography* 20 (1896): 515–19.

Ramsay, David. *The History of the American Revolution*. 2 vols. Philadelphia: R. Aitken & Son, 1789.

———. *History of the Revolution of South Carolina*. 2 vols. Trenton: Isaac Collins, 1785.

Record of the Service of Connecticut Men in the War of the Revolution. Hartford: Connecticut Adjutant General's Office, 1889.

"Records of the South Carolina Line." *South Carolina Historical and Genealogical Magazine* 5–7 (1904–6).

Resolutions, Laws, and Ordinances, Relating to the Pay, Half Pay, Commutation of Half Pay, Bounty Lands and Other Promises Made by Congress to the Officers and Soldiers of the American Revolution. Washington, D.C.: Thomas Allen, 1838.

Rhode Island Historical Tracts: No. 6, The Centennial Celebration of the Battle of Rhode Island. Portsmouth, R.I., 1878.

Roberts, Lemuel. *Memoirs of Captain Lemuel Roberts*. Bennington, Vt.: Anthony Haswell, 1809.

Roberts, Thomas. "Journal of Sergeant Thomas Roberts." In *Journals of the Military Expedition of Major General John Sullivan against the Six Nations of Indians in 1779*, edited by Frederick Cook, 240–45. Auburn, N.Y.: Knapp, Peck & Thomson, 1887.

Rodney, Caesar. *Letters to and from Caesar Rodney, 1756–1784*. Philadelphia: University of Pennsylvania Press, 1933.

Rodney, Thomas. "Diary of Captain Thomas Rodney, 1776–1777." *Papers of the Historical Society of Delaware* 8 (1888): 3–53.

Rogers, William. *The Journal of a Brigade Chaplain in the Campaign of 1779 Against the Six Nations*. Providence, R.I.: Sydney S. Ryder, 1879.

Romilly, Sir Samuel. *Observations on the Criminal Law as it Relates to Capital Punishments*. London: T. Cadell and W. Davies, 1810.

Rowe, John. *Letters and Diary of John Rowe, Boston Merchant, 1759–1762, 1764–1779*. Boston: W. B. Clarke Company, 1903.

Rush, Benjamin. *Directions for Preserving the Health of Soldiers*. Lancaster, Pa.: John Dunlap, 1777.

———. *Essays, Literary, Moral and Philosophical*. Philadelphia: Bradfords, 1798.

———. *Letters of Benjamin Rush*. 2 vols. Edited by L. H. Butterfield. Princeton: Princeton University Press, 1951.

Russell, Peter. "The Siege of Charleston; Journal of Captain Peter Russell, December 25, 1779, to May 2, 1780." *American Historical Review* 4 (1898–99): 478–501.

Salmon, Thomas. *A New Geographical and Historical Grammar: Wherein the Geographical Part is truly modern and the Present State of the Several Kingdoms of the World is so Interpreted as to Render the Study of Geography Both Entertaining and Instructive.* 11th ed. London: W. Johnston, 1769.

Senter, Isaac. "The Journal of Isaac Senter, Physician and Surgeon to the Troops Detached from the American Army Encamped at Cambridge." *Magazine of History* 42 (1915): 11–60.

Serle, Ambrose. *The American Journal of Ambrose Serle, Secretary to Lord Howe, 1776–1778.* Edited by Edward H. Tatum Jr. San Marino, Calif.: Huntington Library, 1940.

Seymour, William. "A Journal of the Southern Expedition, 1780–1783." *Papers of the Historical Society of Delaware* 2 (1896): 3–42.

Sherman, Sylvia J. *Dubrose Times: Selected Depositions of Maine Revolutionary War Veterans.* Augusta: Maine State Archives, 1975.

Sherrill, Charles A. *Revolutionary War Pension Applications from Franklin County, Tennessee.* N.p.: Privately published, 1982.

Simcoe, John Graves. *Simcoe's Military Journal: A History of the Operations of a Partisan Corps, Called the Queen's Rangers.* New York: Bartlett & Welford, 1844.

Simes, Thomas. *The Military Guide for Young Officers.* 2 vols. Philadelphia: J. Humphries, R. Bell, and R. Aitken, 1776.

Smith, Samuel. "Memoirs." In *Crumbs for Antiquarians*, edited by Charles I. Bushnell, 1:1–41. New York: Privately published, 1864.

Sproule, Moses. "The Western Campaign of 1779: The Diary of Quartermaster Sergeant Moses Sproule of the Third New Jersey Regiment in the Sullivan Expedition of the Revolutionary War, May 17–October 17, 1779." Edited by R. W. G. Vail. *New-York Historical Society Quarterly* 41 (1957): 35–69.

Stevens, Elisha. *Fragments of Memoranda Written by him in the War of the Revolution.* Meriden, Conn.: Privately published, 1893.

Stevenson, Roger. *Military Instructions for Officers Detached in the Field.* Philadelphia: R. Aitken, 1775.

Stiles, Henry R., ed. *Letters from the Prisons and Prison Ships of the Revolution.* New York: Privately published, 1865.

Stillman, Samuel. *Death, the Last Enemy, Destroyed by Christ, a Sermon preached March 27, 1776 before the Honorable Continental Congress on the Death of the Honorable Samuel Ward, Esq., one of the Delegates from the colony of Rhode Island.* Philadelphia: Joseph Cruikshank, 1776.

Stone, Hiram. "The Experiences of a Prisoner in the American Revolution." *Journal of American History* 2 (1908): 527–29.

Strike, Henry. "A British Officer's Revolutionary War Journal, 1776–1778." Edited by S. Sydney Bradford. *Maryland Historical Magazine* 56 (1961): 150–75.

Strong, Nathan. *The Reason and Design of Public Punishments*. Hartford, 1777.

Stubblefield, George. "Orderly Book of the Company of Captain George Stubblefield, Fifth Virginia Regiment, from March 3, 1776, to July 10, 1776, Inclusive." *Collections of the Virginia Historical Society*, n.s., 6 (1887): 141–91.

Sullivan, John. *Letters and Papers of Major General John Sullivan, Continental Army*. 8 vols. Edited by Otis G. Hammond. Concord: New Hampshire Historical Society, 1930.

Sullivan, Thomas. "Before and After the Battle of Brandywine: Extracts from the Journal of Sergeant Thomas Sullivan of H.M. Forty-Ninth Regiment of Foot." *Pennsylvania Magazine of History and Biography* 31 (1907): 406–18.

——. "The Common British Soldier—from the Journal of Thomas Sullivan, 49th Regiment of Foot." *Maryland Historical Magazine* 62 (1967): 219–53.

Summers, William, ed. "Obituary Notices of Pennsylvania Soldiers of the Revolution." *Pennsylvania Magazine of History and Biography* 38 (1914): 443–60.

Sun-tzu. *The Art of War*. Translated and edited by Ralph D. Sawyer. San Francisco: Westview Press, 1994.

Sweat, William. "Captain William Sweat's Personal Diary of the Expedition against Ticonderoga, May 2–November 7, 1758." Edited by Paul O. Blanchette. *Essex Institute Historical Collections* 93 (1957): 36–57.

Tallmadge, Samuel. *Orderly Books of the Fourth New York Regiment, 1778–1780, The Second New York Regiment, 1780–1783*. Edited by Alman W. Lauber. Albany: University of the City of New York, 1932.

Tammany Society. *An Historical Account of the Interment of the Remains of 11,500 American Seamen, Soldiers and Citizens*. New York: Frank White & Company, 1808.

Tennent, John. *Every Man His Own Doctor or The Poor Planter's Physician*. Philadelphia: Franklin, 1734.

Thacher, James. *A Military Journal During the American Revolutionary War, From 1775–1783*. Boston: Richardson and Lord, 1823.

Thacher, Thomas. *A Brief Rule to the Common People of New England How to order themselves and theirs in the Small-Pocks or Measels*. Boston: John Foster, 1677.

Theobald, J. *Every man his own Physician*. Boston: W. Griffin, 1767.

Tilden, John Bell. "Extracts from the Journal of John Bell Tilden." *Pennsylvania Magazine of History and Biography* 19 (1895): 51–63, 208–33.

Tilton, James. *Economical Observations on Military Hospitals and the Prevention and Cure of Diseases Incident to an Army*. Wilmington, Del.: J. Wilson, 1813.

Tissot, Simon André. *Advice to the People in General, with Regard to their health*. Philadelphia: John Sparhawk, 1771.

Trenchard, John. *A Short History of Standing Armies in England*. London, 1698.

Trumbull, Benjamin. "A Concise Journal or Minutes of the Principal Movements Towards St. John's of the Siege and Surrender of the Forts There in 1775." *Collections of the Connecticut Historical Society* 7 (1899): 137–73.

——. "Journal of the Campaign at New York, 1776–7." *Collections of the Connecticut Historical Society* 7 (1899): 175–218.

VanderBeets, Richard. *Held Captive by Indians: Selected Narratives, 1642–1836.* Knoxville: University of Tennessee Press, 1973.

Van Hovenburgh, Rudolphus. "Journal of Lieutenant Rudolphus Van Hovenburgh." In *Journals of the Military Expedition of Major General John Sullivan against the Six Nations of Indians in 1779*, edited by Frederick Cook, 275–84. Auburn, N.Y.: Knapp, Peck & Thomson, 1887.

Van Swieten, Gerard. *Diseases Incident to Armies with the Method of Cure, and The Nature and Treatment of Gunshot Wounds.* Introduction by Sir John Ranby. Philadelphia: Robert Bell, 1776.

Vaughan, Zebulon. "The Journal of Private Zebulon Vaughan, Revolutionary Soldier, 1770–1780." Edited by Virginia Steele Wood. *Daughters of the American Revolution Magazine* 113 (1979): 100–114, 256–57, 320–25, 478–87.

Vollmer, A. *Military Obligation: The American Tradition—A Compilation of the Enactments of Compulsion from the Earliest Settlements of the Original Thirteen Colonies in 1607 through the Articles of Confederation, 1789.* Washington D.C.: Selective Service System, Government Printing Office, 1947. Reprint. New York: Arno Press, 1979.

Von Bilguer, Johannes Ulrich. *A Dissertation on the Inutility of the Amputation of Limbs.* London: R. Balwin, 1764.

Von Clauswitz, Carl. *On War.* Translated and edited by Michael Howard and Peter Paret. Princeton: Princeton University Press, 1984.

Von Riedesel, Baroness (Friederike Charlotte Louise). "Her Revolutionary War Journal." In *Narratives of the American Revolution*, edited by Hugh F. Rankin, 289–427. Chicago: R. R. Donnelley & Sons, 1976.

Von Steuben, Friedrich. *Regulations for the Order and Discipline of the Troops of the United States, Part 1.* Philadelphia: Styner and Cist, 1779.

Waldo, Albigence. "Diary of Surgeon Albigence Waldo, of the Connecticut Line." *Pennsylvania Magazine of History and Biography* 21 (1897): 299–323.

Washington, George. *George Washington's Papers.* Microfilm. Washington, D.C.: Library of Congress, 1961.

——. *George Washington's Rules of Civility and Decent Behaviour in Company and Conversation.* Edited by John Allen Murray. New York: G. P. Putnam's Sons, 1942.

——. *The Papers of George Washington: Colonial Series.* 10 vols. to date. Edited by W. W. Abbot. Charlottesville: University Press of Virginia, 1983–.

——. *The Papers of George Washington: Revolutionary War Series.* 12 vols. to date. Edited by Philander D. Chase. Charlottesville: University Press of Virginia, 1985–.

——. *Writings of George Washington.* 39 vols. Edited by John C. Fitzpatrick. Washington, D.C.: Government Printing Office, 1934.

Watts, John. *Letterbook of John Watts, Merchant and Councillor of New York. Collections of the New-York Historical Society* 61 (1928).

Weedon, George. *Valley Forge Orderly Book of General George Weedon*. New York: Arno Press, 1971.

Wells, Bayze. "Journal of Bayze Wells of Farmington, May, 1775–February, 1777." *Collections of the Connecticut Historical Society* 7 (1899): 239–96.

Wesley, John. *Primitive Physick: or An Easy and Natural Method of Curing Most Diseases*. Philadelphia: Andrew Steuart, 1764.

White, Joseph. "A Narrative of Events as They Occurred from Time to Time in the Revolutionary War." *American Heritage* 4 (1956): 74–79.

Wild, Ebenezer. "Journal of Ebenezer Wild." *Proceedings of the Massachusetts Historical Society* 26 (1890): 78–160.

Willard, Margaret Wheeler. *Letters on the American Revolution, 1774–1776*. Boston: Houghton Mifflin, 1925.

Willcutt, Jesse. *Revolutionary War Pension Applications of Jesse and Katherine Willcutt*. Livonia, Mich.: Flash Productions, 1975.

Williams, Ennion. "Journal of Major Ennion Williams on his Journey to the American Camp at Cambridge in New England, 1775." In *Journals and Diaries of the War of Revolution with Lists of Officers and Soldiers, 1775–1783*, edited by William Henry Egle, 5–21. Harrisburg, Pa.: E. K. Meyers, 1893.

Winthrop, William. *Military Law and Precedents*. 2 vols. Boston: Little, Brown, 1896.

Wolfe, James. *Instructions to Young Officers*. London: J. Millan, 1778.

Young, Thomas. "Memoir of Major Thomas Young: A Revolutionary Patriot of South Carolina." *Orion: Monthly Magazine of Literature and Art* 3 (1843): 84–105.

Young, William. "Journal of Sergeant William Young." *Pennsylvania Magazine of History and Biography* 8 (1884): 255–78.

Secondary Sources

Alberts, Robert C. *The Most Extraordinary Adventures of Robert Stobo*. Boston: Houghton Mifflin, 1965.

Alexander, Arthur J. "How Maryland Tried to Raise Her Continental Quotas." *Maryland Historical Magazine* 42 (1947): 184–96.

Allen, Oliver. *The Tiger: The Rise and Fall of Tammany Hall*. New York: Addison Wesley, 1993.

Ames, Susie M., ed. *County Court Records of Accomack-Northampton, Virginia, 1632–1640*. Washington, D.C.: American Historical Association, 1954.

Anderson, Benedict. *Imagined Communities: Reflections on the Origin and Spread of Nationalism*. New York: Verso, 1991.

Anderson, Fred. *Crucible of War: The Seven Years' War and the Fate of Empire in British North America, 1754–1766*. New York: Alfred A. Knopf, 2000.

——. *A People's Army: Massachusetts Soldiers and Society in the Seven Years' War*. Chapel Hill: University of North Carolina Press, 1984.

Anderson, Olive. "The Treatment of Prisoners of War in Britain during the American

War of Independence." *Bulletin of the Institute of Historical Research* 28 (1955): 63–83.

Anon. "Funeral Processions in Boston." *Boston Society Publications* 4 (1907): 125–49.

Applegate, Howard Lewis. "Effect of the American Revolution on American Medicine." *Military Medicine* 126 (1961): 551–53.

———. "The Need for Further Study in the Medical History of the American Revolutionary Army." *Military Medicine* 126 (1961): 616–18.

———. "Remedial Medicine in the American Revolutionary Army." *Military Medicine* 126 (1961): 450–53.

Aresty, Esther B. *The Best Behavior: The Course of Good Manners—from Antiquity to Present—as Seen through Courtesy and Etiquette Books*. New York: Simon and Schuster, 1970.

Ariès, Philippe. *Western Attitudes toward Death: From the Middle Ages to the Present*. Baltimore: Johns Hopkins University Press, 1976.

Armbuster, Eugene. *The Wallabout Prison Ships, 1776–1783*. New York: Privately published, 1920.

Axtell, James. *The European and the Indian: Essays in the Ethnohistory of Colonial North America*. New York: Oxford University Press, 1981.

Babits, Lawrence E. *A Devil of a Whipping: The Battle of Cowpens*. Chapel Hill: University of North Carolina Press, 1998.

Bancroft, George. *Letter on the Exchange of Prisoners during the American War of Independence*. New York: New-York Historical Society, 1862.

Barck, Dorothy C. Introduction to *Uniforms of the American, British, French and German Armies in the War of the American Revolution, 1775–1783*, by Charles M. Lefferts. Old Greenwich, Conn.: WE Inc., 1971.

Barker, A. J. *Prisoners of War*. New York: Universe Books, 1975.

Barker, Francis. *The Tremulous Private Body: Essays on Subjection*. New York: Methuen, 1984.

Bass, Robert D. *Swamp Fox: The Life and Campaigns of General Francis Marion*. New York: Henry Holt & Company, 1959.

Baumgarten, Linda. *What Clothes Reveal: The Language of Clothing in Colonial and Federal America*. Williamsburg and New Haven: Colonial Williamsburg Foundation and Yale University Press, 2002.

Bayne-Jones, Stanhope. *The Evolution of Preventive Medicine in the United States Army, 1607–1939*. Washington D.C.: Office of the Surgeon General, Department of the Army, 1968.

Beattie, J. M. *Crime and the Courts in England, 1660–1800*. Princeton: Princeton University Press, 1986.

Bell, Whitfield J., Jr. *John Morgan: Continental Doctor*. Philadelphia: University of Pennsylvania Press, 1965.

Berlin, Robert Harry. "The Administration of Military Justice in the Continental Army during the American Revolution, 1775–1783." Ph.D. diss., University of California, Santa Barbara, 1976.

Bernath, Stuart. "George Washington and the Genesis of American Military Discipline." *Mid-America* 49 (1967): 83–100.

Black, Jeremy. *European Warfare, 1660–1815*. New Haven: Yale University Press, 1994.

Blassingame, John. *The Slave Community: Plantation Life in the Antebellum South*. New York: Oxford University Press, 1979.

Blauner, Robert. "Death and Social Structure." *Psychiatry* 29 (1966): 378–94.

Boatner, Mark Mayo, III. *Encyclopedia of the American Revolution*. New York: David McKay Company, 1966.

Bodle, Wayne K. *The Valley Forge Winter: Civilians and Soldiers in War*. University Park: Pennsylvania State University Press, 2002.

Bodle, Wayne K., and Jacqueline Thibaut. *Valley Forge Historical Research Report*. Valley Forge, Pa.: U.S. Department of the Interior, National Park Service, 1980.

Bolton, Charles Knowles. *The Private Soldier under Washington*. New York: Charles Scribner's Sons, 1902.

Bowen, H. V. *War and British Society, 1668–1815*. Cambridge: Cambridge University Press, 1998.

Bowman, Allen. *The Morale of the American Revolutionary Army*. Washington, D.C.: American Council on Public Affairs, 1943.

Bowman, Larry. *Captive Americans: Prisoners during the American Revolution*. Athens: Ohio University Press, 1976.

Boyd, Thomas. *Light-Horse Harry Lee*. New York: Charles Scribner's Sons, 1931.

Bradford, S. Sydney. "Discipline in the Morristown Winter Encampments." *Proceedings of the New Jersey Historical Society* 80 (1962): 1–30.

Breeden, James O. "Body Snatchers and Anatomy Professors: Medical Education in Nineteenth-Century Virginia." *Virginia Magazine of History and Biography* 83 (1975): 321–45.

Brereton, J. M. *The British Soldier: A Social History from 1661 to the Present Day*. London: Bodley Head, 1986.

Brewer, John. *The Sinews of Power: War, Money, and the English State, 1688–1783*. Cambridge: Harvard University Press, 1990.

Brown, Richard Maxwell. *The South Carolina Regulators*. Cambridge: Belknap Press, 1963.

Brumwell, Stephen. *Redcoats: The British Soldier and War in the Americas, 1755–1763*. New York: Cambridge University Press, 2002.

Burt, Olive Woolley. *American Murder Ballads and Their Stories*. New York: Oxford University Press, 1958.

Bushman, Richard L. *The Refinement of America: Persons, Houses, Cities*. New York: Vintage Books, 1993.

Bynum, Caroline Walker. *The Resurrection of the Body in Western Christianity, 200–1336*. New York: Columbia University Press, 1995.

Callahan, North. *George Washington: Soldier and Man*. New York: William Morrow & Company, 1972.

Calloway, Colin. *The American Revolution in Indian Country: Crisis and Diversity in Native American Communities*. New York: Cambridge University Press, 1995.

Cantlie, Sir Neil. "Inspector General of Hospitals—Robert Jackson (1750–1827), Army Medical Department." *Proceedings of the Royal Society of Medicine* 65 (1972): 1123–26.

Carlton, Charles. *Going to the Wars: The Experience of the British Civil Wars, 1638–1651*. New York: Routledge, 1994.

Carp, E. Wayne. *To Starve the Army at Pleasure: Continental Army Administration and American Political Culture, 1775–1783*. Chapel Hill: University of North Carolina Press, 1984.

Cash, Philip. *Medical Men at the Siege of Boston, April, 1775–April, 1776: Problems of the Massachusetts and Continental Armies*. Philadelphia: American Philosophical Society, 1973.

Chase, Malcolm, and Christopher Shaw. *The Imagined Past: History and Nostalgia*. New York: Manchester University Press, 1989.

Childs, John. *Armies and Warfare in Europe, 1648–1789*. New York: Holmes and Meier Publishers, 1982.

Clark, Thomas D. "Kentucky in the Northwest Campaign." In *After Tippecanoe: Some Aspects of the War of 1812*, edited by Philip P. Mason, 78–98. East Lansing: Michigan State University Press, 1963.

Clodfelter, Michael. *Warfare and Armed Conflicts: A Statistical Reference to Casualty and Other Figures, 1618–1991*. 2 vols. London: McFarland & Company, 1992.

Cohen, Daniel A. *Pillars of Salt, Monuments of Grace: New England Crime Literature and the Origins of American Popular Culture, 1674–1860*. New York: Oxford University Press, 1993.

Cohen, Sheldon S. *Yankee Sailors in British Gaols: Prisoners of War at Forton and Mill, 1777–1783*. Newark: University of Delaware Press, 1995.

Colley, Linda. *Britons: Forging the Nation, 1707–1837*. New Haven: Yale University Press, 1992.

Commager, Henry S., and Richard B. Morris. *The Spirit of 'Seventy-Six*. 2 vols. Indianapolis: Bobbs-Merrill, 1958.

Corvisier, André, and John Childs. "Losses of Life." In *Dictionary of Military History and the Art of War*, edited by André Corvisier and translated by Chris Turner, 463–70. English ed. edited by John Childs. Cambridge: Blackwell Reference, 1994.

Craven, Wesley Frank. *The Legend of the Founding Fathers*. New York: New York University Press, 1956.

Cray, Robert E., Jr. "Commemorating the Prison Ship Dead: Revolutionary Memory and the Politics of Sepulture in the Early Republic, 1776–1808." *William and Mary Quarterly*, 3rd ser., 56 (1999): 565–90.

Cremin, Lawrence A. *American Education: The Colonial Experience*. New York: Harper & Row, 1970.

Curtis, Edward E. *The Organization of the British Army in the American Revolution*. New Haven: Yale University Press, 1926.

Davis, David Brion. *The Problem of Slavery in the Age of Revolution, 1770–1823*. Ithaca, N.Y.: Cornell University Press, 1975.

Dederer, John Morgan. *War in America to 1775: Before Yankee Doodle*. New York: New York University Press, 1990.

DeLacy, Margaret. *Prison Reform in Lancashire, 1700–1850: A Study in Local Administration*. Stanford: Stanford University Press, 1986.

Demos, John. "From This World to the Next: Notes on Death and Dying in Early America." In *Facing Death: Where Culture, Religion, and Medicine Meet*, edited by Howard M. Spiro, Mary G. McCrea Curnen, and Lee Palmer Wandel, 160–65. New Haven: Yale University Press, 1996.

De Watteville, H. *The British Soldier: His Daily Life from Tudor to Modern Times*. New York: G. P. Putnam's Sons, 1955.

Duffy, Christopher. *The Army of Frederick the Great*. New York: Hippocrene Books, 1974.
———. *The Military Experience in the Age of Reason*. London: Routledge & Kegan Paul, 1987.

Duffy, John. *Epidemics in Colonial America*. Baton Rouge: Louisiana State University Press, 1953.

Duncan, L. C. "Medical Men in the American Revolution, 1775–1783." *Army Medical Bulletin* 25 (1931): 369–78.

Dunning, Arend. "Lessons from the Dead." *New Scientist* 137 (1993): 44–47.

Dwyer, William M. *The Day Is Ours! November 1776–January 1777: An Inside View of the Battles of Trenton and Princeton*. New York: Viking Press, 1983.

Earle, Alice Morse. "Death Ritual in Colonial New York." In *Passing: The Vision of Death in America*, edited by Charles O. Jackson, 30–41. Westport, Conn.: Greenwood Press, 1977.

Elias, Norbert. *The History of Manners: The Civilizing Process*. Vol. 1. New York: Pantheon Books, 1978.

Elting, John, ed. *Military Uniforms in America: The Era of the American Revolution, 1755–1795*. San Rafael, Calif.: Presidio Press, 1974.

Engelman, Rose C., and Robert Joy. *Two Hundred Years of Military Medicine*. Fort Detrick, Md.: Historical Unit, U.S. Army Medical Department, 1975.

Exhibit of Books Illustrating the History of Military Medicine. Durham, N.C.: Duke University Hospital, 1941.

Fede, Andrew. "Legitimized Violent Slave Abuse in the American South, 1619–1865: A Case Study of Law and Social Change in Six Southern States." *American Journal of Legal History* 29 (1985): 93–150.

Fenn, Elizabeth. *Pox Americana: The Great Smallpox Epidemic of 1775–82*. New York: Hill & Wang, 2001.

Finke, Detmar H. "Insignia of Rank in the Continental Army, 1775–1783." *Military Collector and Historian* 8 (1956): 71–73.

Fitzroy, Herbert W. K. "The Punishment of Crime in Provincial Pennsylvania." *Pennsylvania Magazine of History and Biography* 60 (1936): 242–69.

Fleetwood, John. *History of Medicine in Ireland*. Dublin: Browne and Nolan, 1951.

Flexner, James Thomas. *George Washington in the American Revolution, 1775–1783*. Boston: Little, Brown, 1967.

Foucault, Michel. *Discipline and Punish: The Birth of the Prison*. New York: Vintage Books, 1979.

French, Allen. *The First Year of the American Revolution*. Boston: Houghton Mifflin, 1934.

French, Roger. "The Anatomical Tradition." In *Companion Encyclopedia of the History of Medicine*, 2 vols., edited by Roy Porter and W. F. Bynum, 1:81–101. London: Routledge, 1993.

Frey, Sylvia. *The British Soldier in America: A Social History of Military Life in the Revolutionary Period*. Austin: University of Texas Press, 1981.

———. "Courts and Cats: British Military Justice in the Eighteenth Century." *Military Affairs* 43 (1979): 5–11.

———. *Water from the Rock: Black Resistance in a Revolutionary Age*. Princeton: Princeton University Press, 1992.

Fritz, Paul S. "The Undertaking Trade in England: Its Origins and Early Development, 1660–1830." *Eighteenth Century Studies* 28 (1994–95): 241–53.

Frothingham, Richard. *Life and Times of Joseph Warren*. Boston: Little, Brown, 1865.

Gatrell, V. A. C. *The Hanging Tree: Execution and the English People, 1770–1868*. New York: Oxford University Press, 1994.

Gelfand, Tony. "The History of the Medical Profession." In *Companion Encyclopedia of the History of Medicine*, 2 vols., edited by Roy Porter and W. F. Bynum, 2:1119–50. London: Routledge, 1993.

———. "The Origins of a Modern Concept of Medical Specialization: John Morgan's Discourse of 1765." *Bulletin of the History of Medicine* 50 (1976): 511–35.

Genovese, Eugene. *Roll, Jordan, Roll: The World the Slaves Made*. New York: Pantheon Books, 1974.

Gibson, James E. *Dr. Bodo Otto and the Medical Background of the American Revolution*. Baltimore: Charles C. Thomas, 1937.

Gilbert, Arthur N. "The Changing Face of British Military Justice, 1757–1783." *Military Affairs* 49 (1985): 80–84.

Gillett, Mary C. *The Army Medical Department, 1775–1818*. Washington, D.C.: Center of Military History, U.S. Army, 1990.

Goebel, Julius, Jr., and T. Raymond Naughton. *Law Enforcement in Colonial New York: A Study in Criminal Procedure (1664–1776)*. New York: Commonwealth Fund, 1944.

Gordon, Maurice Bear. *Aesculapius Comes to the Colonies: The Story of the Early Days of Medicine in the Thirteen Original Colonies*. Ventnor, N.J.: Ventnor Publishers, 1949.

Graham, James. *The Life of General Daniel Morgan of the Virginia Line of the Army of the United States*. New York: Derby & Jackson, 1859.

Greenberg, Douglas. "Crime, Law Enforcement, and Social Control in Colonial America." *American Journal of Legal History* 26 (1982): 293–325.

——. "The Effectiveness of Law Enforcement in Eighteenth-Century New York." *American Journal of Legal History* 19 (1975): 173–203.

Greven, Philip J. *Four Generations: Population, Land, and Family in Colonial Andover, Massachusetts*. Ithaca, N.Y.: Cornell University Press, 1970.

——. *The Protestant Temperament: Patterns of Child-Rearing, Religious Experience, and the Self in Early America*. New York: Alfred Knopf, 1977.

Gross, Robert A. *The Minutemen and Their World*. New York: Hill & Wang, 1976.

Guy, Alan J. *Regimental Agency in the British Standing Army, 1715–1763: A Study of Georgian Military Administration*. Manchester, Eng.: John Rylands University Library, 1980.

Haarman, Albert W., and Donald W. Holst. "The Friedrich von Germann Drawings of Troops in the American Revolution." *Military Collector and Historian* 16 (Spring 1964): 1–9.

Haber, Samuel. *The Quest for Authority and Honor in the American Professions*. Chicago: University of Chicago Press, 1991.

Hanson, Willis T., Jr. *A History of St. George's Church in the City of Schenectady*. 2 vols. Schenectady, N.Y.: Privately published, 1919.

Hare, John S. "Military Punishments in the War of 1812." *Journal of the American Military Institute* 4 (winter 1940): 225–39.

Hatch, Lewis Clinton. *The Administration of the American Revolutionary Army*. New York: Longmans, Green, 1904.

Hatch, Nathan. "The Puzzle of American Methodism." *Reflections* (Yale Divinity School) 88 (1993): 13–20.

Hay, Douglas. "Property, Authority, and the Criminal Law." In *Albion's Fatal Tree: Crime and Society in Eighteenth-Century England*, edited by Douglas Hay et al., 17–63. New York: Pantheon Books, 1975.

Hayter, Tony. *The Army and the Crowd in Mid-Georgian England*. Totowa, N.J.: Rowman and Littlefield, 1978.

——. "The Army and the First British Empire, 1714–1783." In *The Oxford Illustrated History of the British Army*, edited by David Chandler, 111–32. New York: Oxford University Press, 1994.

Heitman, Francis, ed. *Historical Register of Officers of the Continental Army during the War of the Revolution*. Washington, D.C.: Rare Book Shop Publishing Company, 1914.

Heller, Francis H. "Military Law in the Continental Army." *University of Kansas Law Review* 25 (1977): 353–60.

Henry, H. M. *The Police Control of the Slave in South Carolina*. Emory, Va.: Emory and Henry College, 1914.

Hickey, Donald R. *The War of 1812: The Forgotten Conflict*. Urbana: University of Illinois Press, 1989.

Higginbotham, Don. *Daniel Morgan: Revolutionary Rifleman*. Chapel Hill: University of North Carolina Press, 1961.

Hillard, E. B. *The Last Men of the Revolution*. Edited by Wendell D. Garrett. Hartford, 1864. Reprint. Barre, Mass.: Barre Publishers, 1968.

Hindle, Brooke. *The Pursuit of Science in Revolutionary America, 1735–1789*. Chapel Hill: University of North Carolina Press, 1956.

Hindus, Michael Stephen. *Prison and Plantation: Crime, Justice, and Authority in Massachusetts and South Carolina, 1767–1878*. Chapel Hill: University of North Carolina Press, 1980.

Hobsbawm, Eric. "Inventing Traditions." In *The Invention of Tradition*, edited by Eric Hobsbawm and Terence Ranger, 1–14. New York: Cambridge University Press, 1983.

Hopkins, Douglas R. *The Greatest Killer: Smallpox in History*. Chicago: University of Chicago Press, 2000.

Houlbrooke, Ralph. *Death, Religion, and the Family in England, 1480–1750*. Oxford: Clarendon Press, 1998.

Houlding, J. A. *Fit for Service: The Training of the British Army, 1715–1795*. Oxford: Clarendon Press, 1981.

Howard, Michael. *War in European History*. New York: Oxford University Press, 1976.

Huntington, Richard, and Peter Metcalf. *Celebrations of Death: The Anthropology of Mortuary Ritual*. New York: Cambridge University Press, 1979.

Ignatieff, Michael. *A Just Measure of Pain: The Penitentiary in the Industrial Revolution, 1750–1850*. New York: Pantheon Books, 1978.

Isaac, Rhys. *The Transformation of Virginia, 1740–1790*. Chapel Hill: University of North Carolina Press, 1982.

Ivers, Larry E. *British Drums on the Southern Frontier: The Military Colonization of Georgia, 1733–1749*. Chapel Hill: University of North Carolina Press, 1974.

Jackson, Luther P. "Virginia Negro Soldiers and Seamen in the American Revolution." *Journal of Negro History* 27 (1942): 247–87.

Jaeger, C. Stephen. *The Origins of Courtliness: Civilizing Trends and the Origin of Courtly Ideals, 939–1210*. Philadelphia: University of Pennsylvania Press, 1985.

Jarvis, Rupert C. *Collected Papers on the Jacobite Risings*. 2 vols. New York: Manchester University Press, 1971.

Jensen, Merrill. *The New Nation: A History of the United States during the Confederation, 1781–1789*. New York: Alfred Knopf, 1958.

Johnson, James M. *Militiamen, Rangers, and Redcoats: The Military in Georgia, 1754–1776*. Macon: Mercer University Press, 1992.

Jones, Colin. *The Charitable Imperative: Hospitals and Nursing in Ancien Régime and Revolutionary France*. New York: Routledge, 1989.

Jones, Douglas Lamar. "The Strolling Poor: Transiency in Eighteenth-Century Massachusetts." *Journal of Social History* 8 (1975): 28–54.

Jones, J. R. *Country and Court: England, 1658–1714*. Cambridge: Harvard University Press, 1978.

Jordan, John W. "The Military Hospitals at Bethlehem and Lilitz during the Revolution." *Pennsylvania Magazine of History and Biography* 20 (1896): 137–57.

Joy, Robert J. T. "The Natural Bonesetters with Special Reference to the Sweet Family of Rhode Island." *Bulletin of the History of Medicine* 28 (1954): 416–41.

Kaplan, Sidney. "Rank and Status among Massachusetts Continental Officers." *American Historical Review* 56 (1951): 318–26.

Kealey, Linda. "Patterns of Punishment: Massachusetts in the Eighteenth Century." *American Journal of Legal History* 30 (1986): 163–86.

Keller, Kate Van Winkle. "Fiddle, Dance, and Sing with George Bush: A New Source of Eighteenth-Century Popular Music." *Sonneck Society Bulletin* 18 (1992): 47–49.

———. *Songs from the American Revolution*. Sandy Hook, Conn.: Hendrickson Group, 1992.

Kelly, Howard A., and Walter L. Burrage. *American Medical Biographies*. Baltimore: Remington Company, 1920.

Kenney, Alice P. "The Bathtub Court-Martial." *New-York Historical Society Quarterly* 50 (1966): 281–97.

Kett, Joseph. *The Formation of the American Medical Profession: The Role of Institutions, 1780–1860*. New Haven: Yale University Press, 1968.

Kimmel, Ross M. "A Revolutionary War Uniform." *Military Collector and Historian* 27 (summer 1975): 60–62.

Kirkpatrick, T. Percy C. *History of the Medical Teaching in Trinity College Dublin and the School of Physic in Ireland*. Dublin: Hanna and Neale, 1912.

Knouff, Gregory T. "The Common People's Revolution: Class, Race, Masculinity, and Locale in Pennsylvania, 1775–1783." Ph.D. diss., Rutgers University, 1992.

Kohn, Richard H. "The Social History of the American Soldier: A Review and Prospectus for Research." *American Historical Review* 86 (1981): 553–67.

Kollmann, Gerald. "Reflections on the Army of the American Revolution." In *New Wine in Old Skins: A Comparative View of Socio-Political Structures and Values Affecting the American Revolution*, edited by Erich Angermann et al., 153–76. Stuttgart: Ernst Klett Verlag, 1976.

Laqueur, Thomas. "Naming and Memory in the Great War." In *Commemorations: The Politics of National Identity*, edited by John R. Gillis, 150–67. Princeton: Princeton University Press, 1994.

Lawrence, Ghislaine. "Surgery (Traditional)." In *Companion Encyclopedia of the History of Medicine*, 2 vols., edited by Roy Porter and W. F. Bynum, 2:961–83. London: Routledge, 1993.

Leach, Douglas Edward. *Roots of Conflict: British Armed Forces and Colonial Americans, 1677–1763*. Chapel Hill: University of North Carolina Press, 1986.

Lee, Frederic S. "The School of Medicine." In *A History of Columbia University, 1754–1904*, 307–34. New York: Columbia University Press, 1904.

Lee, Wayne E. *Crowds and Soldiers in Revolutionary North Carolina: The Culture of Violence and Riot in War*. Gainesville: University Press of Florida, 2001.

Lemisch, Jesse. "Listening to the 'Inarticulate': William Widger's Dream and the Loy-
alties of American Revolutionary Seamen in British Prisons." *Journal of Social History* 3 (1969): 1–29.

Lender, Mark Edward. "The Social Structure of the New Jersey Brigade: The Continental Line as an American Standing Army." In *The Military in America from the
Colonial Era to the Present*, edited by Peter Karsten, 27–44. New York: Free Press,
1980.

Lesser, Charles H. *The Sinews of Independence: Monthly Strength Reports of the Continental Army*. Chicago: University of Chicago Press, 1976.

Lewis, Jan. "Domestic Tranquility and the Management of Emotion among the Gentry of Pre-revolutionary Virginia." *William and Mary Quarterly*, 3rd ser., 39 (1982):
135–49.

Lifton, Robert Jay. *The Broken Connection: On Death and the Continuity of Life*. New
York: Simon and Schuster, 1979.

Lindsey, William R. "Treatment of American Prisoners of War during the American
Revolution." *Emporia State Research Studies* 22 (1973): 5–32.

Linebaugh, Peter. "The Tyburn Riots against the Surgeons." In *Albion's Fatal Tree:
Crime and Society in Eighteenth-Century England*, edited by Douglas Hay et al.,
65–117. New York: Pantheon Books, 1975.

Lossing, Benson J. *Pictorial Field Book of the Revolution*. 2 vols. New York: Thomas
Addison Emmet, 1900.

Mackesy, Piers. *The War for America, 1775–1783*. Cambridge: Harvard University Press,
1964.

Major, Ralph. *Fatal Partners, War and Disease*. New York: Doubleday, Doran,
1941.

Martin, James Kirby. "A 'Most Undisciplined Profligate Crew': Protest and Defiance
in the Continental Ranks, 1776–1783." In *Arms and Independence: The Military
Character of the American Revolution*, edited by Ronald Hoffman and Peter J. Albert, 119–40. Charlottesville: University Press of Virginia, 1984.

Martin, James Kirby, and Mark Edward Lender. *A Respectable Army: The Military Origins of the Republic, 1763–1789*. Arlington Heights, Ill.: Harlan Davidson, 1982.

Masur, Louis. *Rites of Execution: Capital Punishment and the Transformation of American Culture, 1776–1865*. New York: Oxford University Press, 1989.

Mayer, Holly. *Belonging to the Army: Camp Followers and Community during the American Revolution*. Columbia: University of South Carolina Press, 1996.

McBarron, Charles H., Jr. "Continental Army Uniforms and Specifications,
1779–1781." *Military Collector and Historian* 14 (summer 1962): 35–41.

McCaffrey, James M. *Army of Manifest Destiny: The American Soldier in the Mexican
War, 1846–1848*. New York: New York University Press, 1992.

McCusker, John J. *Money and Exchange in Europe and America, 1600–1775: A
Handbook*. Chapel Hill: University of North Carolina Press, 1978.

McDade, Thomas D. *The Annals of Murder: A Bibliography of Books and Pamphlets on*

American Murders from Colonial Times to 1900. Norman: University of Oklahoma
Press, 1961.

McGowen, Randall. "The Body and Punishment in Eighteenth-Century England."
Journal of Modern History 59 (1987): 651–79.

McKeown, Thomas, and R. G. Brown. "Medical Evidence Related to English Population Changes in the Eighteenth Century." *Population Studies* 9 (1955): 119–41.

Meaders, Daniel E. "South Carolina Fugitives as Viewed through Local Colonial
Newspapers with Emphasis on Runaway Notices, 1732–1801." *Journal of Negro History* 60 (1975): 288–319.

Mencken, August. *By the Neck: A Book of Hangings*. New York: Hastings House Publishers, 1942.

Meranze, Michael. *Laboratories of Virtue: Punishment, Revolution, and Authority in
Philadelphia, 1760–1835*. Chapel Hill: University of North Carolina Press, 1996.

Metzger, Charles H. *The Prisoner in the American Revolution*. Chicago: Loyola University Press, 1971.

Middlekauff, Robert. *The Glorious Cause: The American Revolution, 1763–1789*. New
York: Oxford University Press, 1982.

——. "Why Men Fought in the American Revolution." *Huntington Library Quarterly* 43 (1980): 135–48.

Millett, Allan R., and Peter Maslowski. *For the Common Defense: A Military History of
the United States of America*. New York: Free Press, 1994.

Mintz, Max M. *Seeds of Empire: The American Revolutionary Conquest of the Iroquois*.
New York: New York University Press, 1999.

Morgan, Edmund S. *American Slavery, American Freedom*. New York: W. W. Norton,
1975.

Moss, Bobby Gilmer. *Roster of South Carolina Patriots in the American Revolution*. Baltimore: Genealogical Publishing Company, 1983.

Myers, Gustavus. *The History of Tammany Hall*. New York: Privately published,
1901.

Myers, Minor, Jr. *Liberty without Anarchy: A History of the Society of the Cincinnati*.
Charlottesville: University Press of Virginia, 1983.

Nadelhaft, Jerome J. *The Disorders of War: The Revolution in South Carolina*. Orono:
University of Maine at Orono Press, 1981.

Namias, June. *White Captives: Gender and Ethnicity on the American Frontier*. Chapel
Hill: University of North Carolina Press, 1993.

Nash, Gary B. *The Urban Crucible: The Northern Seaports and the Origin of the American Revolution*. Abridged ed. Cambridge: Harvard University Press, 1986.

Neagles, James C. *Summer Soldiers: A Survey and Index of Revolutionary War Courts-
Martial*. Salt Lake City: Ancestry, 1986.

Neill, Edward D., ed. *Biographical Sketch of Doctor Jonathan Potts, Director General of
the Hospitals of the Northern and Middle Department in the War of the Revolution, with
Extracts from his Correspondence*. Albany, N.Y.: J. Munsell, 1863.

Neimeyer, Charles Patrick. *America Goes to War: A Social History of the Continental Army*. New York: New York University Press, 1996.

Oliphant, John. *Peace and War on the Anglo-Cherokee Frontier, 1756–63*. Baton Rouge: Louisiana State University Press, 2001.

Papenfuse, Edward C., and Gregory A. Stiverson. "General Smallwood's Recruits: The Peacetime Career of the Revolutionary War Private." *William and Mary Quarterly*, 3rd ser., 30 (1973): 117–32.

Paret, Peter. *Understanding War: Essays on Clauswitz and the History of Military Power*. Princeton: Princeton University Press, 1992.

Peckham, Howard H. *The Toll of Independence: Engagements and Battle Casualties of the American Revolution*. Chicago: University of Chicago Press, 1974.

———. *The War for Independence: A Military History*. Chicago: University of Chicago Press, 1958.

Pike, Martha V., and Janice Gray Armstrong. *A Time to Mourn: Expressions of Grief in Nineteenth Century America*. Stony Brook, N.Y.: Museums at Stony Brook, 1980.

Posey, John Thornton. *General Thomas Posey: Son of the American Revolution*. East Lansing: Michigan State University Press, 1992.

Preyer, Kathryn. "Penal Measures in the American Colonies: An Overview." *American Journal of Legal History* 26 (1982): 326–53.

Prude, Jonathan. "To Look upon the 'Lower Sort': Runaway Ads and the Appearance of Unfree Labor in America, 1750–1800." *Journal of American History* 78 (1991): 124–59.

Purcell, Sarah J. *Sealed with Blood: War, Sacrifice, and Memory in Revolutionary America*. Philadelphia: University of Pennsylvania Press, 2002.

Quarles, Benjamin. *The Negro in the American Revolution*. Chapel Hill: University of North Carolina Press, 1961.

Quimby, Robert S. *The U.S. Army in the War of 1812: An Operational and Command Study*. East Lansing: Michigan State University Press, 1997.

Rankin, Hugh F. *Francis Marion: The Swamp Fox*. New York: Thomas Y. Crowell Company, 1973.

———. *North Carolina Continentals*. Chapel Hill: University of North Carolina Press, 1971.

Resch, John. *Suffering Soldiers: Revolutionary War Veterans, Moral Sentiment, and Political Culture in the Early Republic*. Amherst: University of Massachusetts Press, 1999.

Richter, Daniel. "War and Culture: The Iroquois Experience." *William and Mary Quarterly*, 3rd ser., 40 (1983): 528–59.

Risse, Guenther B. "Medical Care." In *Companion Encyclopedia of the History of Medicine*, 2 vols., edited by Roy Porter and W. F. Bynum, 1:45–77. London: Routledge, 1993.

Roeber, A. G. "Authority, Law, and Custom: The Rituals of Court Day in Tidewater Virginia, 1720 to 1750." *William and Mary Quarterly*, 3rd ser., 37 (1980): 29–52.

Roediger, David R. "And Die in Dixie: Funerals, Death, and Heaven in the Slave Community, 1700–1865." *Massachusetts Review* 22 (spring 1981): 163–83.

Rogal, Samuel. "Pills for the Poor: John Wesley's Primitive Physick." *Yale Journal of Biology and Medicine* 51 (1978): 81–90.

Rosenberg, Charles E. *The Care of Strangers: The Rise of America's Hospital System.* New York: Basic Books, 1987.

Rosenzweig, Roy, and David Thelen. *The Presence of the Past: Popular Uses of History in American Life.* New York: Columbia University Press, 1998.

Rossie, Jonathan Gregor. *The Politics of Command in the American Revolution.* Syracuse: Syracuse University Press, 1975.

Rosswurm, Steven. *Arms, Country, and Class: The Philadelphia Militia and "Lower Sort" during the American Revolution, 1775–1783.* New Brunswick, N.J.: Rutgers University Press, 1987.

Rothman, David. *The Discovery of the Asylum: Social Order and Disorder in the New Republic.* Boston: Little, Brown, 1990.

Royster, Charles. "The Continental Army in the American Mind, 1775–1783." 4 vols. Ph.D. diss., University of California, Berkeley, 1977.

——. *Light-Horse Harry Lee and the Legacy of the American Revolution.* New York: Alfred A. Knopf, 1981.

——. *A Revolutionary People at War: The Continental Army and American Character, 1775–1783.* Chapel Hill: University of North Carolina Press, 1979.

Rutman, Darrett B., and Anita H. Rutman. "Of Agues and Fevers: Malaria in the Early Chesapeake." *William and Mary Quarterly*, 3rd ser., 33 (1976): 31–60.

Saffron, Morris H. "The Influence of Dublin on American Medicine." *Proceedings of the XXIII International Congress of the History of Medicine* 1 (1972): 841–45.

——. *Surgeon to Washington: Dr. John Cochran, 1732–1807.* New York: Columbia University Press, 1977.

——. "The Tilton Affair." *Journal of the American Medical Association* 236 (1976): 67–72.

Sampson, Richard. *Escape in America: The British Convention Prisoners, 1777–1783.* Chippenham, Eng.: Picton Publishing, 1995.

Sawyer, Jeffrey K. "'Benefit of Clergy' in Maryland and Virginia." *American Journal of Legal History* 34 (January 1990): 49–68.

Scheer, George F., and Hugh F. Rankin. *Rebels and Redcoats.* New York: World Publishing Company, 1957.

Schwoerer, Lois. *"No Standing Armies!": The Antiarmy Ideology in Seventeenth-Century England.* Baltimore: Johns Hopkins University Press, 1974.

Selesky, Harold E. *War and Society in Colonial Connecticut.* New Haven: Yale University Press, 1990.

Selig, Robert A. "A German Soldier in America, 1780–1783: The Journal of Georg Daniel Flohr." *William and Mary Quarterly*, 3rd ser., 1 (July 1993): 575–90.

Sellers, John R. "The Common Soldier in the American Revolution." In *Military His-*

tory of the American Revolution, edited by Stanley J. Uderdal, 151–61. Washington, D.C.: Proceedings of the Sixth Military History Symposium, U.S.A.F. Academy, 1974.

Selwyn, Sydney. "Sir John Pringle: Hospital Reformer, Moral Philosopher and Pioneer of Antiseptics." *Medical History* 10 (1966): 266–74.

Shelton, Hal Terry. "From Redcoat to Rebel: General Richard Montgomery in the American Revolution." Ph.D. diss., University of Houston, 1991.

Shy, John. "Charles Lee: The Soldier as Radical." In *George Washington's Generals*, edited by George Athan Billias, 22–53. Westport, Conn.: Greenwood Press, 1980.

———. "Logistical Crisis and the American Revolution: A Hypothesis." In *Feeding Mars: Logistics in Western Warfare from the Middle Ages to the Present*, edited by John A. Lynn, 161–79. San Francisco: Westview Press, 1993.

———. "A New Look at Colonial Militia." *William and Mary Quarterly*, 3rd ser., 20 (1963): 175–85.

———. *A People Numerous and Armed: Reflections on the Military Struggle for American Independence*. New York: Oxford University Press, 1976.

———. *Toward Lexington: The Role of the British Army in the Coming of the American Revolution*. Princeton: Princeton University Press, 1965.

Silverman, Kenneth. *A Cultural History of the American Revolution: Painting, Music, Literature, and the Theatre in the Colonies and the United States from the Treaty of Paris to the Inauguration of Washington, 1763–1789*. New York: Thomas Y. Crowell Company, 1976.

Skemp, Sheila L. *Judith Sargent Murray: A Brief Biography with Documents*. New York: Bedford Books, 1998.

Sloane, David C. *The Last Great Necessity: Cemeteries in American History*. Baltimore: Johns Hopkins University Press, 1991.

Smith, Jonathan. "How Massachusetts Raised Her Troops in the Revolutionary War." *Proceedings of the Massachusetts Historical Society* 55 (1922): 345–70.

Sobel, Mechal. *The World They Made Together: Black and White Values in Eighteenth-Century Virginia*. Princeton: Princeton University Press, 1987.

Society of Old Brooklynites. *A Christmas Reminder, Being the Names of About Eight Thousand Persons, A Small Portion of the Number Confined on Board the British Ships During the War of the Revolution*. Brooklyn: Eagle Print, 1888. Reprint. Sarasota, Fla.: Aceto Bookmen, 1995.

Spindel, Donna J. "The Administration of Criminal Justice in North Carolina, 1720–1740." *American Journal of Legal History* 25 (1981): 141–62.

Stafford, Mary, and Rick Stafford. "Reader: Remember Death." *Harvard Magazine* 77 (1974): 32–35.

Stannard, David E. *The Puritan Way of Death: A Study in Religion Culture and Social Change*. New York: Oxford University Press, 1977.

Starr, Paul. *The Social Transformation of American Medicine*. New York: Basic Books, 1982.

Steele, Ian K. *Betrayals: Fort William Henry and the Massacre*. New York: Oxford University Press, 1990.

———. *Warpaths: Invasions of North America*. New York: Oxford University Press, 1994.

Stewart, Michael R. "Grave Site Delineation, Archeological Evaluation of a 4 Acre Tract: Woods School Cemetery." Unpublished report. Doylestown, Pa.: DelVal Soil and Environmental Consultants, 1992.

Stiles, Henry R. *A History of the City of Brooklyn*. 3 vols. Brooklyn: By Subscription (City of Brooklyn), 1867–69.

Stilgoe, John R. *Common Landscape of America, 1580–1845*. New Haven: Yale University Press, 1982.

Stookey, Byron. "Samuel Clossy, A.B., M.D., F.R.C.P. of Ireland: First Professor of Anatomy, King's College (Columbia), New York." *Bulletin of the History of Medicine* 38 (1964): 153–67.

Tarbox, Increase N. *Life of Israel Putnam ("Old Put"), Major General in the Continental Army*. Boston: Lockwood, Brooks and Company, 1876.

Teaford, Jon. "The Transformation of Massachusetts Education, 1670–1780." In *The Social History of American Education*, edited by B. Edward McClellan and William J. Reese, 23–38. Chicago: University of Illinois Press, 1988.

Teeters, Negley K. '. . . *Hang by the Neck* . . . ': *The Legal Use of Scaffold and Noose, Gibbet, Stake, and Firing Squad from Colonial Times to the Present*. Springfield, Ill.: Thomas Books, 1967.

———. "Public Executions in Pennsylvania, 1682–1834, with Annotated Lists of Persons Executed and of Delays and Reprieves of Persons Sentenced to Death in Pennsylvania 1682 to 1834." *Journal of the Lancaster County Historical Society* 64 (1960): 152–63.

Thomas, Keith. *Religion and the Decline of Magic*. New York: Charles Scribner's Sons, 1971.

Titus, James. *The Old Dominion at War: Society, Politics, and Warfare in Late Colonial Virginia*. Columbia: University of South Carolina Press, 1991.

Ulrich, Laurel Thatcher. *A Midwife's Tale: The Life of Martha Ballard, Based on Her Diary, 1785–1812*. New York: Alfred A. Knopf, 1990.

Vinovskis, Maria A. "Angels' Heads and Weeping Willows: Death in Early America." *Proceedings of the American Antiquarian Society* 86 (1976): 273–302.

Volm, Matthew H. *The Hessian Prisoners in the American War of Independence and Their Life in Captivity*. Charlottesville: University Press of Virginia, 1937.

Waldstreicher, David. *In the Midst of Perpetual Fêtes: The Making of American Nationalism, 1776–1820*. Chapel Hill: University of North Carolina Press, 1997.

Ward, Christopher. *The War of the Revolution*. New York: Macmillan, 1952.

Weighley, Russell F. "American Strategy from Its Beginnings through the First World War." In *Makers of Modern Strategy from Machiavelli to the Nuclear Age*, edited by Peter Paret, 408–43. Princeton: Princeton University Press, 1986.

Wells, Robert V. *Facing the King of Terrors: Death and Society in an American Community, 1750–1990*. New York: Cambridge University Press, 2000.

Wiebe, Robert H. *The Opening of American Society: From the Adoption of the Constitution to the Eve of Disunion*. New York: Alfred Knopf, 1984.

Wiener, Frederick Bernays. *Civilians under Military Justice: The British Practice since 1689, Especially in North America*. Chicago: University of Chicago Press, 1967.

———. "Courts Martial and the Bill of Rights: The Original Practice, Part II." *Harvard Law Review* 72 (1958): 266–304.

Wilbur, Keith C. *The Revolutionary Soldier, 1775–1783*. Philadelphia: Chelsea House Publishers, 1969.

Wilson, Charles Reagan, and William Ferris, eds. *Encyclopedia of Southern Culture*. Chapel Hill: University of North Carolina Press, 1989.

Winslow, Ola Elizabeth. *A Destroying Angel: The Conquest of Smallpox in Colonial Boston*. Boston: Houghton Mifflin, 1974.

Winthrop, Robert C. *Report of a Committee Appointed by the Massachusetts Historical Society on Exchanges of Prisoners During the American Revolutionary War*. Boston: Massachusetts Historical Society, 1861.

Wood, Gordon S. *The Radicalism of the American Revolution*. New York: Alfred Knopf, 1992.

Wood, Peter. *Black Majority: Negroes in Colonial South Carolina, 1670 through the Stono Rebellion*. New York: W. W. Norton, 1974.

Wooden, Allen C. "James Tilton, M.D. (1745–1822), Military Medical Reformer." In *Acta Congressus Internationalis XXIV Historiae Artis Medicinae*, edited by J. Antall, G. Buzinkay, and F. Némethy, 393–96. Budapest: Semmeleveis Medical Historical Museum, 1974.

Wright, Robert K., Jr. *The Continental Army*. Washington, D.C.: Center of Military History, U.S. Army, 1984.

———, ed. "Military Police." In *Army Lineage Series*, 3–12. Washington, D.C.: Center of Military History, 1992.

Wyatt-Brown, Bertram. *Southern Honor: Ethics and Behavior in the Old South*. New York: Oxford University Press, 1982.

Young, Alfred F. "George Robert Twelve Hewes, 1742–1840: A Boston Shoemaker and the Memory of the American Revolution." *William and Mary Quarterly*, 3rd ser., 38 (1981): 561–623.

———. *The Shoemaker and the Tea Party*. Boston: Beacon Press, 1999.

———, ed. *Beyond the American Revolution: Explorations in the History of American Radicalism*. De Kalb: Northern Illinois University Press, 1993.

Zahniser, Marvin R. *Charles Cotesworth Pinckney, Founding Father*. Chapel Hill: University of North Carolina Press, 1967.

Zinsser, Hans. *Rats, Lice, and History: Being a Study in Biography, Which, after Twelve Preliminary Chapters Indispensable for the Preparation of the Lay Reader, Deals with the Life History of Typhus Fever*. Boston: Little, Brown, 1935.

Zuckerman, Michael, et al. "Deference and Defiance in Eighteenth-Century America? A Round Table." *Journal of American History* 85 (1998): 11–97.

INDEX

Abbey, Jacob, 11

Abercromby, James, 9

Academies, military, 42

Acquittal rates, 82, 115–16, 271 (n. 105)

Adams, Captain, 173

Adams, John, 22, 44, 95–96, 133, 152, 228

Adams, Samuel, 50

Adams, Zabdiel, 237

Adlum, John, 68–69

Advice to the People in General, 127

Adye, Stephen Payne, 88

African Americans, 8, 16, 100, 177–78, 217, 230

Allen, Ethan, 202, 218–19, 223, 225–27, 230

Allen, Jacob, 31

Allgood, John, 148

Almy, John, 149

American Legion, xiii, 241

Amherst, Jeffrey, 211

Anburey, Thomas, 182–83

Anderson, Enoch, 39, 62, 113

André, John, 215, 266 (n. 26)

Andrews, John, 89

Angell, Israel, 141, 147, 172–73

Apothecaries, 129

Apprentices, 10, 80–81, 90

Archer, Mrs., 223

Armstrong, John, 98

Armstrong, Samuel, 37

Arnold, Benedict, 155, 185, 266 (n. 26)

Articles of war: Associators, 79; British, 21, 77–78, 90–91, 93, 95, 102, 123, 225; Connecticut, 94; Continental, 21, 75, 94–96, 98–99, 102–3, 106, 115, 120, 124; Massachusetts, 21, 93, 96; militia, 75, 77, 79, 90–91; New Hampshire, 94; provincial, 75, 91–93; Rhode Island, 94; South Carolina, 96, 98

Asberry, William, 20

Associators, 79, 117, 240

Bailey, Thomas, 52

Bangs, Isaac, 31, 51

Banyar, Goldsbrow, 177

Barber, Francis, 195

Barber, Isaac, 107

Bard, Samuel, 131

Barker, Stephen, 151

Barton, William, 195

Bateman, Susan, 20

Bates, James, 166

Baylor, George, 30

Beal, Benjamin, 101

Beasley, Daniel, 249

Beatty, Erkuries, 66

Beccaria, Cesare, 85, 246

Bedinger, George, 11

Bedinger, Henry, 11, 222–23, 233

Beebe, Lewis, 67, 147–48, 155, 171, 192–93

Bellew, Robert, 63

Bird, Edward, 107

Bixby, Samuel, 2, 171–72

Black soldiers. *See* African Americans;
Continental army: African American
soldiers; Slaves

Blackstone, William, 77, 85

Blassie, Michael, ix

Blatchford, John, 73

Bloomfield, Joseph, 107, 117

Bodies: burial of, 163, 175, 229–32; dissection of, 176, 178, 196–98, 229; embalming of, 166; at peace, 178–79; of
prisoners, 200, 233–34; resurrection
of, 177–78; status of, xi, 177; treatment
of, x–xi, xiv, 74, 78, 85–86, 114, 177–
78, 182, 190, 249; wolves devouring,
194–95

Bond, William, 187

Books: captivity narratives, 176; courtesy,
26, 40–41, 62; on death, 179; fiction,
34; medical, 124, 127, 138–39; military,
42–44, 89, 115, 260 (n. 14); order or
orderly, 67, 74, 100, 103, 105, 139

Boston Massacre, 237–38

Bostwick, Elisha, 5, 194

Boudinot, Elias, 219–20, 224, 226

Bowers, John, 148

Bowers, Samuel, 148

Boyd, Thomas, 217, 220

Boyle, John, 169

Boylston, Zabdiel, 154

Brackenridge, Hugh Henry, 240

Braddock, Edward, 23, 92, 181

Bradstreet, John, 205

Brandywine, Battle of, 14, 133, 228

Brickett, James, 60

Brief Rule to the Common People, 127

British army, ix, 1, 5, 61–62, 104; and
burials, 164, 177, 179–83, 185, 195; and
dissection of soldiers, 184; and enlistment bounties, 6; and medical care,
123–24, 131–34, 137, 154; and pay, 6;
and prisoners of war, 199, 203, 205,
210, 212–16, 223; and punishment, 75–
77, 81, 84–86, 89, 92, 96, 103, 266
(n. 30); and recruitment, 2, 6, 125; in
Seven Years' War, 10, 22, 89–90; status
of NCOs in, 5–6, 29, 216; status of
officers in, 2, 21–23, 28–29, 41, 46, 61,
202, 218; status of soldiers in, 6, 23, 68,
197, 216; and training, 42; and uniforms, 55; in War of 1812, 245

Brocklesby, Richard, 124, 126, 138, 158

Brooklyn Navy Yard, 250

Brooks, John, 51

Brown, Obadiah, 150

Browne, Montfort, 215

Buchan, William, 127–28, 152–53

Bull, William, 210

Bunker Hill, Battle of, ix, 1, 133, 183–84,
188, 195–96, 238

Burgoyne, John, 62, 182–83

Burial, civilian, 165–67; in dead houses,
168; Moravian, 168; and naming, 168;
of paupers, 175–76, 178; rituals of, 164,
167–68, 174–75; of slaves, 168, 176; in
South, 168

Burial, military, x, 43, 148, 163–67, 174,
183, 203, 249, 250; in dead houses, 194;
of Donop, 63, 186; with honors of war,
163–64, 185, 187–89; of Montgomery,
185; of NCOs, 180–81, 189; of officers,
179–81, 183–84, 187–88, 232; parties,
182, 186–87; of prisoners, 200, 229–
32, 250; reinterment, 250–51; rituals of,
164–67, 179–81, 183, 187, 192; of soldiers, 179, 183, 189–98

Burke, Thomas, 64

Burr, Aaron, 28

Burrows, David, 150–51

Burrows, Jonathan, 11, 150–51

Camps. *See* Housing

Carleton, Guy, 61, 185, 194

Carpenter, Samuel, 20

Carr, Josiah, 189

Carter, Landon, 31

Cheesman, Jacob, 171, 185

Chesterfield, Lord, 26–27, 34, 180

Chubbuck, Simeon, 51

Church, Benjamin, 126, 157, 159

Clime, John, 106

Clossey, Samuel, 178

Clothing, 41, 44–45, 49, 51, 54–59, 119, 124–25, 136, 142–43, 192, 203, 220–21, 223–24

Cochran, John, 136, 154, 158, 160

Coe, Benjamin, 13

Cohen, William S., ix

Cole, Hamlin, 229

Colman, Dudley, 146

Community, military, xi, 165–66, 180. *See also* Continental army

Concord, Massachusetts, 12

Connecticut Courant, 12, 45

Conscription. *See* British army: and recruitment; Continental army: and recruitment; Continental Congress: and recruitment; Provincial armies: and recruitment; Seven Years' War: and recruitment; War of 1812: and recruitment

Continental army: African American soldiers in, 16–17; as community, xix, 69, 71, 76; Connecticut troops, 13, 17, 103, 112; creation of, xii, xvii, 1; Delaware troops, 59, 61, 113; and desertion, xvii, 19, 53, 58, 68, 75, 101, 106, 110, 112–14, 142, 151, 166, 196; and enlistment, xiv, 53, 75, 81, 96, 105, 117, 166, 240, 274 (n. 38); and enlistment bounties, xvii, 3, 12, 15, 45; foreign-born troops, 12, 14, 16, 71, 97–98, 150, 240; Georgia

troops, 8, 112; German troops, 30; and land bounties, 4; Maryland troops, 14–17, 29, 114; Massachusetts troops, 3, 12, 17, 22, 33; and mutiny, 33, 47, 99, 112–13; NCOs in, 33, 47, 116; New Hampshire troops, 68, 103; New Jersey troops, 12–13, 30, 33, 101, 141; New York troops, 103; North Carolina troops, 15–17; officers in, xv, 29–32, 97, 101, 115; and pay, 41, 44–46, 97, 223–24; Pennsylvania troops, 3, 66, 99; and recruitment, xvi, 2–5, 8, 10–17, 40, 96–97; Rhode Island troops, 17, 33, 49, 70, 101, 141, 172; South Carolina troops, 14–16, 18–19, 97–99, 103, 112, 115, 119, 142, 187; status in, xv, xviii, xix, 2–4, 15, 23, 35, 39–40, 44, 49, 51–53, 67–68, 71, 81, 97–98, 101, 104–5, 117, 146, 153, 162, 164, 166, 173–74, 193, 198, 237, 239–42, 249; as subject for analysis, xiii; substitution in, 13–14, 16, 100, 240; Virginia troops, 5, 11–14, 58. *See also* Honor; Prisoners of war; Status, social; Veterans

Continental Congress, xii, xv, xix, 1, 48, 115, 144, 238; and creation of Continental army, xv, 2, 28–29, 64, 75, 80–81, 94–96, 124, 126; and Hospital Department, 126, 131, 135–36, 157–58; and military pay, 46–47, 220; and pension provisions, 47; and prisoners of war, 214–15, 219–20, 225–26; and punishments, 95–96, 268–69 (n. 65); and recruitment, 12, 17–18; and army supply, 48–49; and Washington, 239

Continental navy, 73, 103

Convicts, 10, 14, 80–81, 177–78, 240

Cook, Captain, 166

Cornwallis, Lord Charles, 42

Courts-martial, 60–61, 64–65, 73–76,

79, 93–109 passim, 112, 114–16; in War
of 1812, 247
Craigie, Andrew, 160
Craven, W. Frank, xi
Criminals. *See* Convicts
Cromwell, Oliver, 123
Cross, Stephen, 207–9
Croswell, Andrew, 89
Cudjo (slave), 13
Culbertson, Lieutenant, 173
Cumberland, Duke of, 212
Cummins, Lieutenant, 60

Daugherty, Michael, 60
David, Ebenezer, 144–45, 147, 187
Davis, Captain, 188–89
Davis, Joshua, 173
Davis, Matthew, 250
Dean, Joshua, 242
Dearborn, Henry, 155, 185
Death, 123, 162, 166, 168, 174, 181, 192, 203,
222, 227, 235, 238–39, 249, 251; and
emotions, 169, 234; and naming, 164,
169–74, 249; peace at, 177, 179, 196
Death penalty. *See* Punishment, civilian:
capital; Punishment, military: capital
Deference, xvi, xviii, 3, 25, 27, 41, 44, 59,
65–67, 249
Demere, Paul, 210
Democratic Republican party, 250
Denny, Austin, 244
De Saxe, Marshal, 44
Desertion. *See* Continental army: and
desertion; U.S. Army: and desertion;
War of 1812: and desertion
Dieskau, Baron Jean-Armand, 62, 210
Digby, William, 173, 182
Dinwiddie, Robert, 9, 48, 91–93
*Directions for Preserving the Health of Sol-
diers*, 137, 160
Discipline, xv, 3, 21–23, 25, 40–41, 43,
47, 59–60, 67, 74, 78, 80–81, 92–100

passim, 109, 123, 137, 162, 196, 203,
240, 248. *See also* Deference;
Fraternizing
Disease, 47–48, 51, 70, 112, 122–23, 125,
128, 133, 141–42, 172, 200, 222, 227,
240, 244; dysentery, 120, 132–34, 144,
146, 248; fever, 120, 132, 144, 146, 154,
160, 240, 248; and inoculation, 153–
56, 228, 233; malaria, 132, 141; measles,
248; scurvy, 133; smallpox, 120, 132, 135,
141, 146, 149–50, 153–56, 192, 222, 228,
233; yellow fever, 132, 141. *See also* Medical care; Wounds
Diseases Incident to Armies, 137
Dissection. *See* Bodies; British army: and
dissection of soldiers
Dixon, Robert, 189
Doctors, 50, 120, 122, 128–29, 153, 176,
192, 227, 229, 248; social status of, 50,
67, 131–32, 156, 159, 170–71; surgeons,
120, 123, 124, 129, 157–58, 160, 178, 196
Domestic Medicine, 127
Donop, Carl von, 62–63, 186
Draft. *See* British army: and recruitment;
Continental army: and recruitment;
Continental Congress: and recruit-
ment; Provincial armies: and recruit-
ment; Seven Years' War: and recruit-
ment; War of 1812: and recruitment
Dress. *See* Clothing; Uniforms
Dring, Thomas, 223, 228, 230, 233–34
Duffy, Patrick, 114
Dukerson, Lieutenant, 115
Durkee, John, 152

Eddy, Thomas, 246
Eden, William (Lord Auckland), 85
Education, xiii, 4; of officers, 42, 65
Eliot, Joanna, 51
Elliott, Barnard, 3, 5, 60, 119, 187–88
Enlistment. *See* British army; Continen-
tal army; Provincial armies

Enslin, Frederick, 115

Epidemics. *See* Disease

Erving, John, 169

European armies, xviii, 1–2, 5–6, 22–25, 28, 42, 46, 62; and burials, 164, 177, 179, 183; and medical care, 122–23, 134, 136; and prisoners of war, 202–6, 208, 211

Eutaw Springs, Battle of, 146, 166

Every Man His Own Doctor, 127

Ewald, Johann, 44

Executions. *See* Punishment, civilian: capital; Punishment, military: capital

Fayssoux, Peter, 229

Fergus, James, 135, 149, 187

Firing squads. *See* Punishment, military: capital

Fitch, Jabez, 223, 231

Fletcher, Ebenezer, 145, 228

Florida expedition, 107, 112–13, 141

Food, 41, 52, 70, 112, 124, 132, 136, 142, 220–21, 223–24, 246, 248

Ford, Colonel, 188

Forrestal, James, xiii

Fort Frontenac, 205

Fort Necessity, 206

Fort William Henry, 209

Fourth of July, xiv, 3, 237–39, 243

Fox, Henry, 62

Franklin, Benjamin, 126

Fraser, Simon, 182

Fraternizing, 59–60, 87

Frazer, Persifor, 50, 65, 173

Frederick, King of Prussia, 42, 44; *Instructions*, 42

Freeman's Farm, Battle of, 182, 186

Freemasons. *See* Masons

French army, 28, 42, 62, 180, 183, 205–7

Freneau, Philip, 199–201, 234

Friendly Instructor, 179

Funerals. *See* Burial, civilian; Burial, military

Gage, Thomas, 181, 211, 218

Gardner, Caleb, 146

Gates, Horatio, 161, 183, 226

Gentility. *See* Status, social: and gentry

Gentry. *See* Status, social: and gentry

Gephardt, Richard, x

Germain, Lord George Sackville, 213–14

Germann, Friedrich von, 57, 262 (n. 44)

Germantown, Battle of, 239

Gerry, Elbridge, 95

Gilbert, Benjamin, 33–34, 150

Gilmore, Thomas, 149

Gilmore, William, 186–87

Glover, John, 17, 57

Goring, George, 212

Goss, Thomas, 83

Grant, James, 182, 211

Graydon, Alexander, 3, 5, 17, 31

Greene, Nathanael, 18, 39, 45, 49, 64, 66, 103–4, 120, 135, 137, 143–44, 146, 160

Greenleaf, Moses, 51

Greenman, Jeremiah, 33, 44, 63, 189

Grimke, John, 112

Grose, Francis, 28

Grotius, Hugo, 204

Gustavus Adolphus (King of Sweden), 123

Habersham, John, 224

Hailey, Barnabas, 13–14

Hale, Nathan, 151, 215

Hale, Thomas, 148

Hamilton, Douglas, 146

Hancock, John, 25, 45–46, 95

Hand, Edward, 180, 188

Hanford, Levi, 87, 221, 231

Hangings. *See* Punishment, civilian: capital; Punishment, military: capital

Harlem Heights, Battle of, 190

Harleston, Isaac, 31

Hartley, Thomas, 106

Hausegger, Nicholas, 30

Hawkins, Francis, 26

Henry, John Joseph, 185, 189–90, 193

Henry, Patrick, 40

Hessians, 44, 61, 68, 180, 183, 202, 214

Hewes, George R. T., 45, 89

Hitchcock, General, 188

Hobart, Noah, 82

Holcomb, Benjamin, 56

Holland, John, 61–62, 263 (n. 57)

Honor, ix–x, xvi, 1, 16, 21, 28, 31–32, 37–
    40, 61–71 passim, 82, 93, 100–101,
    113–15, 131, 142–43, 159, 162, 168–69,
    174, 180–82, 185, 197, 203, 206, 209–
    10, 214, 218, 224–27, 235, 242–43,
    249–51

Hospital Department, 124, 126, 131, 136,
    146, 156, 158–59, 228, 247–49

Hospitals, civilian, 126–27, 247–48

Hospitals, military, 121, 125, 147, 148;
    general, 121, 125–26, 131–32, 142, 146,
    151, 156–62, 171, 192; Hôtel des Inva-
    lides, 272 (n. 8); for prisoners, 208;
    regimental, 125–26, 131, 133, 156–60;
    Royal Chelsea Hospital, 123; Royal
    Kilmainham Hospital, 123; in War of
    1812, 247–48

Housing, 44, 49; and hygiene, 117, 122–
    25, 136–39, 143, 162, 248; for officers,
    50–52, 54, 120, 141, 220; for prisoners,
    218–22; for soldiers, 50–54, 120, 122,
    139, 141

How, David, 151, 172

Howe, Robert, 63, 98, 112, 138

Howe, William, 133, 184, 195, 202, 214–
    15, 228

Hubbardton, Battle of, 145, 195

Hughes, Absalom, 13–14

Humphries, Captain, 186

Hunt, Edward, 83

Huntington, Ebenezer, 54, 70–71, 162,
    172

Huyn, Johann von, 183

Ide, Ichabod, 11

Ide, Israel, 11

Independence Day. *See* Fourth of July

Independent Chronicle (Boston), 101

Indians, 8, 141, 176, 209, 245, 249;
    Cherokees, 143, 182, 210–11, 216–17,
    227; graves of, 195; Iroquois, 110, 217;
    Mohawks, 210; as prisoners, 204,
    207–8, 210, 216; scalping by, 176–77;
    scalping of, 177; Shawnee, 249;
    Tecumseh, 249

Ingalls, Phineas, 150

Instructions to Young Officers, 42

Interment. *See* Burial, civilian; Burial,
    military

Irvine, Matthew, 153

Jackson, William, 239

James, Elisha, 101–2, 190

James, Sarah, 101–2

James, Thomas, 101

James II, 7

Jefferson, Thomas, 85

Jesup, Thomas, 246

Jews, 232

Johnson, Lieutenant, 116

Johnson, William, 62, 176–77, 210

Jones, John, 126, 159

Jones, Lieutenant, 188–89

Justice, military. *See* Law, military

King, Gregory, 6

Kirby, Tarrance, 249

Kirkwood, Robert, 107

Knowlton, Thomas, 171

Knox, Henry, 241

Lacey, John, 32, 34, 66, 154, 193–94

Lafayette, Marquis de, 105

Lamb, John, 66

Lambert, George, 115

Langford, Lieutenant, 31

Larabee, Samuel, 149

Laurens, Henry, xix, 97, 105–6

Laurens, John, xix, 70–71

Law, military, xv, 3, 6, 41, 60, 76, 92, 99, 104, 106, 120

Law of Nations, 204

Learned, Ebenezer, 172

Leaunden, Joseph, 114

Le Blond, Guillaume, 44

Lee, Captain, 108

Lee, Charles, 16, 18, 44, 98, 120, 142, 144, 215, 224, 226

Lee, Henry "Light-Horse Harry," 64, 114, 142–44, 162, 196

Leffingwell, Ebenezer, 112

Leslie, William, 185

Letter of Advice, 26

Letters (Lord Chesterfield), 27, 34

Lewis, George, 31

Linn, William, 29

Literacy, xiv, 4, 18, 33, 53, 69, 127, 249

Livingston, William, 175

Logan, Alexander, 135, 148

Logistics. *See* Supply

Long Island, Battle of, 38, 112, 172, 223

Loring, Joshua, 219, 226

Loring, Nathaniel, 175

Lyngard, Richard, 26

Mann, James, 248

Manoeuvres or Practical Observations on the Art of War, 44

Manual Exercise, 42

Manuals. *See* Books

Marion, Francis, 31, 103, 138, 143–44

Maroney, Alexander Milliner, 12

Martin, Joseph Plumb, 11, 13, 52, 57, 80, 120, 190, 237

Marvin, Elihu, 152

Masons, ix, 34, 189, 224

Mather, Cotton, 153–54

Maurice of Orange, 123

Maxwell, William, 30

Mayer, Holly, xix

McCullough, Lieutenant, 187

McDougall, Alexander, 52, 65, 107

McDowell, William, 187

McIntosh, Lachlan, 16, 43, 103, 140

McMichael, James, 54

Medical care, xvii, 117, 121–22, 203, 223; apothecaries, 121; biblical injunction concerning, 138; bleeding, 119; bone-setters, 121; emetics, 121, 152; medicines, 121; midwives, 121

Meers, Abram, 109

Meigs, Return J., 64

Mercer, Hugh, 239

Messer, Sharlene, 271

Middlekauff, Robert, 253 (n. 6)

Middleton, Peter, 131

Miles, Samuel, 202, 219, 222

Military Guide for Young Officers, 179–80

Military Instructions for Officers, 43

Militia, xvi, xix, 1, 3, 5–8, 19, 24, 54, 63, 68–69, 100, 108, 117, 121, 135, 140, 143, 145, 188, 199, 214, 222, 237

Mills, Captain, 68

Mobility, social, xvii, 23, 25, 32–34, 41, 66, 128, 249

Monmouth, Battle of, 148, 186

Monro, Donald, 124–25, 136, 248

Monro, George, 209

Monroe, James, 245

Montcalm, Marquis de, 209

Montesquieu, 204

Montgomery, Richard, 20, 61, 185, 238–39

Moody, Eleazar, 26

Moody, Moses, 51

Morgan, Daniel, 11, 39, 107, 138

Morgan, John, 126, 129–32, 155–60

Morristown, 51, 160

Mortality rates, 3, 122–23, 132–36, 153–54, 160, 170, 183, 190, 193, 197, 200,

245, 249, 273 (nn. 28, 34), 274 (nn. 36, 38)
Morton, Robert, 104
Moulton, Simeon, 221
Moultrie, William, 65, 96, 106, 108, 187
Muhlenberg, Henry Melchior, 128, 179
Mutiny Acts. *See* Articles of war

Napoleonic Wars, 243
Nash, Francis, 239
Nash, Solomon, 148
National myth, xiv, 237–39, 242
Native Americans. *See* Indians
NCOs. *See* Officers, noncommissioned
Newtown, Battle of, 195
Nickols, Samuel, 190
Nicola, Lewis, 43–44, 59, 75, 180
Norris, James, 195
Norton, George, 139
Nott, Captain, 171
Noyen, Pierre-Jacques, 205

Observations on the Diseases of the Army, 125, 160
Officers, xvi; burial of, 170–71, 180, 186–87; corruption of, 46; and duels, 60, 65; as gentlemen, 2, 21–22, 40, 45–46, 50, 63, 104, 114, 120, 131, 145, 162, 241; and medical care, 145–47, 154; resignation of, 46; and seniority, 30, 63–64; and training, 42, 65, 137, 151, 245, 264 (n. 69); as veterans, 241–42; in War of 1812, 245. *See also* British army: status of officers in; Continental army: officers in; Housing: for officers; Punishment, military: of officers; Uniforms: of officers
Officers, noncommissioned (NCOs), xvi, 42–43, 55, 113, 116, 233; burial of, 180–81, 188–89. *See also* British army: status of NCOs in; Continental army: NCOs in; Prisoners of war: NCOs as; Pro-

vincial armies: NCOs in; Punishment, military: of NCOs
Onesimus (slave), 153
Orme, Robert, 23
Osborn, Sarah, 140
Osborne, George, xi
Oxford English Dictionary, 38

Padget, Frederick, 228
Painter, Thomas, 11
Palmer, Seaman, 233–34
Pardons. *See* Punishment, civilian: and reprieves; Punishment, military: and reprieves
Parker, Oliver, 46
Parliament, British, 7, 77, 125, 211–12, 216
Peale, Charles Willson, 140, 152, 162, 172, 197
Peek, Captain, 116
Pennsylvania Evening Post, 101
Pennsylvania Gazette, 126, 197
Pennsylvania Journal, 90
Pennsylvania Packet, 22, 137
Pensions, xiv, 4, 242–43; applications for, 74, 135, 156, 186, 225, 227, 234, 242, 244, 255 (n. 10)
Perry, David, 90
Peterborough, New Hampshire, xviii, 14, 226, 244, 288 (n. 19)
Petit, Jean-Louis, 129
Physicians. *See* Doctors
Piatt, Daniel, 195
Pinckney, Charles, 14, 19, 60, 67
Poor, Enoch, 188
Porter, Elisha, 50
Posey, Thomas, 32
Potts, Jonathan, 146
Primitive Physick, 127
Princeton, Battle of, 152, 185, 187–88, 239
Pringle, John, 124–26, 131, 136, 138, 158, 160, 248
Prisoners of war, 73, 144–45, 193,

199–235, 250, 283 (n. 4); burial of, 229–34, 250; and cartels, 202, 212, 214, 216, 218, 249; in English civil war, 211; and enlisting in enemy forces, 224, 226; exchange of, 202–5, 212–16, 222; and hostages, 206; legal status of, 211–14, 218; loyalist, 216–17; NCOs as, 202, 232–33; officers as, 200, 202–3, 206, 218, 220, 223, 226–27, 232, 234; parole of, 206–7, 220, 229, 249; philosophy of, 204, 211; and ransoms, 204, 208–9, 211; in Scottish Highland rebellion, 212–13; soldiers as, 200, 202–3, 206, 219, 226, 232, 234; in South Carolina, 216–17; and status, 200, 202–3, 206, 218, 225–26, 232, 234; as traitors, 211; in War of 1812, 249

Prisons: hospitals, 227–28; jails, 200, 220–21, 249; penitentiaries, 246; prison ships, 200, 221, 230, 234–35, 240, 249, 251; prison ships in New York, 199–200, 223, 250, 283 (n. 4); prison ships in South Carolina, 200, 229, 283 (n. 4); sugar houses, 200, 221

Provincial armies, 1, 5–6, 8, 23, 62, 177, 182; African Americans in, 9; and bounties, 8; in Connecticut, 8, 24, 132; and discipline, 9; Indians in, 9; in Massachusetts, 9–10, 24, 48, 132, 207; and medical care, 131–32; NCOs in, 24; in North Carolina, 9; officers in, 24, 207; and pay, 9, 48; and prisoners of war, 205–10; and ranger companies, 177; and recruitment, 8–10; in South Carolina, 10; and substitution, 8; and supply, 48; in Virginia, 9–10, 23, 48, 92–93, 206

Prussian army, 6, 28, 42, 75

Punishment: biblical guidelines for, 75, 82–83, 89, 94, 99, 104

Punishment, civilian: branding, 82; capital, 82–83, 246, 265 (n. 16); execution

rates, 83, 246; fines, 82; in New York, 83–84; public, xi, 22, 74, 246; and reformers, 85, 88; and reprieves, 83; reprimand, 82; of servants, 91; of slaves, 83–85, 91, 97, 105, 114, 246, 265 (n. 16); and social status, 76, 84; in South Carolina, 83–84; and state constitutions, 99; stocks, 82; whipping, 82

Punishment, military: capital, 73–74, 79, 99, 104, 109–14, 196, 246–47, 266 (n. 26); being cashiered, 114–15; in Continental army, 76, 81, 103, 105; corporal, 74, 77, 80; execution rates, 110, 246, 270 (n. 92), 289 (n. 27); extralegal, 105, 107, 116; fines, 74, 90, 94, 246; running the gauntlet, 86–87, 99, 103, 108; informal, 107–8; lash, 86–102 passim, 107, 142–43, 246; in militia, 76, 77, 80–81, 90–92, 100, 246; of NCOs, 74; tying by neck and heels, 91; of officers, 74, 80, 86, 100, 114–15; piquet, 86–87, 99, 103, 246–47, 269 (n. 75); in provincial armies, 76, 81, 90–92; being reduced to ranks, 74; and reformers, 88–89; and reprieves, 99, 109, 112–13, 247, 270 (n. 92), 289 (n. 27); reprimand, 74, 115; of soldiers, 74; in War of 1812, 246–47; wooden horse, 87, 99, 103

Putnam, Israel, 51, 71, 105

Putnam, Rufus, 34, 106

Quakers, 79

Quebec expedition, 33, 39, 61, 141, 145, 154–55, 171, 185, 188–89, 193, 203, 238–39

Quincy, Josiah, 18

Racial attitudes, 9–10, 16–18, 97

Rage militaire, 1, 3

Ramsay, David, 15, 61, 149

Recruitment. *See* British army: and re-

cruitment; Continental army: and recruitment; Continental Congress:
and recruitment; Provincial armies:
and recruitment; Seven Years' War:
and recruitment; War of 1812: and
recruitment

Redemptioners. *See* Servants

Reed, Joseph, 95, 171, 219

Reed, Philip, 114

Regular army. *See* Continental army

*Regulations for the Order and Discipline of
the Troops of the United States*, 43, 137

Regulator movement, 83–84

Resch, John, 244, 288 (n. 19)

Revere, Paul, 175

Rêveries, 44

Reynolds, Catherine, 83

Ricky, John, 101

Riedesel, Baroness von, 182–83

Rights of War and Peace, 204

Riter, Franklin, xiii

Rites of war. *See* Burial, military: with
honors of war

Roberts, Lemuel, 52, 153, 227

Rodney, Thomas, 152, 162, 185, 188

Rogers, William, 110, 188–89

Ross, Dr. W. M., 246

Rundel, Joseph, 50–51, 149

Rush, Benjamin, 85, 119, 126, 133–35, 137,
142, 152, 160–62, 185, 198, 228; on
Washington, 160

Russel, Ensign, 65

Rutherford, Griffin, 166–67

Rutherford, James, 166

Rutledge, John, 97, 98

Sabin, Josiah, 155–56

Sacrifice, 46, 159, 167, 173, 197, 208,
237–38, 240–41, 243

Saratoga, Battle of, 39, 56, 62, 182–83,
194

School of Good Manners, 26

Schuyler, Philip, 61–62, 185

Scott, Craig, 279

Scott, William "Long Bill," 226

Senter, Isaac, 153

Servants, xv, 2, 10, 14, 80–81, 84, 90, 107,
267 (n. 39); of officers, 50–51, 223–24,
240

Service, military, xiii–xviii, 2–11, 13–18,
21, 24–25, 32–33, 38, 41–47 passim, 53,
63, 68–69, 71, 74, 77–81, 86, 88,
90–93, 103–6, 109, 132, 157, 176, 214,
243. *See also* British army; Continental
army; Provincial armies; U.S. Army

Seven Years' War, 6, 30, 75, 124, 140, 216;
and burials, 181; disease in, 125–26, 131,
133–34; officers in, 23–24, 62; and pay,
48; and prisoners of war, 62, 205–10;
and punishment, 88–91; and recruitment, 8–10

Shakespeare, William, 163–64, 169–70

Sherburne, Henry, 146

Sherman, Isaac, 64

Sherman, Roger, 99

Shippen, William, 126, 130, 135, 158, 160,
178

Simes, Thomas, 89, 179–80

Slavery, xv, xix, 18, 78, 81, 105

Slaves, 9–10, 13, 19, 48, 78, 80–81, 92,
97–98, 178, 196, 217, 240. *See also*
Punishment, civilian: of slaves

Smallpox. *See* Disease: smallpox

Smallwood, William, 29, 39

Smith, Captain, 202

Smith, John, 10, 70, 116

Smith, Samuel, 186

Society of Old Brooklynites, 251

Society of the Cincinnati, 241–42

Songs, 37, 69, 71, 238

Sources, historical, 4–5

South Carolina Gazette, 84

Spectator, 27

Speer, John, 171

Spirit of Laws, 204

Sprout, Ebenezer, 33

St. Clair, Arthur, 108

Standing army, 7, 12, 76–77, 85, 94, 117, 237, 244–45

Status, social, xi, xv, xvii, 1–2, 10, 15, 18, 20, 22–23, 41, 92, 114, 122, 174, 177–78, 249; and gentry, xv, 25–28, 30–34, 38–40, 46, 54, 64, 82, 84, 92, 105, 129, 145, 147, 165, 168–69, 190, 206. *See also* Continental army: status in; Doctors: social status of; Prisoners of war: and status; Punishment, civilian: and social status

Stephen, Adam, 92

Stephenson, Hugh, 11

Steuben, Baron Friedrich von, 23, 43–44, 67, 137, 162

Stevens, Elisha, 68, 163

Stevens, Judith (Sargent Murray), 104

Stevenson, Roger, 43, 89

Stewart, Alexander, 146

Stewart, Michael, 282 (n. 80)

Stillman, Samuel, 162

Stirling, Lord (William Alexander), 30, 215

Stobo, Robert, 206–7

Stono Rebellion, 19

Stony Point, Battle of, 64

Stricker, George, 30

Sullivan, James, 22

Sullivan, John, 22, 59, 66, 99, 108, 110, 116, 188, 195, 217

Supply, 47–49, 52, 70, 133–34, 136, 245–46, 248

Sweat, William, 48, 132–33

Swieten, Gerhard van, 137

Tammany Society, 250–51

Tatler, 27

Tecumseh, 249

Telley, William, 101

Tennent, John, 127

Thacher, James, 104, 134, 155, 157, 196

Thacher, Thomas, 127

Thirty Years' War, 204

Thomas, John, 155

Tilden, Ezra, 144, 192, 194

Tilden, John Bell, 50–51, 66, 147

Tilghman, Tench, 56

Tilton, James, 137, 142, 148, 153, 158–61, 248

Tissot, Simon André, 127–28

Tomb of the Unknowns, ix

Trask, Israel, 11, 50

Treatise of Artillery, 44

Treatise of Military Exercise, 43

Treatise on the Attack and Defense of Fortresses, 42

Treaty of Westphalia, 204

Trenchard, John, 7, 77

Trumbull, Benjamin, 144

Trumbull, John, 30

Trumbull, Jonathan, 30

Trumbull, Jonathan, Jr., 30

Tudor, William, xii, xix, 16, 44, 78, 94–95, 98, 105–6

Turner, David, 101–2

Turner, Varsal, 101–2

Tyrrel, Sergeant, 112

Uniform Code of Military Justice, xiii

Uniforms, 55–56; of officers, 56; of soldiers, 56–59. *See also* Clothing

U.S. Army: creation of, 244–45; and desertion, 247; Hospital Department, 247; and pay, 245, 261 (n. 20); punishments in War of 1812, 246–47; status of soldiers in, 245

U.S. Congress: and creation of U.S. Army, 244–45; and pensions for Revolutionary War veterans, xiv, 4, 243; and reinterment of Revolutionary War dead, 250–51

U.S. Constitution, 244, 264 (n. 5)

Valley Forge, 46, 51, 54, 110, 116, 140–41, 147

Van Anglin, Captain, 108, 116

Varnum, James, 147

Vattel, Emmerich, 204, 206

Vauban, Sébastien Le Prestre de, 42

Vaughan, Zebulon, 32, 39, 52, 106, 116, 153, 171

Veterans, xiii, xiv, 4, 200, 225, 237, 241, 243–44

Vietnam War, x

Waiters. *See* Servants

Waller, William, 212

Warner, Seth, 155

War of 1812, 242, 245–49; and bounties, 245; death in, 249; desertion in, 247; and medical care, 247–49; officers in, 245; and pay, 245; prisoners of war in, 249; punishment in, 246–47, 289 (n. 27); and recruitment, 245, 248; soldiers in, 245

Warren, John, 195

Warren, Joseph, ix–x, 20, 188, 195–96, 238–39

Washington, George: on burials, 185–86, 188, 196–97; on civil rights, xv; defamation of, 98; on food, 52; and gentlemanly conduct, 24–25, 27, 38, 46, 65–66; and honor, 38, 40, 65; advises Lafayette, 105; and medical care, 136, 138–39, 151, 156–58; mythic status of, 239; and Posey, 32; and prisoners of war, 206, 211, 214–16, 218, 224, 226; and punishment, 74–75, 91–100 passim, 105–6, 109–11, 113–14; in Seven Years' War, 9–10, 35, 181; smallpox, 154–56; and Society of the Cincinnati,

241; and status of soldiers and officers, 20–22, 28, 30–31, 34–35, 40, 44–46, 186, 198; on training army, 43–44; on uniforms, 55–59

Washington, William, 146

Watts, John, 169

Wayne, Anthony, 64, 66, 138–39

Webb, Samuel, 103

Wells, Austin, 11, 186–87

Wells, Bayze, 147, 190

Weltner, Ludowick, 30

Wesley, John, 127

Wharton, Florence, 191, 282 (n. 80)

Whigs, 7, 77, 152

Whitney, Lieutenant, 60

Wild, Ebenezer, 110

Williams, Ennion, 1–3, 27

Williams, John, 50

Williams, Major, 224

Williams, Otto, 171

Wolfe, James, 6, 42–43, 177

Women, xiii, xix, 20, 37–39, 50–51, 54, 83, 101, 104, 121, 126–27, 140, 149, 205, 208, 213, 223

Wooster, David, 239

World War I, 241

World War II, xii

Wounds, 123–24, 132–33, 145–46, 148, 150–52, 160, 163, 181–82, 194, 205, 209, 228–29. *See also* Disease; Medical care

Wraxall, Peter, 62

Yorke, Joseph, 213

Young, William, 44

Youth's Behavior, 26

Zinsser, Hans, 122–23